FOODS AND NUTRITION

Munn Rankin and Hildreth's

Foods and Nutrition

BARBARA LAKE, B.Sc. (H. & S.S.)
Formerly Head of Department of Home Economics
F. L. Calder College, Liverpool

and

MARY WATERWORTH, B.Sc. (H. & S.S.)
Formerly Head of Food Studies
F. L. Calder College, Liverpool

Bell & Hyman
London

Published in 1981 by
BELL & HYMAN LIMITED
Denmark House
37–39 Queen Elizabeth Street
London SE1 2QB

First published in 1939 by
Allman & Son Ltd (now incorporated in Mills & Boon Ltd)

Thirteenth edition 1980
Reprinted 1983

British Library Cataloguing in Publication Data

Lake, B.
  Foods and nutrition.—13th rev. ed.
  1. Nutrition
  I. Title   II. Waterworth, M.   III. Rankin,
  William Munn
  613.2   TX353

ISBN 0 7135 2060 4

Printed in Great Britain by
Biddles Ltd, Guildford, Surrey

CONTENTS

ACKNOWLEDGEMENTS

The following have been good enough to give permission for the reproduction of copyright data:

The Controller, HM Stationery Office, and the Medical Research Council for figures from McCance and Widdowson's *The Composition of Foods* (Paul and Southgate) p. 89

The Controller, HM Stationery Office, and the Department of Health and Social Security for the figures on recommended daily amounts of food energy and nutrients from *Report on Health and Social Subjects* 15 (p. 18)

The Food and Agriculture Organization of the United Nations for data from the *Handbook of Human Nutrition* (p. 20) and tables from *Protein Requirement* (pp. 91, 93)

Messrs Churchill Livingstone for tabulated data from *Human Nutrition and Dietetics*, 6th edition, by Davidson, Passmore, Brock and Truswell (p. 26).

NUMBERED TABLES

LIST OF FIGURES

PREFACE TO THE TWELFTH EDITION

Since 1939, through a whole series of editions and regular revisions, Munn Rankin and Hildreth's *Foods and Nutrition* has held its place among texts for students of Home Economics and allied studies. In preparing yet another and more radical revision, involving substantial re-writing, our care has been to retain those features for which the work has always been valued.

Section A is devoted to the science upon which all studies of human nutrition are based. Inevitably the content of organic chemistry is considerable. The aim has been to set this down as concisely as is consistent with clarity and the need to direct non-chemists to other texts; there is no attempt here to provide readers with their introduction to chemistry. Human physiology is another study of immense importance to nutritionists and it is difficult to defend anything less than a comprehensive study of body systems, except on the grounds of practicability. The inclusion herein shows what is essential rather than desirable. Biochemistry is an expanding area with ill-defined boundaries between organic chemistry and physiology. The contributions of biochemistry to nutrition in the years since this book was first published are most significant and must be acknowledged at all levels of study. In an attempt to summarize the present state of knowledge, the sacrifice of detail to simplicity is admitted while hoping that essential accuracy remains.

In Section B, attention turns to the study of food commodities and to the processes involved in their manufacture and preparation for the table. Traditional information retained from previous editions takes its place beside the contribution from modern food science and technology. Attention has been paid to revisions in Food Legislation and to possible effects of EEC Regulations.

Details of experimental procedures, appropriate to food studies, have always been a feature of this work. The value of the investigational approach in Home Economics teaching still needs to be urged and it is hoped that the wide range of exercises included will encourage teachers and students to plan programmes which will have significant findings for choices of materials and methods to be used in meal preparation. Admittedly, some experiments demand laboratory facilities and supervisors practised in the techniques, but most are suitable for translation into Home Economics rooms equipped with units or trolleys reserved for the purpose. In addition, it is hoped that, where Food Science is being offered as a component in Applied Science courses or as an option in Chemistry, this book will become a resource for experimental details and for background into the foods which are the objects of study.

In its revised form, this book will be suitable for students of 'A' level Domestic Science/Home Economics/Cookery and for college students taking courses in Catering, Institutional Management, Food Technology and Home Economics.

We wish to express our thanks to Mrs Anne Dew who read substantial parts of the manuscript and made helpful suggestions, now incorporated. Mrs Joan Bryant, of Mills and Boon, earns our gratitude for unfailing patience and encouragement. Various bodies have kindly given permission for the publication of copyright data, and this is acknowledged separately. The plate on page 29 is reproduced by kind permission of the Principal, F. L. Calder College, Liverpool.

Liverpool, 1975   B.L. and M.W.

PREFACE TO THE THIRTEENTH EDITION

The publication in 1978 of a new and extended edition of the Composition of Foods followed in 1979 by revised recommendations concerning energy and nutrient intakes in the U.K. has prompted a revision of the text. This provided an opportunity to reflect current thinking in nutrition and to make some minor amendments in the light of the valued comments from colleagues and former students.

Liverpool, 1980   B.L. and M.W.

SECTION A.—NUTRITION AND THE SCIENCE OF FOOD

CHAPTER I

GENERAL CONSIDERATIONS

1.1 THE STUDY OF FOOD

Our food is almost entirely organic, having plant and animal origins, with only salt, water and a few minor additives deriving from mineral sources. Thus the study of food draws appreciably on organic chemistry, with emphasis upon the three types of macronutrients: carbohydrates, lipids, proteins. There must also be an appreciation of the physical dispersions in the complex mixtures which occur in most foods, if there is to be understanding of their behaviour during cooking and handling. Where foods are formed of whole plant or animal structures, a study of tissues is also necessary.

Within the body foods operate as biochemicals and cell chemistry is the key to food functions, with physiology relating these to the working of the body as a whole.

1.2 FOOD SUPPLIES

Food production originates with photosynthesis in green plants, whether on land or in the sea, whereby carbon dioxide and water are used in the production of carbohydrates (see 2.2). This is an energy-utilizing process, the source being the sun's radiation. Chemical energy, stored within carbohydrates, is thus made available to the plant itself or to animals eating that plant. More concentrated energy stores are laid down in animals, and in some plant organs, by the conversion of carbohydrate into lipids.

Growth of plants (and therefore of food crops) requires more than an energy source. Proteins, as constituents of all living cells, have to be synthesized by plants and, for this, a nitrogen source is needed. A fertile soil will contain soluble nitrogenous matter, provided either by the process of decay, whereby dead remains of plants and animals are degraded, or by the introduction of inorganic fertilizers. This nitrogen, plus other necessary elements, gives soil fertility, the key to increased crop yields from agricultural land. To capitalize upon this, there must be control of pests and selective breeding of food plants and stock animals. Success with all such measures has produced reaction from a section of the public which fears the effects of introducing chemicals, foreign to foods, into the diet. They advocate natural methods of food production in which inorganic fertilizers and chemical pesticides are eschewed and dependence upon organic composts and biological pest control is re-established. This policy arouses considerable enthusiasm among its adherents although established scientific opinion holds back support for its claims.

'Natural foods' and 'health foods' are not synonymous. Indeed the latter embraces a wide range of products, sold for specific health-promoting purposes; some, for example, contain a high level of synthetic vitamins. It is difficult to justify additional expenditure on such foods over conventional foods. At the same time the limitations in nutritional knowledge must be admitted and no one should claim to have given the final verdict on a dietary programme.

Considerations other than health can influence food habits. Some religions impose dietary restrictions; many accord particular significance to both feasts and fasts. Vegetarianism derives largely from a reverence for life. Because it excludes many favourite foods whose nutritional properties cannot be gainsaid, the appeal of its philosophy is not universal. The future may bring economic sanctions upon meat consumption with increased dependence upon vegetarian foods. Such considerations provide impetus for the development of new foods from plant sources such as are described in Chapter XV. In spite of the sophisticated processing involved in their production, these merely present plant proteins in a modified form and are a far cry from truly synthetic foods. So far there is very little progress in the synthesis of nutrients, with the exception of vitamins, which, for medication and food fortification, are manufactured rather than extracted from natural materials.

1.3 ENOUGH OF THE RIGHT FOODS

One of the fundamental responsibilities of an administration is provision of food and it is to this end that governments and the United Nations Organization appoint committees of nutrition experts to provide recommendations for daily nutrient intakes *per capita*. From these, total food requirements for communities are calculated and translated into food production targets and food import quotas. The recommended daily amounts for energy and nutrients for the UK (DHSS, 1979) are summarized in Table 1.1 on page 18 and frequent references are made to them in subsequent chapters. They embody the results of researches into the nutritional needs of the various population categories in this country and amounts of nutrients quoted are considered to be adequate for practically all healthy persons within each category. This means that for a large proportion they will be more than adequate. The recommendations for amounts of food energy differ in that they are identical with the average requirements for persons within each category. Consequently each category will include some persons for whom they are excessive, some for whom they are inadequate.

Both for nutrients and for food energy, the recommended daily amounts are intended to be applied to groups and not to individuals. It is necessary to know a great deal more than age, sex and occupation before an individual's precise dietary requirements can be stated.

Table 1.2 (FAO, 1974) (p. 20) draws from the several publications of recommended intakes of nutrients by FAO and is intended for international application, especially in those countries where there is the greatest need for improved nutritional standards. All such recommendations require for their interpretation data on composition of foods (see, for example, Paul and Southgate, 1978, *The Composition of Foods* and *Manual of Nutrition*). Trained professionals, such as caterers, dietitians and food administrators can competently handle such detailed information in meal and diet planning and in policy decisions for food and agriculture programmes. On the other hand, lay persons, concerned with feeding themselves or their families, cannot be expected to work to that scale. Nutrition teaching programmes should therefore help the general public towards sound eating habits by translating expert findings concerning nutrient chemicals into the everyday language of foods and meals.

1.4 DIETARY GOALS

The growing concern within Western Society about diseases associated with affluence and attributable to over-nutrition has stimulated a number of governments to adopt a new and positive approach to nutrition education for the public at large. In 1975 the Swedish *Diet and Exercise Programme* was published. Its dietary recommendations anticipated the more precise *Dietary Goals for the 1980s* set for the United States in the McGovern Report (1977). Six in number, these goals are concerned with overall reductions in intakes of fats, cholesterol, sugar and salt and with an increase in dependence upon complex carbohydrates (starches and fibre). Other governments and medical authorities see this approach as practicable and adaptable and several have followed with their own versions adapted to specific needs and priorities.

Government initiative in the United Kingdom has not so far resulted in the setting of definitive goals but in the publication of a series of booklets entitled *Prevention and Health*; the third of these, *Eating for Health* (DHSS 1978) is concerned with nutrition. The subject matter gives the background information for understanding the ten points of the summary which make recommendations along the following lines:

for babies and young children—

encourage breast feeding
avoid cultivation of a 'sweet-tooth'
ensure vitamin D supplements for those at risk

for all—

choose a wide range of foods to obtain all necessary nutrients
control energy intake to avoid obesity
limit intakes of fats and sugar
increase dependence on bread, fruit and vegetables including potatoes

for many—

protein intakes could be reduced without harm

for some—

less salt could be beneficial

and

alcohol is not necessary for anyone

Nutrition Education is the title of another government publication, a report from a working party set up jointly by the British Nutrition Foundation, the DHSS and the Health Education Council (BNF 1978). This ends by referring back to the Working Party a number of subjects for further attention. These include *breastfeeding, rickets, obesity* and *dental caries*, a list which underlines the problems which are present currently in the UK and which ought to be soluble, given the public knowledge and also the will.

REFERENCES

BNF (1978). *Nutrition Education*, HMSO.
DHSS (1978). *Prevention & Health: Eating for Health*, HMSO.
DHSS (1979). *Recommended daily amounts of food energy and nutrients for the United Kingdom*, Report on health and social subjects 15, HMSO.
FAO (1974). *Human nutritional requirements*, FAO nutritional studies 28, HMSO.
Paul, A. A. and Southgate, D. A. T. (1978). *McCance and Widdowson's The Composition of Foods*, MAFF/MRC, HMSO.
MAFF (1976). *Manual of nutrition*, HMSO.

FURTHER READING

Pirie, N. W. (1969). *Food resources conventional and novel*, Penguin.
Borgstrom, G. (1974). *World Food Resources*, Intertext Books (Blackie & Son Ltd.).

Table 1.1

Recommended daily amounts of food energy and some nutrients for population groups in the United Kingdom

(a) Age range years	Occupational category	(b) Energy MJ	(b) Energy kcal	(c) Protein g	Thiamin mg	Riboflavin mg	(d) Nicotinic acid equivalents mg	(e) Total folate µg	Ascorbic acid mg	(f) Vitamin A retinol equivalents µg	(g) Vitamin D cholecalciferol µg	Calcium mg	Iron mg
BOYS													
under 1		5·0	1200	30	0·3	0·4	5	50	20	450	7·5	600	6
1		5·75	1400	35	0·5	0·6	7	100	20	300	10	600	7
2		6·5	1560	39	0·6	0·7	8	100	20	300	10	600	7
3–4		7·25	1740	43	0·6	0·8	9	100	20	300	10	600	8
5–6		8·25	1980	49	0·7	0·9	10	200	20	300	(i)	600	10
7–8		9·5	2280	57	0·8	1·0	11	200	20	400	(i)	600	10
9–11		10·5	2500	63	0·9	1·2	14	300	25	575	(i)	700	12(i)
12–14		11·0	2640	66	1·1	1·4	16	300	25	725	(i)	700	12(i)
15–17		12·0	2880	72	1·2	1·7	19	300	30	750	(i)	600	12(i)
GIRLS													
under 1		4·5	1100	27	0·3	0·4	5	50	20	450	7·5	600	6
1		5·5	1300	32	0·4	0·6	7	100	20	300	10	600	7
2		6·25	1500	37	0·5	0·7	8	100	20	300	10	600	7
3–4		7·0	1680	42	0·6	0·8	9	100	20	300	10	600	8
5–6		8·0	1900	47	0·7	0·9	10	200	20	300	(i)	600	10
7–8		8·5	2050	51	0·8	1·0	11	200	20	400	(i)	600	10
9–11		9·0	2150	53	0·8	1·2	14	300	25	575	(i)	700	12(i)
12–14		9·0	2150	53	0·9	1·4	16	300	25	725	(i)	700	12(i)
15–17		9·0	2150	53	0·9	1·7	19	300	30	750	(i)	600	12(i)
MEN													
18–34	Sedentary	10·5	2510	63	1·0	1·6	18	300	30	750	(i)	500	10
	Moderately active	12·0	2900	72	1·2	1·6	18	300	30	750	(i)	500	10
	Very active	14·0	3350	84	1·3	1·6	18	300	30	750	(i)	500	10
35–64	Sedentary	10·0	2400	60	1·0	1·6	18	300	30	750	(i)	500	10
	Moderately active	11·5	2750	69	1·1	1·6	18	300	30	750	(i)	500	10
	Very active	14·0	3350	84	1·3	1·6	18	300	30	750	(i)	500	10
65–74 }	Assuming a sedentary life	10·0	2400	60	1·0	1·6	18	300	30	750	(i)	500	10
75+ }		9·0	2150	54	0·9	1·6	18	300	30	750	(i)	500	10
WOMEN													
18–54	Most occupations	9·0	2150	54	0·9	1·3	15	300	30	750	(i)	500	12(i)
	Very active	10·5	2500	62	1·0	1·3	15	300	30	750	(i)	500	12(i)
55–74 }	Assuming a sedentary life	8·0	1900	47	0·8	1·3	15	300	30	750	(i)	500	10
75+ }		7·0	1680	42	0·7	1·3	15	300	30	750	(i)	500	10
Pregnancy		10·0	2400	60	1·0	1·6	18	500	60	750	10	1200(h)	13
Lactation		11·5	2750	69	1·1	1·8	21	400	60	1200	10	1200	15

Notes to Table 1

(a) Since the recommendations are average amounts, the figures for each age range represent the amounts recommended at the middle of the range. Within each age range, younger children will need less, and older children more, than the amount recommended.

(b) Megajoules (10^6 joules). Calculated from the relation 1 kilocalorie = 4·184 kilojoules, that is to say, 1 megajoule = 240 kilocalories.

(c) Recommended amounts have been calculated as 10% of the recommendations for energy

(d) 1 nicotinic acid equivalent = 1 mg available nicotinic acid or 60 mg tryptophan.

(e) No information is available about requirements of children for folate. Graded amounts are recommended between the figure shown for infants under 1 year, which is based upon the average folate content of mature human milk, and the 300 μg daily which is suggested for adults.

(f) 1 retinol equivalent = 1 μg retinol of 6 μgβ-carotene or 12 μg other biologically active carotenoids.

(g) No dietary sources may be necessary for children and adults who are sufficiently exposed to sunlight, but during the winter children and adolescents should receive 10 μg (400 i.u.) daily by supplementation. Adults with inadequate exposure to sunlight, for example those who are housebound, may also need a supplement of 10 μg daily.

(h) For the third trimester only.

(i) This intake may not be sufficient for 10% of girls and women with large menstrual losses.

Table 1.2
Recommended Intakes of Nutrients by the FAO

Age	Body weight	Energy (1)		Protein (1, 2)	Vitamin A (3, 4)	Vitamin D (5, 6)	Thiamin (3)	Riboflavin (3)	Niacin (3)	Folic acid (5)	Vitamin B₁₂ (5)	Ascorbic acid (5)	Calcium (7)	Iron (5, 8)
	kg	MJ	kcal	g	mg	mg	mg	mg	mg	µg	µg	mg	g	mg
Children														
1	7·3	3·4	820	14	300	10·0	0·3	0·5	5·4	60	0·3	20	0·5–0·6	5–10
1–3	13·4	5·7	1360	16	250	10·0	0·5	0·8	9·0	100	0·9	20	0·4–0·5	5–10
4–6	20·2	7·6	1830	20	300	10·0	0·7	1·1	12·1	100	1·5	20	0·4–0·5	5–10
7–9	28·1	9·2	2190	25	400	2·5	0·9	1·3	14·5	100	1·5	20	0·4–0·5	5–10
Male adolescents														
10–12	36·9	10·9	2600	30	575	2·5	1·0	1·6	17·2	100	2·0	20	0·6–0·7	5–10
13–15	51·3	12·1	2900	37	725	2·5	1·2	1·7	19·1	200	2·0	30	0·6–0·7	9–18
16–19	62·9	12·8	3070	38	750	2·5	1·2	1·8	20·3	200	2·0	30	0·5–0·6	5–9
Female adolescents														
10–12	38·0	9·8	2350	29	575	2·5	0·9	1·4	15·5	100	2·0	20	0·6–0·7	5–10
13–15	49·9	10·4	2490	31	725	2·5	1·0	1·5	16·4	200	2·0	30	0·6–0·7	12–24
16–19	54·4	9·7	2310	30	750	2·5	0·9	1·4	15·2	200	2·0	30	0·5–0·6	14–28
Adult man (moderately active)	65·0	12·6	3000	37	750	2·5	1·2	1·8	19·8	200	2·0	30	0·4–0·5	5–9
Adult woman (moderately active)	55·0	9·2	2200	29	750	2·5	0·9	1·3	14·5	200	2·0	30	0·4–0·5	14–28
Pregnancy (later half)		+1·5	+350	38	750	10·0	+0·1	+0·2	+2·3	400	3·0	30	1·0–1·2	(9)
Lactation (first 6 months)		+2·3	+550	46	1200	10·0	+0·2	+0·4	+3·7	300	2·5	30	1·0–1·2	(9)

(1) *Energy and protein requirements.* Report of a joint FAO/WHO expert group, FAO, Rome, 1972. (2) As egg or milk protein. (3) *Requirements of vitamin A, thiamin, riboflavin and niacin.* Report of a joint FAO/WHO expert group, FAO, Rome, 1965. (4) As retinol. (5) *Requirements of ascorbic acid, vitamin D, vitamin B₁₂, folate and iron.* Report of a joint FAO/WHO expert group, FAO, Rome, 1970. (6) As cholecalciferol. (7) *Calcium Requirements.* Report of a FAO/WHO expert group, FAO, Rome, 1961. (8) On each line the lower value applies when over 25 per cent of calories in the diet come from animal foods, and the higher value when animal foods represent less than 10 per cent of calories. (9) For women whose iron intake throughout life has been at the level recommended in this table, the daily intake of iron during pregnancy and lactation should be the same as that recommended for nonpregnant, nonlactating women of childbearing age. For women whose iron status is not satisfactory at the beginning of pregnancy, the requirement is increased, and in the extreme situation of women with no iron stores, the requirement can probably not be met without supplementation.

CHAPTER II

ENERGY

2.1 THE CONCEPT OF ENERGY

The energy utilized by living organisms is the same in all respects as that possessed by inanimate matter and it is useful to recall fundamental ideas concerning its nature.

2.1.1 Energy is conserved

Energy cannot be created or destroyed. In order to obtain a particular form of energy, it is necessary to take another available form and convert it. Electrical energy, so useful to man, can be obtained from the energy of motion in a waterfall. Chemical energy stored within the molecules of nutrients can be liberated by living cells and used for activities such as muscle contractions.

2.1.2 Energy and work are directly related

When work, in the physicist's meaning of the word, is done, energy is expended. For example, lifting an object from the floor to a shelf is doing work against gravity and energy is required. But that is not the end of the energy since it cannot be destroyed. Rather it is retained by the object on the shelf or, to express this more correctly, stored in the surrounding gravitational field. It can now be called potential energy: energy due to position. The amount of energy thus stored will relate precisely to the amount of work done on the object, i.e., to the weight of the object (its mass multiplied by gravity) and the vertical distance between floor and shelf. Work done can be calculated by measuring distances moved against known forces and the units for work, joules, are also used for energy used in performing work.

A joule is defined as the work done or the energy expended when a force of one newton is applied through a distance of one metre, one newton being that force which will give a mass of one kilogramme an acceleration of one metre per second squared.

2.1.3 Energy has numerous forms

Heat is the kinetic energy of matter, causing the continuous movement of its constituent particles. Radiation includes visible light, thermal radiations, ultraviolet light, gamma rays and microwaves. Chemical energy holds together the constituent atoms of molecules, while electrical energy organizes the subatomic particles. Mechanical energy is possessed by moving bodies.

2.1.4 Energy needs only one unit

The fact that such diverse manifestations as movement, electricity and heat are essentially the same and interchangeable underlines the logic of measuring all in the same unit. The common unit for all forms of energy is the joule. Defined above in mechanical energy terms, the joule can also be defined in electrical terms as:

The electrical energy expended or the work done in conveying a current of one ampere across a one volt potential difference for one second. Alternatively, one joule of electricity is expended when an appliance with the power of one watt operates for one second.

Heat energy supplied to matter causes its temperature to rise and this was used as the basis for establishing units for heat energy —the calorie and the British thermal unit—which are of little use for mechanical and electrical energy.

The calorie is defined as the heat required to raise the temperature of one gramme of water from 15° C to 16° C.

The British thermal unit refers to one pound of water and a one Fahrenheit temperature interval. These units have also been used for the chemical energy in fuels and nutrient molecules, which can only be assessed when it is liberated by the break-down of these molecules during combustion. All such liberated energy will be in the form of heat so that traditionally it was measured in calories, or rather kilocalories, for foods and British thermal units for fuels.

To apply the joule, which is the SI unit for the measurement of heat energy, is merely a matter of arithmetic, the units being related as follows:

$$1 \text{ kilocalorie (kcal)} = 4 \cdot 184 \text{ kilojoules (kJ)}$$

It should be noted that when daily intakes of energy are mentioned, the unit used is the megajoule (1000kJ) taken to the first place of decimals, i.e. to the nearest 100kJ, because this shows an appropriate degree of accuracy. The energy available from foods is expressed in kJ per 100g.

2.1.5 **Energy cannot be destroyed but it can be wasted**

When energy is utilized as, for example, when petrol, rich in chemical energy, is exploded in an internal combustion engine, only part becomes mechanical energy moving the car, while the remainder is wasted as heat, necessitating an efficient cooling system. The term 'wasted' implies that the heat cannot be recovered and put to some useful form of work. An expression of the efficiency of the conversion would be the mechanical energy as a percentage of the energy value of the petrol used. An internal combustion engine will rarely exceed a 25 per cent efficiency and the same is true of the human body taking physical exercise. Usually about three-quarters of the energy from food is dissipated in the form of heat. Small wonder that contracting one's muscles is the surest way of keeping warm.

But what of the energy which is 'used up' doing mechanical work? Some will be stored away if the work includes lifting loads to higher potentials, winding watch springs or charging batteries with the help of a dynamo, but most will certainly be done against friction for this is how we move our bodies from place to place. And work done against friction converts mechanical energy into heat. Tracing energy conversion chains will show that eventually all energy resolves itself into heat which is taken up by the constantly vibrating material particles of our environment. For this reason heat is sometimes spoken of as the lowest form of energy.

2.2 ENERGY AND CHEMICAL CHANGE

Chemical energy has been discussed as energy stored within molecules and holding together the constituent parts, the atoms. If this is correct, it is reasonable to expect large molecules containing many atoms to store more energy than small molecules. A useful generalization is that energy is liberated when large molecules are broken down by chemical change into small molecules while energy is absorbed when large molecules are built up from small ones.

From the angle of food studies, probably the most significant anabolic (building up) reaction is photosynthesis. This is an endergonic (energy-requiring) reaction. Similarly the most significant catabolic (breaking down) reaction is that implicit in respiration—the oxidation of foods. This is an exergonic (energy-releasing) reaction. Word equations which summarize the complex chemistry involved, show how the one is the reverse of the other.

(i) Photosynthesis—energy-requiring

carbon dioxide + water (+ energy) → carbohydrate + oxygen

(ii) Respiration—energy-releasing

carbohydrate + oxygen → carbon dioxide + water (+ energy)

Later in the text more will be shown of the sequences of chemical changes which ensure that chemical energy from food is made available to the body by a series of carefully controlled reactions and not violently, as when burning occurs.

2.3 ENERGY EXPENDITURE BY THE BODY

The body's uses for energy, although interrelated, are listed below under four separate headings.

2.3.1 Performance of mechanical work

Performance of mechanical work amounts to moving or compressing loads and involves muscular contractions. There are two types of contraction—voluntary and involuntary. Voluntary contractions of skeletal muscles made deliberately are used to move the limbs, trunk and face. During physical exercise they increase markedly; during sleep they are very much reduced. Involuntary contractions of the muscles of internal organs keep vital processes, such as circulation and digestion, going. They continue throughout life although with less force during sleep.

Within muscle cells, energy is released from energy-rich molecules derived from food and used to change the muscle fibre protein molecules chemically so that they increasingly overlap to shorten muscle fibres. Only about a quarter of the energy made available is usefully employed. The rest is released as heat.

2.3.2 Synthesis of essential materials

The cells are factories admitting small-molecule raw materials and producing large-molecule products: e.g. fatty acids and glycerol into triglycerides for storage in adipose tissue; amino-acids into proteins for growth and replacement or for components of secretions. These are anabolic reactions requiring the provision of energy in a suitable form.

2.3.3 Production of electrical potentials

The control by cell membranes of the passage of ions in particular directions is important in the functioning of both muscles and nerves.

These ionic gradients amount to electrical potential differences and their maintenance requires an expenditure of energy. This is continuous and much of the energy expenditure of the body during rest is for this purpose.

2.3.4 Maintenance of body temperature
The internal body temperature of a healthy person is kept near to 37° C even though there is often an appreciably lower environmental temperature. A difference of 17 degrees is very usual ensuring a continuous transfer of heat from the body to the environment. The loss must be made good by energy from food. However there is usually more than enough heat available for this purpose from the low (approximately 25 per cent) efficiency of the body in converting chemical energy into mechanical work. During waking hours muscular contractions usually provide sufficient heat to maintain body temperature. Feeling cold will stimulate more contractions in the form of shivering. Only during sleep is it necessary for the deliberate release of heat (thermogenesis) to occur.

Babies and old people may have some difficulty in thus maintaining their temperatures and should not be exposed to low environmental temperatures when resting.

2.3.5 Basal metabolic rate
When the body is resting and no voluntary muscular contractions are occurring, energy continues to be expended for involuntary contractions of the muscles of the internal organs and for cell and nerve activity. Basal metabolic rate (BMR) has been defined to provide some concept of a level below which energy expenditure will not fall throughout the 24 hours. All activity will increase the expenditure rate above BMR.

An individual's BMR is measured some 12 hours after the last meal while he is lying down wearing only lightweight clothing in a comfortably warm room. At other times during the day energy expenditure rate, even when resting, will be increased by the rather explosive energy release which follows ingestion of food, a phenomenon known as specific dynamic action (SDA) and by the maintenance of postures such as sitting. The less precise term, resting metabolic rate, which will be about 10 per cent above BMR, may reasonably be applied to eight hours of bed rest and other forms of rest in each 24 hours. At all other times the rate will be resting metabolic rate plus that required for physical activity involving skeletal muscle contractions.

Results of BMR determinations show variations between individuals and also variations within an individual's lifetime. A cursory glance might indicate that BMR increased with body weight but more careful analysis indicates that BMR is directly related to 'lean body mass', i.e. excluding fatty tissue. BMR divided by lean body mass in kilograms gives a fairly consistent result for adults (see Table 2.1). Such BMR/lean body mass ratios for children are higher than for adults and those for elderly people show a slight decline. This is reasonable when it is remembered that activities of cells synthesizing materials for growth and maintenance account for much of the energy expenditure measured by BMR. Some residents in tropical countries (both natives and immigrants) show lower metabolic rates (about 10 per cent lower) than the average for other countries.

Table 2.1

Resting Rate of Energy Expenditure (kJ per min)—Average Values for Adults According to Body Weight

Subject	Body weight (kg)							
	45	50	55	60	65	70	75	80
Man of average build, i.e. 10% body weight as fat	—	3·9	4·2	4·5	4·8	5·1	5·3	5·6
Woman of average build, i.e. 20% body weight as fat	3·3	3·5	3·8	4·1	4·4	4·7	4·9	5·2

2.4 ESTIMATING REQUIREMENTS

Statements about dietary requirements tend to be made concerning individuals, e.g. a sixteen-year-old girl will require 9·0MJ of energy, 53g of protein, 0·9mg thiamin, etc. per day (Department of Health and Social Security (1979)). In fact, the recommendations are intended to be applied in the main to groups of people, even whole populations, for the purpose of calculating a total requirement and translating this into the bulk of food to be produced and imported. One of the most important of these calculations is that directed to energy.

It is necessary to select samples from the population representing age–sex–occupation categories and find out how much energy each expends in a typical day. There are three distinct methods of doing this.

2.4.1 Direct calorimetry

Probably the most important reason for including a description of the difficult and costly experiment using direct calorimetry in a text-book such as this is that its use by Atwater and Benedict at the turn of the century showed conclusively that the principle of conservation of energy applies to man and his food as much as to an engine and its fuel (Davidson *et al.*, 1975). It proved that the energy man expends is equal to the energy he obtains from food.

When it is remembered that all forms of energy are converted ultimately into heat, it will be appreciated that all that is necessary is for the energy value of the food eaten to be calculated and the heat given off to be collected and measured. In practice this is highly complicated. The subject is enclosed in a sealed and insulated air-conditioned chamber. Within this he eats and rests and engages in a variety of activities, the energy for which will end as heat (providing he is not winding watches, lifting objects to higher levels or gaining body weight—all of which store energy). The temperature within the calorimeter is kept constant by water flowing through pipes which surround it. The water takes up the heat being produced and this is the sole means by which heat is extracted from the calorimeter. By calculating the product of the mass of water flowing through the system and its rise in temperature, a measure of the energy expended is obtained. At the same time the energy value of the food eaten is calculated.

2.4.2 Indirect calorimetry

An additional success of the direct calorimetry experiments was the proof that energy expenditure is related quantitatively to oxygen consumption. Therefore by measuring oxygen used in respiration for a given period it is possible to calculate the energy expended in the same time. This is a much simpler operation and most subsequent work has been based on this indirect method.

If the only food molecules being oxidized by the cells were of glucose, every litre of oxygen consumed would result in 20·8kJ (4·95kcal) of energy, calculated as follows:

$$C_6H_{12}O_6 + 6O_2 \rightarrow 6CO_2 + 6H_2O + \text{energy}$$

$C_6H_{12}O_6 +$	$6O_2$	$\rightarrow$	$6CO_2$	$+$	$6H_2O$	$+$	energy
180g	$6 \times 22\cdot4$ litres		$6 \times 22\cdot4$ litres		6×18g		2·78MJ
(mass of one mole)	(volume of six moles)		(volume of six moles)		(mass of six moles)		

or 1 litre of oxygen gives $\dfrac{2\cdot78}{6 \times 22\cdot4}$ MJ $= 20\cdot8$kJ

This is known as the energy equivalent for one litre of oxygen for glucose. Other nutrients have slightly different energy equivalents as shown in Table 2.2.

Table 2.2
Energy Equivalent of 1 Litre Oxygen

	kJ	kcal
Starch	21·13	5·047
Animal fat	19·62	4·686
Protein	19·26	4·600

A useful approximation for a food mixture such as is normally utilized is 20kJ per litre of oxygen consumed. Three methods are available for measuring oxygen consumption: the Benedict–Roth spirometer, the Douglas bag and portable spirometers.

Benedict–Roth Spirometer   The Benedict–Roth spirometer requires the subject to breathe in oxygen from a container with a water-float seal. The expired gas is passed through a carbon dioxide absorber and returned to the oxygen container. Gradually the oxygen is consumed causing a rise in the water level within the container, duly recorded on a rotating drum. (This is a sophisticated adaptation of the simple experiment with the candle burning under a bell-jar while floating on water. As the oxygen is consumed the water will be seen to rise within the bell-jar.) The Benedict-Roth spirometer gives a direct reading of rate of oxygen consumption but it requires the subject to be attached to a somewhat cumbersome apparatus so that its use is restricted to measurements of resting rates of metabolism or for energy expenditure rates during stationary occupations (see Fig. 2.1).

Douglas Bag   The Douglas bag collects for analysis all air respired by the subject during a given period. Typical results for the composition of expired and inspired air, after drying, are given in Table 2.3 from which oxygen consumption can be calculated.

Calculation:

In expired air, for 79·40 parts by volume of nitrogen, there are 16·60 parts oxygen.

In inspired air, for 79·40 parts by volume of nitrogen, there are 21·03 parts oxygen and 0·04 parts carbon dioxide.

∴ oxygen consumed when 100·47 volumes of air are inspired = 21·03 − 16·60 = 4·43 volumes.

FIG. 2.1. Indirect calorimetry. A spirometer is used to measure oxygen consumption of a subject performing physical work at a measurable rate.

Table 2.3
Air Composition Results (Douglas Bag)

	Inspired air by volume (%)	Expired air by volume (%)
Oxygen	20·93	16·60
Nitrogen	79·03	79·40
Carbon dioxide	0·04	4·00

The Douglas Bag with face mask and hose restricts activity somewhat but is a very reliable method of indirect calorimetry.

Portable Respirometers Portable respirometers measure total volume of expired air while reserving a small sample for subsequent analysis. These have provided results for diverse activities including sports and athletics. Examples of results obtained by indirect calorimetry giving energy expenditure rates for different occupations are shown in data collected by Durnin and Passmore (1967), a selection of which is shown below:

Light work at 10–20kJ/min
Light industry
Most domestic work with
    modern appliances
Gymnastic exercises
Building industry
Agricultural work (mechanized)
Golf

Moderate work at 20–30kJ/min
General labouring (pick and
    shovel)
Agricultural work (non-
    mechanized)
Ballroom dancing
Gardening
Tennis

Heavy work at 30–40kJ/min

Coal-mining (hewing and
    loading)
Football
Country dancing

*Very heavy work at above
40kJ/min*
Lumberwork
Furnace men (steel industry)
Swimming (crawl)
Cross-country running

Sedentary occupations and intellectual activity consume relatively small amounts of energy compared with those requiring muscular work. The feelings of exhaustion which frequently result from mental work are not indications that the body is lacking in energy supplies.

Having obtained by indirect calorimetry the rates of energy expenditure by a subject when resting and performing his range of daily activities, it is necessary to observe him, stop-watch in hand, and draw up a schedule showing how he spends a typical 24 hours. Then by multiplying each energy expenditure rate by the appropriate time and totalling, a result for the whole day's energy consumption can be found.

2.4.3   Dietary surveys

It can readily be appreciated that an individual adult in good health, able to perform the physical activities demanded by his job and recreations and maintaining a steady body weight must be obtaining an adequate supply of energy from his diet. It is therefore useful to measure food intakes and calculate energy supplied to a representative range of such individuals. Dietary surveys however have inherent drawbacks, for those questioned have difficulty in recalling what they have eaten and volunteers who weigh all their food intakes may modify their eating habits artificially during the course of the exercise. Possibly equally dependable evidence may be gained by calculating the energy value of the whole food consumption of a large group, generally considered to be in good health and given free access to food. From this a useful average per head of population may be derived.

2.5 RECOMMENDED DAILY AMOUNTS OF FOOD ENERGY

A number of national and international organizations make recommendations mainly for the benefit of those concerned with providing adequate food supplies for whole populations. Such publications give valuable guidance to those providing meals in institutions and to a lesser extent to any who plan individual diets and family meals. Attention here will be confined to the recommendations of an international organization, the Food and Agricultural Organization (FAO) (with the World Health Organization) of the United Nations, and to those of the Department of Health and Social Security (DHSS), applicable to the United Kingdom.

2.5.1 **International**
The FAO's current recommendations for energy (FAO, 1972) are based largely on dietary surveys which show how much energy is utilized in practice by a representative community. In order to devise a means for applying these to individual conditions, the day is divided into three eight-hour periods: eight hours bed rest, eight hours occupational activity and eight hours non-occupational activity. Knowledge of appropriate energy expenditure rates is applied to a reference man and a reference woman, each in the age range 20–39 years, engaged in moderately active occupations and weighing respectively 65kg and 55kg.

Reference man

In bed—8 hr at approx. basal metabolic rate (4·4kJ/min)	2·1MJ (500kcal)
At work—8 hr moderate activity (averaging 12·1kJ/min)	5·8MJ (1400kcal)
Non-occupational activity—8 hr (range 6·25–13·1kJ/min)	3·0–6·3MJ (700–1500kcal)

Range of energy expenditure over 24 hr	10·9–14·2MJ (2600–3400kcal)
Mean energy expenditure over 24 hr	12·5MJ (30000kcal)
Mean energy expenditure per kg body weight	0·19MJ (46kcal)

Reference woman

In bed—8 hr at approx. basal metabolic rate (3·75kJ/min)	1·8MJ (420kcal)
At work—8 hr moderate activity (averaging 8·75kJ/min)	4·2MJ (1000kcal)
Non-occupational activity—8 hr (range 5·0–8·5kJ/min)	2·4–4·1MJ (580–980kcal)
Range of energy expenditure over 24 hr	8·4–10·1MJ (2000–2400kcal)
Mean energy expenditure over 24 hr	9·2MJ (2200kcal)
Mean energy expenditure per kg body weight	0·17MJ (40kcal)

Similar break-down figures for reference men and women in light activity, very active and exceptionally active occupational categories are given by FAO. The adjustments necessary for age and other variables will be discussed later.

2.5.2 National

The Department of Health and Social Services (1979) divides the population into age and sex categories and an average body weight is stipulated for each. There is no difference in the energy recommended by FAO for its reference man and woman and the DHSS's recommendations for men and women in similar age and occupation categories.

It is very necessary for individuals to be aware of the many variables which can operate to modify such figures before applying them to their own cases.

2.6 VARIATIONS IN REQUIREMENTS

2.6.1 Body size and composition

It is reasonable to expect that the larger the body size the greater will be the energy requirement. If body weight is taken as the measure of size, then the greater the weight the more energy will be used in moving one's body around. If instead surface area is taken as the measure of size, the larger the surface area the more readily will heat be lost from the body by cooling. However, neither measure of size gives a direct relationship with energy. Possibly heavy persons are less physically active than lightweights; their bulk may slow them down or else they may learn to perform their mechanical work with less expenditure of energy.

Energy requirements are more directly related to 'lean body mass' than to total body mass and this explains why a man is considered to require more than a woman of equal weight and comparable age and activity. Women lay down more fat than men.

In general it is fair to assume that for thin-to-average persons of comparable age and activity, the greater the -body weight the greater the energy requirement. This is not true when additional weight amounts to obesity or where it reduces physical activity.

2.6.2 Age

During life, energy requirements rise from a minimum during infancy to a maximum probably attained at adolescence or during the early years of employment. Thereafter comes a gradual falling off.

During growth, energy requirements are certainly related to body weight but not uniformly at all ages. FAO gives the requirement of a one-year-old child weighing 11·4kg as 4·9MJ per day which works out at 431kJ per kilogramme body weight. This requirement per kilogramme body weight will never be reached again but shows a falling off so that, for a ten-year-old boy, it is given as 310kJ per kilogramme and at fifteen, it is 222kJ per kilogramme. The high energy requirement/body weight ratio for children is due to the energy needed for synthesis used for growth.

The end of school or student years brings for many young people a reduction in physical activity due to employment which ties them to a desk or work bench. A diminishing number follow strenuous occupations which cause expenditure to exceed that during adolescence. Whether or not recreational activities level out or heighten discrepancies is not predictable. Almost certainly there will be a slowing down of both occupational and recreational activities from the age of about forty and this calls for a reduction in energy intake.

Ageing will also produce a reduction in the resting metabolic rate probably due to a reduction in the proportion of tissue cells actively engaged in synthetic processes. FAO suggest a gradual reduction after 40 years of age until by 70 the requirement is only 70 per cent of what it was at 20. In the UK, DHSS (1979) recommendations indicate a reduced requirement for men after 35 years of age but only after the age of 55 for women. Failure to adjust food intakes appropriately is one cause for the weight increases which are associated with middle age.

2.6.3 Climate
It used to be suggested that energy requirements related to mean environmental temperatures so that in cold climates they were raised and in hot climates they were lowered. The latest recommendations from FAO (1972) abandon this, acknowledging the means by which man manipulates his microclimate. His uses of clothes, and heating, cooling and ventilating devices allow him to achieve a mean skin temperature of 33° C within a wide variation of meteorological conditions. Should external climatic conditions and his responses to them restrict his physical activity (and this can result from extremes of both heat and cold) his energy requirement will drop.

2.6.4 Physical activity
It has been found convenient by both FAO and DHSS, to distinguish between occupational and non-occupational activities and to accord to each an eight-hour allocation each day.

Occupations are variously defined according to their energy demands. DHSS provides a guide for interpreting their occupational categories for men:

(i) *Sedentary:* office workers, drivers, teachers, journalists, clergy, doctors, shopworkers.

(ii) *Moderately active:* those engaged in light industry and assembly plants, railwaymen, postmen, building workers, bus conductors, most agricultural workers.

(iii) *Very active:* miners, steel workers, dockers, forestry workers, army recruits. Also some agricultural workers, building and unskilled labourers.

For women, only two occupational categories are stipulated, the main one being 'most occupations', plus a 'very active' category to allow for the few women who are professional athletes, dancers and the like.

FAO allows four categories for both sexes, 'light activity', 'moderately active', 'very active' and 'exceptionally active' (see Table 2.4). The international organization takes account of communities in which there is as yet little mechanization, certainly not in the home, and of women whose working roles do not follow the traditions of the UK.

Non-occupational activities vary enormously in their energy requirements and there is no general rule which relates particular types of recreational activity to occupational categories. Rugby teams are drawn from coal-miners as well as office workers, and television-addiction affects sedentary workers as much as labourers. Non-occupational activities are not limited to recreation but include the many day-by-day personal and family chores such as washing, dressing, eating and probably quite an amount of domestic work. Any recommendations must allow for a range to cover these unpredictable demands.

Table 2.4

24-hour Range of Energy Expenditure

FAO (1972)	Light activity	Moderately active	Very active	Exceptionally active
Reference man	9·7–13·0MJ (2300–3100 kcal)	10·9–14·2MJ (2600–3400 kcal)	13·0–16·3MJ (3100–3900 kcal)	15·1–18·4MJ (3600–4400 kcal)
Reference woman	7·5–9·2MJ (1800–2200 kcal)	8·4–10·1MJ (2000–2400 kcal)	10·1–11·8MJ (2400–2700 kcal)	11·7–13·4MJ (2800–3200 kcal)

DHSS (1979)	Sedentary		Moderately active		Very active
65kg man	9·0–10·5MJ (2150–2510kcal)		11·5–12·0MJ (2750–2900kcal)		14·0MJ (3350kcal)

2.6.5 Pregnancy and lactation

Pregnancy and lactation increase a woman's energy requirements. The growth of the foetus and the placenta requires energy for synthesis. .There is an increase in fatty tissue—a natural defence against possible future food shortage which could jeopardize the foetus. The increase in the mother's weight will result in increased energy expenditure if she continues to move about normally. All this effects a noticeable increase in basal metabolic rate amounting to about 20 per cent during the last few weeks of pregnancy.

The home circumstances of a pregnant woman will determine the excess of food required over normal intake. If she continues to be physically active, possibly looking after other children, she will require more than the woman who has abandoned an active job to await her first child. Indeed some women have to guard against undue formation of adipose tissue in such circumstances. Regular weight recording throughout pregnancy is a wise precaution which can indicate either an excessive food intake, or, if the weight increase rises suddenly, an abnormal condition.

The DHSS (1979) figures recommend an addition of 1MJ (240kcal) per day during the second and third trimesters. FAO (1972) suggest 0·6MJ (150kcal) per day for the first trimester and 1·5MJ (375kcal) for the second and third trimesters. The difference is bound up in the responsibility of the international organization to countries in which under-nourished expectant mothers are much more evident than in the UK. Indeed both organizations are concerned with calculations of total community requirements and the allowances which should be made for pregnancies rather than for an individual's concern for her own diet. A woman who is healthy and well-nourished will have, after the first three months or so, a natural inclination to eat rather more food than normally. If this is well-chosen and her weight is approved by her medical advisers, she need make no deliberate effort to 'eat for two'.

Lactation has much in its favour. The malnutrition in children reported by world health authorities is by and large confined to the weaned. Sucklings in contrast are well-nourished. The increased secretion by the glands of the mother is normally met by an increased food intake, together with some use of the mother's food reserves—her adipose tissue. If she is deprived of food, there will be considerable dependence upon her bodily reserves.

There is evidence that from the energy conversion angle, the nursing mother is quite efficient. The energy value of her milk production is about 80 per cent of that of the additional food she consumes. On this is based the calculation of additional energy allowances. A woman who has laid down some fat during pregnancy will be able to utilize some of this during lactation and her additional food intake need not be so large. FAO (1973) recommend an additional allowance of 2·3MJ (550kcal) per day as against DHSS (1979) who recommend 2·5MJ (600kcal). Some women might look more favourably upon breast feeding if they realized that it would assist them to regain their pre-pregnancy figures by utilizing their reserves of fatty tissue for milk secretion.

2.7 MEETING ENERGY REQUIREMENTS

2.7.1 Combustion of foods

When food is burned in air, chemical changes occur. Some of the products will be gases including carbon dioxide and water vapour. Most foods will leave a solid residue. If this is black, carbon is present which can be converted to carbon dioxide by further application of heat, especially in an ample supply of air. Eventually a near-white residue or ash remains comprising the incombustible mineral matter in the food. This method of oxidation of food molecules results in the evolution of their chemical energy in the form of heat.

If a known mass of a particular food is oxidized completely by burning within a bomb calorimeter and the heat produced is measured, the heat of combustion for that food can be calculated in kilojoules per gramme. The procedure involves filling the calorimeter with oxygen under pressure and incorporating a platinum catalyst so that the food can be ignited by an electric current. The container is surrounded by a known mass of water to absorb the heat which can then be calculated by noting the rise in temperature of the water. A simplified version of the bomb calorimeter is the Nuffield food calorimeter designed to be operated in school laboratories.

2.7.2 Available energy from foods

Within the body energy is obtained by the oxidation of foods, but this differs from burning in that the protein content of foods is not completely oxidized. Absorbed carbohydrates and fats can be completely converted into carbon dioxide and water vapour, but in the case of amino-acids, the digestion products of proteins, the nitrogen component is removed and converted into the compounds urea, uric acid and creatinine which are excreted. These compounds have an energy content which is lost from the body.

Another limitation on the availability of energy from food is that some parts are not absorbed through the walls of the small intestine but pass out of the body with the faeces. The heat of combustion of the urine and faeces must be subtracted from the heat of combustion of food to give an estimation of the available energy from food.

As a result of experiments early this century, Atwater established some results for available energy of the three categories of macronutrients in food: proteins, fats and carbohydrates (Davidson, et al., 1975). He made allowances for energy lost in urine constituents and analysed faeces showing that absorption rates for protein, fat and carbohydrate are respectively, 92, 95 and 99 per cent. His findings are embodied in the widely used Atwater factors, given as:

Protein	17kJ/g (4kcal/g)
Fat	37kJ/g (9kcal/g)
Carbohydrates (starch and glucose)	16kJ/g (3·75kcal/g)
Ethanol	29kJ/g (7kcal/g)

Used in conjunction with composition of food tables, these factors enable an estimate of available energy for foods to be calculated. For example: 100g white bread contains 8·0g protein, 1·4g fat and 51·7g available carbohydrate (Food no. 20 in McCance and Widdowson, 1967.)

Available energy from protein	$8·0 \times 17$kJ $=$	136·0kJ
Available energy from fat	$1·4 \times 37$kJ $=$	51·8kJ
Available energy from carbohydrate	$51·7 \times 16$kJ $=$	827·2kJ
Available energy from 100g white bread	$=$	1015·0kJ

The wide application of Atwater's factors has been criticized because they were based on a limited number of subjects on a particular diet and some modifications have been suggested. It should also be remembered that food composition tables have limited reliability. Foods do not always comply exactly with the figures produced from analyses of carefully selected but limited numbers of samples. The fat content of meats is a case in point; it varies enormously affecting the energy value of such foods. Individuals will further vary the proportions of nutrients by personal preferences expressed in the amount of fat eaten from a cut of meat, the amount of butter eaten with bread, sugar in tea, etc. Nevertheless, provided they are used with discretion, the Atwater factors, together with food composition tables, can give useful indications of the energy available from food. This conclusion receives support in the findings from work in Glasgow involving subjects of differing ages and various diets (Southgate and Durnin, 1970).

The appropriate contribution of each of the principles (proteins, fats and carbohydrates) to the total energy content of the diet has been a matter for much research and discussion. There are firm recommendations for protein which are discussed in Chapter V but currently there are none giving definite proportions for fats and carbohydrates. Diets studied show considerable variations between communities. In general, increased prosperity raises the level of fat consumption, averaging 40–45 per cent of the total energy intake. In poor countries the contribution of fat to energy needs is 15 per cent or lower. Thus there is a wide range of difference tolerated, always provided the diets are customary. Suddenly imposed alterations in fat/carbohydrate proportions can produce distaste for the diet and other distress symptoms (see 10.5.3).

2.8 ENERGY AND THE CONTROL OF BODY WEIGHT

The general public tends to use the word 'energy' differently from the scientist. To feel 'in need of energy' is, for the layman, an expression of lassitude, a lack of vitality. Merely to eat more food, supplying the scientist's idea of energy, will not correct the condition; paradoxically, a good meal may bring an immediate sensation of drowsiness. Possibly owing to this confusion in terms, the unit of measurement for energy has taken hold and the public at large refers to 'calories' rather than 'energy' when discussing that quality in food which is concerned with weight control and body fat. It is unfortunate that scientists now have to ask the public to abandon 'calories' and accept 'joules' (or rather their multiples, 'kilo-' and 'megajoules') as measures of the energy from foods.

The intake of energy must exceed expenditure in the form of heat plus performance of mechanical work whenever body weight is increasing. During the growing years weight must necessarily increase with formation of additional tissues of all types including adipose tissue. With the end of growth, body weight settles down and for the most part remains at a fairly constant level. At this stage intake and expenditure of energy must balance, if not on a day-to-day basis then over a few days taken together. This implies that either food intakes and energy expenditures must remain at remarkably constant levels or else an alteration in intake must be matched by an alteration in expenditure or vice versa. This control, which results in the body weight of many adults remaining more or less constant, has been likened to a thermostat whereby the amount of fuel being burned varies with the rate of heat loss from the oven. The thermostat can be set to any chosen temperature but the body-weight controller setting is difficult to alter and for many the level it has selected is not the one they would have chosen. The majority of those concerned about slimming are not worried because their weight is rising but because it has settled at a level above that which pleases them or is considered healthy.

Certain stages in adult life are associated with alterations in static body weight. Middle age and, for women, pregnancy and menopause can result in a higher setting for the control mechanism. If in earlier years a desirable weight has been achieved without conscious limitation of food intake, it is often difficult to adjust to a new diet. Nevertheless weight reduction will only occur when energy intake is exceeded by energy expenditure. A slimmer's programme must involve either a reduction in the energy value of the diet or an increase in the expenditure of energy by taking exercise. A combination of both is the most promising course. Meanwhile it should be remembered that many thin persons can indulge in quite high intakes without weight gain. Their bodies must be able to metabolize and not store up these energy sources because their controls are set low. It is also highly probable that these thin persons take more exercise than their obese counterparts.

REFERENCES

Andrew, B. L. (1972). *Experimental physiology*, Churchill Livingstone.

Bell, G. H., Davidson, J. N. and Scarborough, H. (1972). *Textbook of physiology and biochemistry*, Churchill Livingstone.

Davidson, Sir Stanley, Passmore, R., Brock, J. F., and Truswell, A. S. (1979). *Human nutrition and dietetics*, 7th edition, Churchill-Livingstone.

DHSS (1979). *Recommended daily amounts of food energy and nutrients for groups of people in the United Kingdom*, HMSO.

DHSS (1978). *Prevention and Health: Eating for Health*, HMSO.

Durnin, J. V. G. A., and Passmore, R. (1967). *Energy, work and leisure*, Heinemann.

FAO (1972). *Energy and protein requirements*, Report of joint FAO/WHO expert group, FAO, Rome.

Paul, A. A. and Southgate, D. A. T. (1978). *McCance and Widdowson's The Composition of Foods*, MAAF/MRC, HMSO.

Southgate, D. A. T., and Durnin, J. V. G. A. (1970). *British Journal of Nutrition*, 24, 517.

CHAPTER III

CARBOHYDRATES

3.1 CHEMICAL CHARACTERISTICS OF CARBOHYDRATES

Each member of the carbohydrate group of compounds contains the elements carbon, hydrogen and oxygen and the atoms of hydrogen and oxygen are usually present in the same proportion as in water, i.e. two hydrogens to one oxygen. This gave rise to the name which means hydrate of carbon, though now it is known that they are not hydrates in the chemical sense. Among the commonest members of the group are the different sugars, starches and celluloses, derived from plant sources. A few animal foods provide significant amounts of carbohydrate, notably lactose in milk and glucose and fructose in honey.

Chemically all carbohydrates are related to polyhydric alcohols and contain hydroxyl groups (—OH), giving them some typical properties and reactions: affinity for water and, in reaction with acids, ester formation.

The simple sugars, having the smallest molecules among the carbohydrates, may be considered the units from which the more complex sugars and the large molecule carbohydrates are derived; links develop among the unit molecules, with the elimination of the elements of water by the process of 'condensation'. Thus a molecule of maltose may be regarded as built up from two molecules of glucose; and a sucrose molecule from a molecule of glucose and one of fructose.

$$2C_6H_{12}O_6 \quad - \quad H_2O \quad \longrightarrow \quad C_{12}H_{22}O_{11}$$

two glucose molecules — minus — one water molecule — condense to — one maltose molecule

$$C_6H_{12}O_6 \quad + \quad C_6H_{12}O_6 \quad - \quad H_2O \quad \longrightarrow \quad C_{12}H_{22}O_{11}$$

one glucose molecule — plus — one fructose molecule — minus — one water molecule — condense to — one sucrose molecule

By the reverse process of condensation, hydrolysis, water is taken up by the complex carbohydrates which are broken down into simpler carbohydrates and ultimately the simplest sugars. Thus starch yields finally only glucose, inulin only fructose, while sucrose yields equal amounts of glucose and fructose.

3.2 CLASSIFICATION

Carbohydrates are conveniently classified with reference to simple sugar molecules.

(i) *Monosaccharides* Each molecule is a simple sugar and hydrolysis does not yield any simpler carbohydrate.

Examples: Pentoses $C_5H_{10}O_5$ (5C molecules): arabinose, xylose and ribose.

Hexoses $C_6H_{12}O_6$ (6C molecules): glucose, fructose and galactose.

(ii) *Disaccharides* Each molecule on hydrolysis yields two simple sugar molecules.

Examples: Sucrose, maltose and lactose. These examples share the molecular formula $C_{12}H_{22}O_{11}$ and yield hexoses on hydrolysis.

(iii) *Oligosaccharides* Each molecule on hydrolysis yields a small number (3–10) of simple sugar molecules.

Examples: Raffinose, a trisaccharide of glucose, fructose and galactose, occurring in molasses
stachyose, a tetrasaccharide occurring in beans

(iv) *Polysaccharides* Each molecule is a long chain polymer and yields on hydrolysis many simple sugar molecules.

Examples: Starches
celluloses
glycogen
dextrins
inulin

General formula $(C_6H_{10}O_5)_n$ where n is a large number.
All give hexoses on complete hydrolysis

Hemicelluloses: Yield xylose and other monosaccharides on complete hydrolysis.
Pectic substances: Chief products of hydrolysis are galacturonic acid and methanol.

3.3 THE MONOSACCHARIDES

The most important monosaccharides from the standpoint of human food are all hexoses with the molecular formula $C_6H_{12}O_6$. Other groups are likewise named from the number of carbon atoms per molecule, e.g. trioses $C_3H_6O_3$ and pentoses $C_5H_{10}O_5$, this latter including ribose, a sugar important in the chemistry of nucleic acids

All the hexoses (glucose, fructose and galactose) are sugars, white crystalline solids, soluble in water and sweet to taste. When gently heated dry, they first melt, then caramelize, the colour gradually darkening from pale yellow to dark brown, and on further heating, give off water and thick acrid fumes. Finally charring occurs, leaving a shiny black coke. Solutions of sugars in water are known as syrups.

3.3.1 Molecular structures
The distinctions between these compounds and their respective properties are explained with reference to structural formulae.

GLUCOSE. This is the α-form. In the β-form the positions of —H and —OH at C1 are reversed.

FRUCTOSE. α-form. In the β-form positions of —CH₂OH and —OH at C2 are reversed.

Alternative ring structure for FRUCTOSE.

GALACTOSE. α-form. In the β-form positions of —OH and —H at C1 are reversed.

These structural formulae attempt to show the three-dimensional ring structure with the thickened lines indicating the front edge of a horizontal table. The carbon atoms have been numbered to enable the reactive group in each to be identified. In both glucose and galactose molecules, reactivity in the form of reducing action is associated with carbon atom number 1, while in fructose it is associated with carbon atom number 2. When such a carbon atom is involved in a linkage with another monosaccharide unit to form a disaccharide or part of a polysaccharide chain, its reactivity is prevented. This will be shown later to account for the reducing activity of some, but not all, of the disaccharide sugars.

3.3.2 Reducing sugars

Reducing action affecting copper salts in alkaline solution is the operative principle in Fehling's and Benedict's reactions used to identify and estimate reducing sugars in foods and other biochemical materials. Fehling's solution is usually made up from separate solutions of copper sulphate (solution I or A) and a solution containing caustic soda and sodium potassium tartrate (solution II or B). The copper II oxide which forms on heating the mixture is reduced to a red precipitate of copper I oxide by any sugar present which contains a reducing group. Glucose, galactose, maltose and lactose all contain reducing groups and therefore are called reducing sugars. Sucrose alone among the common sugars has no reducing group (see 3.4.1) and therefore does not give a positive result for Fehling's and Benedict's tests (see Expt. 3(i) c and d).

Monosaccharides can be distinguished from disaccharides by using Barfoed's reagent, a solution containing copper acetate and acetic acid. Only the monosaccharides will reduce copper salts in acid solution.

3.3.3 Glucose

Glucose is found in grapes, hence the alternative name grape sugar. A solution of the sugar placed in the tube of a polarimeter is seen to turn the plane of polarization to the right, so that it is said to be dextro-rotatory, hence the third name dextrose. This property indicates that glucose has at least one asymmetric carbon atom, where every bond is joined to a different group.

Glucose is an important biochemical being present in the blood at controlled concentrations. The normal fasting level in venous blood ranges from 60 to 100mg per 100ml of blood. The presence of glucose in urine is a symptom of the disease diabetes and accordingly a specific test of easy application has been devised. This is the Clinistix test and, provided it is applied strictly in accordance with directions, it provides valuable evidence of the presence of glucose. It employs glucose oxidase, the enzyme for oxidation of glucose to gluconic acid and hydrogen peroxide. The colour indicator is sensitive to oxidizing agents and hence to hydrogen peroxide.

The occurrence of glucose in food plants is widespread but content is usually limited and there are few good food sources. It is made on an industrial scale from maize starch by hydrolysis effected by heating in dilute sulphuric acid. It crystallizes from concentrated aqueous solution in a granular form which includes water of crystallization (monohydrate). It is readily soluble in water. Its sweetness is 75 per cent that of sucrose for which it is used as a cheaper alternative in some confectionery. In the absence of air it is fermented by yeast giving alcohol and carbon dioxide and much is used in brewing in place of maltose.

3.3.4 Fructose

Fructose is found widely distributed with glucose in fruits and also in honey. It is the sweetest of all the sugars. Its other name, laevulose, derives from its effect on the plane of polarized light—a rotation to the left. When sucrose, which is dextro-rotatory, is hydrolysed yielding equal quantities of glucose and fructose, the resulting mixture, is found to be laevo-rotatory, hence the name, invert sugar. The angle of rotation (to the left) of the fructose exceeds that (to the right) of the glucose.

$$C_{12}H_{22}O_{11} \ + \ H_2O \ \longrightarrow \ C_6H_{12}O_6 \ + \ C_6H_{12}O_6$$

sucrose		glucose	fructose
dextro-		dextro-	laevo-
$[\alpha]_D = +66°$		$[\alpha]_D = +53°$	$[\alpha]_D = -92°$

invert sugar
laevo-
$[\alpha]_D = -39°$

3.3.5 Galactose

Galactose is of significance as a product, with glucose, of the hydrolysis of the disaccharide lactose (milk sugar). Galactose combines with lipids and proteins to give important compounds. These include the cerebrosides, well represented in the lipid material in nerve and brain tissue, which contain a sugar unit, usually galactose, in their molecular structures. Much of the polymeric carbohydrate component of the glyco-proteins in cellular membranes is based on monomers of galactose or galactose derivatives.

3.4 THE DISACCHARIDES

The disaccharides include three common sugars: (i) cane or beet sugar, known as sucrose, the familiar form of sugar; (ii) malt sugar or maltose; and (iii) milk sugar or lactose. These all have the common molecular formula $C_{12}H_{22}O_{11}$ but differ somewhat in their properties, both chemical and physical, and fundamentally in the arrangement of the component elements and groups within their molecules. Their reactions with Fehling's and Benedict's solutions are explained with reference to structural formulae.

3.4.1 **Molecular structures and reducing action of disaccharides**

Two monosaccharide molecules condense to give one disaccharide molecule:

$$(C_6H_{11}O_5)\ O\!H + HO\,(C_6H_{11}O_5) \rightarrow (C_6H_{11}O_5)\!-\!O\!-\!(C_6H_{11}O_5) + H_2O$$

This shows how two monosaccharide units come to be linked via an atom of oxygen. The respective carbon atoms to which this oxygen attaches account for the different properties of the resulting disaccharides.

MALTOSE

A glucose unit linked by C1 via oxygen to C4 of a second glucose unit. The arrangement of —H and —OH at C1 of the second glucose unit is left unresolved because maltose has both α- and β-forms.

Reducing Action Although the reactive group associated with C1 in the first glucose unit is involved in the linkage, the C1 in the second unit is free and able to cause reducing action. Hence the positive results given by maltose to Fehling's and Benedict's tests.

LACTOSE

A galactose unit linked by C1 via oxygen to C4 of a glucose unit. Again the formula is intended to show that lactose has both α- and β-forms.

Reducing Action   Like maltose, lactose has one C1 linked but the other C1 free to give it reducing properties, as shown by positive reactions to Fehling's and Benedict's tests.

SUCROSE

A glucose unit linked by C1 via oxygen to C2 of a fructose unit. As a component of sucrose, fructose has a five-membered ring.

Reducing Action   In sucrose, both reactive groups, the C1 of glucose and the C2 of fructose are used in the linkage and therefore none remain to give reducing properties. Hence the negative results when Fehling's and Benedict's test are applied. NB Sucrose is a non-reducing sugar.

3.4.2 Hydrolysis

On hydrolysis (breakdown by reaction with water) disaccharides yield monosaccharides. This can be achieved by heating solutions with acids or by the use of the appropriate enzymes such as are produced in the small intestines of mammals.

$$\text{maltose} + \text{water} \xrightarrow{\text{maltase}} \text{glucose}$$

$$\text{lactose} + \text{water} \xrightarrow{\text{lactase}} \text{glucose} + \text{galactose}$$

$$\text{sucrose} + \text{water} \xrightarrow{\text{sucrase}} \text{glucose} + \text{fructose}$$

The mixture of glucose and fructose thus obtained is sometimes called invert sugar (see 3.3.4) and accordingly the enzyme sucrase may be referred to as invertase. Yeast cells likewise need to digest sucrose before it can be absorbed and used for energy production and so they also secrete the appropriate enzymes. It is possible to extract invertase from yeast cells and use it for the experimental study of enzyme activity. Maltase is also produced by yeast cells to enable them to utilize maltose. Yeasts have no specific enzyme for lactose and therefore do not grow in milk.

3.4.3 Sucrose
Sucrose, the most familiar of sugars, occurs widely in nature: in ripe sugar cane—15–20 per cent; in sugar beet—7–17 per cent; in maple sap—2–3 per cent; and in a variety of ripe fruits, e.g. strawberry--5–6 per cent, pineapple—11 per cent.

It is from sugar cane and beet that by far the greatest quantity of sugar is manufactured, the former cultivated mainly in the tropics and the latter in temperate countries. Prior to this deliberate production of sucrose, honey, which contains some sucrose and much invert sugar, was the sugary material used for sweetening purposes.

3.4.4 Maltose
Maltose is found in malt, the young germinating grain of barley, wheat or oats, and is formed by the action on the starch of the endosperm by diastase, an amylytic enzyme secreted by the outer layer of the scutellum which separates the embryo from the endosperm. Malt is the primary substance from which beer is made. After damp grains of barley have been allowed to germinate in the dark for a sufficiently long period at a suitable temperature, they are dried and killed by heat. When the malt is boiled with water the sugar dissolves out and forms a sweet solution, wort, from which maltose may be obtained by evaporation and crystallization.

Maltose is not as sweet as sucrose. It is dextro-rotatory to a much higher degree ($[\alpha]_D = +137°$) than sucrose, glucose or lactose.

3.4.5 Lactose

Lactose is found in mammalian milks in appreciable amounts—3–6 per cent. It is said to be 'fairly' soluble in water rather than 'readily' soluble and gritty crystals of lactose tend to complicate the preservation of milk by methods involving evaporation. It is only mildly sweet to taste.

While being unaffected by food-spoilage yeasts, lactose is utilized by lactic acid bacilli, normally present in fresh milk, and as a result lactic acid is produced. The resulting acidity causes the souring of milk, characterized by changes of taste and consistency. The most abundant milk protein, casein, is water soluble at pH 7 to 6 but as the pH falls, indicating increased acidity, the solubility of casein is reduced. At pH 4·6, the iso-electric point, casein is rendered completely insoluble and it separates from water, forming curds.

3.5 THE POLYSACCHARIDES

Polysaccharides all have large molecules in the form of long chains either straight or branching. The commonest, starch and cellulose as well as glycogen, the storage carbohydrate in animal tissues, are polymers of hexose and share the general formula $(C_6H_{10}O_5)_n$. Partial hydrolysis will yield shorter chain polymers, dextrins being formed this way from starch, and further action will provide the disaccharide maltose. Complete hydrolysis yields the constituent hexose sugars.

Hemicelluloses are polysaccharides which include pentoses in their polymers. They have no food value, being indigestible, and are concerned, with normal cellulose, in plant cell wall structure.

Pectic substances, which include the extractable material pectin, are not true carbohydrates, but, being chemically similar, it is convenient to consider them in this context.

3.5.1 Starch

Starch is widely distributed in plants and is mainly found in storage form in roots, tubers, stem pith and seed endosperm. It is the commonest reserve form of carbohydrate. It is synthesized by the process of photosynthesis in leaves from carbon dioxide gas absorbed from the atmosphere through the leaf stomata and water taken up from the soil by the roots and transmitted to the leaves by the vascular system. This synthesis takes place only when cell protoplasm is accompanied by chlorophyll and in the presence of sunlight. Oxygen is liberated, usually equal in volume to the carbon dioxide absorbed. Plants can utilize solar energy, animals cannot and therefore animals are dependent on plants for their continued existence.

Starch is held in the plant cells in the form of plastids or granules with typical shapes for different types of plants. As the storage organ ripens these gradually fill the cells.

Source	% starch in dried substance
Potato tubers	72–84
Wheat grains	66–72
Maize grains	68–72

Extraction of starch from roots, tubers and grains is achieved by crushing and maceration with water and allowing it to sediment from the milky liquid. This is followed by washing and slow drying. Industrial starch is much used as sizing material for strengthening the warp threads of cotton before weaving.

Two glucose polymers have been found in starch granules, amylose and amylopectin. Amylose, comprising 10–15 per cent of the whole, is a straight chain polymer, each molecule consisting of several hundred alpha D-glucose units linked together, C1 to C4 as in maltose. Amylopectin, the more abundant component, has larger molecules with several thousand alpha D-glucose units linked together in branching chains utilizing both C1 to C4 and C1 to C6 links.

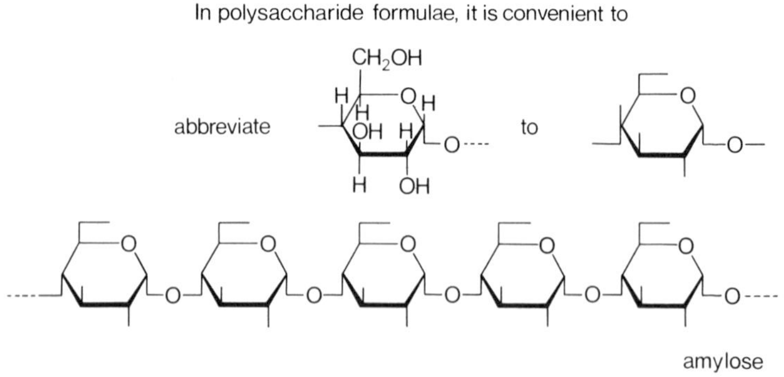

In polysaccharide formulae, it is convenient to

abbreviate   to

amylose

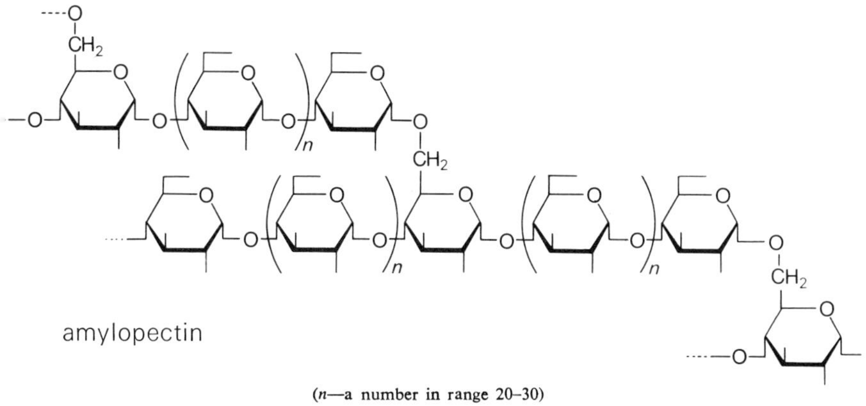

amylopectin

(n—a number in range 20–30)

Within the starch granule these molecules are densely packed, especially at the boundary, giving a particle which is insoluble in cold water. However, with heat, water is able to penetrate and cause the granule to swell, a phenomenon important in cooking. Heating in water above 85° C will cause granules to fragment. The starch molecules with their abundant hydroxyl (—OH) groups, each strongly hydrophilic, will attract water and form a colloidal dispersion in which the free flow of water will be impeded. In culinary terms, thickening will have occurred. On cooling, provided the concentrations are correct, all free flow of water will be prevented and a gel will result. The large starch molecules will have coalesced, forming a three-dimensional lattice within which the water is trapped.

When the cooking of whole grains (e.g. rice) and whole tubers (e.g. potatoes) is carried out, starch gels are formed within the cell walls which, though softened, tend to remain intact, giving the texture typical of such foods. Some separation of cell from cell can occur as when potatoes 'fall' or are mashed but the results differ from the starch gels obtained by the cooking in water of flours and extracted starches.

3.5.2 Cellulose

Cellulose is widely distributed throughout the plant kingdom as the chief constituent of cell walls. It is a polysaccharide with molecules consisting of long chains of beta D-glucose units linked C1 to C4. The beta-form of glucose differs from the alpha-form which features in the starch polymers in the arrangement of the —H and the —OH around the C1. The number of glucose units in a cellulose molecule is always large, usually amounting to several thousands.

cellulose

There is no enzyme in the human alimentary canal to break down such a linkage and cellulose is not utilized as food. Its function in the diet of humans is the provision of bulk resulting in an indigestible residue which stimulates bowel activity. Much of the cellulose present in cereals is removed as bran by flour milling and used for animal feed. Ruminants are able to derive considerable amounts of energy from cellulose because bacteria present in their alimentary tracts break it down to fractions which can be assimilated and metabolized. It has appeared sensible to separate unavailable carbohydrate from human food and use it to raise meat-producing herds especially in view of the majority preference for white bread. However the growing body of medical opinion associating low residue diets with diseases of the colon and the cardio-vascular system favours the consumption of wholemeal flour.

Much use is made of cellulose derivatives in slimmers' foods in which they are included for their capacity for absorbing large amounts of water. They swell up within the stomach giving a feeling of repletion while contributing nothing to the energy total.

Cellulose occurs with materials such as lignins in woody tissues and hemicelluloses which form an amorphous cell wall component in plant tissues generally and especially in seeds. Hemicelluloses are polysaccharides yielding other hexose sugars and also pentoses and uronic acids (carboxylated monosaccharides) on hydrolysis. Hemicellulose polymers are smaller than those of cellulose and significantly more soluble in alkaline solution. This probably accounts for the softened texture of leaf vegetables and dried peas and beans when cooked in water containing sodium bicarbonate. Lignins are not polysaccharides but complex branching polymers based on phenylproponoid units. They occur closely linked to polysaccharides in walls of cells said to be lignified.

Like cellulose, lignins and hemicelluloses pass undigested through the body.

3.5.3 Pectin
Pectic substances together with hemicelluloses form about 30 per

cent of cell wall substance, providing an amorphous cement in which are embedded the cellulose fibres. Although not strictly carbohydrates, pectic substances have similar polymer structures to the polysaccharides, but with galacturonic acid replacing glucose as the predominant monomer.

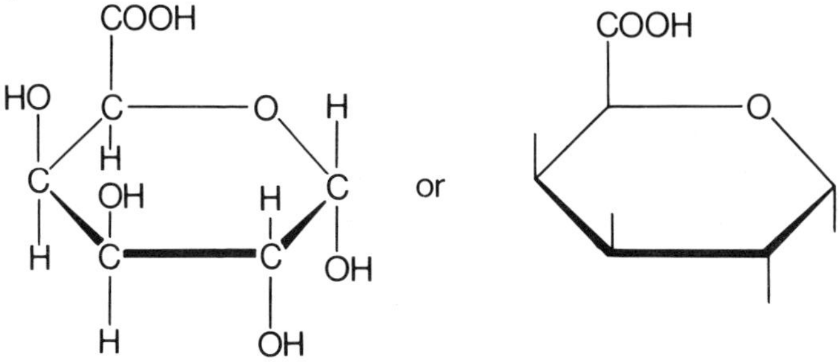

D—galacturonic acid

The methyl ester of this acid is another significant monomer.

The name pectin is given to such of these pectic substances as can be extracted by boiling plant tissues in water and which will gel in acid solution in the presence of a high concentration of a low molecular weight substance. This property is employed in jam making: the fruit supplies the pectin and the acid, and sucrose is used to aid gel formation. Incidentally, glycerol or ammonium sulphate will also give gels with pectin although neither would produce an acceptable jam.

Pectin polymers are mainly pectinic acid which contain both esterified and non-esterified D-galacturonic acid units. The relative number of esterified units has been described as 'more than negligible' and that shown in the following formula should not be taken as definitive.

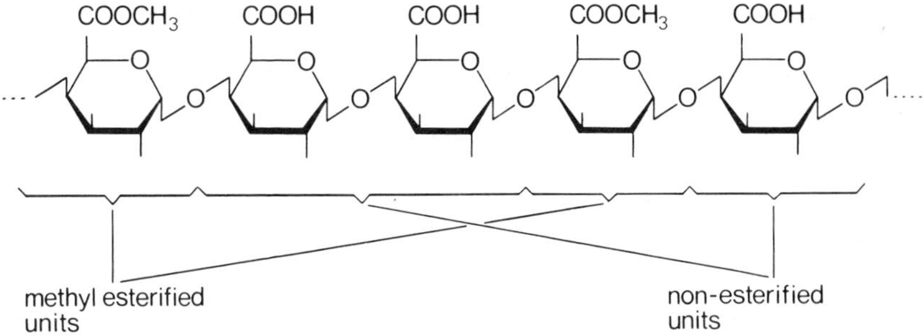

methyl esterified units

non-esterified units

PECTINIC ACID—Pectin

3.5.4 Dextrins

Dextrins are partial breakdown products of amylopectin. Their molecules are fragments of the original polymer and this allows more ready dispersion in water. Such dispersions, in high concentration, have a viscosity and stickiness. In the past, they were used as gums on labels and postage stamps and as size for stiffening fabrics.

Some dextrinization occurs when starchy foods are baked and dextrins contribute something to the characteristic taste and texture of bread crust. Manufactured dextrin is obtained from starch by controlled hydrolysis utilizing either acids and heat, or diastatic activity of malt extracts. The product dries to a glassy solid which is ground to a powder, slightly buff-coloured and readily soluble in water. The test for dextrins is a wine-red colour with iodine. In fact not all the polysaccharides polymers which count as dextrins give this but the probability of colour-producing dextrins occurring within a mixture is high enough to make this a useful test.

Being derived from starch, dextrins have the same nutritional value.

3.5.5 Glycogen

Glycogen has the same empirical formula as starch and cellulose. Its molecule is built up of many glucose units forming a branching chain structure resembling that of amylopectin but with shorter branch chains. It is found in the liver and muscles of mammals as a reserve carbohydrate from which energy can be derived. Its reserve function is related to the maintenance of blood glucose level rather than to long-term storage against shortage of food supplies.

Extracted glycogen is a white powder, giving opalescent dispersions in water which colours violet–red with iodine.

On complete hydrolysis, glycogen yields only glucose. While being a compound of immense biochemical interest, the amounts consumed from foods are insignificant. Liver and muscle stores become depleted by metabolic activity before and immediately after animal slaughter.

3.5.6 Inulin

Inulin is a polysaccharide found dissolved in the cell sap of certain tubers such as Jerusalem artichokes and dahlias where it replaces starch as the reserve carbohydrate. It can be separated as a white powder by evaporation or precipitation with alcohol. The powder is readily distinguished from starch by lack of colour on treatment with iodine. It is hydrolysed by a specific enzyme inulase, each molecule yielding forty fructose molecules and one glucose molecule.

3.5.7 Alginates

Alginic acid, obtained from seaweed, is a polyuronide with its linear polymers formed of D-mannuronic acid units linked C1 to C4. While not truly a carbohydrate, it is included here for reasons which apply to the pectic substances. Sodium alginate is used in food preparation because, with a strong affinity for water, it serves as a thickening agent. Many manufactured foods contain alginates as thickeners rather than starch probably because of the clarity of the gel. This is seen in the quick-setting glazes sold for use in fruit flans. Fruit squashes in which there is no settling out of fruit solids very likely contain alginates, as do many ice creams and frozen desserts.

PRACTICAL EXERCISES

*All experiments require standard precautions; those marked * involve particular hazards and should be supervised*

Expt. 3.1   QUALITATIVE TESTS FOR CARBOHYDRATES IN SOLUTION

Apply the following tests to dilute (approx. 1%) solutions of available carbohydrates, e.g. starch, dextrin, glucose, fructose, maltose, lactose and sucrose. For each conclude whether poly-, di- or monosaccharide, and whether reducing or non-reducing.

*(i) **Molisch Test** (Given by ALL soluble carbohydrates)
To 2cm³ solution in a test tube, add a few drops Molisch reagent (alcoholic solution of alpha napthol). Mix well. Add 1–2cm³ concentrated sulphuric acid CAREFULLY, pouring down the inside of the tube to form a lower layer. Leave to stand.

Positive result Purple colour at interface indicating soluble carbohydrate present.

(ii) **Iodine Test** (Test for carbohydrate polymers)
To 2cm³ solution in a test tube, add a few drops iodine solution.

Positive results
   (a) Blue colour—indicating unbranched polymer chains (i.e. amylose) present.
   (b) Reddish brown/black colour—indicating branched polymers, i.e. amylopectin, dextrins or glycogen.
   (c) Dark purple/black colour—indicating mixtures of branched and unbranched polymers as in starch.

(iii) **Fehling's Test** (Given by all reducing sugars)
To 1cm³ solution in a test tube, add 1cm³ each of Fehling's solutions I and II. Mix and heat in a boiling water bath for 2 minutes.

Positive result Orange–red precipitate—indicating reducing carbohydrate present, i.e. glucose, fructose, lactose or maltose.

(iv) **Benedict's Test** (Given by all reducing sugars. Similar to Fehling's but more specific and less sensitive)
To 1cm³ of solution in a test tube, add 2cm³ Benedict's solution. Mix and heat for 2 minutes in a boiling water bath.
Positive result Yellow or red precipitate indicates reducing carbohydrate present.

THEORY for Fehling's and Benedict's Tests Both reagents contain copper II salts. The presence of copper II ions is readily shown by blue colour. On heating with a reducing agent, the copper II ions are reduced to copper I ions which in alkaline solution convert to insoluble copper I oxide, the orange–red precipitate. The electrons needed to change copper II ions to copper I ions come from the reducing agent which is thereby oxidized, e.g.

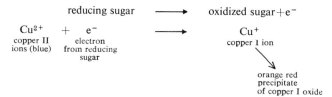

Barfoed's test utilizes the reduction of copper II ions but in acid solution. It is only given by monosaccharides and serves to distinguish them from reducing disaccharides.

(iv) **Barfoed's Test** (Test for reducing monosaccharides)
Use ONLY solutions already shown to contain reducing sugars. To 1cm³ of solution in a test tube, add 5cm³ Barfoed's reagent. Mix well and boil in a water bath for 3 or 4 minutes but NOT longer.

Positive result Red precipitate or coloration, indicating presence of reducing monosaccharide such as glucose or fructose.

(v) **Fearon's Test** (Test for reducing disaccharides)
Use ONLY solutions already shown to contain reducing sugars. To 4cm³ solution in a test tube, add 4 drops 5% aqueous methylamine hydrochloride. Mix and boil in a water bath for 30 seconds ONLY. Cool and add 4 to 5 drops 20% sodium hydroxide and return to water bath.

Positive result Red colour indicates reducing disaccharides such as maltose and lactose. (NB. A yellow colour which does NOT turn red will be given by reducing mono- and trisaccharides, and is NOT a positive.)

(vi) **Glucose Oxidase Test—Clinistix** (Specific test for glucose)
Clinistix paper sticks are impregnated with glucose oxidase and orthotolidine. The enzyme will convert glucose into gluconic acid and hydrogen
peroxide which oxidizes orthotolidine to a blue pigment. Test ONLY solutions
already found to contain reducing monosaccharides. Carry out the test
EXACTLY according to the directions on the pack having particular regard
for timing and for checking the colour against the chart. (NB. Atmospheric
oxidation of orthotolidine will in time cause blue colour to develop if
dampened sticks are exposed. Hence the importance of timing.)

Expt. 3.2 IDENTIFICATION OF A CARBOHYDRATE IN A SOLUTION KNOWN TO
CONTAIN A SINGLE CARBOHYDRATE

The following procedure may be followed for identifying a carbohydrate
in aqueous solution. (NB. There is no simple means of positively identifying sucrose—the most familiar of the sugars.)

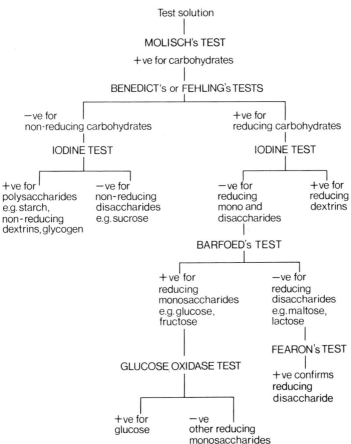

Expt. 3.3 DETECTION OF SUCROSE IN THE PRESENCE OF REDUCING SUGARS

Use a mixture of 4 parts 1% aqueous sucrose and 1 part 1% aqueous glucose. To 15cm³ of mixture in a small conical flask, add 10cm³ each of Fehling's solution and I and II. Boil thoroughly so that glucose is removed by oxidation. Supernatent liquid should be blue; if not add more Fehling's solutions and re-boil.

Filter to remove red precipitate, collecting filtrate in another conical flask. Add hydrochloric acid (concentrated) dropwise to filtrate until green and acidic (check with litmus paper, blue turns red). Boil thoroughly to hydrolyse sucrose to monosaccharides. Make alkaline by adding 40% aqueous sodium hydroxide dropwise until it will turn red litmus paper blue. Re-boil.

Positive result Orange–red precipitate indicating sucrose present in original mixture.

*Expt. 3.4 QUANTITATIVE DETERMINATION OF CONCENTRATION OF A SOLUTION KNOWN TO CONTAIN ONE REDUCING SUGAR

This may be adapted to determine total available carbohydrate in a foodstuff if hydrolysis to monosaccharide is carried out and the extract treated as if it contained only glucose.

Benedict's Method

Reagents

Benedict's quantitative reagent
0·3% glucose solution
Solution of named reducing sugar in unknown concentration
Sodium carbonate—anhydrous

Principle Benedict's quantitative reagent consists of copper sulphate, sodium carbonate, sodium citrate, potassium thiocyanate and a small amount of potassium ferrocyanide. Reducing sugars convert Cu^{++} to Cu^{+}, and in the presence of the potassium thiocyanate, a white precipitate of copper I (cuprous) thiocyanate is formed instead of red copper I (cuprous) oxide (as when the qualitative reagent is used). The small amount of potassium ferrocyanide assists in maintaining Cu_2O in solution. Since the precipitate formed is white, the loss of blue colour in the solution due to the complete reduction of the copper is easily observed. Use of Na_2CO_3 as the alkali instead of NaOH (as in Fehling's solution) minimizes the destruction of small amounts of sugar.

Method Pipette 10cm³ Benedict's quantitative reagent into a small conical flask and add 2g anhydrous Na_2CO_3. Now add a piece of porous pot and heat the solution GENTLY to boiling. Keeping the mixture just boiling, run in the sugar solution in small amounts (say 0·5cm³) from a burette, boiling well after each addition until the blue or green colour disappears. The end point is reached when further addition of solution after boiling fails to cause any change in colour. When nearing the end point, it is advisable to boil gently for 30 seconds after the addition of each drop of sugar to avoid overshooting.

Read the burette to the nearest 0·05cm³. Do at least two careful titrations; if these do not agree satisfactorily, more must be done until agreement is reached.

10cm³ Benedict's solution should be equivalent to:

> 20·0mg glucose
> 21·2mg fructose
> 20·6mg sucrose—after hydrolysis
> 27·1mg lactose
> 28·2mg maltose

Check technique on the given 0·3% glucose solution. Then determine the concentrations of the sugar solutions provided, calculating mg sugar per 100cm³ solution and converting to a % concentration.

Caution The titration figure for the sugar solution against 10cm³ Benedict's reagent MUST fall between 5cm³ and 10cm³. If the first titration is less than 5cm³ the sugar solution must be diluted quantitatively; if above 10cm³, more Benedict's reagent must be employed.

Expt. 3.5   MICROSCOPIC EXAMINATION OF STARCH GRANULES

Obtain specimens of starch extracted from different sources, i.e. potato, maize, rice, wheat, together with one of unknown origin, e.g. laundry starch.

Disperse minute quantities of each known starch in turn on to a microscope slide in a drop of water. Cover with a coverslip and examine under low and high power of a microscope. Draw each, indicating comparative sizes and characteristic features which allow for identification.

Similarly examine and draw unknown starch and make suggestions regarding its identity.

NB. Novices fail often because too much starch is used so that clumping of granules occurs. It is almost impossible to use too small an amount.

If while an unstained preparation of starch granules is being observed through the microscope, a drop of iodine solution is added against the coverslip edge, as it diffuses through the starch suspension, blue–black staining of granules will be observed.

*Expt. 3.6   INVESTIGATION OF STARCH PRODUCTION IN GREEN LEAVES

Place a green leaf in a beaker of boiling water for a few minutes to render cell walls permeable. Turn off heat and remove leaf into a test tube of methylated spirit (FLAMMABLE). Cause the methylated spirit to boil by holding the test tube in the hot but no longer boiling water in the beaker. The chlorophyll will be dissolved out into the hot methylated spirit, leaving a de-colourized leaf which, on soaking in iodine, will blacken where starch is present.

In order to conclude conditions under which starch is present in green leaves as a result of photosynthesis, carry out the above on:

(*a*) A leaf taken from a plant after several hours exposure to sunlight
(*b*) A leaf taken from a potted plant (e.g. geranium) which has been in a dark cupboard for 24 hours.
(*c*) A leaf from a variegated form of geranium, dead-nettle, etc.

NB. It is important to distinguish between the blue–black colour given by starch in iodine and the dark brown colour of iodine-stained cellulose. Take the precaution of washing out excess iodine and holding the leaf up to the light to discriminate.

*Expt. 3.7   DETECTION OF CELLULOSE IN THE ABSENCE OF STARCH

In plant tissues shown to contain no starch, the presence of cellulose, forming the cell walls, can be demonstrated as follows. Soak the tissue in a pool of iodine on a white tile and allow thorough staining to occur. Then drag a part of the tissue across the tile into a pool of 60% sulphuric acid (CORROSIVE).

Positive result   Blue–black colour in contrast to the dark brown of adjacent iodine-stained tissue, indicating cellulose present.

Expt. 3.8   DETECTION OF CARBOHYDRATES IN FOODSTUFFS

(i) Sugars and Dextrins
Make a cold water extract by thoroughly shaking the fragmented foodstuff in cold water and filtering. Test filtrate for presence of soluble carbohydrate and then distinguish between poly-, di- and monosaccharides, reducing and non-reducing sugars with tests given under Expt. 3.1.

If appreciable amounts of soluble protein are present, interference with precipitation can occur and it may be necessary to remove by coagulation and filtration. Slight acidification with dilute acetic acid followed by boiling will achieve this.

NB. Fehling's and Benedict's tests are only given in alkaline solution and some foods may be sufficiently acid to require additional alkali. A green colour rather than the familiar orange–red is an indication. A yellow colour is due to the precipitate coming out as a colloid. Further boiling will cause the particles to coalesce and assume their proper colour.

(ii) Starches
Addition of iodine to food in its original state will usually show starch by intense blue–black colour. If in doubt whether a dark colour is due to starch or to darkly stained cellulose:

> either   hold a thin slice of stained material up to the light to distinguish between blue–black and dark brown
> or   disperse the stained food in water and look for distinctly blue–black colour diffusing into the water.

(iii) Cellulose
If starch is also present, it is necessary to remove it by hydrolysis in 40% hydrochloric acid, heating the mixture for about an hour over a water bath. The undissolved material, recovered by filtration with washing, should be tested for cellulose as under Expt. 3.7.

FURTHER READING

Burkitt, D. P. & Trowell, H. C. (eds) (1975). *Refined Carbohydrate Foods and Disease*, Academic Press.

Norman, R. O. C., and Waddington, D. J. (1975). *Modern organic chemistry,* Mills and Boon.

Taylor, R. J. (1974). *Carbohydrates,* Unilever Educational Booklet Advanced Series No. 10, Unilever Research Division.

CHAPTER IV

LIPIDS

4.1 IDENTITY AND CLASSIFICATION OF LIPIDS

Greasiness is a property readily appreciated. It implies lack of affinity for water and solubility in organic liquids, termed grease-solvents. The substances so described include mineral oils and waxes, animal fats and oils and vegetable oils and waxes. All owe their characteristic consistency to significant hydrocarbon groups within their molecules, either as chain or ring structures. These groups show a hydrophobic (water-hating) tendency. This hydrocarbon content also accounts for the high energy yield when these substances are broken down as in oxidation. Thus most will burn readily and many serve as energy sources for living organisms.

Mineral oils and waxes cannot be utilized by animals, although some bacteria can tap their energy reserves and bring them into the food chain (see 15.7). It is usual to confine the term lipid to greasy substances occurring within plant and animal tissues.

Lipids are classified into:

(i) Simple lipids—Triglycerides together with di- and mono-glycerides and free fatty acids

(ii) Complex lipids—Phospholipids, steroids, terpenes.

4.2 SIMPLE LIPIDS

4.2.1 **Triglycerides**

All fats and oils in human food are predominantly triglycerides. These are esters formed by reaction between alcohols and acids:

| One molecule glycerol | three fatty acid molecules | one triglyceride molecule | three molecules water |

This esterification reaction is reversed when triglycerides are hydrolysed.

$$\text{triglyceride} + \text{water} \rightarrow \text{glycerol} + \text{fatty acids}$$

Enzymes called lipases can bring this about, as in intestinal digestion. Otherwise high temperatures and elevated pressures are needed.

Glycerol, also known as glycerin, is an alcohol with three hydroxyl (—OH) groups per molecule and therefore capable of combining with three fatty acid molecules, each of which is likely to differ from the others.

The fatty acids which contribute to triglycerides consist of molecules with a single carboxyl group (written HOCO., as in the equation on p. 61, or, elsewhere as —COOH) attached to a straight hydrocarbon chain, shown above as R′, R″ or R‴. Hydrocarbon chains consist of numbers of carbon atoms joined to each other and to hydrogen atoms thus:

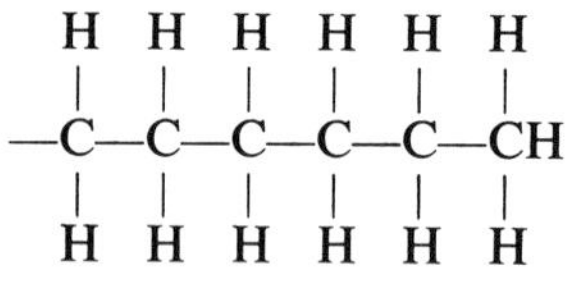

Such a chain is perhaps better shown as

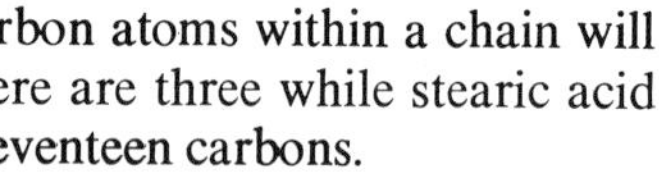

or written shortly as

$$-(CH_2)_5CH_3$$

The number of carbon atoms within a chain will vary; for example, in butyric acid there are three while stearic acid has a hydrocarbon chain containing seventeen carbons.

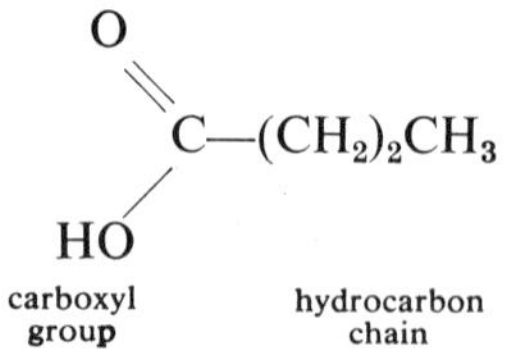

Butyric acid

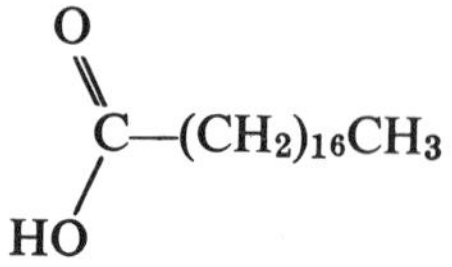

carboxyl group   hydrocarbon chain

Stearic acid

4.2.2 Unsaturation

In butyric and stearic acids, there are two hydrogen atoms for each carbon atom in the chain with an extra hydrogen at the end. Some fatty acids, e.g. oleic, have a lower proportion of hydrogen to carbon. This is termed unsaturation and is attributed to the existence of double bonding between one or more pairs of adjacent carbon atoms. Two carbon atoms joined by a single bond can combine with hydrogen atoms thus:

$$
\begin{array}{cc}
H & H \\
| & | \\
-C\!-\!C- & \text{'saturated'} \\
| & | \\
H & H
\end{array}
$$

Two carbon atoms joined by a double bond can combine with only two hydrogen atoms thus:

$$
\begin{array}{cc}
H & H \\
| & | \\
-C\!=\!C- & \text{'unsaturated'}
\end{array}
$$

as in

$$
\underset{HO}{\overset{O}{\underset{\diagup}{\overset{\diagdown}{C}}}}\!-\!(CH_2)_7CH\!=\!CH(CH_2)_7CH_3 \quad \text{Oleic acid}
$$

Some other unsaturated fatty acids have two, three or four double bonds within the hydrocarbon chain. These are said to be polyunsaturated. Fatty acids may be classified by the occurrence of double bonds in their hydrocarbon chains.

(i) Saturated fatty acids—no double bonds
e.g. palmitic $C_{15}H_{31}COOH$ or $CH_3(CH_2)_{14}COOH$

(ii) Mono-unsaturated fatty acids—one double bond
e.g. oleic $C_{17}H_{33}COOH$ or $CH_3(CH_2)_7CH\!=\!CH(CH_2)_7COOH$

(iii) Polyunsaturated fatty acids—two or more double bonds
e.g. linoleic $C_{17}H_{31}COOH$ or
$CH_3(CH_2)_4CH\!=\!CHCH_2CH\!=\!CH(CH_2)_7COOH$ (two double bonds) linolenic $C_{17}H_{29}COOH$ (three double bonds) arachidonic $C_{19}H_{31}COOH$ (four double bonds)

It should be noted that the general formula for a saturated fatty acid is $C_nH_{2n+1}COOH$. The number of hydrogen atoms in a molecule of an unsaturated fatty acid must fall below $2n$ where n is the number of carbon atoms in the hydrocarbon chain. Incidentally, only fatty acids with odd numbers of carbon atoms in their hydrocarbon chains are utilizable by living organisms and therefore feature in foodstuffs.

The most abundantly occurring fatty acids in foodstuffs are shown in Table 4.1. Others are present in less significant amounts. A large number of different triglycerides, each containing a distinctive combination of three fatty acid residues per molecule, results from synthesis by living cells. The majority will include both saturated and unsaturated hydrocarbon chains. Naturally occurring lipid material, whether in animal or plant tissues, comprises mixtures of these various triglycerides.

4.2.3 Di- and Monoglycerides

Digestive hydrolysis of triglycerides (see 9.5.4) proceeds in stages giving intermediate products, diglycerides and monoglycerides. Hence these are normal metabolites. Glycerol monostearate has appreciable emulsifying power and is deliberately added in some food preparations (see 6.2.3).

$$
\begin{array}{ccccc}
\text{H} & & \text{H} & & \\
| & & | & & \\
\text{HC—OCO.R}' & & \text{HC—OCO.R}' & & \\
| & & | & & \\
\text{HC—OCO.R}'' & & \text{HC—OCO.R}'' & & \\
| & & | & & \\
\text{HC—OCO.R}''' & + \text{H}_2\text{O} & \rightarrow \quad \text{HC—OH} & + & \text{HOCO.R}''' \\
| & & | & & \\
\text{H} & & \text{H} & &
\end{array}
$$

one molecule   one molecule   one molecule
triglyceride   diglyceride   fatty acid

$$
\begin{array}{ccccc}
\text{H} & & \text{H} & & \\
| & & | & & \\
\text{HC—OCO.R}' & & \text{HC—OCO.R}' & & \\
| & & | & & \\
\text{HC—OCO.R}'' & + \text{H}_2\text{O} & \rightarrow \quad \text{HC—OH} & + & \text{HOCO.R}'' \\
| & & | & & \\
\text{HC—OH} & & \text{HC—OH} & & \\
| & & | & & \\
\text{H} & & \text{H} & &
\end{array}
$$

one molecule   one molecule   one molecule
diglyceride   monoglyceride   fatty acid

4.3 EDIBLE FATS AND OILS

4.3.1 Physical states

The significant difference between a fat and an oil is physical state. Fats are solids and oils are liquids at room temperature. Raise a fat above its melting point and it changes to oil. This will have been preceded by a softening effect which, for some fats, extends over a wide temperature range. Unlike pure substances, fats do not have precise melting points. They are mixtures of numerous triglycerides each with its own melting point. Some are solids at room temperature, others liquids. The solid triglycerides are tiny crystals dispersed through the rest which are oils. This gives fats such as butter, margarine and lard their plastic texture so that, while holding their solid state, they can be distorted easily by pressure. The softening which accompanies a rise of temperature is due to a proportion of the crystals melting to oil. A hard fat such as mutton dripping which cracks under pressure contains a high proportion of crystalline triglycerides and relatively few oils. Olive oil is obviously a mixture of triglycerides all of which are liquids at room temperature. When stored in a refrigerator, those with the highest melting points will be seen to solidify as discernible crystals.

4.3.2 Fatty acid distribution

Table 4.1

Range and Proportion of Important Fatty Acids* obtained by Hydrolysis of Dietary Fats and Oils

Fatty acid in parts %	Corn oil	Olive oil	Cotton seed oil	Lard	Beef tallow	Mutton fat	Butter
Saturated							
Myristic $C_{13}H_{27}COOH$	1	1	1	1	2	2	10
Palmitic $C_{15}H_{31}COOH$	6	9	21	28	32	34	30
Stearic $C_{17}H_{35}COOH$	2	1	2	8	15	19	11
Butyric C_3H_7COOH	—	—	—	—	—	—	3
Caproic $C_5H_{11}COOH$	—	—	—	—	—	—	2
Unsaturated							
Oleic $C_{17}H_{33}COOH$	37	80	25	56	49	43	30
Linoleic $C_{17}H_{31}COOH$	54	8	50	5	2	2	3
% Unsaturated fatty acids	91	88	75	61	51	45	33
Iodine value	122·6	81·1	105·7	58·6	49·5	40·0	36·1

* Several other fatty acids are also obtained but in less significant amounts.

4.3.3   Degree of unsaturation

It will be appreciated from the information in Table 4.1 that unsaturated fatty acids are widely distributed. Indeed all the dietary oils and fats are unsaturated to some extent. The percentage yield of unsaturated fatty acids is probably not so significant as a comparison of the numbers of double bonds. Significant amounts of the polyunsaturates, as in corn and cottonseed oil, greatly increase the degree of unsaturation over that of oils such as olive where mono-unsaturates predominate. A measure of degree of unsaturation is given by the iodine value of a fat or oil. The double bond is a reactive point in the hydro-carbon chain and halogens (chlorine, bromine, iodine) are readily added.

$$-\underset{\substack{|\\H}}{\overset{\substack{H\\|}}{C}}=\underset{\substack{|\\H}}{\overset{\substack{H\\|}}{C}}- \quad + \quad I_2 \quad \rightarrow \quad -\underset{\substack{|\\I}}{\overset{\substack{H\\|}}{C}}-\underset{\substack{|\\I}}{\overset{\substack{H\\|}}{C}}-$$

The iodine value is defined as the number of grammes of iodine which are required to saturate 100g of a fat.

4.3.4   Unsaturation and melting points

For a crystalline substance to melt, the energy supplied must be sufficient to separate the constituent particles. The heavier the particles and the closer their packing, the greater the energy required for separation and hence the higher the melting point. Double bonds interfere with the assumption by triglycerides of their most stable crystalline forms. Hence a high degree of unsaturation is associated with a relatively low melting point, such as is shown by an oil. Conversely the higher melting points of solid fats are associated with greater saturation. Liquid oils can be converted into solid fats by the process of hydrogenation whereby the numbers of double bonds are reduced.

4.3.5   Hydrogenation

The need to increase available dietary lipids by making a wide variety of plant and marine animal oils palatable, coupled with the British and North American preference for fats rather than oils, has resulted in products such as margarine with its butter-like qualities and cooking fats which resemble lard. Both are made from oils which are converted to plastic fats by a process of hydrogenation whereby double bonds are saturated by the addition of hydrogen under catalytic control. Hydrogen gas is bubbled through oil con-

taining a nickel catalyst on whose surface molecules of hydrogen
and triglycerides are absorbed and rendered reactive.

$$\underset{\text{unsaturated}}{-\overset{\displaystyle \overset{H}{|}}{C}=\overset{\displaystyle \overset{H}{|}}{C}-} \;+\; H_2 \;\; \xrightarrow[\text{catalysts}]{\text{nickel}} \;\; \underset{\text{saturated}}{-\overset{\displaystyle \overset{H}{|}}{\underset{\displaystyle \underset{H}{|}}{C}}-\overset{\displaystyle \overset{H}{|}}{\underset{\displaystyle \underset{H}{|}}{C}}-}$$

If hydrogenation were allowed to proceed to completion so that
no double bonds remain, the resulting fat will be a hard crystalline
solid, lacking the plastic qualities of butter and lard which allow
spreading, rubbing-in to flours and creaming. Therefore, either
part only of the oil is hydrogenated completely and then blended
with the untreated oil, or hydrogenation is applied to the whole
batch of oil and stopped while some double bonds still remain.
Both the physical properties of the end product and nutritional
considerations prompt manufacturers in their choice of method as
well as the fatty acid make-up of original oils (see 14.5 and 14.6).

4.3.6 Plastic fats

The division between the crystal content and the oil is critical for
the performance of plastic fats. The production of thin films either
for spreading on bread, wrapping around flour particles when
rubbing-in, or enclosing air bubbles during creaming, demands a
crystal-lattice structure which can readily be deformed and reformed. Loss of this crystal lattice would allow free flow, i.e.
behaviour equivalent to that of an oil. Crystal formation depends
upon molecular shapes and those given by triglycerides will depend
on the fatty acids which contribute the 'three tails' of hydrocarbon
chains attached to the glycerol residue (see Fig. 4.1).

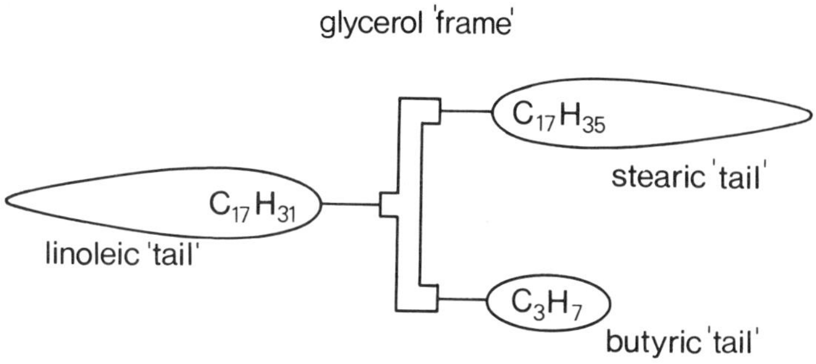

glycerol 'frame'

Fig. 4.1. Stylized representation of a triglyceride

The most abundant fatty acids, palmitic, stearic, oleic and linoleic, all have similar chain lengths (C_{15} or C_{17}) but inclusion of a short chain such as that from butyric will produce an unbalanced shape, likely to complicate crystal formation. A process of interesterification whereby fatty acids are switched about between glycerides can give plastic fats with crystal structures which result in improved creaming, shortening or spreading properties. The relatively inferior creaming properties of lard can now be overcome, enabling it to compete with hydrogenated vegetable shortenings as an 'all-purpose' baking fat.

4.3.7 Oxidation

The reactivity of double bonds is utilized in iodine value determinations and hydrogenation. It is also concerned with most rancidity changes (see 14.5). Oxidation is a chain reaction which proceeds from a methylene group ($=CH_2$), adjacent to a double bond, and results in addition of oxygen to form hydro-peroxides. These react further giving a variety of breakdown products, aldehydes and ketones, responsible for the flavour and odour of rancidity. Oxidation is promoted by heat, light, available oxygen and the catalytic properties of metallic impurities. Antioxidants prevent oxidative rancidity by reacting preferentially with the available oxygen.

Another result of oxidation in the vicinity of double bonds is the creation of cross-bridges between chains and the joining of molecules giving polymers. This is the main principle operating in the drying of oils such as linseed oil, the basis of traditional paints. Similar polymerization of peroxides occurs in frying oils, subjected to repeated heating, and results in gum-like products.

4.3.8 Frying

Oil, or fat above its melting point, is a useful medium for cooking because much higher temperatures can be obtained than with water. Recommended frying temperatures are as high as can be achieved short of decomposition which would be indicated by smoke formation. Oils suitable for frying can be raised to temperatures in the region of 175–200° C without decomposition, provided they are free from contamination. Impurities lower the 'smoke point', the temperature at which decomposition commences, especially free fatty acids which accumulate as a result of hydrolysis.

$$\text{triglyceride} + \text{water} \rightarrow \text{fatty acids} + \text{glycerol}$$

This reaction is provoked by repeated heating of the oil bath so that, in time, it is not possible to attain the necessary temperature for frying without some decomposition occurring.

Margarine and butter always contain an appreciable amount of water, together with some milk solids, and dripping will contain non-lipid material unless carefully clarified. In consequence these fats have limited application in frying. The water will vapourize during heating, causing dangerous 'spitting' and foaming with possible hazards from overflowing.

Deep-fat frying always constitutes a fire risk because of the flammable vapour produced by hot oil. Control depends upon air exclusion because in absence of oxygen, no burning will occur. The acrid smell of burning fat is from the acrolein, formed from glycerol, a product of hydrolysis, by dehydration.

$$
\begin{array}{ccc}
\mathrm{CH_2OH} & & \mathrm{CH_2} \\
| & -2\mathrm{H_2O} & \parallel \\
\mathrm{CHOH} & \longrightarrow & \mathrm{CH} \\
| & & | \\
\mathrm{CH_2OH} & & \mathrm{C{=}O} \\
& & | \\
& & \mathrm{H} \\
\text{glycerol} & & \text{acrolein}
\end{array}
$$

4.3.9 Emulsifying Agents

The use of dietary fats and oils as ingredients in food preparation not only adds to the nutritional value of a dish but greatly increases its palatability. Many flavouring materials, occurring in small amounts in foods, are fat-soluble and therefore are 'brought out' by the addition of fat which may have little intrinsic taste. However there is a toleration limit to the greasiness of a dish and it is very general practice in cookery to make and stabilize emulsions of oil in water, thereby achieving quite high contents of 'invisible' fat. Emulsifying agents (see 6.2.3), with their dual hydrophilic (water-loving) and lipophilic (fat-loving) properties, are very effective in holding oil and water together in a fine state of division. The naturally occurring lecithin is responsible for the consistency of egg yolk which contains some 30 per cent fat without any evidence of greasiness. Indeed the lecithin content of egg yolk allows more oil and water to be emulsified in mayonnaise. Lecithin is a phospholipid differing from a triglyceride in having only two fatty acid residues and a phosphoric acid-choline residue instead of the normal three fatty acid residues attached to the glycerol frame (see Fig. 4.2). The molecular structure of lecithin is:

$$CH_2OCO.R'$$
$$|$$
$$R''.OCOHC$$
$$|$$
$$CH_2.PO_4^-.(CH_2)_2.N^+(CH_3)_3$$

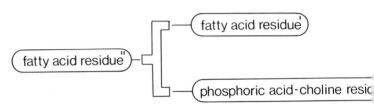

FIG. 4.2. Stylized representation of Lecithin

The hydrophilic tendency is associated with the phosphoric acid-choline residue portion while the remainder of the molecule is lipophilic.

Glyceryl monostearate (GMS) is a much-used emulsifying additive (see 14.7) with two hydroxyl groups (—OH) providing the hydrophilic portion and the stearate chain $(C_{17}H_{35}-)$ the lipophilic portion. The molecular structure of GMS is:

$$CH_2OCO.C_{17}H_{35}$$
$$|$$
$$HOHC$$
$$|$$
$$CH_2OH$$

High-ratio fats and low energy-value margarine spreads employ emulsifying additives extensively (see 14.11).

4.4 COMPLEX LIPIDS

Complex lipids have considerable biochemical importance; some have dietary significance. Only a brief survey is given here.

4.4.1 Phospholipids

Phospholipids are lipid-like compounds which contain phosphate groups and usually nitrogen also. They occur naturally in nerve tissues and cell membranes. Snake venom contains phospholipase, an enzyme capable of breaking down the phospholipids vital for nerve functioning.

Lecithin Lecithin is found in egg yolk and, in much lower concentration, in milk. It is the most familiar of the phospholipids.

4.4.2 Steroids

Steroids differ significantly in chemical structure from phospholipids. Their structures are built upon polycyclic carbon skeletons. Molecular weights are quite high and they form hard solids; their name derives from the Greek *stereos,* meaning solid. Examples include the sex hormones, the D vitamins (see 8.5.1), cortisone and cholesterol.

Cholesterol Cholesterol is found in nearly all body tissues, particulary those of the central nervous system. It is secreted by the liver in bile and, within the gall bladder, it may form aggregates known as gall stones. It can also deposit within arteries, restricting the aperture, a condition known as atherosclerosis. Concern is shown for blood cholesterol levels and their relation to heart disease (Royal College of Physicians 1976). Research into dietary intakes of cholesterol is being undertaken; major sources include egg yolk, milk, butter, cheese, offal and shell fish. Vegetable foods exclude cholesterol and the substitution of margarines made from seed oils rather than from animal fats is sometimes advocated. However recent evidence indicates that the body readily synthesizes about 80 per cent of its cholesterol from acetate units which are metabolic break-down products of all triglycerides, whatever their source. Other researches point to the possibility of lowering blood cholesterol levels by reducing intakes of fats high in saturated fatty acids, with partial substitution by fats with a high degree of polyunsaturation (see 4.3.3, 14.5).

The positive function of cholesterol in the body is not wholly understood. Probably it has a structural role in cell membranes and a synthetic role in the production of sex hormones. The molecular structure of cholesterol is:

4.4.3 Terpenes

The terpenes are a category of lipids including many compounds responsible for the odours, flavours and colours of plants. Essential oils, e.g. sandalwood, eucalyptus, peppermint, clove, lavender and camphor, extracted from plants for perfumes or food flavourings, contain volatile terpenes or their alcohols or aldehydes. The carotenoids which give the red–orange colouring to carrots, tomatoes and many other fruits and vegetables and which are present in green plant tissues, though masked by chlorophyll, are larger molecular weight terpenes, e.g. β-carotene (see 8.4.1).

The lipid nature of terpenes accounts for their solubility in other lipids and hence to the ability of fat, used in cooking, to bring out the flavour of vegetables. When making tomato soup, surface droplets of fat will colour intensely with carotene while the watery stock is only slightly tinted.

PRACTICAL EXERCISES

*All experiments require standard precautions; those marked * involve particular hazards and should be supervised*

Expt. 4.1   DETECTION OF LIPIDS IN FOODS

(i) **Grease-spot Test** (Given by all extractable lipids but also by mineral oils and waxes, not present in foods)
Apply to a solid food by wrapping a fragment in filter paper and leaving in a warm place long enough to dry out any water.

Positive result   Translucent stain on filter paper indicating lipid present in sufficient quantity to be extracted.

(ii) **Sudan III Test for traces of lipid** (Applicable to foods in fragmented form: powders, crumbs, gratings, etc.)
Sudan III is a red dye used in alcoholic solution from which it is readily absorbed by lipids.
  Place a standard amount (level spatula) of fragmented food in a test tube with 5cm³ Sudan III solution and shake thoroughly. Filter, collecting the filtrate in another test tube. Repeat with an equivalent amount of lipid-free material (e.g. starch) and compare the depth of colour of the filtrates.

Positive result   A paler filtrate than that from starch, indicating lipid present. The residues on the filter papers, when dried, will give further evidence of Sudan III absorption.

Expt. 4.2 DEMONSTRATION OF ACROLEIN FORMATION

The acrid smell of burnt fat is due to acrolein formation and is evidence of the glycerol residue in the molecular structure of triglycerides.

Heat 1 or 2 drops of glycerol in a dry hard glass test tube with an equal volume of potassium hydrogen sulphate crystals, a dehydrating agent. Note the characteristic smell.

*Expt. 4.3 COMPARISON OF DEGREES OF UNSATURATION OF FATTY ACIDS AND TRIGLYCERIDES

NB. WORK IN VENTILATED CONDITIONS

Prepare solutions of stearic, palmitic and oleic acids (and of any other fatty acids available) in test tubes using 1g acid in 5cm³ chloroform and a solution of bromine (CORROSIVE) in chloroform (FLAMMABLE and TOXIC), giving a deep amber colour. Add a blank test tube containing only 5cm³ chloroform. Using a Pasteur pipette, add bromine dropwise to each solution in turn and to the blank, counting the number of drops to give each a uniform yellow colour.

Positive result Bromine will be decolourized by unsaturated fatty acids. Saturated fatty acids will have results (in terms of drops of bromine solution) equivalent to the blank. Repeat with chloroform solutions of various fats and oils.

NB. This test only gives some indication of degrees of unsaturation and is not intended as a quantitative exercise.

*Expt. 4.4 INVESTIGATION OF LIPID SOLUBILITY

NB. WORK IN VENTILATED CONDITIONS

Solvents Use water and industrial spirit (FLAMMABLE) and such of the following as are available: chloroform, ether, carbon tetrachloride, acetone (all FLAMMABLE and/or TOXIC).

Introduce a small pea-sized piece of fat into each of a series of test tubes. Half-fill each with one of the solvents and shake well. Look for evidence of solubility. If not obvious, filter, collecting filtrate on a watch glass. Allow to evaporate (NO HEAT SOURCE) and look for a greasy smear which indicates some solubility.

*Expt. 4.5 SOME PROPERTIES OF LECITHIN

(i) **Solubility**
Add a knife-point of lecithin to equal volumes of (*a*) ether, (*b*) deionized water, in test tubes. Shake each thoroughly and describe the dispersions formed. To (*b*) add an oil, dropwise, shaking between additions to demonstrate emulsification. To (*a*) add an excess of acetone and note precipitation of lecithin. Extraction with ether and precipitation with acetone allows lecithin to be separated from other lipids.

(ii) **Phosphate content**
To a knife point of lecithin in a test tube add 2cm³ dilute sodium hydroxide and heat for 2 minutes in a boiling water bath. Neutralize with dilute nitric

acid and add ammonium molybdate solution, sufficient to double the volume. Return to the water bath for a few minutes.

Positive result Yellow colour or precipitate indicating phosphate present.

*Expt. 4.6 EXAMINATION OF CHOLESTEROL CRYSTALS

Mix a knife-point of cholesterol in about 4cm³ industrial spirit. Boil thoroughly by holding test tube in hot (90–95° C) water (NO FLAME). Cool and allow a few drops to crystallize on a microscope slide. Examine and draw typical crystal shapes.

*Expt. 4.7 QUANTITATIVE DETERMINATION OF LIPID IN A FOOD

Soxhlet Extraction
Weigh out 5g of the food into a dry Soxhlet thimble (see Fig. 4.3). Suspend the thimble in a beaker and dry it to constant weight in a steam oven. Place it in the Soxhlet condenser attached to a previously weighed flask containing sufficient ether to fill the thimble and half fill the flask. Now attach the reflux condenser to the extraction tube. Heat the flask by means of a water bath or electric hotplate so as to keep the ether gently boiling. The ether vapour passes up the side-tube of the extractor to the reflux condenser where it is condensed and runs back on to the food in the thimble. When the thimble is practically full, the ether is returned to the flask by an automatic syphoning device, carrying with it some of the fat from the food. In this way, although a comparatively small quantity of ether is used, the food is being constantly extracted with fresh fat-free solvent.

After siphoning over 24 times, stop the experiment just before the next lot of ether is on the point of siphoning over. The Soxhlet flask will then contain all the fat in the substance and little ether. The flask is then dried off in air and weighed to constant weight. The fat is then washed out of the Soxhlet flask by a fat solvent, and the flask dried and weighed again. The percentage weight of fat in the food can now be calculated.

Calculation

$$\begin{aligned}
\text{Original weight of food sample} &= x \text{ g} \\
\text{Weight of flask} + \text{extracted lipid} &= y \text{ g} \\
\text{Weight of flask} &= z \text{ g}
\end{aligned}$$

$$\text{Per cent lipid in food} = \frac{y-z}{x} \times 100$$

REFERENCE

Royal College of Physicians of London and British Cardiac Society (1976). *Report: Prevention of Coronary Heart Disease*, J. Roy. Coll. Physns.

FURTHER READING

Taylor, R. J. (1967). *The chemistry of the glycerides*, Unilever educational booklet, Information Division, Unilever Ltd.
Taylor, R. J. (1969). *Essential fatty acids—a review*, Information Division, Unilever Ltd.

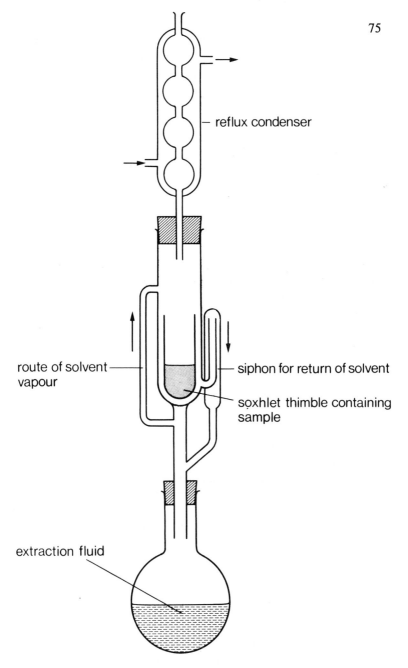

FIG. 4.3. Soxhlet apparatus for lipid extraction

CHAPTER V

PROTEINS

5.1 CHEMICAL COMPOSITION OF PROTEINS

Proteins are the most highly complex substances known. More than carbohydrates and lipids, they are essential components of all organisms, plant and animal: the living substance, protoplasm, being a complex of many proteins. Their essential elements are, carbon, hydrogen, oxygen and nitrogen. Many contain sulphur in addition, some phosphorus also and a few contain metallic elements such as iron, copper and zinc (see Table 5.1).

Table 5.1
Composition of Protein as Chemical Elements

	% dry weight
Carbon	51 – 55
Hydrogen	6 – 7·7
Oxygen	20 – 24
Nitrogen	15 – 19
Sulphur	0·3 – 2·3
Phosphorus (when present)	0·4 – 0·8

The majority of proteins have a nitrogen content of around 16 per cent. This fact is utilized when deriving values for the protein content of foods. The total nitrogen in a food is obtained by Kjeldahl's method and converted to an estimation of protein content by multiplying by the factor 6·25 ($= 100/16$) for most foods; it is 6·38 for milk and 5·68 for vegetables.

Compared with molecules of most other substances, protein molecules are particularly large. Exact information regarding molecular formulae is scarce, only a few proteins so far having been fully investigated. The particle weights given in Table 5.2 are estimates only.

Table 5.2

Comparative Weights of Protein Particles

	Particle weights (one carbon atom = 12)
Egg albumin	45 000
Haemoglobin	68 000
Serum albumin	69 000
Serum globulin	156 000
Fibrinogen	400 000

Related to the immense size of these molecules is the fact that the water-soluble proteins have the characteristic properties of hydrophilic colloids. In their natural states, as constituents of plant and animal tissues and secretions, they are associated with a high level of bound water, amounting to 30 per cent of protein weight.

5.2 CLASSIFICATION OF PROTEINS

Within the animal body, proteins fulfil many different roles, forming structural material, contractile tissue, nerve-impulse conductors, hormones, enzymes, buffers and oxygen carriers. Consequently a very large number of proteins have been distinguished and classified as simple or conjugated, globular or fibrous, defined as follows:

SIMPLE PROTEINS: On hydrolysis yield only amino-acids.
CONJUGATED PROTEINS: On hydrolysis yield both amino-acids and other distinctive substances which in the protein molecule form the prosthetic group.
GLOBULAR PROTEINS: Rounded or compact-shaped molecules; soluble in water or in dilute aqueous solutions of electrolytes; easily denatured.
FIBROUS PROTEINS: Fibrous molecules; insoluble in water and dilute salt solutions. Many twisted into helices, giving elasticity. Others in form of pleated sheets.

Simple proteins may be globular or fibrous; conjugated proteins are essentially simple globular proteins linked to non-protein material. Some defy strict classification and myosin will be quoted as falling between the globular and fibrous categories with actin occurring in both forms.

5.2.1   Classification of significant food proteins

I (A) Simple globular proteins

- (i) Albumins: dissolve in water giving a colloidal dispersion. Easily coagulated by heat. Occur in egg white (ovalbumin), milk (lactalbumin), blood plasma.
- (ii) Globulins: insoluble in pure water but dissolve in dilute solutions of salts. Heat coagulable. Occur in egg white, milk (lactoglobulin), blood plasma and muscle cells.

I (B) Simple fibrous proteins—insoluble in water and dilute solutions of salts

- (i) Collagens: the most abundant body proteins, present in connective tissue as 'white fibres'. Inelastic. High tensile strength. Converted by prolonged contact with boiling water to gelatin, a hot water soluble protein, more susceptible to enzymic digestion than collagen.
- (ii) Elastins: form 'yellow elastic fibres' present in elastic tissues such as artery walls and skin and, together with the more abundant collagenous white fibres, in the connective tissue of muscles. Elastin is unchanged by cooking.

II Conjugated proteins—classified according to nature of prosthetic (non-protein) group

- (i) Glycoproteins contain carbohydrate, e.g. mucin in saliva.
- (ii) Lipoproteins, combining lipid with simple protein, provide a means of lipid transport in blood and material for cell membrane formation.
- (iii) Phosphoproteins contain phosphate groups, the most notable being casein from milk.
- (iv) Chromoproteins include pigment groups such as haem in haemoglobin and flavin in flavoprotein.
- (v) Nucleoproteins combine nucleic acids with simple protein and form the polymeric material within nuclei, considered to be responsible for replication during cell division.

5.3   Structure of Proteins

As with most other macromolecular substances, proteins have a polymeric structure. This is appreciably more complex than that of carbohydrates due to the nature of the monomers employed, the amino-acids. These are small relatively simple molecules, soluble in water and capable of diffusing through animal membranes. Hence they can be transported around the body in the blood and pass through cell membranes.

5.3.1 **Amino-acids**

Hydrolysis of proteins from foods or from body tissues yields 20 distinct amino-acids. The number of different proteins which can be formed from them by condensation polymerization is vast. Proteins vary according to:

    (i) the number of different amino-acids included;
    (ii) the proportions in which the different amino-acids occur;
    (iii) the sequence of amino-acids in the polymer chains.

Nearly all amino-acids have the following molecular structure:

$$HN-\underset{\underset{R}{|}}{\overset{\overset{H}{|}}{C}}-C\underset{OH}{\overset{O}{<}}$$

described as a carbon atom, C, to which is attached: a hydrogen atom, H; a carboxyl group, —COOH (acidic); an amino group, —NH_2 (basic); and a residual group, —R, which varies with each amino-acid, being as simple as a single hydrogen atom or methyl group (—CH_3), or larger and more complex with significant properties, e.g. acidic or basic, hydrophilic or hydrophobic, sulphur-containing and reducing (see Table 5.3).

Table 5.3
Examples of Amino-Acid Formulae

Glycine $NH_2-\underset{\underset{H}{|}}{\overset{\overset{H}{|}}{C}}-CO.OH$ R =   H

Alanine $NH_2-\underset{\underset{CH_3}{|}}{\overset{\overset{H}{|}}{C}}-CO.OH$ R = —CH_3

Glutamic $NH_2-\underset{\underset{(CH_2)_2CO.OH}{|}}{\overset{\overset{H}{|}}{C}}-CO.OH$ R = —$(CH_2)_2CO.OH$ acidic

Lysine	NH_2—$\overset{\overset{\text{H}}{\mid}}{\underset{\mid}{C}}$—CO.OH $(CH_2)_4NH_2$	$R = $ —$(CH_2)_4NH_2$	basic
Serine	NH_2—$\overset{\overset{\text{H}}{\mid}}{\underset{\mid}{C}}$—CO.OH CH_2OH	$R = $ —CH_2OH	hydrophilic
Leucine and isoleucine	NH_2—$\overset{\overset{\text{H}}{\mid}}{\underset{\mid}{C}}$—CO.OH C_4H_9	$R = $ —C_4H_9	hydrophobic
Cysteine	NH_2—$\overset{\overset{\text{H}}{\mid}}{\underset{\mid}{C}}$—CO.OH CH_2SH	$R = $ —CH_2SH	sulphur-containing and reducing

5.3.2 Primary structure of proteins—formation of polypeptide chains

Because they each contain both an acidic group and a basic group, two amino-acid molecules will react together to form a dipeptide and water.

$$HN-\overset{\overset{\text{H}}{\mid}}{\underset{\mid}{C}}-\overset{\overset{O}{\diagup\!\diagup}}{C}-OH + HN-\overset{\overset{\text{H}}{\mid}}{\underset{\mid}{C}}-\overset{\overset{O}{\diagup\!\diagup}}{C}-OH \rightarrow HN-\overset{\overset{\text{H}}{\mid}}{\underset{\mid}{C}}-\overset{\overset{O}{\diagup\!\diagup}}{C}-N-\overset{\overset{\text{H}}{\mid}}{\underset{\mid}{C}}-\overset{\overset{O}{\diagup\!\diagup}}{C}-OH + H_2O$$

a dipeptide

The resulting dipeptide also contains both an acidic and a basic group either one able to react with another amino-acid molecule to form a tripeptide, again with the elimination of water.

$$HN-\overset{\overset{\text{H}}{\mid}}{\underset{\mid}{C}}-\overset{\overset{O}{\diagup\!\diagup}}{C}-N-\overset{\overset{\text{H}}{\mid}}{\underset{\mid}{C}}-\overset{\overset{O}{\diagup\!\diagup}}{C}-N-\overset{\overset{\text{H}}{\mid}}{\underset{\mid}{C}}-\overset{\overset{O}{\diagup\!\diagup}}{C}-OH$$

a tripeptide

Within living cells, this process continues, linking large numbers of amino-acids to form long polypeptide chains in which each

amino-acid residue joins to its neighbour by —$\overset{\overset{O}{\parallel}}{\underset{}{C}}$—$\overset{}{\underset{\overset{\mid}{H}}{N}}$—, the peptide linkage.

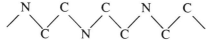

Fragments of polypeptide chain in which R, R′, R″ and R‴ may or may not differ from each other

The sequence of amino-acid residues in a polypeptide chain gives the primary structural feature of a protein. The 'zig-zag' of the polypeptide formula is an attempt to show something of the three-dimensional structure which is supported by a 'backbone' of

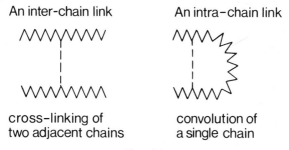

with projecting R groups, one from each component amino-acid. Some R groups are comparatively large, amounting to bulky side chains which interfere with close packing of molecules. The R

An inter-chain link   An intra-chain link

cross-linking of   convolution of
two adjacent chains   a single chain

FIG. 5.1

groups play a significant part in cross-links formation whereby adjacent chains are joined and single chains are convoluted (see Fig. 5.1).

5.3.3 Types of cross-links

The three most significant types of cross-links are hydrogen bonds, salt-links and disulphide links.

Hydrogen bonds Hydrogen bonds form between 'polar' groups which attract each other (rather as do the poles of a magnet) when in proximity, e.g. carbonyl groups ($=CO$) attract imino groups ($=NH$). Inspection of the polypeptide formula above will show these groups occurring regularly along its length, allowing frequent and regular hydrogen bonding between it and another chain. The total effect is considerable even though a single hydrogen bond is weak.

--- represents
hydrogen bonding

Salt links   Salt links form between ionized R groups, a positively charged —NH_3^+, attracting a negatively charged —$CO.O^-$, just as a positive ion will attract a negative ion when a salt is dissolved in water. Such ionization occurs in R groups which have been described as either basic or acidic (see 5.3.1) when the protein is dispersed in water. Salt links only operate when there is proximity between charged groups. They are stronger than hydrogen bonds but weaker than covalent bonds.

Salt–link formation

Disulphide links Disulphide links form between two adjacent sulphydryl groups (formula —SH and also called 'mercapto'). This is covalent bonding and stronger than the links described before. For it to occur, an oxidizing agent must be present to remove hydrogen. Disulphide links can only be broken when the opposite chemical change occurs, i.e. reduction.

Disulphide bond formation

5.3.4 Proteins and polypeptides distinguished
The distinction between a protein and a polypeptide is not always clear. Sometimes protein molecules consist of single polypeptide chains; others contain two or more chains linked together. A differentiation which may be usefully applied is that protein molecules display typical molecular shapes or conformations which are the result of secondary and, for globular proteins, tertiary features employing some or all of the cross-links described above. For polypeptides, primary structure alone need be considered.

5.3.5 Secondary structure of proteins—the α-helix
There is evidence for polypeptide chains within fibrous proteins forming helical structures (see Fig. 5.2(a)) or right-handed spiral coils in which successive turns are held in place by hydrogen bonding—known as intra-chain bonding. Such structures account for the marked elasticity of some fibrous proteins such as keratin in wool and hair. Super-coiling of a number of such helices into a 'rope' gives considerable strength and limits extensibility. The postulated structure for collagen is a three-stranded rope (see Fig. 5.2(b)).

Evidence of molecular structure of globular protein is sparse. It is possible that their polypeptides also form helices, at least in parts, before further conformations occur.

5.3.6 Tertiary structure of proteins—formation of globular proteins
Few globular protein structures (see Fig. 5.2(c)) have been described

to date. Evidence from X-ray studies of haemoglobin and myo-globin suggests formation of compact shapes from a folding back on itself of one or more protein strands which have, at least in parts, the secondary helical structure. The folds are held secure by any or all of the types of cross-links described above (see 5.3.3 and Fig. 5.1). R groups which are hydrophobic appear to be tucked into the interior while hydrophilic R groups are external, a factor favouring solubility in water and diffusibility.

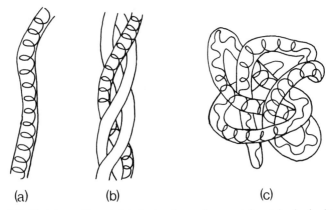

(a)   (b)   (c)

Fig. 5.2. Sketches of postulated structures for proteins (*a*) single helix; (*b*) triple coiled helices; (*c*) a globular protein

The achievement of the requisite molecular shape is necessary for performance of specific function, for loss of shape (e.g. when denaturing occurs) is accompanied by loss of biological activity.

5.4 DENATURATION OF PROTEINS

From a biological standpoint denaturation means loss of function; in the cooking of foodstuffs, it is associated with coagulation or with curdling. At a molecular level, it is described as the untwisting or unfolding of protein molecules. Globular proteins are much more susceptible than fibrous proteins and therefore denaturation can be considered loss of tertiary structure. A number of agencies can be employed, all of which are considered to interfere with cross-links.

5.4.1 Denaturing agencies

(i) Heat disrupts hydrogen bonds and, to a lesser extent, salt links. These operate by attraction which is only effective when peptide chains are sufficiently close together. Applying heat gives them energy to move apart.

(ii) Vigorous agitation such as whipping or shaking can result in physical separation and the loss of hydrogen bonds and salt links.

(iii) Organic solvents such as ethanol (the familiar alcohol) disrupt hydrogen bonds because they are capable of hydrogen bonding themselves to exposed polar groups.

(iv) Acids and alkalis provide charged ions which alter the charges on protein molecules and thus interfere with salt links. (This is considered more fully in section 5.5.)

(v) Salts of heavy metals, providing such ions as mercury II Hg^{2+}, silver Ag^+ and lead II Pb^{2+}, disrupt salt links by producing salt links of their own.

(vi) Alkaloidal agents such as tannic acid and picric acid also disrupt salt links and form new bonds between themselves and protein chains.

5.4.2 Destruction of enzymes

Attention will be paid later to theories of enzyme action (see 10.2). Here it is sufficient to acknowledge that all enzymes are proteins and that activity is associated with their molecular surfaces. Therefore denaturing, by altering their natural shapes, will effectively prevent activity. When, in food processing, enzyme destruction is deliberate, heat is the agency most commonly employed. The preservative actions of alcohol and acids such as vinegar are partly explained by reference to the denaturing effects on autolytic enzymes.

5.4.3 Coagulation, gel formation and curdling

By and large, fibrous proteins are insoluble in water due to their large-sized particles and the utilization of their hydrophilic R groups for cross-links in coiling and supercoiling. Conversely globular proteins have lower molecular weights, compact shapes and exposed hydrophilic groups which enable them to disperse in water or in dilute solutions of salts. Such aqueous dispersions are not true solutions for the dispersed particles are too large to diffuse through animal membranes. Rather they are hydrophilic colloids called sols because of their free flowing consistencies. Denaturing usually increases the viscosity, a change observed in cookery when a mixture such as egg custard thickens on heating. Obviously this is due to an increase in the water-binding properties of the protein particles, no doubt due to increased exposure of hydrophilic groups by unfolded protein chains. Continued denaturing can cause renewed cross-link formation but between rather than within protein molecules so that larger aggregates are produced. This effect is known as coagulation of proteins. If this is done so that the surface area remains extensive, the protein will continue to bind water and may indeed set into a gel, a structure in which there is no free flow of water.

Within a gel the protein strands form a three-dimensional lattice which traps the water in its interstices. If instead the protein strands form closely packed aggregates, surface areas will diminish and the water-binding power of the protein will fall. This is characterized by a separation of protein curds from the dispersing water, for example, as is seen when egg custard is inadvertently boiled or when acid and milk are mixed. As gel formation is frequently the desirable end-point in cooking and curdling something to avoid, it is worth noting that denaturing changes which proceed slowly and steadily are likely to favour gel formation while rapid exposure to denaturing agencies is more likely to end with curd formation. Take for example the addition of lactic acid to milk in sufficient quantity to cause ordinary souring; addition of all acid at once will cause immediate precipitation of curds but slow steady acid production by bacterial action will result in a gel in which the whole of the water in the milk is held within the framework.

Heat is the most frequently applied agency for gel formation but some protein sols only convert to gels when allowed to cool, gelatin jellies being examples. Probably the reformation of cross-links and the building of the lattice occur as protein strands lose energy and move less freely. Gelatin gels are exceptional in being able to revert to sols on heating. Other protein gels will shrink when further heat is applied and some of the bound water will be exuded. Note the effect of over-cooking scrambled eggs and the diminished size of an over-done joint of meat.

Egg albumin is particularly susceptible to denaturation by mechanical agitation. Hence the possibility of whipping egg white into a stable foam for use in meringues and soufflés. The casein in milk is denatured by the enzyme rennin but the formation of the junket gel requires calcium ions to be present. Indeed the responses of proteins to denaturing changes, brought about by cooking, are much affected by other substances present in the water. For example, sugar makes egg protein less susceptible to heat coagulation and higher baking temperatures are needed for sweet custards than for savoury. Gluten strand formation in bread dough, involving the breaking and remaking of disulphide links, is facilitated by the presence of reducing and oxidising agents. The pH of a protein dispersion influences the ease with which denaturing can be provoked; a pinch of cream of tartar assists foaming of egg white and stale milk will curdle on heating. In fact the nearer a protein dispersion is to its iso-electric point the more readily will it respond to denaturing agencies.

5.5 Iso-electric Point of Proteins

Owing to the presence of ionizable groups, a globular protein molecule in water will bear both positive and negative charges, i.e. $-NH_3^+$ and $-CO.O^-$. In its natural state, a globular protein such as the casein in milk or the albumin in egg white, will bear an excess of one type of charge, either negative over positive or vice versa. The resultant charge will be the same on all the protein particles in the dispersion and this will help to keep them in solution. Since 'like charges repel', the negative charges on casein particles in milk keep them moving and prevent them from coalescing. Adding acids, which provide positive hydrogen ions, will neutralize the negative charge and curd formation will result.

$$-COO^- \;+\; H^+ \;\longrightarrow\; -COOH$$

charged particles   become   uncharged particles
in solution   which precipitate

For a protein dispersion with an overall positive charge on its particles, precipitation will occur when an alkali, providing negative hydroxyl ions, is added.

$$-NH_3^+ \;+\; -OH^- \;\longrightarrow\; -NH_2 \;+\; H_2O$$

charged particles   become   uncharged particles
in solution   which precipitate

Thus a change in the pH (acidity or alkalinity) of a solution can affect the solubility of a protein. Charged protein particles are more soluble than uncharged. The pH of a protein solution which gives uncharged particles and lowest solubility is known as the iso-electric point of the protein.

The most significant iso-electric point in foodstuffs is that of the major milk protein, casein. Fresh milk has a pH of approximately 6·4. In this state the casein particles have an overall negative charge. As staling occurs, the pH drops (due to bacterial conversion of lactose into lactic acid), there is a reduction in the overall charge and casein solubility is lowered. At pH 4·6, the iso-electric point for casein, no charge remains and the consistency is that of sour milk. If, as mentioned before (5.4.3), the change in pH is gradual, the protein will bind the water and gel. When the change is accelerated by heating or pouring the milk into the acid, curds form. This governs the procedure for making milk jelly—'add fruit juice to milk, slowly'. Reversing this (and also using warm ingredients) will produce large curds which are bound to separate out, giving a two-layered jelly.

Casein curds can be redissolved by adding additional strong acid and taking the pH down below the iso-electric point. In this range, the protein particles will once more carry an overall charge which will now be positive due to an excess of hydrogen ions. This is utilized in the Gerber method for determination of fat in milk (see Expt. 13.6) when concentrated sulphuric acid is used.

5.6   EFFECT OF SALT CONCENTRATION ON PROTEIN SOLUBILITY

Neutral salts such as sodium chloride (common salt) have appreciable effects on the solubility of globular proteins. (In these circumstances, myosin ranks as a globular protein.) In general, solubility is increased by the presence of salts in low concentration, due to interference by the introduced ions with inter-molecular links in the form of hydrogen bonds or salt links; a phenomenon known as 'salting-in'. This justifies the recommendation to add a little salt to the stock pot. Some cookery writers take this further and advise against adding salt in meat cookery until the process is well advanced.

In contrast, solubility decreases when salt concentrations are high resulting in 'salting-out'. This is due to unequal competition for water between the abundant and fully charged ions and the merely polar side groups of the protein molecules. Consequently the latter are deprived of water and tend to set up inter-molecular links, resulting in protein coagula which separate out from the water. This is a likely explanation of the firm texture of salted meats and of the enzyme-inhibiting effects of salt concentrations.

5.7   HYDROLYSIS AND DIGESTION

Protein hydrolysis reverses peptide formation. As peptide links are broken, smaller lengths of polypeptide chain are produced until eventually, all are degraded to the constituent amino-acids.

$$
\begin{array}{c}
\text{R} \\
\text{C} \\
\diagup\text{H}\diagdown \\
\text{N} \\
\text{H}
\end{array}
\begin{array}{c}
\text{O} \\
\text{C} \\
\diagup\diagdown\text{H} \\
\text{C} \\
\text{R}
\end{array}
+ \text{H}_2\text{O} \rightarrow
\begin{array}{c}
\text{R} \\
\text{C} \\
\diagup\text{H}\diagdown \\
\text{NH} \\
\text{H}
\end{array}
+
\begin{array}{c}
\text{O} \\
\text{HOC} \\
\diagdown\text{H}\diagup \\
\text{C} \\
\text{R}
\end{array}
$$

This provides the means of investigating the composition of proteins. In the laboratory, hydrolysis may be achieved by the use of heat with mineral acids or alkalis. In the mammalian alimentary tract, proteolytic enzymes are employed in sequence to achieve conversion of ingested protein, with its large and often insoluble molecules, into soluble diffusible amino-acids.

5.8 DISTRIBUTION OF DIETARY PROTEINS

Because proteins are essential components of living cells they are widely distributed in animal and vegetable products, with the exception of deliberate extracts of such things as fats, oils and sugar. The amounts of protein vary enormously, not just from food to food, but between different samples of the same food, due largely to variations in water and fat contents. The figures quoted in Table 5.4 are of foods whose protein content is reasonably constant. For others, it is only safe to make statements such as 'lean meat is unlikely to contain more than 25g per 100g and 20g per 100g is the highest expected in fish'.

Table 5.4
Protein Content of Selected Foods (Paul and Southgate, 1978)

Ref. no.	Food	Protein (g/100g)	Ref. no.	Food	Protein (g/100g)
257	Sirloin, roast, lean & fat	23·6	33	Bread, white	7·8
258	Sirloin, roast, lean only	27·6	20	Rice, boiled	2·2
275	Lamb chop, grilled	23·5	569	Baked beans	5·1
321	Chicken, roast, meat only	24·8	621	Peas, fresh, boiled	5·0
468	Plaice fillet, fried	18·0	822	Almonds, shelled	16·9
165	Eggs, whole, raw	12·3	640	Potatoes, old, boiled	1·4
152	Cheddar cheese	26·0	652	Potato crisps	6·3
124/5	Cows' milk, fresh whole	3·3	637	Plantain, boiled	1·0

5.9 PROTEIN QUALITY

The body's primary need for protein from the diet is as a source of amino-acids from which it can build its own protein molecules of the many different types needed for tissue formation and for secretions. Food proteins differ in their abilities to meet these needs and this necessitates a concept of protein quality. Any amino-acids not used by the body for protein synthesis are broken down and used for energy production. This can be counted the secondary function of proteins, because it can equally well be performed by carbohydrates and lipids. However it is important to remember that the body serves its energy needs before those of growth and tissue maintenance, and in an energy-deficient diet, protein will be diverted from its primary function.

5.9.1   Biological estimations

Experimental evidence gained by feeding one protein at a time in calculated amounts to experimental animals (and to a few human subjects) shows that for the great majority of proteins, part only can be utilized by the body for protein synthesis while the remainder is broken down and its nitrogen excreted as urea. This is the basis for expressing protein quality as a percentage.

$$\text{protein quality} = \frac{\text{weight of protein utilized for synthesis of tissues and secretions}}{\text{weight of protein digested and absorbed}} \times 100$$

Calculations of protein are in fact always based on nitrogen estimations (see Expt. 5.5, Kjeldahl's method) and therefore a more precise value for protein quality is given by:

$$\text{biological value (BV)} = \frac{\text{nitrogen retained}}{\text{nitrogen absorbed}} \times 100$$

When a protein is eaten as the sole source of dietary nitrogen, in amounts capable of just meeting the body's need for nitrogen, the percentage of nitrogen used for protein synthesis is the biological value of that protein.

The difference between the amount of nitrogen absorbed and the amount taken in as food is small, being that in undigested protein. For most purposes this can be ignored and a simpler experimental procedure employed giving,

$$\text{net protein utilization (NPU)} = \frac{\text{nitrogen retained}}{\text{nitrogen ingested}} \times 100$$

Results of such feeding experiments provide values for food proteins which put them in rank order with egg protein and human milk protein highest, having NPU values approaching 100, indicating virtually complete utilization. Food proteins from animal sources—meat, fish and cow's milk—rate NPU values of 70–80. The extracted animal protein, gelatin, rates very low indeed, virtually zero NPU. In general, proteins from vegetable sources are lower in quality than animal protein but some, notably soya bean and rice proteins, are not significantly lower in biological value than the major animal proteins. A selection only of NPU values is given in Table 5.5 and readers are warned against comparing results obtained from different sources and therefore not by identical experimental procedures.

Table 5.5
NPU values of selected Food Proteins (FAO, 1965)

Protein	NPU	Protein	NPU
Egg	100	Potato	71
Pork	84	Rice	67
Fish	83	Wheat flour	52
Beef	80	Beans	47
Cow's milk	75	Gelatin	0

All biological experiments are lengthy and costly and for this reason a chemical method for estimating protein quality has been evolved.

5.9.2 Chemical score (or amino-acid score)
Variations in quality of proteins are due to differences in the amounts of essential amino-acids which they supply. Essential amino-acids are listed as:

For adults and children—isoleucine
                                leucine
                                lysine
                                methionine
                                phenylalanine
                                threonine
                                tryptophan
                                valine
Plus, for children—   histidine

These must be supplied by dietary proteins; other amino-acids, called 'non-essential', can be made within the body.

For protein synthesis, all essential amino-acids must be supplied together, each in sufficient amount. If the supply of one essential amino-acid runs out, protein synthesis will cease. In the experiments to determine biological value (or NPU), one protein is used at a time and the essential amino-acid which runs out first is called the limiting amino-acid. Proteins with biological values of 100 or thereabout, notably egg protein, have no limiting amino-acid but contain all the essential amino-acids in precisely the proportions required. Such a protein can be used as a reference protein against which other proteins are compared and given a chemical score:

$$\text{chemical score of test protein} = \frac{\%\text{ of limiting amino-acid in test protein}}{\%\text{ of same amino-acid in reference protein}} \times 100$$

Many calculations make use of egg protein as a reference. FAO calculates chemical scores using its own 'reference amino-acid pattern', based on estimations of needs for individual amino-acids.

It should be noted that very nearly all food proteins contain all essential amino-acids. Those with high biological values contain them in proportions approaching those required by the body. Lesser biological value proteins are limited by a low proportion (not a lack) of one or two essential amino-acids. If an essential amino-acid is missing from a protein, its biological value will be zero, for when it is used alone, no synthesis of protein will be possible. Gelatin and zein (from maize) are examples of the rare zero biological value proteins in foods. All other familiar proteins possess biological value and providing sufficient is consumed, could alone supply requirements for growth and tissue maintenance.

5.10 SELECTION OF DIETARY PROTEINS

Of all nutrients, protein is likely to be the one in scarcest supply and therefore highest in cost. This applies especially to the major animal proteins which find such favour in most human diets. The selection and efficient use of proteins is an important consideration and attention should be paid both to the quantity and the quality of protein in various foods. Eggs, meat, fish and cheese are prized because they contain protein of high quality in relatively high percentage contents. Soya bean products, including the meat analogues now available (see 15.6), also qualify on both these grounds. Other plant foods may contain appreciable amounts of protein which is only of moderate biological value (e.g. marrowfat peas) or conversely, small amounts of protein of a higher quality (e.g. rice).

5.10.1 Protein mixtures

The text so far has considered single proteins used in isolation. This is a false situation. In most dietary patterns, several protein sources are used in the same meal, giving a protein mixture which may well have a resultant biological value greater than that of any single component. The reason for this relates to the idea of limiting amino-acids and is known as the supplementary value of proteins.

A shortage of a particular amino-acid in one protein can be compensated by an excess in another. Thus a combination of two protein-providing foods with different limiting amino-acids is sound practice, such as bread and cheese, beef and spaghetti, fish and chips. Table 5.6 shows limiting amino-acids and chemical scores for a selection of food proteins compared with egg protein.

Table 5.6
Chemical Scores and Limiting Amino-Acids of Selected Food Proteins based on Egg Essential Amino-Acid Pattern (FAO, 1965)

Food	Chemical score	Limiting amino-acid
Egg	100	—
Meats	80–70	S (= sulphur-containing methionine and cysteine)
Fish	75	Tryptophan
Milk—cow's	60	S
Potato	70	S
Rice	75	Lysine
Wheat	50	Lysine

The practice can be extended with a view to increasing the efficient use of a shortage commodity at the domestic level by regularly mixing sources of proteins used at each meal. For the relief of communities suffering protein deficiency, high biological value mixtures have been formulated from selected plant sources.

5.10.2 Vegetarian diets
Vegetarians who reject all animal foods need to pay particular attention to selection of foods to obtain good quality protein mixtures. Even so, they will need to ensure that they consume a sufficient quantity of food. Plant proteins are not inferior *per se*, and hence their former classification as second class or incomplete is rejected, but they do tend to occur in smaller amounts and to be of moderate biological value only. In order to meet protein needs it is necessary to compensate lower quality by larger quantity and vegetarian diets are likely to be bulky.

5.10.3 Deficiency diseases
In communities where there is a low standard of nutrition with subsistence mainly on roots or plantains protein deficiency can occur because the appetite is geared to energy requirement and not to

protein needs. Elsewhere total food supplies may be inadequate and protein deficiencies will be aggravated because, if needs for energy are not met from carbohydrates and fats, proteins will be employed as energy providers and not for their exclusive function of providing amino-acids for protein synthesis. The disease kwashiorkor is a protein deficiency disease; marasmus is the disease caused by diets deficient in both protein and energy.

5.11   RECOMMENDED INTAKES

The ability of the body to store protein is limited and is largely discounted in making recommendations for daily intakes. Indeed, stress should be laid on spreading scarce and expensive protein supplies throughout the meals of the day and the days of the week. If at any time the intake of protein exceeds needs, the excess will be broken down into urea, which is excreted, and an energy-providing fraction. As energy can be supplied by the cheaper carbohydrates and fats, this is protein wastage.

In adults there is a constant need for protein to replace that broken down as cells and secretions are renewed. Back in 1936 the League of Nations Technical Committee recommended 1g protein per kg body weight per day. Although much more is now known of protein composition and metabolism, this remains a useful guide for caterers and administrators to apply.

The DHSS (1979) links protein requirements to energy and suggests that proteins should contribute at least 10 per cent of the dietary intake of energy. Recommendations average 54g per day, for most women, and 60–72g per day, for most men, of protein mixtures rating NPU values around 70. These relate closely to the 1936 figures. Such levels are achieved in the majority of British diets. While acknowledging evidence that appreciably lower intakes would suffice without protein deficiency, the DHSS fear that lowered levels would result in diets unpalatable to the British public and could jeopardize the supplies of other nutrients, notably vitamins of the B-group which often occur in association with proteins.

The latest recommendations from FAO (1972) are somewhat less demanding at 41g per day for women and 53g per day for men when the chemical score is 70, increased to 48g and 62g respectively when the protein quality falls to a chemical score of 60. Whether comparisons are valid between dietary proteins rated according to NPU (UK) and chemical score (FAO) is a moot point, but it is likely that the international organization will make the more modest recommendations because their advice is intended for use in impoverished communities.

Children, adolescents and pregnant or lactating women, have special needs for protein over and above those for replacing tissues and producing secretions. They have to provide the materials for growth and increased secretion. To a lesser extent, convalescents from tissue-wasting illnesses (including fevers), injuries and surgery will have special needs. Recommendations for children and adolescents allow them a greater amount of protein per kilogram body weight than for adults. Additional allowances for women during the later stages of pregnancy are recommended with substantial additions throughout lactation, in view of the protein content of milk.

PRACTICAL EXERCISES

*All experiments require standard precautions; those marked * involve particular hazards and should be supervised*
Unless otherwise indicated, the tests should be carried out on a selection of extracted proteins, both globular and fibrous, of known origins, viz. egg albumin, casein, fibrin (from clotted blood), gluten, gelatin and keratin (wool or hair) and also foods noted for their protein content.

*Expt. 5.1 THERMAL DECOMPOSITION OF PROTEINS WITH INDICATIONS OF CONSTITUENT ELEMENTS

Strongly heat some dry protein in an ignition tube held by tongs in a horizontal position. Note the typical smell—burning hair—and test the fumes emitted with:

(a) Moist red litmus paper
    Result Blue colour due to alkaline fumes (NH_3) indicating nitrogen content.
(b) Moist lead acetate paper (POISONOUS)
    Result Dark colour due to hydrogen sulphide indicating sulphur content.

Condensed water vapour inside the tube is indicative of hydrogen and oxygen content, while the black residue is carbon.

Expt. 5.2 WATER SOLUBILITY OF PROTEINS

Test each protein available for water solubility by adding a SMALL quantity, in powdered or fragmented form, to half a test tube of water and shaking thoroughly. Foaming is evidence of solubility, even if slight. If insoluble in cold water, try the effect of heating.

Classify the proteins tested as 'cold-water soluble', 'hot-water soluble' and 'insoluble'. Make suggestions concerning the types of dispersions which have formed.

Retain solutions/suspensions (labelled) for use in Expt. 5.3.

Expt. 5.3   TESTS FOR THE PRESENCE OF PROTEIN

There is no exclusive test for protein; most of the following are given by many but not all proteins and Biuret which is given by all proteins (although slowly by insoluble ones) is also given by some non-protein compounds. Therefore it is necessary to carry out THREE or more of the tests (usually Biuret, Millon's and Xanthoproteic) and obtain at least TWO positives before concluding protein present in an unknown substance.

(i) **Biuret Test** (Given by compounds having two or more peptide linkages) Mix 5cm³ 2M sodium hydroxide and 3 drops 1% copper sulphate. Reserve some of this mixture for colour comparisons. Add 1cm³ Biuret mixture to an equal volume of solution/suspension under test and leave to stand.

Positive result   Violet to pink colours indicate proteins, peptones, peptides or other soluble compounds with two or more peptide links. Small molecule peptones give pink tones.

*(ii) **Millon's Test** (Given by compounds containing the hydroxy-phenyl group, C_6H_4OH)
Millon's reagent (mercury dissolved in nitric acid) is both POISONOUS and COSTLY. Use minimum quantities. To about 2cm³ solution/suspension under test, add 2 drops Millon's reagent and heat in a water bath.

Positive result   Brick red colour or precipitate indicates amino-acid tyrosine, free or combined in a protein. Tyrosine is present in nearly all proteins, although sometimes at low levels. Chloride ions interfere with this test.

*(iii) **Xanthoproteic Test** (Given by compounds containing the phenyl group, C_6H_5)
To about 2cm³ solution/suspension under test, add 2 drops concentrated nitric acid (CORROSIVE) and heat in a water bath. Cool and neutralize by adding an ample amount of ammonium hydroxide solution.

Positive result   Yellow colour which deepens on neutralization indicates amino-acids, phenylalanine, tyrosine and tryptophan, free or combined in protein.

(iv) **Sakaguchi's Test** (Given by practically all known proteins because arginine is widely represented)
To 3cm³ solution/suspension under test, add 1cm³ 2M sodium hydroxide, 2 drops 1% alcoholic alpha naphthol and 3 drops 10% sodium hypochlorite. Mix well and allow to stand. Repeat on a 'blank', i.e. a test tube containing water instead of test solution/suspension.

Positive result   Bright red colour, distinct from the slight reddish colour in the blank, indicates the amino-acid arginine, free or in combination in protein.
    NB. Sodium hypochlorite solution is unstable—use of domestic bleach which contains a stabilizer eliminates this complication.

(v) **Sulphide Test** (Given by compounds which decompose to give inorganic sulphides in alkaline solution)
To 1cm³ solution/suspension under test, add 2cm³ dilute sodium hydroxide. Boil thoroughly in a water bath, noting dissolution of insoluble protein. Either add a few drops lead acetate solution or dip in a lead acetate test paper.

Positive result Brown/black colour indicates presence of amino-acids, cystine and cysteine, free or combined.
    NB. The third sulphur-containing amino-acid methionine does NOT give a positive.

*Expt. 5.4 DENATURATION OF PROTEIN

Precipitation from solution is taken as evidence of denaturation. Use a 2% solution of egg albumin. The dispersion should be clear. If instead egg white (often called albumen) is used, make up a 10% solution and filter off insoluble globulins. Place approximately 3cm³ of the albumin solution in each of four test tubes, (*a*), (*b*), (*c*), and (*d*).

To (*a*) add 4cm³ industrial spirit (alcohol) and shake;
    (*b*) add 2cm³ mercuric chloride solution (POISONOUS);
    (*c*) add 2cm³ tannic acid solution and mix;
    (*d*) heat, gently at first and then bring to boiling.

Record results, describing any coagulum formed. While these apply in particular to egg albumin, the effects of organic solvents, salts of heavy metals, 'alkaloids', e.g. tannic acid, and heat are similar for most soluble proteins. Apply them to explanations of:

(*a*) 'Pickling of anatomical specimens in alcohol'
(*b*) 'Swallowing egg white as an antidote for lead poisoning'
(*c*) 'Applying tannic acid ointment to burns and why this is no longer advocated'
(*d*) 'Destroying enzymes by heat'.

*Expt 5.5 DETERMINATION OF THE PERCENTAGE OF PROTEIN IN A FOOD— Kjeldahl Method

The food material is combusted in a Kjeldahl flask (Fig. 5.3) with concentrated sulphuric acid which oxidizes the organic matter, and the nitrogen present is converted into ammonium sulphate. Excess caustic soda is now added and the mixture distilled. The nitrogen is expelled as ammonia which is absorbed in a known volume of standard acid. The excess of standard acid is determined by titration with standard alkali. The amount of nitrogen can then be estimated and this, when multiplied by the proper factor, gives the amount of protein.
    Weigh out accurately between 1 and 5g of the food into a round-bottomed Jena flask of 200–300cm³ capacity (usually termed a Kjeldahl flask). Add 20cm³ of concentrated sulphuric acid, about 0·5g of copper sulphate which assists oxidation, and about 5g of powdered potassium sulphate to raise the boiling point. Kjeldahl catalyst tablets are available to replace the copper sulphate and potassium sulphate additions. Place the flask in a fume-cupboard in a sloping position and heat gently until the

contents of the flask are either pale coloured or clear.

Cool the flask carefully and when quite cold dilute the contents of the flask with about 70cm³ of water. Add this water carefully and shake and cool after each addition.

When quite cold, connect the flask to the distillation apparatus. This is fitted with a 'spray bulb' to retain any alkali, which may spurt upwards, and a dropping funnel.

The end of the condenser just dips below the surface of 50cm³ M/10 HCl plus H_2O in a flask which should preferably be on a movable base so that as the flask fills it can be lowered to keep the tip of the condenser just below the surface of the acid. This is necessary to prevent sucking back. Place in the flask a few pieces of broken earthenware or zinc dust to prevent bumping during boiling. Pour a few drops of litmus into the flask. Fill the dropping funnel with 50cm³ or more of 40% caustic soda solution. When the apparatus is all fitted together run in the caustic soda solution from the dropping funnel until the contents of the flask are strongly alkaline. Close the tap and heat the flask to boiling so that the ammonia is distilled off. To test when all the ammonia has been distilled off, allow a drop of the distillate to fall on red litmus paper. When the operation is complete, remove the flask and titrate its contents against M/10 caustic soda using screened methylred as indicator.

Calculate the amount of acid neutralized by the ammonia and hence the weight of nitrogen in the food material. The average percentage of nitrogen in a protein is 15–16%. Hence the weight of protein can be obtained by multiplying by the factor 6·25.

Calculation

Weight of food sample $\qquad = Wg$

Titration result $\qquad = T\text{cm}^3$ M/10 NaOH

∴ Ammonia produced had neutralized 50–Tcm³ M/10 HCl

Nitrogen contained in 50–Tcm³ M/10 ammonia $\quad = \dfrac{14(50-T)}{1000 \times 10}$ g

∴ % Nitrogen in food $\quad = \dfrac{14(50-T)}{10\,000} \times \dfrac{100}{W}$

% Protein in food $\quad = \dfrac{14(50-T)}{100W} \times 6\cdot25$

REFERENCES

DHSS (1979). *Recommended Daily Amounts of Food Energy and Nutrients for groups of people in the UK*, HMSO.

FAO (1965). *Protein requirements*, Report of a joint FAO/WHO expert group, FAO, Rome.

FAO (1972). *Energy and protein requirements*, Report of a joint FAO/WHO expert group, FAO, Rome.

Paul, A. A. and Southgate, D. A. T. (1978). *McCance and Widdowson's The Composition of Foods*, MAFF/MRC, HMSO.

FURTHER READING

Fisher, P., and Bender, A. (1970). *The value of food*, Oxford University Press.

Lawrie, R. A. (ed.) (1969). *Protein as human food*, Proceedings of the sixteenth Easter school in agricultural science, University of Nottingham, Butterworth.

Norman, R. O. C., and Waddington, D. J. (1975). *Modern Organic Chemistry*, Mills and Boon.

Taylor, R. J. (1969). *The chemistry of proteins*, Unilever educational booklet, Information Division, Unilever Ltd.

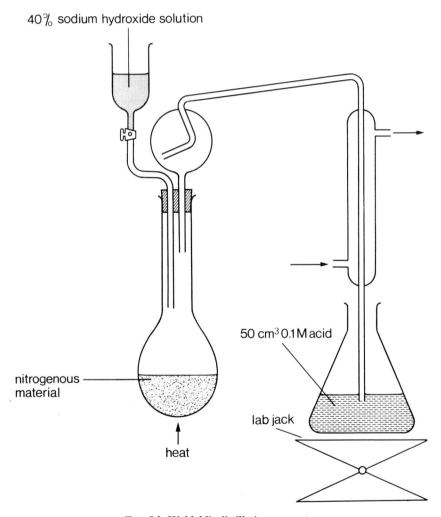

FIG. 5.3. Kjeldahl's distillation apparatus

CHAPTER VI

WATER

Water is at once the most familiar and the most exceptional of all chemical compounds. Its familiarity can lead to the unjustified neglect of water in listing nutritional requirements. The widespread distribution within foodstuffs and its influence on consistencies, makes the study of water a significant component of food science.

6.1 POLARITY OF THE WATER MOLECULE

The well-known formula for a molecule of water, H_2O, does not disclose the significant spatial arrangement of the two hydrogen atoms and one oxygen atom. This is better shown, within the limits of two dimensions, by

$$\underset{H\qquad H}{\overset{O}{\diagup_{105°}\diagdown}}$$

The bonds between the hydrogen atoms and the oxygen involve electrons (negative particles) which are in constant motion. The probability is very high that, at any given moment, there will be more electrons on the 'oxygen side' of the molecule than on the 'hydrogen side'. A molecule is, overall, neutral, containing equal numbers of negatively charged electrons and positively charged protons. Therefore an unequal distribution of electrons will produce negativity in the region of excess electrons and positivity elsewhere. This is depicted by

$$\underset{\delta^+ \qquad\quad \delta^+}{\underset{H\qquad\quad H}{\overset{\overset{\delta^-}{O}}{\diagup\quad\diagdown}}}$$

where δ^- stands for 'partially negative' and δ^+ for 'partially positive'. The molecule's oppositely charged 'sides' give it polarity and, because 'unlike charges attract', water molecules attract each other

The attraction shown by ...... constitutes a hydrogen bond between the oxygen of one molecule and one or other of the hydrogens of another. The attraction between water molecules is similar to pins attracted to a magnet, each pin becoming a small magnet with north and south poles. They cling together in a mass or, if adjusted with care, can form a linear arrangement (Fig. 6.1(a)).

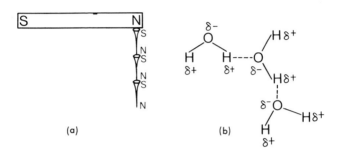

(a)   (b)

FIG. 6.1. Spatial arrangements of (a) magnetized pins and (b) of water molecules

In liquid water, the molecules are a disorganized mutually-attractive mobile mass. In ice, there is a more static orderly arrangement, with a three-dimensional lattice structure due to the polarity being associated with three points on each molecule (see Fig. 6.1(b)).

The concept of the polar molecule of water can be used to account for the distinctive properties of water.

6.1.1 Hydrophilic and hydrophobic properties

Hydrophilic and hydrophobic mean water-loving and water-hating respectively, and when applied to organic molecules or parts thereof indicate responses to the proximity of water. Hydrophilic organic molecules will contain groups such as hydroxyl (—OH), carbonyl (—CO), carboxyl (—COOH) and amino (—NH$_2$) which attract water because they also have polarity. Organic molecules which are hydrophobic to the extent that they will not mix with water are either composed entirely of carbon and hydrogen, e.g. mineral oils, or mainly so, e.g. lipids. Their greasiness is attributed to the non-polarity of hydrocarbon groups.

For a substance to be wholly miscible with water the influence of its hydrophilic group(s) must outweigh that of the hydrocarbon portions. For example, ethanol (C$_2$H$_5$OH) is soluble in water because the hydrophilic tendency of —OH is greater than the hydrophobic tendency of C_2H_5.

The two tendencies operate in some molecules so that they concentrate at surfaces, their hydrophilic portions in the water and their hydrophobic portions projecting out into the air or other non-polar substance. These are surface active agents of which emulsifying agents and detergents are examples (see 6.2.3).

6.1.2 Ionization

The component parts of molecules of compounds called electrolytes are linked by electrical attraction. When they dissolve in water, the polarity of the water molecules provides a counter-attraction and the electrolyte molecules split into charged ions. The positive ions are drawn by the negative polarity of the oxygen of water molecules; the negative ions by the positive polarity of the hydrogens. All salts in aqueous solutions exist as ions; acids and alkalis ionize at least to some extent in water. Some organic macro-molecules, notably proteins, include ionizable groups such as $-COOH \rightarrow -COO^- + H^+$ and $-NH_2 + H^+ \rightarrow -NH_3^+$, so that they carry charges, positive or negative, and sometimes both (see 5.3.3).

6.2   WATER-BASED DISPERSIONS

Water is a remarkable solvent. Its bi-polarity ensures its attraction for both positive and negative ions and for groups with either δ +ve or δ −ve polarity. Thus it is able to dissolve most inorganic materials, to some extent at least, and organic compounds that do not mix with water are easily distinguished.

6.2.1   True solutions

Inorganic ions, such as those of the metallic elements (Na^+, K^+, Ca^{2+}, Fe^{2+} and Fe^{3+}) and non-metallic elements (chloride, Cl^- and iodide, I^-), together with radicals (hydroxyl OH^-, sulphate SO_4^{2-} and phosphate PO_4^{3-}) form solute particles small enough to be dispersed easily in water. The same is true for small-size hydrophilic organic molecules—e.g. the sugars, ethanol, acetic, lactic and citric acids, and urea. True solutions are transparent to light and both solute and solvent will pass through diffusion membranes as well as filters.

True solutions are homogeneous mixtures of solute and solvent. Amounts of a solute dissolved in a given amount of a solvent can be varied; the greater the amount of solute the higher is the concentration. For a solid solute in water there will be a maximum concentration at which point no more solid will dissolve and the solution is described as saturated. In many cases, solubility is greater in hot water than in cold and when such a hot saturated solution is allowed to cool, some of the solute separates out, usually in the form of crystals. This will occur with sugar solutions (usually referred to as syrups). The size of the crystals depends on the rate of formation. Large crystals form slowly. Rapid cooling of hot saturated syrups, beating and 'seeding' (addition of a few pre-formed crystals) all accelerate the process and result in tiny crystals. In food preparation, small crystals are usually favoured. For sugar confectionery (fudge and fondants) small crystals create the typical smooth texture and the preparation involves simultaneous cooling and beating. Formation of small ice crystals depends on speed of formation and requires quick-freezing and, for ice-cream, this is accompanied by beating.

Boiling of water occurs when its vapour pressure equates with atmospheric pressure. Presence of solute particles, with their attraction for water molecules, hinders evaporation and more energy has to be provided before the vapour pressure reaches atmospheric pressure, i.e. solutes elevate the boiling point of water. The greater the solute concentration, the larger the elevation. This is used to measure concentrations of solutions by reading their boiling points, e.g. in jam making when a boiling point of $105°$ C indicates the soluble solids concentration (70 per cent) required to give a set.

Solutes likewise depress freezing points; hence the need to bring temperatures down below $0°$ C in order to freeze foods.

6.2.2 Hydrophilic colloids

Molecules or aggregates of molecules too large to pass through diffusion membranes can be dispersed in water provided they possess hydrophilic tendencies and that other factors do not predispose their coalescence. Globular proteins are considered water-soluble but the dispersions they form are colloidal and not true solutions. They provide noteworthy examples of loss of solubility due to formation of aggregates of molecules, too large to be dispersed in water (see 5.4.3).

Other hydrophilic colloidal systems in food processing are those formed by cooked starch, pectins and alginates. Blood and other body fluids within and without the cells, contain materials in colloidal dispersion which are thereby prevented from diffusing freely into surrounding tissues. Plasma proteins, for example, have roles to play within the blood and need to be retained. When barriers have to be penetrated, such colloidal-sized particles are broken down to diffusible dimensions by, for example, digestive reactions.

Many colloidal dispersions appear cloudy; some dilute samples look clear except when viewed in a beam of light, in which all colloidal dispersions show dispersion of light—the Tyndall effect.

6.2.3 Emulsions

Two immiscible fluids, e.g. oil and water, water and air, air and oil, lack the mechanism of mutual attraction to bring about dispersions unaided. Unstable emulsions can be made by mechanical means such as whisking or beating. One fluid, the disperse phase (DP), is divided up into small discrete amounts which are dispersed in the second fluid, the continuous phase (CP). By the introduction of a thickening or stiffening material, formed emulsions can be stabilized. The increase in the viscosity of the continuous phase provides a mechanical impediment to the movement of particles of the disperse phase. Examples from food preparation are:

   (i) Thickened gravy—the dripping providing the oil (DP) and the stock providing the water (CP), made viscous by the cooked starch of the flour.
  (ii) Egg white beaten to a foam is an air (DP) in water (CP) emulsion, stiffened by denatured albumin.
 (iii) Creamed plastic fat is another foam, with air (DP) dispersed in oil, the liquid triglycerides (CP), stiffened by crystals of fat, solid triglycerides. (This example does not belong under 'water-based dispersions' but is included to further appreciation of emulsions in foodstuffs.)

The formation and stabilization of oil-in-water emulsions is greatly facilitated by the use of emulsifying agents which have particles with dual affinities, one 'end' being hydrophilic (and lipophobic—lipid-hating), the other 'end' being lipophilic—lipid-loving —(and hydrophobic). Here it should be noted that not only are hydrocarbon groups hydrophobic but also lipophilic. Attention is drawn to the structures of lecithin and glycerol monostearate (see 4.3.9, 4.2.3), both naturally occurring emulsifying agents. Utilizing the 'head and tail' symbol for such dual-affinity molecules, their distribution within an oil-in-water emulsion is shown, two-dimensionally, in Fig. 6.2.

The oil droplets are effectively 'tied' to the surrounding water so that they do not rise to the surface and form an oily layer. In addition, the larger droplets are broken down into smaller ones to provide a sufficient area of interface between oil and water to accommodate the emulsifying agent particles. This furthers the process of emulsification. The action is precisely that of soap or non-soap detergent particles in the removal of greasy soiling matter. Bile salts are further examples of emulsifying agents.

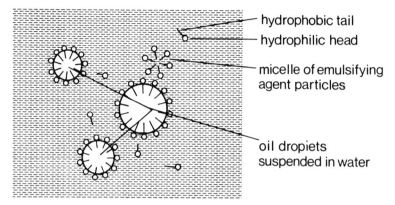

FIG. 6.2. Action of Emulsifying Particles

6.2.4 **Bound water**

Hydrophilic colloids have the ability to bind water to their surfaces by polar attraction. In the case of proteins this ability will vary according to their state of denaturation (see 5.4.3), being at a maximum at the point of gel formation. Shrinkage of a gel causes loss of some bound water and curdling reduces bound water appreciably. Starch granules bind water as cooking proceeds. Although cellulose is insoluble and usually occurs in foods in the form of fibres in leaves and stems or as flakes in bran, it has very considerable water-binding power due to the abundance of hydrophilic hydroxyl groups in its molecular structure (see 3.5.2).

Concentrated true solutions of materials such as salt and sugar, when used in preservation, bind their solvent water effectively, making it unavailable for enzymic and microbial activity. Water of crystallization is bound within the crystal structures of sugars in crystallized fruits and fondants.

The total water in foodstuffs can be very high: turnip 93 per cent, potatoes 76 per cent, green peas 78 per cent, raw beef 71 per cent. Even 'dry stores' contain appreciable amounts, lentils 12 per cent, wheat flour (average) 12·5 per cent. The crispest of cornflakes contain 3 per cent water and, like many other dehydrated foodstuffs, they are hygroscopic, i.e. absorb moisture when exposed to the atmosphere. Only part of the total water in foods is bound. The remainder, described as free water, will evaporate under ordinary atmospheric conditions of temperature, humidity and pressure. Free water, as distinct from bound water, can be utilized by micro-organisms in foodstuffs. Thus it is the free water content of a food, rather than the total water content, which is significant to its keeping qualities.

6.2.5 Diffusion and osmosis

Diffusion occurs in fluids (liquids and gases) because their particles are free to move. It results in homogeneous mixtures of gases and of the solute and solvent particles in solutions. Although this movement, which is due to kinetic energy, is random, the overall effect is directional. This results in a transfer of particles from a region of high concentration to one of lower concentration until uniformity is achieved, i.e. diffusion follows the concentration gradient.

Certain membranes in foods and living tissues are semipermeable, allowing passage of some but not all fluid particles. Water molecules are among the smallest and permeate many internal membranes, although the outer surfaces of both plant and animal structures have to be able to retain water. Dissolved particles in true aqueous solution, notably glucose, amino-acids and ions of mineral elements, are small enough to diffuse through cell membranes and follow the concentration gradients. Consequently equal concentrations should be expected within and without a cell. When this does not obtain, as in the case of sodium and potassium ions (see 6.5.1), energy has to be expended to oppose diffusion (see 2.3.3).

The flavouring of foods during cooking employs diffusion (e.g. passage of salt from brine, or sugar from syrup into foods cooked therein) and exchange of soluble flavouring materials between different foods within the same dish. This applies not only to water-soluble matter but also to the diverse organic substances which impart flavour when diffused into the fat content of a food.

By the same rule, water-soluble nutrients can be lost from foods into surrounding cooking liquors. The B group vitamins, ascorbic acid and ions of mineral elements are noteworthy examples. For maximum conservation, volumes of liquors should be as small as is compatible with efficient cooking. Thus effective diffusion, proceeding until concentrations of water-soluble nutrients are equal within and without the food, will cease sooner than it would were larger volumes of water employed.

When two aqueous solutions of differing concentrations are separated by a semipermeable membrane, there will be random passage of water molecules from one side to the other in both directions. Remembering the attraction which exists between true solute particles and water, one is able to appreciate that the greater pull will come from the solution containing the higher concentration of solute. Thus the effective movement will be out of the dilute solution and into the concentrated solution, until eventually concentrations are equalized.

Osmosis is the passage of water through a semipermeable membrane from the more dilute into the more concentrated of two solutions.

Pressure is exerted in the direction of the flow and may well oppose gravity, as can be demonstrated (see Expt. 6.3). The magnitude of osmotic pressure will depend upon the difference in the initial concentrations of the two solutions—the greater the difference, the higher the osmotic pressure. But for valid comparisons, concentrations must be measured in terms of numbers of solute particles in a given volume of solvent, emphasizing the dependence upon attraction by individual particles for water. This accommodates the evidence of high osmotic pressures shown by electrolytes (ionization raising the numbers of dissolved particles) and of negligible osmotic pressure from colloids (outsize dimensions severely limiting the numbers of particles in solution).

In biological systems, osmotic pressure is utilized to move water as, for example, in the roots of plants. In foods, concentrated solutions of salt or sugar are employed as preservatives to control microbial activity by osmotic withdrawal of water (exosmosis) from contaminating cells. Endosmosis operates in the re-hydration of foods such as prunes.

6.3 WATER AS A HEAT RESERVOIR

The mutual attraction among water molecules accounts for water's high thermal capacity. A rise in temperature signifies increased kinetic movement which will only be achieved if the energy input is sufficient to overcome these forces of attraction. Consequently a larger amount of heat has to be given to water than to the same mass of any other common material, to produce a particular temperature rise. Water heats up more slowly than adjacent materials exposed to the same heat sources. By the time it is hot, water will have absorbed appreciable amounts of heat. With the heat source withdrawn, water, by the same principle, will be slow to cool. This heat storage can be applied to many uses in cooking. It should also be realized that not only hot water but cool and even cold water has a heat content which has to be removed when the temperature needs to be lowered. This heat can be sensed coming from the back of a refrigerator which is cooling food down from room temperature to that required for its storage.

Once water is cooled to 0° C further removal of heat results not in a temperature drop but in freezing. Ice with its orderly structure has a lower heat content than water at the same temperature. Evaporation of water to steam is, by contrast, a heat-storing change. Steam produced from boiling water will contain not only the heat supplied to raise the temperature to boiling point but also the latent heat used to separate the molecules sufficiently to convert the liquid into a gas. Consequently steam is a valuable means of conveying heat to foodstuffs during cooking.

6.3.1 Specific heats

Amounts of heat involved in temperature changes are expressed in terms of specific heat.

The specific heat of a substance is the amount of heat required to raise the temperature of one gramme by one degree Celsius.

The specific heat of water is 4·18 joules or 1 calorie; that of ice is about half this value. For all foods except those with a high fat content, it is acceptable to apply the values for water or for ice to fresh and frozen foods respectively when calculating heat exchanges in food processing.

6.3.2 Latent heats

When solids change to liquids and liquids change to gases, heat is taken in. Equal amounts of heat are given out when these changes are reversed. The precise amounts of heat involved in changes of state, without alteration of temperature, depend upon both the masses and the materials and are calculated from latent heat values.

Latent heat of fusion is the amount of heat required to convert one gramme of a solid to a liquid without change of temperature.
Latent heat of vaporization is the amount of heat required to convert one gramme of a liquid to a gas without change in temperature.

While fusion only takes place at a temperature known as the melting point, vaporization will occur at all temperatures up to a maximum which is the boiling point.

The latent heat of fusion of ice is 334·4J (80cal) per gramme. The latent heat of vaporization of water is 2257·2J (540cal) per gramme.

6.4   WATER AS A NUTRIENT

Some two-thirds of the weight of the body is due to water. It is present in and around all cells and it provides the fluid basis of the blood, the lymph, glandular secretions and the excretions. Adipose tissue has the lowest water content, 10 per cent; bone comes next with 25 per cent, and the remaining tissues average 80 per cent.

Water is constantly being lost from the body in urine, breath, perspiration and faeces. Unless this is replenished, life cannot be supported. It may be possible to live without food for three weeks or more but three days is nearer the maximum period for survival without water.

6.4.1   Functions of water in the body

(i) Water provides a transport medium for suspended and dissolved substances from one part of the body to another. In a watery medium, foodstuffs are moved along the alimentary canal. Within the water of plasma digested nutrients are carried from the intestines to the liver and on to all other tissues. Waste nitrogenous materials are collected and passed to the kidneys. Hormones produced by the endocrine glands are transported to responsive sites and mobile structures such as blood cells and chylomicrons (see 9.6.2) follow the water flow through the blood vessels. Dissolved in the water within and without cells, diffusible materials are able to penetrate cell membranes.

(ii) Water is the medium for excretion of waste nitrogenous material in the form of urine, formed in the kidneys. Urine excretion is also the means employed to rid the body of an excess of any water-soluble material, thus maintaining the constant internal composition of the body.

(iii) The ionizing power of water enables the critical functioning of sodium and potassium ions at cell membranes and the sheaths of nerve fibres whereby electrical potentials can be established.

(iv) The high thermal capacity of water enables the body to work at a near-constant internal temperature. Quite large amounts of heat, produced in active tissues such as muscles and liver, can be taken up by the water of the blood with only small temperature rises. As the blood flows into the cooler peripheral tissues, this heat can be lost from the body again without appreciable falls in temperature.

(v) The principal means by which heat is lost from the body is by evaporation of perspiration. The heat required for this (latent heat of vaporization) is taken from the skin tissues. This is continuous and essential for body temperature control. If evaporation of perspiration is prevented, heat stroke will follow.

(vi) Certain external surfaces of the body need to be bathed in water to maintain their integrity. These include the cavity of the mouth and throat, the nasal and respiratory passages and the conjunctiva of the eye.

(vii) Water is a necessary chemical reagent entering into the many hydrolysis reactions of digestion and metabolism.

6.4.2 Water balance

In good health, the total amount of water in the body remains remarkably constant, in spite of continued output and variable intakes. Obviously a system of controls exists to adjust output to intake.

The fluid intakes of adults vary with personal habits and social customs. A very general estimate might be one to one-and-a-half litres per day. In addition to dietary intakes in the form of drinks and the water in foods, there is an appreciable contribution of water from the oxidation of carbohydrates and lipids. The total water available must be sufficient to replace losses. The signal to increase intake by drinking, the thirst mechanism, is a rise in the concentration of blood salt to which a centre in the hypothalamus of the brain is sensitive. This valuable mechanism has certain drawbacks. If the need for water is to replace losses from copious sweating, such as occurs when manual work is carried out at high temperatures or when there is fever in illness, there will also have been losses of salt. Hence the blood salt concentration may not rise sufficiently to produce a thirst. Drinks should be administered frequently in such circumstances as a matter of routine and not merely on request. Losses of salt should also be made good to prevent 'heat-fatigue'. In addition, the thirst mechanism fails for babies and helpless patients if they cannot make their requests understood. Anyone charged with nursing needs to ensure that water intake is adequate under all circumstances. A useful gauge for assessing requirements for fluid intake is the volume of urine produced.

Output can be controlled in respect of urine production. If the intake of fluids is below the requirement, the body responds by excreting less water in the urine. The control operates through another centre in the hypothalamus which detects a rise in blood concentration. This relays a message to the pituitary gland which secretes the anti-diuretic hormone (ADH). The response by the kidneys to ADH is the secretion of a more concentrated urine, whereby water is retained by the body until blood concentration returns to normal. Conversely if intake of fluids rises so that blood concentration falls, the production of ADH by the pituitary is inhibited and diuresis occurs, i.e., the production of large volumes of dilute urine.

Again there are limitations on this aspect of control. The retention of water in the body by the concentration of urine can only be taken so far. The amount of urea produced, from amino-acid metabolism, will determine the lower limit to urine volume, i.e. the obligatory water loss. The greater the protein intake, the higher will be the obligatory water loss. In addition certain substances such as alcohol and coffee taken with water, have diuretic effects and increase the volume of urine whether or not this is required for the adjustment of blood concentration. The regular drinking of fairly copious amounts of plain water has much to commend it.

6.5   WATER AND ELECTROLYTES

Electrolytes are compounds which ionize in water. The presence of ions in body fluids has considerable significance.

6.5.1   Distribution of sodium and potassium ions

The potassium ion is the principal cation (positive ion) inside the cells, while the sodium ion is the most abundant outside. If diffusion were allowed to proceed unchecked, there would be movement of potassium ions out of, and of sodium ions into, the cells until the concentrations of both achieved uniformity within and without. Only by expenditure of energy are the different concentrations maintained. Contraction of muscle cells and impulse conduction along nerve fibres is accompanied by a reversal in the distribution of potassium and sodium ions indicating a fundamental involvement in cell functioning.

6.5.2   pH

Water itself ionizes but to a very slight degree. All molecules remain whole except for one in 500 million and that splits into a positive hydrogen ion and a negative hydroxyl ion. In a mixture of these ions and water molecules, it should be expected that the ions will combine giving water molecules:

$$H^+ \; + \; OH^- \; \rightarrow \; H_2O$$

But in order to acknowledge that this will not go to completion, the very slight reverse tendency should be shown:

$$H^+ \; + \; OH^- \rightleftarrows H_2O$$

This low level of ionization of water is nevertheless very significant, providing the key to the concept of acidity, alkalinity and neutrality.

In pure water, the number of hydrogen ions will always equal the number of hydroxyl ions and, because the degree of ionization is predictable, a value of 10^{-7} moles per litre can be given for the concentrations of each. If a source of hydrogen ions is added to the water, the hydrogen ion concentration will rise—say to 10^{-6} moles per litre or 10^{-3} or even higher. On the other hand, if a source of hydroxyl ions is added to water, hydrogen ions will be removed by the forward reaction:

$$H^+ \; + \; OH^- \; \rightarrow \; H_2O$$

The hydrogen ion concentration will be lowered—say to 10^{-8} or 10^{-11}, or lower still to 10^{-14}. But no lower because that is the minimum hydrogen ion concentration given by water ionization even in the presence of an overwhelming concentration of hydroxyl ions.

Aqueous solutions of acids and acid salts provide hydrogen ions; the stronger the acid the more hydrogen ions there are. Measurement of hydrogen ion concentration provides a useful expression of acidity. Alkalis and alkaline salts in water provide hydroxyl ions, thereby lowering the hydrogen ion concentration. Again its measure would indicate degree of alkalinity. But the very small numbers involved, 10^{-2}, 10^{-7}, 10^{-14} etc., have a certain remoteness and instead the pH scale has been adopted. The powers of ten of hydrogen ion concentrations, without their negative signs, provide the numbers in the scale. Examples:

	Hydrogen ion concentration moles per litre	pH
Pure water	10^{-7}	7
Vinegar	10^{-3}	3
(dilute solution of acetic acid)		
soap flakes in water	10^{-9}	9

pH ranges: pH = 7   neutrality
          pH below 7   acidity
          pH above 7 up to 14   alkalinity

It is worth stressing that, although pH is based on measurement of hydrogen ion concentration, the higher that is, the lower the pH and vice versa.

6.5.3 pH of blood and acid–base balance

The pH of blood is maintained constant, within very narrow limits, just on the side of alkalinity, 7·35–7·45. This is despite the fact that the residues from some foods are alkaline while those from others are acidic. In general, animal foods form acidic products due to their protein contents, the sulphur and phosphorus therein forming radicals of strong acids. By contrast, plant foods, even the most acidic fruits, leave alkaline residues. Plant acids are either oxidized in the energy-producing cycles, or else, being weak acids, they form alkaline salts with sodium or potassium ions.

The body has two mechanisms for dealing with either type of residue and thus acidosis (lowering of blood pH) and alkalosis (raising of blood pH) is avoided.

(i) Carbon dioxide is an acid gas and its loss from the blood into the lungs will raise the pH. The rate of loss of CO_2 can be finely adjusted to control blood pH.

(ii) When acid residues are being produced by the diet, the urine will be acidic. Conversely, alkaline residues will cause the formation of alkaline urine.

The condition of acidosis can be induced by the formation of ketone bodies (see 10.5.3) and by excessive production of lactic acid as a result of prolonged and strenuous exercise (see 10.4.7). Acidosis is a serious condition which disturbs the carbon dioxide transport system of the blood by taking the pH below the level with which the mechanisms just described can cope.

PRACTICAL EXERCISES

All experiments require standard precautions

Expt. 6.1 DETECTION OF WATER IN FOODS

Cobalt chloride is blue when anhydrous, pink when in solution and hydrated crystalline form. The change from blue to pink gives an exclusive test for water. Impregnated test paper is available which normally appears pale pink due to atmospheric water.

Thoroughly dry a strip of cobalt chloride paper so that it is bright blue. Fold it around a fragment of food and press between dry glass plates (microscope slides).

Positive Result Pale pink colour, indicates water present in sufficient amounts to be expressed.

Expt. 6.2 USE OF A DIFFUSION MEMBRANE TO SEPARATE A TRUE AQUEOUS SOLUTE FROM A HYDROPHILIC COLLOID

Prepare a dilute solution of starch in hot water and add a pinch of salt. Allow to cool and use to half fill a test tube. Stretch a damp cellophane jam jar cover over the mouth of the test tube and fasten securely with an elastic band. Allow to dry and form a seal. Meanwhile place some deionized water in a beaker, checking to ensure that both starch and chloride ions are absent by performing the iodine (Expt. 3.1) (ii) and the silver nitrate tests (Expt. 7.2 (ii) on samples. Support the test tube inverted in the deionized water so that the cellophane membrane is just below the surface. Leave for 30 minutes while, at 5 minute intervals, samples are withdrawn from the beaker and treated for starch and chloride ion content.

Draw conclusions concerning the diffusion of dissolved particles through the membrane.

Expt. 6.3 DEMONSTRATION OF OSMOSIS

(i) Prepare a 20 per cent solution of sucrose in water and colour it with a dye to make it more visible. Tie a tight knot in one end of a 10cm length of visking tubing. Insert a filter funnel in the other end and fill the tubing bag with sucrose solution. Remove the funnel and replace with a length (about 40cm) of glass tubing with a capillary bore. The visking tubing should fit securely around the glass tubing and some of the syrup will be displaced into the bore. Support vertically with the visking tubing bag dipping below the surface of some water in a beaker. Mark on the glass tube, the initial level of the sugar solution. Observe at 15 minute intervals, recording changes in the sucrose solution level until a steady level is achieved.

Comment on the evidence for osmotic pressure which this exercise provides.

(ii) Select two similar samples of prunes (say two, A and B, with five prunes in each sample.) Record the initial weight of each sample. Treat as follows:

(*a*) Soak A overnight in tap water at room temperature
(*b*) Soak B overnight in 20 per cent sucrose solution at room temperature.

Drain on absorbent paper and re-weigh. Also record appearance and texture in response to touching gently. Offer an explanation of findings in terms of osmosis.

Finally attempt to reverse the changes in sample A by soaking in the sugar solution.

FURTHER READING

Davidson, Sir Stanley, Passmore, R., Brock, J. F. and Truswell, A. S. (1979). *Human nutrition and dietetics*, 7th edition, Churchill-Livingstone.
Davis, K. S., and Day, J. A. (1964). *Water, the mirror of science*, Heinemann.

CHAPTER VII

MINERAL ELEMENTS

7.1 NATURE AND OCCURRENCE

To maintain growth, repair wastage and supply energy, the body continually requires not only foods consisting mainly of proteins, fats and carbohydrates, but also foods which contain, in much smaller quantities, certain mineral elements. The term mineral is taken as referring to all chemical elements other than carbon, hydrogen, oxygen and nitrogen. Of the 90 odd chemical elements designated mineral, 20 or so occur in anticipated quantities in the human body. The following are listed in order of decreasing abundance: calcium, phosphorus, potassium, sulphur, sodium, chlorine, magnesium, iron, zinc, copper and iodine. The contribution of calcium to the weight of an adult man weighing 70kg will be rather more than 1kg; that of iron 5g or less. Other minerals which occur in trace amounts only are cobalt, selenium, molybdenum, silicon, aluminium, chromium, arsenic, boron, fluorine and nickel.

Within the body, the bony skeleton has the highest mineral content; 35 per cent of bone consisting of calcium phosphate mainly with lesser amounts of other insoluble salts of calcium and magnesium. Elsewhere in the body, mineral cations (especially potassium and sodium) and anions (phosphates, chlorides, etc.) are dispersed in blood, cell and tissue fluids and glandular secretions. Sulphur occurs in combination in protein, and phosphorus, in the form of phosphate groups, is a component of many organic molecules active in metabolism. Iron is an essential component of haemoglobin and myoglobin, the oxygen-carrying pigments in blood cells and muscles respectively. Several respiratory enzymes, including the cytochromes of the electron transport chain (see 10.4.5), contain iron. The body's very small amount of iodine is concentrated in the thyroid gland and its hormones and thereby it plays a vital role. Other elements present in very low levels are known to be just as essential, e.g. zinc for the production of insulin, and cobalt and copper for their contribution to the production of haemoglobin. Some trace elements have as yet no identifiable role but research will continue in the hope of being able to influence dietary practices in the interests of health. The association of fluorine with dental enamel is a case in point.

The mineral elements are ingested in both organic and inorganic forms: as parts of certain proteins; as simpler organic compounds in the cell and tissue fluids; as inorganic ions in the same fluids; from food additives, especially the familiar sodium chloride, and calcium carbonate, the additive in white flour.

Foods which consist of whole tissue structures whether plant or animal are certain to provide a good selection of mineral elements because of their involvement in the metabolism of all species. Milk and eggs, being intended as sole sources of nourishment for the young of other animals, are a special case and will be shown to be valuable mineral element sources. However there are so many variables between the several mineral elements with regard to sources, factors limiting availability, functions in the body, individual requirements, etc., that general statements made about them as a whole are of little value. Individual consideration must be given to those for which there is sufficient evidence.

7.2 SODIUM AND POTASSIUM

In the form of their cations, the two metallic elements, sodium and potassium, which are very similar chemically, play important roles in cell functioning (see 6.5.1). The cations of sodium and potassium together with the anions from weak acids most abundant in body fluids, i.e. phosphates, carbonates, citrates, etc., give the component ions of alkaline salts. These are responsible for alkalinity of bile and pancreatic juice and help to stabilize the pH of blood just on the alkaline side of neutrality. In addition sodium in the blood controls the thirst mechanism (see 6.4.2).

There is appreciably more potassium in the body as a whole and yet far more sodium must be supplied by the diet. The body retains its potassium adequately and it is so widespread in foods that only a freakish diet could produce a deficiency. On the other hand, sodium as salt is lost from the body in sweat and in urine and must be replaced from food. Again sodium is widespread and most people cultivate a taste for salt so that only in conditions which provoke excessive sweating is there need for a deliberate intake. Stokers, miners and athletes are usually provided with palatable salt-containing drinks. Symptoms of a sodium deficiency are those of 'heat-fatigue'—muscular weakness, drowsiness and mental confusion. If physical exercise is attempted, muscular cramps occur: hence the conditions called 'miners' cramp' and 'stokers' cramp'.

There is no limit on the absorption of sodium and potassium due to the formation of insoluble salts.

7.3 CALCIUM

Most of the body's calcium is in the hard structures of bone and teeth, mainly in the form of hydroxyapatite, $Ca_{10}(PO_4)_6(OH)_2$. Its crystalline form gives rigidity and hardness to these tissues. Equally important is the calcium content of the blood which maintains a uniform concentration around 10mg per 100ml. Blood calcium is essential for the clotting mechanism. Calcium ions are probably concerned with all cell functioning; certainly they are involved in muscle contraction, possibly in the myosin–actin interaction.

A dynamic equilibrium exists between the calcium in the blood and that in the bones. The bone calcium is constantly being dissolved out into the blood under the influence of cells called osteoclasts and replaced from the blood under the influence of other cells called osteoblasts. This allows for bone growth in childhood and adolescence and, in adult life, provides for maintenance and the adjustment of bone shape to meet stresses on the skeleton in action. In adults, the calcium withdrawn will equal the calcium laid down over a short period; during the growing years, the amount laid down must exceed that withdrawn.

Throughout, there will be urinary excretion of calcium and, consequently, there is a need for regular dietary intakes. If this fails, the amounts laid down in the skeleton will be jeopardized while withdrawal will continue, keeping the blood calcium level constant. This does not produce discernible effects on bone structure in adults; at least, none have been reported. Probably this is because the amount of calcium in the bone is vast compared with the amount in blood. For children, deficient intake could be serious if it interfered with the process of ossification whereby the cartilage in the skeleton is replaced by bone. But in these circumstances deficiencies of calcium are not nearly so significant as those of vitamin D which regulates the absorption of calcium from the food in the intestines into the blood and which is also concerned with the parathyroid hormone in controlling the blood calcium level. In women already on a diet very low in calcium (and probably deficient also in vitamin D), the demands of the foetus in pregnancy and the greater withdrawal for milk production during lactation, could precipitate the disease osteomalacia (see 8.5.3). Even so, there is no evidence to support the theory that calcium is withdrawn from teeth to meet the demands of a pregnancy. The condition of osteoporosis, characterized by fragile bones with lowered calcium and protein contents, is an aging symptom. No evidence exists as yet which links it with any dietary deficiency.

The absorption of calcium from food in the intestines is dependent upon the presence of vitamin D, which in turn, requires lipids for its absorption. Other factors also operate. Some products of protein digestion, probably small molecule amino-acids, are considered to facilitate calcium absorption. The coincidence of certain anions limits absorption. Such anions are oxalates from spinach and rhubarb, phytate from whole grain cereals and fatty acid radicals from lipids, all of which form insoluble calcium salts which pass out of the body with the faeces. In consequence, only a small part of the ingested calcium is usually absorbed. But this is not the whole story of calcium absorption. It is possible that the body has the ability to adapt to a low level of available calcium by increasing absorption efficiency. This would account for inconsistencies in some of the evidence, concerning intakes of phytates, which has been used in the debates about whole and refined cereals. The ability of the body to adapt to more stringent conditions when required has great biological advantage but the time taken for such adaptations to take effect makes difficulties for experimental scientists seeking to establish nutrient requirements. (See Davidson *et al.*, 1979).

7.3.1 Recommended intakes

There is little reliable evidence on which to make recommendations for intakes of calcium. Nevertheless there is value in providing some guidance for caterers and administrators. The FAO (1961) recommendations are given as:

	mg per day
0–12 months (not breastfed)	500– 600
1– 9 years	400– 500
10–15 years	600– 700
16–19 years	500– 600
Pregnancy and lactation	1000–1200

At the time when these figures were published, the recommendations for calcium issued by the Medical Research Council in the UK and the National Research Council in the USA were for appreciably higher quantities. It was in the light of these figures that Britain's bread was fortified with chalk and the drinking of abundant quantities of milk was urged and subsidized. Since then, studies of communities existing on substantially smaller amounts of calcium have influenced opinion and, when the DHSS (1969) published figures for Recommended Intakes of Nutrients, those for calcium were, in effect, taken from the FAO (1961), with 500mg calcium per day for adults in all categories. In the DHSS (1979) recommendations for children between 1 and 9 years the recommended amount is raised to 600mg per day.

7.3.2 Meeting requirements

Milk, in all its forms, and cheese are by far and away the most important sources of calcium in the diet (see Table 7.1). White flour in the UK is fortified with calcium carbonate to an extent which more than compensates for losses due to elimination of bran and wheatgerm in milling (see 11.6). Indeed, as a result, white bread provides nearly four times the amount of calcium in wholemeal bread. Another good source is tinned fish, but only when the bones are consumed. Green vegetables are potentially a moderate source but unreliable due to variations in culture conditions and because, in cooking, calcium ions can be leached out into the cooking water. The calcium in hard water makes a contribution within prescribed districts. Few additional sources exist and it must be allowed that, without milk, cheese and fortified white bread, it would be difficult to meet even the more modest recommendations of 1969.

Table 7.1
Portions of Food Supplying approximately 125mg Calcium—about one Quarter of a Day's Requirement

    15g cheese
   100g milk
    30g sardines
   125g white bread
   250g egg (4 large eggs)

7.3.3. Hypercalcaemia

Calcium has its place in animal physiology because it can be maintained in tissues in either a soluble form, suitable for mobility in fluids, or in an insoluble form, suitable for the construction of hard tissues. Under exceptional circumstances, insoluble calcium salts are deposited within the soft tissues. This serious condition, hypercalcaemia, was diagnosed in a number of babies in the 1950s, a time when fortification of baby foods with vitamin D was practised without restriction. Presumably this led to excessive absorption of calcium. Since then, fortification levels have been controlled and the problem of hypercalcaemia appears to have been solved.

7.4   IRON

Iron differs from those mineral elements already considered in that the body appears to have difficulty both in absorbing it from food and in excreting it in urine. In other words, the little that is taken in from the food is well retained.

7.4.1   Iron in the body

Iron compounds in the body function in (i) the transport of oxygen and (ii) the transfer of electrons. Therefore iron is implicated in the oxidation of foodstuffs and the release of energy.

Most of the iron contained in the body is in the form of haemoglobin, the conjugated protein in red blood cells, capable of transporting oxygen from lungs to tissues. Myoglobin is another iron-containing red-coloured pigment in muscles which transports oxygen. Within the cells, oxygen is utilized for energy release and some of the enzymes involved in the oxidation sequences are iron compounds, notably the cytochromes of the electron transport chain (see 10.4.5).

The remainder, about a quarter, of the iron in the body is in storage as the compound ferritin, in which iron is bound to protein. Ferritin is found mainly in the liver, the spleen and the red bone marrow. When red blood cells are broken down, the iron from the haemoglobin is salvaged by the liver and 'recycled' for haemoglobin in new red blood cells, formed in bone marrow.

7.4.2   Absorption of iron

Only a small proportion of the iron in foods is absorbed into the blood stream. As very little iron is lost from the body (except due to injury and menstruation), this is a means of preventing a build-up of excess iron. The body can store iron but only in limited amounts.

There is evidence that absorption responds to increased demands for iron by the body such as when new red blood cells are being formed in the red bone marrow of growing children and pregnant women. Persons accustomed to diets low in iron certainly absorb a higher proportion of their intake than do those ingesting ample amounts. From this, it could seem that iron presents no problem in nutrition but this is not the case. There is a continued high incidence of anaemia—the condition of inadequate haemoglobin jeopardizing oxygen supplies—and iron deficiency is one possible cause.

Groups at risk are:

   (i) children and adolescents, especially at times of 'growth spurts'

when blood volume is increasing;
(ii) girls and women, due to menstruation, especially at adolescence when growth is coincident;
(iii) women undergoing a succession of pregnancies.

Accordingly provision of iron should be considered, together with factors affecting its absorption, whenever diets are being planned and particularly for the categories defined above. At the same time, it must be admitted that treatment of iron deficiency anaemia is more likely to be effective when by medication (i.e. doses of iron II sulphate) than when tackled solely by dietary measures. .

Absorption of iron is favoured by certain coincident nutrients. Ascorbic acid, which is a reducing agent, assists by converting iron in the iron III (ferric) form to the iron II (ferrous) form necessary for absorption. Products of protein digestion are also considered to favour absorption of iron. This may also be due to the reducing properties of the sulphydryl groups (—SH). Another possibility is that ascorbic acid and certain amino-acids form complexes with iron which is then absorbed in that form. Haem iron from meats is better absorbed than inorganic iron from vegetable sources or from eggs.

As with calcium, absorption of iron is reduced due to the formation of insoluble salts by reaction with oxalate and phytate ions and with the free fatty acids which are present in the intestines.

7.4.3 Recommended daily intakes

The ability of the body to store some iron probably makes a daily intake unnecessary and yet it is advisable to include iron in any recommendations for daily nutrient intakes. The variations in absorption rates complicate the decisions. The DHSS (1979) recommendation of 10mg per day for adult men and post-menopausal women is based on a postulated 1mg requirement and a 10 per cent absorption rate. The 12mg recommendation for women in childbearing years allows a mere 2mg per day to compensate for menstrual losses. This is considered to be adequate on the grounds that the absorption rate may well be higher in such women. Recommendations for amounts during adolescence, pregnancy and lactation are, respectively, 12, 13 and 15mg per day. There is also acknowledgement that medicinal supplements may be needed by women with high menstrual losses and during pregnancy.

7.4.4 Meeting requirements

Reliable good dietary sources of iron are not numerous; some foods quoted for their contents are not included regularly in most diets (see Table 7.2). Foods containing the iron stores and haemoglobin of mammalian carcasses are obvious choices for supplying iron; liver and black sausage (pudding) head the list. All other flesh foods and eggs contain useful amounts. Milk and cheese on the other hand contain traces only and should not be counted upon for iron. Predominantly milk diets require supplementation. Whole or high extraction rate cereals are appreciably better than the refined forms. This favours the consumption of oatmeal and wholemeal bread although white flour in the UK has its iron restored (see 11.7). Cocoa and hence chocolate are reliable sources. Other foods with plant origins deserving to be listed among iron-providing foods are black treacle, dried fruit and curry powder. All of these derive at least some of their iron from the utensils used in their production. This accounts for the figures in food tables which show that, when due allowances are made for dehydration concentration, dried apricots contain more than twice the amount of iron in fresh ones. The high value quoted in food composition tables for curry powder (75·0mg/100g) has been confirmed by a recent study which showed some samples with iron contents as high as 95mg per 100g.

Any general statement about the iron content of green vegetables is liable to be misleading. Dark green leaves, especially those outer leaves grown in full sunlight, are better sources than paler interior leaves. Varieties make for differences. The most promising listed, spinach, is probably valueless because of the coincident oxalate. If cooked, leaf vegetables will lose some of their mineral content due to the leaching out of ions from cell sap into cooking water. With all these reservations, it is probably unwise to place much reliance on green vegetables for iron supplies but they have the redeeming feature of an ascorbic acid content. This could help in the absorption of such iron as green vegetables supply or that contributed by other foods eaten at the same meal.

Table 7.2

Portions of Food Supplying 2.5mg Iron—about one Quarter of a Day's Requirement

15g black pudding, grilled
25g lamb's liver, fried
75g lean beef, cooked
100g wholemeal bread
150g white bread
125g egg (2 large)

7.5 PHOSPHORUS

Phosphorus in living material is in the form either of phosphate groups (PO_4) of organic compounds or the phosphate ions (PO_4^{3-}) in solution in tissue fluids or as insoluble calcium phosphate in bones. As with calcium, the body maintains a balance between phosphorus in bone and that in the tissue fluids. The level in the blood is about $3.5mg/100cm^3$, including both plasma and blood cell contents. An excess is readily excreted in urine.

7.5.1 Phosphates in metabolism

Phosphates are implicated in very many metabolic sequences. Several of the B group vitamins only perform their co-enzymic functions when combined with phosphate. Phosphorylation is a necessary preliminary for several compounds entering into reactions, e.g. glucose phosphate formation is the start of glycolysis. The tri- and di-phosphates of adenosine, ATP and ADP, are among the most important biochemicals in living cells, serving to store the energy provided continuously by the oxidation of nutrient molecules and to release it on demand.

7.5.2 Dietary considerations

There is no shortage of phosphorus in foods. Its universal occurrence in cells, both plant and animal, ensures this. No recommendations are made concerning intakes. The value of medicinal doses of phosphates is discounted.

7.6 THE HALOGENS: IODINE, FLUORINE AND CHLORINE

7.6.1 Iodine

Thyroxine and related hormones of the thyroid gland are compounds containing iodine. They are formed and stored in the thyroid gland and released under the control of the pituitary gland. Thyroxine controls metabolic rates (see 2.3.5) and when it is deficient the rate of energy release will fall.

Deficiency of iodine in the diet is associated with the development of simple goitre, which involves the enlargement of the thyroid gland. In times past, when consumption of vegetables tended to be confined to those grown locally, the incidence of goitre was marked in certain geographical areas where the soil iodine level is low. This has ceased to apply with the redistribution and preservation of vegetables. A low iodine intake is certainly implicated but other factors also predispose individuals to this condition.

Although the DHSS (1969) puts forward a suggestion for a daily intake for all of 150μg, it makes no confident recommendation. Researches are hampered by the slow adaptation to increased iodine intakes in cases of deficiency. Dietary sources are vegetables grown on iodine containing soils, some fish and iodized table salt. Contrary to some suggestions, sea water is not a source of iodine and Derbyshire's association with goitre has no connection with its remoteness from the coast.

Pregnancy is a time of increased thyroid activity and it is customary to give iodine with nutritional supplements at this time even though ability to profit from them has not been proved. Probably a better safeguard against goitre following pregnancy would be a sufficient intake of iodine for women throughout adult life.

7.6.2 Fluorine

Evidence points clearly to the value of traces of fluorine in drinking water in preventing tooth decay (DHSS, 1969). Food sources are not considered significant. Levels of fluoride ions of 1ppm are considered adequate to produce marked improvements if taken in drinking water by young children.

7.6.3 Chlorine

This is the most commonly occurring of the chemical elements called the halogens. Chloride ions are found throughout all body tissues and, as a component of hydrochloric acid, they are secreted in gastric juice. Chloride ions are readily absorbed from the diet, the best sources being those to which salt is added for flavouring or for preservation, but all animal and plant tissue foods contain a certain amount. Excess chloride ions are excreted in the urine. In addition some is lost as salt in sweat.

7.6.4 Zinc

Zinc is an essential constituent of the diet. It occurs in many body tissues and in more than 80 identified enzymes. Dietary intakes are rarely deficient. The average UK diet supplies about 20mg daily although vegetarian and low-income diets are likely to provide considerably less. Deficiencies arise from impaired absorption. Retardation of growth and puberty are the severe manifestations reported recently in Iran. Studies there associate non-availability of zinc with consumption of unleavened wholemeal bread containing abundant phytate and fibre, both of which can bind divalent cations such as zinc. Although this is not a problem in the UK, it should be considered when the effects of ingesting larger quantities of bran are assessed (Reilly 1978).

PRACTICAL EXERCISES

All experiments require standard precautions.

Expt. 7.1   Determination of the percentage of mineral ash in a food material

Weigh a clean dry crucible. Add to it about 5g of the food material, e.g. grated cheese, and weigh carefully. Heat the crucible gently over a bunsen flame until most of the organic matter has been destroyed and then strongly in a muffle furnace for several hours. When nothing but a clean ash remains, cool in a desiccator and when cold, weigh. Place in the muffle furnace for a further period of several hours, re-cool in a desiccator and re-weigh. Continue until constant weight is obtained. From the weighings obtained, calculate the percentage of mineral ash in the food.

It is important to remember in these estimations that the percentage of mineral ash is low and that care is needed in weighing and in the first heating to prevent loss of material.

Expt. 7.2   Identification of the mineral constituents of foods

Reduce the food material to ash as described in Expt. 7.1. Note the colour of the ash. This is usually white but in the presence of iron salts a brown tinge may be noticeable. Dissolve the ash in about 20cm³ of distilled water slightly acidified with nitric acid.

The common acid radicles in food are carbonate, chloride, sulphate and phosphate. The common metallic constituents are sodium, potassium, calcium, magnesium and iron.

Carry out the following tests on the solution of ash.

(i) **Carbonate**
To about 3cm³ of the solution add a few drops of dilute hydrochloric acid. Effervescence will indicate the probable presence of carbonate.

(ii) **Chloride**
To about 3cm³ of the solution add a few drops of silver nitrate solution. A white precipitate of silver chloride will indicate the presence of chloride.

(iii) **Sulphate**
To about 3cm³ of the solution add an equal bulk of 10% barium chloride solution. A white precipitate of barium sulphate insoluble in hydrochloric acid will indicate the presence of sulphate.

(iv) **Phosphate**
To about 3cm³ of the solution add 1cm³ of concentrated nitric acid and 3cm³ of 10% ammonium molybdate solution. Heat in a beaker of boiling water. The formation of a yellow colour or precipitate will indicate the presence of phosphate.

(v) **Sodium**
The flame test is most suitable. Dip a platinum wire into the solution or some of the solid ash and heat in the bunsen flame. A yellow flame coloration will indicate the presence of sodium.

(vi) Potassium

The flame test is most suitable and is carried out in the same way as for sodium. A lilac flame coloration will indicate the presence of potassium. If sodium has already been identified the flame should be examined through cobalt blue glass.

(vii) Calcium

Add ammonia to a portion of the solution until it is slightly alkaline and then make it slightly acid with acetic acid. Add about an equal volume of 5% ammonium oxalate solution. A cloudy white precipitate of calcium oxalate which may be slow to form indicates the presence of calcium.

(viii) Magnesium

If a precipiate has been formed in the previous test, remove it by filtration and make the filtrate strongly alkaline with ammonia. Add 1cm³ of 10% sodium phosphate solution. The formation of a crystalline precipitate indicates the presence of magnesium.

(ix) Ferric Iron (Iron III)

Acidify several cubic centimetres of the solution with hydrochloric acid. Add about 1cm³ of 10% ammonium thiocyanate. The formation of a red colour indicates the presence of ferric iron. If negative, take a second portion and add a few drops of hydrogen peroxide and warm. This will oxidize any ferrous iron (iron II) to ferric, which can be detected as above.

REFERENCES

Davidson, Sir Stanley, Passmore, R., Brock, J. F., and Truswell, A. S. (1979). *Human nutrition and dietetics*, 7th edition, Churchill-Livingstone.

DHSS (1969). *Fluoridation studies in the UK and the results achieved after eleven years*, HMSO.

DHSS (1979). *Recommended daily amounts of food energy and nutrients for groups of people in the United Kingdom*, HMSO.

FAO (1961). *Calcium requirements*, Report of a joint FAO/WHO expert group, FAO, Rome.

FAO (1970). *Requirements of ascorbic acid, vitamin D, vitamin B_{12}, folate and iron*, Report of a joint FAO/WHO expert group, FAO, Rome.

Reilly (1978). *Zinc—the unassuming nutrient*, Getting the most out of food: 13th Series, Van den Berghs & Jurgens Ltd.

CHAPTER VIII

VITAMINS

8.1 HISTORICAL SURVEY

Until the decade beginning 1911 it was generally accepted that for all purposes of health, food should consist essentially of the three principles: proteins, fats and carbohydrates—the first for the building, maintenance and repairing of tissue, the latter two for the supply of energy—and, of less importance, a small amount of mixed mineral salts. Nowadays to these are added the 'accessory food factors' or vitamins, as no less essential, though they occur in natural foods in very minute quantities only. Without the vitamins, in their several types, even though all other food principles are provided in full amount and perfect balance, health and in the end life itself cannot be maintained. Instead, therefore, of reckoning the adequacy of a diet as before, in terms only of energy and proteins, account must be taken also of the several vitamins, listed as A, B complex, C, D, E, etc. each of which plays its particular role in maintaining the health of the system, while its absence is attended by some special form of 'deficiency disease'.

Although it is only within quite recent years that our knowledge has been well established of the significance of vitamins in food and of their specific nature and behaviour, it is nevertheless true that for many centuries what are now known as deficiency diseases were in a vague uncertain fashion related to certain types of food. Thus it was recognized as long ago as the time of Chaucer that scurvy could be prevented or even cured by the addition to the diet of sailors and explorers, of fruits and green vegetables. In 1735 Casali in a description of the disease pellagra noted in detail the deficiencies in the diets consumed in every case by the inhabitants of the districts in Spain where this disease was rife. In 1734 Bachstruv demonstrated that scurvy was due to nothing more than a total abstinence from fresh vegetable food and greens, for it could be cured by the addition of relatively very small quantities of these to a faulty diet. In 1747, James Lind, a naval surgeon at Haslar, divided twelve scurvy patients into six groups, and to each group made a different dietetic addition. The pair receiving oranges or lemons were quickly cured and scarcely less quickly those who had cider. He confirmed observations which had been made at the beginning of the eighteenth century that dried vegetables were useless against scurvy and adopted the view that 'no moisture whatsoever could restore the natural juices of the plant lost by evaporation'. He was also struck by the good effect of cows' milk in the treatment of scurvy, supposing it to be 'a truly vegetable liquor, an emulsion prepared of the most succulent wholesome herbs'. Lind recommended that concentrated lemon juice syrup should be served throughout the Navy, but his suggestions were at first largely unheeded so that in 1780, at least 2400 men of the Channel Fleet were affected by scurvy, and the mortality exceeded that from battle and wounds. In 1793 on the persuasion of Dr Blane the naval authorities made trial of Dr Lind's suggestions as to the use of lemons. The *Suffolk* made a voyage of 19 weeks without touching any port; every man on board was given $\frac{3}{4}$oz of lemon juice with 2oz of brown sugar in addition to his usual rations, and on arrival at Madras there had not been a single case of scurvy. Young recommended as an alternative for the use of the Navy the plan of taking to sea for purposes of food, beans, peas, barley, etc. in a state of germination. It was by realizing that there was something present in fresh vegetables and fruit, without which normal health was impaired, that Captain Cook is reported not to have had a single case of scurvy in the course of his many voyages of discovery—a fact in remarkable contrast to the great losses among the crews of the other great explorers, Vasco da Gama, Prince Henry of Portugal, Anson, etc. Nelson maintained an extraordinarily good bill of health throughout his fleets when engaged in continuous blockade, by means of a diet in which fruit and fresh vegetables were common items.

By the beginning of the 19th century the daily ration of one ounce of lemon juice on board ship was compulsory throughout the Navy, with the result that scurvy became very rare. The lemon juice supplied to the Navy was first made from lemons grown in Spain or other Mediterranean countries, but afterwards it was made from West India limes, and scurvy again broke out. The reason for this was not discovered until recently, when it was shown that while the lemon is particularly rich in the anti-scorbutic vitamin C, the lime is unexpectedly poor.

Unfortunately the views of the majority of physicians regarding the influence of anti-scorbutic foods remained vague and diffident, and scurvy continued to devastate the mercantile marine until well into the 19th century, nor was the true cause realized until quite recent times. Yet as far back as 1841, the American doctor Budd had ascribed the action of such foods 'to an essential element which it is hardly too sanguine to state will be discovered by organic chemists or the experiments of physiologists in a not far distant future'.

The first experiments of the modern type on animals were performed in 1881 by Lunin at Basle. He fed six mice on a diet containing every ordinary constituent of milk in quantities quite sufficient to support life, but qualitatively so treated that the 'freshness' was destroyed. All the animals died and Lunin was led to observe that small quantities of substances, as yet unknown, were present in fresh food and 'were essential to life'. He had come upon what is now known as vitamin A.

But what is perhaps the starting point of our present considerable knowledge of the relationships of diet to the deficiency diseases, and of the identification and separation of the several vitamins, was the investigation of the disease beri-beri. In 1897 Eijkman, a Dutch army doctor stationed in Dutch East Indies, proved that beri-beri, a disease characterized by extreme languor and debility, accompanied by an affection of the nerves and sometimes by paralysis, was solely dependent upon the consumption in large quantities of polished rice, as the staple diet. He had been sent over as a member of a commission to study this disease which was then thought to be bacterial in origin. After the return home of the commission, he remained in charge of a laboratory, and needing some fowls for investigation found it convenient to feed them on the scraps, chiefly of polished rice, thrown out from the hospital wards. The fowls presently developed an illness with many of the symptoms of beri-beri, from which they recovered when no longer fed with polished rice, or when fed either with whole rice, or with polished rice to which an extract of rice polishing had been added. Eijkman at first suggested that the disease was due to some poison in the polished rice, or to a state of intoxication being set up by the consumption of excessive quantities of starch, either of which was corrected by the natural antidote in the so-called 'silver skin' which was removed in polishing. Later, led by the researches of others, he came to the conclusion that there was present in the husk of rice grains a substance, small in amount, but absolutely essential to normal nutrition. It was Funk who in 1911, after working on the causation of beri-beri, coined the word 'vitamines' as more convenient than the term 'accessory food substances', which Hopkins had been using for a time, and under the impression that they were nitrogenous compounds allied to the amines. This has proved to be incorrect, and in any case the terminal 'e' is now dropped and the substances are now known as 'vitamins'.

It is very largely due to the methods of Gowland Hopkins of Cambridge University, who was afterwards knighted and received with Eijkman the Nobel prize for medicine in 1929, that the investigations on vitamins have proved so fruitful. His investigations depended largely on the feeding of animals on experimental diets, composed of highly purified material of proteins, fats, carbohydrates and minerals, to which were added or withheld certain substances, very minute in quantity. The purified materials taken alone wholly failed to maintain ordinary life. In 1912 Hopkins published his classical experiments in which the addition of 2 or 3 cubic centimetres of fresh milk to the diet of rats fed upon normally balanced but artificial foods caused an improvement in their rate of growth and health, out of all proportion to that shown in the rest of the rats, which lacked only the milk. All the latter became undernourished, feeble and finally died. The deprival of milk from the normally developing rats, fed otherwise only on the artificial diets, was followed by failure to grow, debility and death, unless the milk was restored in good time.

American workers, Osborne and Mendel of Newhaven, and McCollum and Davis of Wisconsin, by their experiments proved that many natural foods such as milk, sugar and butter-fat contained substances having a marked influence upon growth and health, and that these substances could be extracted from the original food and transferred to artificial foodstuffs, so making these last growth-promoting and life-sustaining. The latter two investigators also proved that vitamins occurred in natural foods in different groups, some being 'fat-soluble' and others 'water-soluble'—a very useful experimental distinction. Thus they showed in 1915 that in addition to the anti-scorbutic vitamin (vitamin C) there were at least two other vitamins, the first, contained in butter-fat, 'fat-soluble A' and the second contained not only in fresh milk but also in the wheatgerm, rice polishings, etc., 'water-soluble B'. During the later stages of the First World War, many intensive researches on nutrition were carried out, from which emerged chiefly, among other matters, proof that rickets was caused by the absence from food and the system of a factor with certain distinctive features which justified its separation from 'fat-soluble A' as 'vitamin D'. After 1919 a vast amount of research was undertaken on vitamins in every civilized country. This resulted not simply in the recognition of many more vitamins, and of the part played by each in the maintenance of animal metabolism, but also of their chemical composition and afterwards, in some cases, their synthesis in the laboratory and manufacture on an industrial scale.

The knowledge of vitamins has penetrated far from the laboratories of science and become in considerable measure the common stock of information of the general community. It has also been exploited by producers and distributors of fresh foods and manufacturers of processed foods and medicaments. Dietetics has been profoundly affected by the recognition of the special importance of the different vitamins and of the advantage of particular foodstuffs in which one or other of them occurs in relative abundance.

8.2 Definition, Classification and Nomenclature

The nutrients which have been subjects for previous chapters—carbohydrates, lipids, proteins and mineral elements—are grouped by their common chemical characteristics. By contrast, the vitamins are not a chemical category. Neither can a common physiological role be claimed for them for, as yet, insufficient knowledge exists concerning the action of some of them within the body. The features which known vitamins have in common are used to define 'vitamin status'. From time to time, the claims of newly discovered substances are investigated and, in consequence, the following list has been compiled, acknowledging the existence of other substances which might well be included.

(i) Fat-soluble

Vitamin A	retinol and its precursor, beta-carotene.
Vitamin D	cholecalciferol (formerly vitamin D_3) and ergocalciferol (formerly vitamin D_2).
Vitamin E	several tocopherols.
Vitamin K	several quinones.

(ii) Water-soluble

B group vitamins

thiamin (formerly vitamin B_1 or aneurin).
riboflavin.
nicotinic acid and nicotinamide (also called niacin in USA).
pantothenic acid.
vitamin B_6 pyridoxine, pyridoxal and pyridoxamine.
biotin.
folic acid and related substances.
vitamin B_{12} cyanocobalamin.

Vitamin C   ascorbic acid together with the oxidized form, dehydroascorbic acid.

8.2.1 Vitamins defined

Vitamins are organic substances which have to be taken in by the body in trace amounts to enable it to function properly. The diet is obviously the main source but, in some cases, there are contributions from the bacteria which exist symbiotically in the gut. The intake is necessary because the body cannot produce these substances; at least, not in sufficient amounts at all times.

Attention is focused on vitamins by the incidence of deficiency diseases, the recognizable symptoms of which can be attributed to shortage of particular nutrients on the grounds that: (i) favourable response is shown to dosage by the nutrient concerned, and (ii) symptoms can be reproduced in experimental animals deliberately deprived.

It must be emphasized that deficiency diseases, in the UK at any rate, are rare, amounting to a low incidence of scurvy, chiefly among elderly persons living alone and a few reported cases of rickets in immigrant children. Undoubtedly the sufficiency of vitamins in our diets provides protection against deficiency diseases but to date there is no evidence that additional amounts will provide any benefits for health. Indeed, excessive intakes of vitamin D have produced harmful effects (see 7.3.3). Recently claims have been made concerning benefits from extra large doses of vitamin C but they are based on a 'multi-function theory' for the role of this vitamin and will be considered later (see 8.13.2).

8.2.2 Vitamin nomenclature

The earliest names for vitamins, 'fat-soluble A' and 'water-soluble B', recognized a useful distinction, that of solubility, which continues to be used in classification but the use of the alphabet has become an encumbrance. Nowadays it is possible to name vitamins with reference to chemical composition. This is most effective when one compound only possesses specific vitamin activity but more often than not it is shared by a number of related compounds. Then it is useful to employ a generic term and, for this, the old literal notation is usually retained. For example, vitamin D can be used as a generic term for the compounds cholecalciferol and ergocalciferol which have different origins but identical activity. The numerous vitamins listed as belonging to the B group are quite distinct and merit no generic term but they all derive from what originally was thought to be the single vitamin B. Consequently they have many common sources which it is useful to speak of as 'supplying B group vitamins'.

8.3 OCCURRENCE OF VITAMINS

8.3.1 In plant and animal tissues

Recognition of the fat-solubility of the vitamins A, D, E and K is helpful in anticipating likely sources—cells in plant and animal tissues capable of concentrating lipid and lipid-like materials. These include adipose tissues, liver cells, egg yolks and the plastid-containing cells in plant leaves and some roots. The water-soluble vitamins, on the other hand, will occur in watery tissues: cell sap, inter- and intra-cellular fluids.

8.3.2 Good dietary sources

To name a good dietary source of any nutrient, consideration must be given both to the amount of that nutrient present in the food in question and also to the frequency with which that food appears in significant amounts in usual diets. Foods with a high content of a nutrient but which are seldom eaten, are of little value unless they are deliberately encouraged as dietary supplements. Note must also be taken of factors limiting the availability of nutrients, e.g. losses in cooking waters, heat instability (which affects some but by no means all vitamins) and limited absorption.

8.4 VITAMIN A

8.4.1 Chemistry

The substance identified as vitamin A is retinol, an alcohol consisting of a large 20-carbon unsaturated hydrocarbon group which gives the molecule its non-polar character plus a hydroxyl (—OH) group, characteristic of alcohols. The formula for retinol, written as $C_{19}H_{24}CH_2OH$, shows it to be an alcohol with the terminal —CH_2OH group which is replaced by the aldehyde group – CHO, when changed into the aldehyde, retinal.

The precursor of the retinol found in animal tissues is the plant pigment beta-carotene, a hydrocarbon $C_{40}H_{50}$ (see 4.4.3) which, when split into two with one part hydroxylated, will give one molecule of retinol, a somewhat inefficient conversion. It is convenient to express all sources in terms of retinol equivalents which make allowances for the inferior absorption of beta-carotene and for its inefficient conversion within the body to retinol (see 8.4.4).

8.4.2　Physiological functions

The mode of action of retinol within the body is not well understood. Evidence from human studies suggests a three-fold involvement: (i) maintenance of moist surface tissues; (ii) growth regulation; and (iii) vision.

(i) Possibly the maintenance of the soft membranous tissues of the body is by control of epithelium formation and prevention of the sequence through to keratin production. Keratin is the non-living, tough and relatively inflexible material of hair, nails and epidermis and is totally unsuitable for the moist surfaces of the body, in particular, the covering of the eye.

(ii) Some evidence links retinol's association with growth to the action of RNA in protein synthesis (see 10.6.4).

(iii) The most positive evidence of function concerns dim light vision. Retinal, the aldehyde formed from retinol, unites with certain lipo-proteins to give rhodopsin, the pigment in the rods of the retina. When light enters the eye, this pigment is bleached; a chemical change which starts a relay to the brain producing the sensation of vision. Pigments in the cones, the other retina receptors, are only sensitive to light of daylight intensity, or the equivalent, and so, to make dim light vision possible, rods must be kept supplied with rhodopsin. This draws upon the retinol supply in the blood which in turn depends upon dietary intake of either preformed retinol (vitamin A) or its precursor, beta-carotene.

8.4.3　Effects of deficiency

Although the effects of vitamin A deficiency are serious, they are rare in the UK. The following list shows them to be distinctly varied, an observation which points to the multi-functioning of the vitamin in the body. Often secondary infections are present in the subjects, complicating diagnosis.

(i) Keratinization of epithelial surfaces of the body, resulting in a build-up of keratin in the pores of the skin and over the surface of the eye causing the condition of xerophthalmia, with subsequent blindness.

(ii) Retarded growth (if deficiencies occur early in life) and bone deformities.

(iii) Night blindness or defective dim light vision.

8.4.4.　Requirements

Healthy individuals are likely to have in their livers sufficient vitamin A to last them for many months without further dietary intake. Therefore deficiencies are rare. The fat-solubility and water-insolubility of retinol accounts for storage in the body but gives rise to the danger of hypervitaminosis which can cause bone damage. A greatly excessive intake of carotene can cause a harmless yellow skin coloration.

The body utilizes both pre-formed vitamin A, retinol, and its precursor or provitamin, beta-carotene. To assess the total retinol activity of a mixed diet, it is necessary to convert milligrammes of carotene to microgrammes of retinol as follows:

(i) Multiply by 1000   milligrammes to microgrammes.
(ii) Divide by   6   carotene to retinol (an inefficient process —see 8.4.1).

International units (IU) are now obsolete and to convert IU vitamin A to microgrammes retinol, multiply by 0·3. For example, a glass of milk (200g) and an apple (100g) would contribute the following:

	Vitamin A	Carotene	Conversion factor	Retinol
Milk	300 IU		×0·3	90μg
Apple		0·03mg	$\times\dfrac{1000}{6}$	5μg
				Total 95μg

Recommended daily intakes of retinol, given by both FAO/WHO (1967) and DHSS (UK) (1979), are, for all adults, 750μg retinol equivalents (2500 IU vitamin A), with 1200μg during lactation. There appears to be no relationship between requirements for the vitamin and physical activity.

8.4.5. Dietary sources

Retinol occurs in animal tissues and secretions, the chief food supplies being milk, butter, egg yolk and some fatty fish. The richest natural sources are fish liver oils but these are usually employed as dietary supplements rather than foods. All table margarine is enriched to 900μg per 100g, making it an important source. Beta-carotene, the most common of the retinol precursors, is the yellow pigment in carrots, apricots, tomatoes and other yellow/orange-coloured and dark green fruits and vegetables.

Retinol is easily absorbed but carotene is not, possibly because it is not always accompanied by sufficient fat to dissolve it out of plant tissues where it is mainly concentrated in subcellular structures called chromoplasts.

Losses of retinol and carotene during normal conditions of food storage and cooking are small and can be ignored.

8.5 Vitamin D

8.5.1 Chemistry

The substances belonging to the vitamin D category are steroids (see 4.5.2). Two similar compounds have identical vitamin D activity. They are cholecalciferol which is produced when 7-dehydrocholesterol, present in animal lipid material, absorbs ultra-violet light, and ergocalciferol, which is formed by the irradiation of plant oils containing ergosterol. Both calciferols are alcohol derivatives of complex hydrocarbons.

8.5.2 Physiological function

Cholecalciferol (vitamin D_3) is considered to function as a hormone precursor. On reaching the liver, it is converted to 25-hydroxycholecalciferol and transported in the blood on a protein carrier to the kidneys where further hydroxylation results in dihydroxycholecalciferol, the substance which is now accorded hormone status. (Kodicek, 1974). Activated by this hormone, the epithelium of the small intestine synthesises a specific calcium-binding protein which transports calcium across the intestinal wall into the blood and facilitates transfer of calcium between blood and bone and other tissues as required (see 7.3).

8.5.3 Effects of deficiency

Disorders affecting calcium–phosphorus metabolism occur when intake and production within the body are deficient. When this arises in young children, the deficiency disease, rickets, occurs characterized by impeded ossification (the process whereby the cartilagenous skeleton is replaced by bone) with consequent deformities. The adult version of rickets is osteomalacia in which calcium in bones is depleted and not replenished, with consequent reduction in bone strength. (The condition osteoporosis is distinct, being a seemingly inevitable feature of ageing and not, as far as is known, due to any nutritional deficiency.)

Both deficiency diseases respond to vitamin D therapy, although once skeletal deformities have · been produced, they cannot be eradicated. Those affected include women in purdah, deprived of exposure to any sunlight. Cases lately reported in the UK were of immigrant children brought from the tropics where the sunlight intensity would counteract deficient dietary intakes. Once in the UK, their bodies would be wrapped up against the cold while changes to a western-type diet were resisted.

8.5.4 Requirements

There is little knowledge on which to recommend intakes for adults. The dual sources, diet and exposure to sunlight, make determinations of requirements particularly difficult. All that can be hoped for is a course steered between too low an intake and the sort of excess which can lead to hypercalcaemia (see 7.3.3).

The recommendations for groups of people in the UK are confined to 7.5μg per day for infants and 10μg per day for each of the following: young children, pregnant women and lactating women. (DHSS 1979.)

To convert the now obsolete international units (IU) into microgrammes, it is necessary to multiply by 0.025.

8.5.5 Sources

The chief source is that produced in adipose tissues below skin exposed to ultra-violet rays in sunlight. Food sources are relatively few. Vitaminized margarine and egg yolk are probably the most important, followed by fatty fish and butter made from summer milk. Dietary supplements in the form of fish liver oils and fortified infant and invalid foods can contribute significant amounts. Contents in milk and cheese are low, probably negligible in winter produce.

Both forms of vitamin D are extremely stable and there is little loss through processing and storage. Losses of around 25 per cent have been reported when vitamin D enriched milk is dried but these are not confirmed and, in any case, fortification levels are adequate to allow for such reductions.

8.6 Vitamin E

Whether or not vitamin E should be regarded as having full vitamin status for man is a matter of opinion. It may well be an essential inclusion in the diet but so far no pathological condition in humans can be shown to result from deficiencies nor can any advantage to health be attributed to increased intakes.

Vitamin E is a generic term for a group of tocopherols which occur naturally in foodstuffs and which have proved vitamin-value for a number of mammalian species.

Tocopherols occur widely in plants, notably in seed embryos, and in milk and eggs. They serve as antioxidants in fats and oils by being preferentially oxidized and therefore delaying the onset of oxidative rancidity. In addition to its natural occurrence, vitamin E is a permitted antioxidant additive in cooking fats and oils.

8.7 VITAMIN K

Once more the term covers a number of distinct but related compounds with the same vitamin activity. All are quinones and fat-soluble, although some show a tendency towards water solubility. The function of the K vitamins is concerned with the synthesis by the liver of prothrombin and other factors required for the clotting of blood. Absorption of vitamin K requires the presence of bile salts and deficiencies have resulted from biliary obstruction rather than from dietary exclusion. The outcome is interference with clotting of blood and serious bleeding with injury or surgery.

Sources of vitamin K in the diet are principally green leaf vegetables supplemented by that which is synthesized in the colon by bacteria. No recommendations are made for daily intakes.

8.8 VITAMINS AND ENERGY-RELEASE

The sequence of reactions whereby the chemical energy in glucose is released and 'packaged' in ATP (adenosine triphosphate) molecules ready for use, is summarized in Fig. 8.1 as

$$\text{glucose} \rightarrow \text{pyruvic acid} \rightarrow \text{acetyl coA} \rightarrow CO_2 + H_2O$$

Very many intermediate changes are involved requiring control by enzymes and their study has thrown light on the mode of action of several B group vitamins. Some details of enzyme action are given later (see 10.4.1, 2, 3, 4 and 5) and then it will be shown that, in the main, enzymes require co-factors for their activation. It is as co-enzymes or co-enzyme producers that certain B group vitamins are known to work.

Acetyl coA is the name given to what may be considered the most crucial of the metabolites, (intermediate products of metabolism) in respiration. Fig. 8.1 shows how it is produced not only during glucose metabolism but also from the beta-oxidation of fatty acids and when certain of the amino-acids, following deamination, are utilized for energy production. Some of the acetyl coA feeds into the citric acid cycle which, followed by the electron transport chain (ETC), results in final conversion to carbon dioxide and water with coincident production of energy-rich ATP. The remaining acetyl coA is used to produce triglycerides for adipose tissue storage against future energy demands. Thus acetyl coA is at the centre of the control of energy release and storage.

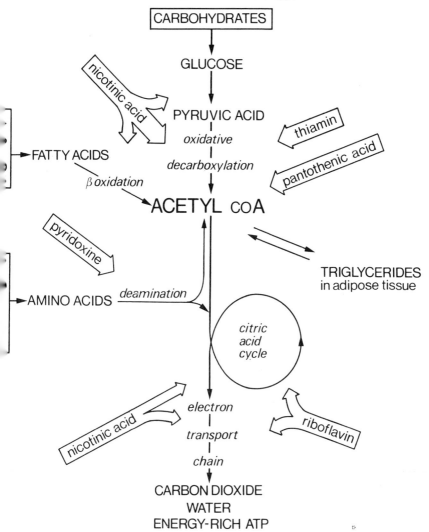

FIG. 8.1. Summary of vitamin involvement in release of energy from nutrient molecules

Following the glucose sequence, nicotinic acid is the first of the vitamins to be implicated, being concerned with the oxidation changes leading to acetyl coA formation from pyruvic acid. Thiamin is also involved in this sequence. Converted to TPP, (thiamin pyrophosphate), it serves as co-enzyme to the carboxylase which catalyses the decarboxylation (removal of carbon dioxide) of pyruvic acid. In thiamin deficiency, pyruvic acid accumulates. Some is converted to lactic acid, with a limited release of energy, but this is only a partial solution for lactic acid in excess in the tissues cannot be tolerated. Thiamin is necessary to ensure that pyruvic acid catabolism can proceed via the citric acid cycle and the electron transport chain.

Formation of acetyl coA, both from pyruvic acid and from fatty acid oxidation, requires the substance co-enzyme A. Admittedly only catalytic amounts are needed but the significance for vitamin study is that pantothenic acid forms part of the co-enzyme A molecule and must be supplied for its formation.

Nicotinic acid and riboflavin, another B vitamin, are needed for production of the hydrogen carriers which remove hydrogen from metabolites of the citric acid cycle for transfer down the electron transport chain and ultimate oxidation to water.

In order that the amino-acids not needed for protein synthesis can be utilized for energy production, deaminations (removal of nitrogen groups) and decarboxylations (removal of carbon dioxide) must take place. Such changes necessitate the co-enzymic function of vitamin B_6. Another B group vitamin, biotin, functions as a co-enzyme for carboxylases related to co-enzyme A activity. Probably sufficient biotin is synthesized in the intestines by bacteria to make a dietary intake unnecessary. In fact insufficient is known about requirements for biotin or for pantothenic acid and vitamin B_6 to justify authoritative recommendations for intakes. Other B group vitamins concerned with energy release are now considered in greater detail.

8.9   THIAMIN

8.9.1   **Chemistry**

Thiamin is a complex organic molecule with sufficient polarity to make it soluble in water. Its single hydroxyl group is readily replaced by a pyrophosphate group and it is the thiamin pyrophosphate thus formed which has co-enzyme activity. In neutral and alkaline conditions, thiamin is unstable to heat but in acid conditions it can withstand temperatures up to 120° C.

8.9.2 Physiological functions

Thiamin pyrophosphate functions as the cocarboxylase in the oxidative decarboxylation of pyruvic acid (see 8.8 and 10.4.3).

8.9.3 Effects of deficiency

The deficiency disease is beri-beri, a serious menace in communities with predominantly carbohydrate diets, exacerbated by the preference for polished rice, which has lost much of the thiamin present in whole grain rice. Elsewhere beri-beri is virtually unknown. The only evidence of deficiency in this country is among chronic alcoholics. In experimentally induced beri-beri, accumulations of pyruvic acid in tissues can be demonstrated. Early symptoms include loss of appetite and nausea. Degeneration of nerve tissues follows with muscular convulsions and cardiac disturbance. An intake of fat will alleviate symptoms in the early stages. Response to treatment with thiamin is good, even in quite advanced cases but if untreated, beri-beri will prove fatal.

8.9.4 Requirements

Thiamin requirements are linked with carbohydrate intake and, for practical purposes, recommendations are related to total energy intakes. Both FAO (1967) and DHSS (1979) give 96µg thiamin/MJ (0·4mg/1000kcal).

8.9.5 Dietary sources

All animal and plant tissues contain thiamin and so it is present in most foods although not in extracted fats, refined sugars or distilled spirits. The most important sources are seeds such as legumes and those cereals of which the germ and the bran layers are eaten. In this country, all white flour is fortified to give 0·24mg/100g, making bread in all its forms a good source. The best source among meat is pork. Brewers' yeast has a high content but little is consumed by the majority of the population.

Thiamin is one of the vitamins about which there should be concern for its availability in cooked and processed foods. It is readily soluble and liable to be leached out into cooking waters. It is sensitive to oxidation and rapidly destroyed by heat when in neutral or alkaline solution. In acid solution, it can withstand temperatures up to 120° C. Losses of the vitamin due to cooking amount to 30–50 per cent from meat and 25–40 per cent from vegetables. Sodium bicarbonate, used as a raising agent in baked flour goods or in the cooking of vegetables, will decrease thiamin stability, as will the use of sulphite preservatives (see 19.8). Losses from foods during prolonged storage will depend on the conditions prevailing. For example, the lower the temperature, the smaller the losses from frozen foods.

8.10   RIBOFLAVIN

8.10.1   Chemistry
The flavins are a group of compounds whose molecules feature fused rings of carbon and nitrogen. Riboflavin is a flavin with a group derived from the pentose sugar, ribose. It is a yellow crystalline solid, sparsely soluble in water and insoluble in lipids. In ultra-violet light, it fluoresces a greenish yellow. It is stable to heat in acid solution but not in alkaline. When exposed to light it decomposes, forming lumiflavin. Like thiamin, riboflavin is only metabolically active when phosphorylated.

8.10.2   Physiological functions
Riboflavin forms the prosthetic group of flavoproteins which function as hydrogen carriers in the oxidation sequences of respiration whereby hydrogen is fed into the electron transport chain and united with oxygen (see 10.4.4 and 5).

8.10.3   Effects of deficiency
There is no recognizable deficiency disease. The symptoms which occur with marked deficiencies are lesions of the tongue, lips and cornea, with watering eyes which are readily dazzled. It should be noted, however, that similar effects result from other factors.

8.10.4   Requirements
There is some difference of opinion as to whether requirements should be related to total energy expenditure or merely to resting metabolism (see 2.3.5). FAO, (1967) advises 0·55mg/1000kcal (4200kJ) total energy expenditure while DHSS (1979) suggests (1·0mg/1000kcal) resting metabolism. In practice, there is no significant difference between the two recommendations. For example, a woman requiring 2200kcal per day expends 1300kcal of this total for resting metabolism. By FAO standards, she requires 1·21mg riboflavin as against 1·3mg by DHSS recommendations. No decrease in requirement is indicated for the aged. Recommendations are for 1·6mg/day in pregnancy and 1·8mg/day during lactation. The increases for pregnancy are related to increased cell mass and those for lactation to the riboflavin content of breast milk.

8.10.5 Dietary sources

The best sources are liver, milk, cheese, eggs, fresh peas and beans and some leaf vegetables. Yeast extract and beef extract are excellent but are only consumed in small quantities and some people take none at all. Beer is a fairly good source, also whole grain breakfast cereals.

The limited solubility in water results in some leaching out during the cooking of green vegetables. Riboflavin is destroyed by sunlight. This is especially significant for milk in glass bottles. The riboflavin converts into an unpleasant tasting substance called lumiflavin which adversely affects the small amount of ascorbic acid in the milk. Nevertheless total losses of riboflavin from foods during preparation and cooking are small compared with those of thiamin and ascorbic acid.

8.11 NICOTINIC ACID

8.11.1 Chemistry

Nicotinic acid is a derivative of the relatively simple pyridine ring:

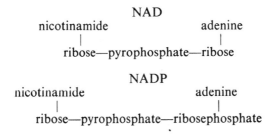

pyridine nicotinic acid nicotinamide

As nicotinamide, it enters into complexes which serve as the co-enzymes, nicotinamide adenine dinucleotide (NAD) and nicotinamide adenine dinucleotide phosphate (NADP)

NAD

nicotinamide   adenine
| |
ribose—pyrophosphate—ribose

NADP

nicotinamide   adenine
| |
ribose—pyrophosphate—ribosephosphate

Nicotinic acid is a very stable compound which can be formed in the body from the amino-acid tryptophan.

8.11.2 Physiological functions

The dinucleotides NAD and NADP function as co-enzymes in the oxidation sequences of respiration. The nicotinic acid moiety acts as a hydrogen acceptor in glycolysis, acetyl coA formation and the citric acid cycle, and feeds this hydrogen into the electron transport chain for oxidation (see 10.4.2, 3, 4 and 5; and 10.5.1).

8.11.3 Effects of deficiency

Pellagra is the deficiency disease. It is endemic in countries subsisting chiefly on maize, the protein of which is limited by tryptophan (see 5.9.2). It is a chronic relapsing disease, characterized by dermatitis, diarrhoea and in far gone cases, dementia.

8.11.4 Requirements

The amount of the vitamin which must be supplied by the diet depends on the coincident intake of tryptophan. Consequently a 'nicotinic acid equivalent' has been defined

One nicotinic acid equivalent =   1mg nicotinic acid
                                 = 60mg tryptophan

Like riboflavin, nicotinic acid requirements are related by DHSS (1979) to resting metabolism and by FAO (1967) to total energy expenditure:

FAO (1967) 1·6mg nicotinic acid/MJ (6·6mg/1000kcal) total energy

DHSS (1979) 2·7mg nicotinic acid equivalents/MJ (11·3mg/1000 kcal) resting metabolism.

An additional 3mg nicotinic acid equivalents are recommended during pregnancy and 6mg during lactation.

8.11.5 Dietary sources

Nicotinic acid is widely distributed in plant and animal foods but only in small amounts. The better sources are meats, especially offal, fish, wholemeal cereals and pulses. In maize and potatoes it is unavailable, being in a 'bound' form known as niacytin. Therefore these sources should be discounted. In fact it is probably safer to discount cereal sources unless they have been fortified. White flour in the UK has the vitamin added to the level of 1·6mg per 100g. Nicotinic acid is very stable to heat, oxidation, acids and alkalis. Some losses occur due to leaching into cooking water.

8.12   B GROUP VITAMINS AND BLOOD

8.12.1   **Vitamin B_{12}**

Pernicious anaemia is a serious, though uncommon, disease, and is distinct from iron-deficiency anaemia. Sufferers have an inborn predisposition, possibly inherited. The anaemia results from the arrested development of red blood cells which, originating as endothelial cells in red bone marrow, pass through a sequence of stages before becoming the mature erythrocytes which circulate in the blood stream. In megaloblastic anaemia, these cells are halted at the megaloblast stage, i.e. as large nucleated cells lacking haemoglobin.

Until 1926, no treatment existed and pernicious anaemia was invariably fatal. At that time, it was found that raw liver fed in large amounts proved effective. Later, intramuscular injections of liver extracts gave promising results. In 1929, the theory was postulated that formation of blood cells requires both an extrinsic factor from food and an intrinsic factor secreted by the stomach. As the intrinsic factor is necessary for the absorption of the extrinsic factor, its absence from gastric secretion results in defective production of the formed elements in blood and consequent anaemia. Prolonged research, involving fractionation of liver extracts, produced in 1948 a red crystalline substance capable of treating pernicious anaemia when given by injection (Smith, 1963). This is vitamin B_{12}, later shown to be the chemical compound, cyanocobalamin. 20mg of crystalline B_{12} are said to be as effective as one ton of fresh liver. This has provided relief for persons born with pernicious anaemia although to date the intrinsic factor which they lack has not been identified nor the cause of its absence explained.

Vitamin B_{12} is quite widely distributed in animal foods but not in plant materials. Vegans, vegetarians who exclude all animal products, are in some danger of deficiency.

8.12.2   **Folic acid and related substances**

During the 1930s, while pernicious anaemia was being investigated but before vitamin B_{12} had been isolated, certain cases of megaloblastic anaemia among the poorly fed of Bombay, including many pregnant women, failed to respond to liver extract (Davidson, 1975). These contrary results were considered to point to the existence of a second nutritional anti-anaemia factor. Successful administrations of yeast preparations and of a spinach extract substantiated this theory and the factor was given the name folic acid. In due course, this was extracted and then synthesized, the pure substance, named pteroyl glutamic acid, being effective in the treatment of nutritional megaloblastic anaemia.

Folic acid and various active folates are present in green vegetables and liver. Beef, wheat flour, ham and eggs all contain a little. Deficiencies may be due to poverty or to improper absorption in conditions such as sprue and steatorrhoea (defective absorption of fats). Pregnancy increases requirement markedly.

8.12.3 Requirements for folate

Requirements for folate are considered to relate to body weight. Having made allowances for the limited absorption of some forms of folate, an estimate of $5\mu g$ folate/kg body weight/day has been derived. On this, the DHSS (1979) recommendations have been calculated, arriving at allowances of $50\mu g$ folate per day for infants, rising to $300\mu g$ daily for adults.

8.13   VITAMIN C—ASCORBIC ACID

Of all the vitamins, ascorbic acid probably receives the most attention from those concerned about the nutritional value of the food they provide for themselves and for others. There also is a tendency among laymen to transfer the attributes of vitamin C to vitamins at large. Hence the generalizations about vitamins being readily 'lost' or 'destroyed' in cooking when, in fact, only ascorbic acid and thiamin are seriously depreciated in this way. Although there is no need for a generic term, (ascorbic acid and its oxidized form, dehydroascorbic acid, being the only compounds with this particular activity) 'vitamin C' has become sufficiently familiar to the general public to deserve retention, although in scientific communications it is now superseded by 'ascorbic acid'.

Paradoxically there remains considerable uncertainty about the mode of action of this familiar vitamin. In spite of repeated researches, it is still not possible to pin-point the roles of ascorbic acid in cell chemistry.

8.13.1 Chemistry

Ascorbic acid is a relatively simple chemical with the molecular formula $C_6H_8O_6$. The structural formula reveals a sugar-like molecule rather than an organic acid; indeed its acid properties are the consequence of the hydrolysis it undergoes when dissolved in water.

The resemblance to glucose results from its synthesis. All species of mammals other than primates (including man) and guinea pigs are capable of producing ascorbic acid by a series of enzyme operated changes from glucose.

$$C_6H_{12}O_6 \xrightarrow{\ -4H\ } C_6H_8O_6$$
glucose   ascorbic acid

Man and guinea pig lack one of the necessary enzymes. In plants ascorbic acids is synthesized from galactose as well as from glucose.

Ascorbic acid in neutral or alkaline solution will readily lose hydrogen to an oxidizing agent.

Both ascorbic acid and dehydroascorbic acid have vitamin value and the reaction is readily reversed. Further oxidation converts dehydroascorbic acid into diketogulonic acid which is completely lacking in vitamin value. This is an irreversible change from which the vitamin cannot be recovered.

Ascorbic acid can be synthesized economically on a commercial scale, the crystalline solid being chemically stable. The reducing properties of ascorbic acid are utilized in food processing, both as an antioxidant preventing enzymic browning (see 17.2) and as a flour improver (see 11.5). The fact that it is a normal constituent of food favours its acceptance as a processing additive, although no enhancement of nutritive value should be anticipated.

8.13.2 Physiological functions

The ease with which ascorbic acid can lose hydrogen and form dehydroascorbic acid which in turn can readily take up hydrogen prompts speculation that it functions in oxidation–reduction reactions which abound in cell chemistry. And yet it is not possible to point to any one reaction and show its dependence upon ascorbic acid as a reducing agent or dehydroascorbic acid as an oxidizing agent.

However there is ample evidence to link ascorbic acid with collagen, the protein which forms the more abundant of the connective tissue fibres, and with mucopolysaccharides in the intercellular cement substance. Analysis of collagen shows a significant content of hydroxyproline, one of the rare amino-acids for which the genetic mechanism appears to lack means of selection from cytoplasm and transfer to the sites of polypeptide synthesis, the ribosomes (see 10.6.4). Instead proline is brought to the collagen synthesizing ribosomes and there hydroxylated as incorporation proceeds. Evidence points to involvement of ascorbic acid in this hydroxylation. The relatively large amounts of collagen distributed throughout the body in all tissues, stresses the fundamental importance of vitamin C related to the normal processes of growth and tissue maintenance. Its function is highlighted when radical tissue replacement is required, as in wound healing, and confirmatory evidence comes from increased concentrations of ascorbic acid found at the seat of a wound.

Another and separate function is suspected for ascorbic acid which is concerned with energy release. At the end of the electron transport chain, where hydrogen is finally converted to water, ascorbic acid may well be involved in catalytic control. Undoubtedly more will be heard of this with progress in research. Mention of it is made here to emphasize that vitamin C is probably multifunctional and claims for value from various levels of intake are difficult either to substantiate or to refute. Currently there is interest in the use of very high intakes for combating the common cold (Pauling, 1970). No support for this theory is forthcoming from FAO (1970).

In plants, ascorbic acid is involved in a still-unspecified way with photosynthesis.

8.13.3 Effects of deficiency

The historical aspects of the deficiency disease scurvy have been considered (see 8.1). Currently in the UK, cases are diagnosed only among a small number of persons, usually elderly and living alone on very limited diets. The problem is social rather than medical for they respond well to dietary supplements if only they can be reached. Symptoms of scurvy are well documented and the interested reader should consult a medical or dietetics textbook, for they cannot be adequately summarized in a work such as this. However two symptoms have been selected for inclusion because they emphasize the function of ascorbic acid in tissue maintenance.

(i) Teeth become loose due to lack of the cement substance which should bind them to the jaw.

(ii) Blood capillaries, lacking adequate support from surrounding connective tissues, are ruptured by blood pressure and cutaneous haemorrhages occur.

Where there is no blatant scurvy but a lower than average intake, wounds are slow to heal but there is no acceleration of normal wound healing with high doses of the vitamin.

8.13.4 Requirements

The wide divergence between recommendations for daily intakes of vitamin C made by countries through the world (UK 30mg, USA 45mg, and West Germany 75mg to take three examples) stems from the different premise which each adopts. The UK recommendations (DHSS 1979) are based on the amounts of the vitamin shown to prevent any symptoms of scurvy in healthy men (Bartley, Krebs and O'Brien 1953) plus a margin for safety. The German recommendations are calculated from the amounts required to maintain tissue saturation. The intermediate recommendations of the Americans derive from a study utilizing radioactive ascorbic acid (Baker *et al*, 1969 and Hodges *et al*, 1971) which showed that the adult body stores some 1·5g ascorbic acid, referred to as a metabolic pool. At the onset of a period of vitamin C deficiency, this metabolic pool is used up at the rate of 45mg per day. The USA recommendations (National Research Council 1974) aim to keep the metabolic pool filled to capacity.

The international recommendations (FAO, 1970) agree with those of the UK and are set at 30mg ascorbic acid per day for adults.

8.13.5 Dietary sources

Ascorbic acid is widely distributed in plant and animal tissues but in very variable amounts. In meats, glandular tissues have higher concentrations than muscle but in general, animal foods are not counted important sources of the vitamin. Rather, dependence is placed upon fruits and vegetables but these need to be selected with knowledge and handled with care to preserve this highly soluble and chemically unstable nutrient.

The large losses which occur are mainly due to:

(i) solubility in water used for washing, blanching and cooking. Leaching out can be limited by use of minimum volumes of water and by washing leaves etc. when whole rather than after shredding;

(ii) oxidation to diketogulonic acid, which is favoured by exposure to air, light, heat, alkali and copper ions. It is catalyzed by ascorbic acid oxidase, an enzyme liberated when cells are damaged. Extreme heat, quickly applied, destroys this enzyme. This is the principle of blanching, an initial process in the preservation of many fruits and vegetables. Ascorbic acid is reasonably stable in acid solution and in the presence of sulphite preservatives. Oxidation can occur in bruised and wilting leaf vegetables and soft fruits so that preserved forms, which are harvested and processed at speed, can compete with them.

The best sources in the British diet are probably citrus fruits because, in the main, they are eaten immediately after peeling and without heating or soaking in water. Blackcurrants have particularly high concentrations but are only available seasonally. Strawberries and raspberries are good enough sources to justify expenditure when available as fresh fruit. Preserved forms, frozen or canned, of all these fruits make appreciable contributions to the overall intake. Tomatoes are popular and many are eaten raw which maximizes their moderate content. Green vegetables are valuable sources especially when dark coloured and full grown but cooking in water inevitably results in losses. Addition of soda to the water to intensify the green colour hastens the destruction of the vitamin due to alkalinity. Peppers are particularly good sources and are now used in sufficient amounts in this country to qualify them as 'good dietary sources'. Potatoes have a moderate ascorbic acid content when new but this diminishes during storage and old potatoes stored through the winter contain very little from March onwards. However potatoes are eaten in such quantities that for nine months of the year they make a very significant contribution. Dehydrated mashed potato, which has recently made an impact on the retail market, is an unreliable source unless fortified with synthetic ascorbic acid.

Vitamin C is valued sufficiently by the public at large to make it a sales attraction for a processed and packaged food. Manufacturers are careful to make claims only when they can guarantee that the concentration in their product does not fall below the stated amount and this will usually necessitate addition of the synthetic vitamin.

In nutrition education, scurvy should not be held out as a threat to every child who refuses to eat cabbage, but it is fair to imply that vitamin C is likely to be a 'nutrient at risk' in many diets if only for the reason that its dietary sources are limited. A sudden and radical change in the diet could trigger a deficiency if it was towards foods which are poor sources of the vitamin. On these grounds, crash slimming programmes can be hazards. An altered life-style, say leaving school and the school dinner for a city job with lunch hours used for window-shopping, could have serious consequences.

PRACTICAL EXERCISES
All experiments require standard precautions

ASCORBIC ACID DETERMINATIONS
The dye 2:6 dichlorophenol indophenol is blue in neutral and alkaline solution and pink in acid solution. It is decolourized by reducing agents such as ascorbic acid and sulphur dioxide. In fresh foods, ascorbic acid is the quickest acting reducing agent present, hence the dye can be used for its estimation provided the titrations are carried out quickly, allowing the same time for each.

Preserved foods often contain sulphites, as preservatives, which produce sulphur dioxide, capable of decolourizing the dye. To prevent this, acetone is added to complex the sulphites. The instability of ascorbic acid is countered by the inclusion, in the extracting water, of a stabilizing agent. This takes the form of an acid: metaphosphoric, acetic, tricloracetic, oxalic. The first is probably the most effective, although being unstable it has to be prepared immediately before use; hence its substitution in simplified versions of the analysis.

A 0.05% solution of the indophenol dye is approximately equivalent to a 0.02% solution of ascorbic acid, i.e. nearly equal volumes react during titration. The procedure for method I (Expt. 8.1) involves preparation of an accurate 0.020% solution of ascorbic acid, suitably stabilized, and an approximately 0.05% dye solution. The latter is standardized by titration against the former and then used to determine the ascorbic acid content of standard dilutions of foods.

Method II (Expt. 8.2) simplifies this procedure by employing tablets of the dye, each one equivalent to 1mg ascorbic acid. These are intended for diagnosis of hypovitaminosis and not for analytical purposes. Even so, they provide a useful insight for students into methods of food analysis.

End points in the titrations are not altogether easy to ascertain and workers require to practise the technique in order to replicate their own results. Red coloured foods present particular difficulties and are probably better avoided at this level of working.

Expt. 8.1 METHOD I FOR DETERMINATION OF ASCORBIC ACID IN FOOD MATERIALS

THIS METHOD REQUIRES AN ANALYTICAL BALANCE

Preparation of stabilizing solution Weight 40g metaphosphoric acid sticks, freed from crusty deposits. Crush and dissolve in water without heating, add 100cm³ glacial acetic acid and make up to 1 litre. This is better used within 10 hours but may be kept overnight in a refrigerator.

Preparation of standard ascorbic acid solution Weigh 0·200g pure ascorbic acid into a weighing bottle. Transfer, with washing, to a 100cm³ standard flask and make up to 100cm³ with the stabilizing solution. This solution should be used within 24 hours.

Preparation of dye solution Dissolve 0·05g 2:6 dichlorophenol indophenol in water, dilute to 100cm³ and filter. This will keep for a few weeks in a refrigerator but will require to be re-standardized before each use.

Standardization of dye solution Fill a burette with dye solution. Pipette 10cm³ standard ascorbic acid solution into a small conical flask. Titrate to a faint pink colour, persisting for 15 seconds. Express the concentration as mg ascorbic acid equivalent to 1cm³.

If Tcm³ is the average of three replicating titrations,
then Tcm³ dye solution $\equiv$ 0·002g or 2mg ascorbic acid
$\therefore$ 1cm³ dye solution $\equiv \frac{2}{T}$ mg ascorbic acid

(i) Determination of Ascorbic Acid in a Fruit Juice (not red-coloured) Obtain the juice by crushing the fruit and straining through double muslin. Commercial products, if concentrated, should be diluted according to directions. Pipette 50cm³ into a 100cm³ standard flask and make up to 100cm³ with the stabilizing solution. Mix well. Pipette a 10cm³ aliquot of this test solution into a small conical flask. FOR PRESERVED FRUIT JUICES, add 2–3cm³ acetone.

Fill the burette with standardized dye solution and titrate to a pale pink end point persisting for 15 seconds. Repeat to obtain three accurate results, each titration taking the same time, not in excess of 2 minutes.

Calculate the ascorbic acid (AA) content in mg per 100cm³ original juice.

If average titration result $= V$cm³ dye ($\frac{2}{T}$ mg AA/cm³)
10cm³ juice (diluted 50:50) contains $V \times \frac{2}{T}$ mg AA
100cm³ juice (original) contains $V \times \frac{2}{T} \times$ 20mg AA

NB. For juices low in ascorbic acid, values of V will be small prejudicing accuracy. In these circumstances, EITHER increase the aliquot taken (20cm³ instead of 10cm³), OR dilute the dye volumetrically.

(ii) Determination of Ascorbic Acid in a Food (green vegetable, fruit, etc.) Chop the food roughly and weigh out 50g of a representative sample. Homogenize thoroughly in a liquidizer together with about 100cm³ stabilizing solution. Transfer contents of the liquidizer to a 250cm³ standard flask or stoppered measuring cylinder, washing with stabilizing solution. Make up to 250cm³ with stabilizing solution. Mix well and allow to sediment, filter supernatant liquid through double muslin and label 'extract'.

Fill burette with standardized dye solution. Pipette a 25cm³ aliquot of extract into a conical flask, adding 5cm³ IF FOOD CONTAINS A PRESERVATIVE.

Titrate to a pale pink end point, persisting 15 seconds, repeating to obtain replicating results at constant time.

Calculate the ascorbic acid (AA) content in mg per 100g original food.

If average titration result $= V$cm³ dye ($\frac{2}{T}$ mg AA/cm³)

25cm³ extract contains $V \times \frac{2}{T}$ mg AA

250cm³ extract or 50g food contains $V \times \frac{2}{T} \times 10$mg AA

100g food contains $40\frac{V}{T}$ mg AA

NB. If V is too small for accuracy, the dye solution should be diluted volumetrically to give titration result in the range 10–15cm³.

Expt. 8.2 METHOD II FOR DETERMINATION OF ASCORBIC ACID IN FOOD MATERIALS (Simplified version using Indophenol Tablets—1 tablet $\equiv$ 1mg AA)

Preparation of dye solution Crush 4 tablets of 2:6 dichlorophenol indophenol and dissolve in a little water. Transfer with washing to a 100cm³ standard flask or stoppered measuring cylinder. Make up volume to 100cm³ and mix well. Label '1cm³ $\equiv$ 0.04mg AA). Use to fill the burette.

(i) Determination of Ascorbic Acid Content of Orange/Lemon/Grapefruit Juice

Squeeze juice from fruit and strain through double muslin or, if a concentrated commercial product, dilute according to directions. Pipette 10cm³ juice into a 100cm³ standard flask or stoppered measuring cylinder. Add 50cm³ dilute acetic acid and make up to 100cm³. Mix. Pipette a 10cm³ aliquot into a small conical flask, adding 2cm³ acetone IF PRESERVED. Titrate adding dye solution from the burette to a pale pink and point, persisting 15 seconds, repeating to obtain replicating results at constant time.

If average titration result $= V$cm³ dye (0·04mg AA/cm³)

10cm³ diluted juice contains $V \times 0·04$mg AA

100cm³ diluted or 10cm³ original juice contains $V \times 0·04 \times 10$mg AA

100cm³ original juice contains $4V$mg AA

(ii) Determination of Ascorbic Acid Content of a Whole Food

Chop food coarsely and weigh out Wg of a representative sample,

where $W =$ 10 for a good ascorbic acid source

20 for a moderate ascorbic acid source

25 for a poor ascorbic acid source.

Homogenize this sample by mashing or liquidizing with 50cm³ dilute acetic acid. Transfer to a stoppered measuring cylinder. Make up to 100cm³ with water and shake well. Allow to settle and decant off the supernatant liquid, filtering if necessary through double muslin, and label 'extract'. Pipette a 10cm³ aliquot into a small conical flask, adding 2cm³ acetone IF ORIGINAL FOOD CONTAINED PRESERVATIVE. Titrate against dye solution to a pale pink end point persisting 15 seconds, repeating to obtain replicating results at constant time.

If average titration result $= V$cm³ dye (0·04mg AA/cm³)

10cm³ extract contains $V \times 0·04$mg AA

100cm³ extract or Wg food contains $V \times 0·04 \times 10$mg AA

100g food contains $V \times 0·04 \times 10 \times \frac{100}{W}$ mg AA $= 40\frac{V}{W}$mg AA

Expt. 8.3   DETECTION OF ASCORBIC ACID IN A FOOD

Prepare a solution of 2:6 dichlorophenol indophenol by dissolving one tablet or a knife-point of the solid in about 20cm³ water. The blue dye turns pink in acid solution and is decolourized by reducing agents, including ascorbic acid and sulphite preservatives.

Obtain an extract of the food under test by chopping or mashing a pea-sized piece, shaking up in half a test tube of dilute acetic acid (to stabilize ascorbic acid) and filtering. If the food has been commercially preserved, add about 1cm³ acetone to the extract to counteract preservatives.

Add dye solution to the extract, dropwise and look for evidence of decolourization. Continue until a pink colour is established.

Positive result   Decolourization of dye occurring IMMEDIATELY is an indication of presence of ascorbic acid. The more dye required to establish a pink colour the greater the amount of ascorbic acid present.

REFERENCES

Baker, E. M., Hodges, R. E., Hood, J., Sauberlich, H. E. and March, S. C. (1969). *Metabolism of ascorbic-1-¹⁴C acid in experimental human scurvy*, American Journal of Clinical Nutrition, 22, 549–558.

Bartley, W., Krebs, H. A., and O'Brien, J. R. P. (1953). *Vitamin C requirement of human adults*, Special Report Series, MRC, HMSO.

Davidson, Sir Stanley, Passmore, R., Brock, J. F., and Truswell, A. S. (1979). *Human nutrition and dietetics*, 7th edition, Churchill-Livingstone.

DHSS (1979). *Recommended daily amounts of food energy and nutrients for groups of people in the United Kingdom*, HMSO.

FAO (1967). *Requirements of vitamin A, thiamin, riboflavin and niacin*, Report of a joint FAO/WHO expert group, FAO, Rome.

FAO (1970). *Requirements of ascorbic acid, vitamin D, vitamin B₁₂, folate and iron*, Report of a joint FAO/WHO expert group, FAO, Rome.

Kodicek, E. (1974). *Lancet* I 325–329.

National Research Council (1974). *Recommended dietary allowances*, Food and Nutrition Board, National Academy of Sciences, National Research Council publication no. 1694.

Pauling, L. (1970). *Vitamin C and the common cold*, Freeman, San Francisco.

Smith, E. L. (1963). *Vitamin B₁₂*, 2nd edition, Methuen.

FURTHER READING

Birch, G. G. & Parker, K. L. (eds) (1974). *Vitamin C: recent aspects of its physiological and technological importance*, Applied Science Publishers.

Darke, S. J., and Stephen, J. M. L. (1976). *Topics of our time 1: Vitamin D deficiency and osteomalacia*, DHSS, HMSO.

Lewin, S. (1976). *Vitamin C: its molecular biology and medical potential*, Academic Press.

Marks, J. (1975). *A Guide to the vitamins: their role in health and disease*, MTP Press.

CHAPTER IX

DIGESTION AND ABSORPTION

9.1 NATURE OF DIGESTION

Food in any meal comprises a fair proportion of substances that are very evidently insoluble in water, as well as beverages that are almost wholly water, and such substances as sugars, acids, mineral ions, etc. which are soluble in the water of beverages or of foodstuffs as prepared for the table. Food in eating enters the alimentary canal, which may be conveniently considered to be a tube passing through the body, and its cavity, in a way, is really external to the system. Anything that is not in a state of solution, or of fine emulsion, is unable to pass through the wall of the alimentary canal and so to enter the system. For food therefore to be made available as a whole to the tissues of the body, as a source of energy and repair material, it must first be converted into such a physical and chemical state that it can pass through the lining of the alimentary canal. This transformation is effected by the process of digestion. This consists essentially of bringing about a change in the chemical substance of the carbohydrates, proteins and fats, largely by reaction with water—hydrolysis—under the action of digestive enzymes (see 10.2). The enzymes are poured out into the cavity of the gut, in the mouth from the salivary glands, in the stomach from the gastric glands, in the duodenum from the pancreas, and in the small intestine from dispersed glands. The digestive enzymes are specific in their action, and are distinguished as those that hydrolyse carbohydrates, those that hydrolyse proteins (proteolytic) and the fat splitting enzymes.

The soluble and simpler derivatives of food substances produced by the hydrolysing action of enzymes are able to diffuse more or less freely through the lining membrane, the epithelium of the alimentary canal, mainly in the small intestine, and enter the circulatory system by means of which they are quickly transported to the tissues for use as fuel or building material, or to storage organs such as the liver and adipose tissue. The odd thing is that the breakdown products of enzymic digestion soon after being assimilated into the system are in large measure restored to their original grade by dehydration and condensation: thus, the amino-acids are integrated again as proteins or polypeptides, the fatty acids are recombined with glycerol as fats, and glucose is condensed as glycogen. Digestion is simply a means of effecting the transfer of food substances across the thin epithelial coating of the alimentary canal from the gut cavity into the circulatory system.

9.2   THE HUMAN DIGESTIVE TRACT

The digestive tract amounts to a tube running through the body, beginning with the mouth and throat and continuing as the alimentary canal. Successive sections of the alimentary canal vary appreciably in shape, length and internal diameter. All, however, conform to a basic plan with regard to the structure of their walls (Fig. 9.1).

9.2.1   Structure of walls of alimentary canal

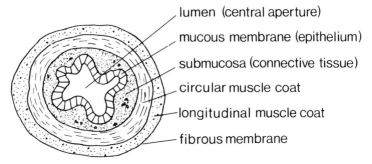

lumen (central aperture)

mucous membrane (epithelium)

submucosa (connective tissue)

circular muscle coat

longitudinal muscle coat

fibrous membrane

FIG. 9.1. Diagram of tissue structures in alimentary canal (cross-section, general plan)

The structure of the alimentary canal is shown diagrammatically in cross-section in Fig. 9.1. The inner layer, the mucous membrane, is formed of a single layer of epithelial cells. Throughout, it serves to lubricate the ingested food by secreting mucus which is a slimy secretion of mucin (a glycoprotein) in water. In some parts the mucous membrane is elaborated to form sac-like glands for the secretion of digestive juices, as in the stomach and small intestines. Also in the small intestine, it forms projections, the villi, which allow absorption of digested materials through to the circulating fluids, blood and lymph. Thus the mucous membrane is specialized along its length for both secretion and absorption.

Below the mucous membrane a layer of connective tissue gives continuity and supports blood vessels, lymph glands and vessels, and nerve fibres.

Next come two distinct bands of simple non-striated muscle fibres. These are involuntary in that their contractions are automatic and cannot be controlled at will. Contraction of the circular band narrows a tubular length of alimentary canal, while contraction of longitudinal fibres produces shortening. Alternating contractions of circular and longitudinal muscles, passing along a section of oesophagus or intestines, produce peristaltic waves which propel food along the whole length of the alimentary canal, except that in the stomach progress is halted. Muscular contractions of stomach walls effectively churn the contents.

On the outside of the canal a membrane of fibrous tissue gives support and protection.

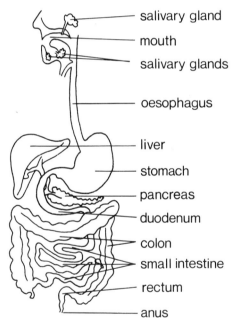

salivary gland

mouth

salivary glands

oesophagus

liver

stomach

pancreas

duodenum

colon

small intestine

rectum

anus

FIG. 9.2. Organs of the digestive tract

9.2.2 Organs of the digestive tract and associated glands

The principal organs of the digestive tract and its associated glands are illustrated in Fig. 9.2. Secretions from the glands are poured through ducts into the mouth, stomach and small intestine. The enzymes they contain promote the chemical changes of digestion. They are helped by the presence of water, by electrolytes which adjust the pH of the food mixture, by the internal body temperature and by the state of subdivision of the food particles which is brought about by chewing in the mouth, churning in the stomach and, for lipids, the emulsification produced by bile.

9.3 DIGESTION IN THE MOUTH

The process of reducing the food to physical and chemical states suitable for absorption is begun in the mouth. In mastication, when at all sufficiently practised, the teeth cut and grind the pieces of food to a small size, and the tongue and mouth muscles generally by their movement mix up the food with the saliva secreted by the salivary glands. The very act of mastication stimulates the glands to secrete saliva, but the secretion of saliva is more of a reflex action, in response to the stimulus of taste and to a less extent of that of smell. Pavlov showed by his experiments on the conditioned reflex in dogs, that the note of the dinner bell may be sufficient to initiate secretion. This evidence has often been used to support the contention that the thought of food will stimulate salivation in humans. Research does not confirm this; the alternative postulation is that, when hungry, thoughts of food make one more aware of saliva already in the mouth. On the other hand fear appears to dry the mouth; a condition afflicting nervous orators.

The secretion of the salivary glands proceeds in the main from three pairs of glands; the parotid, in front of the ears, the submaxillary and the sublingual, respectively below the lower jaw and in the floor of the mouth. The mixed secretion of the several glands consists mainly of water, with small amounts of dissolved inorganic salts giving a pH of 6·8. It is slimy, because of a little mucin, and reactive to starch because of the enzyme ptyalin. Saliva acts as a moistener and lubricator of food, so as to admit of its easy passage down the gullet or oesophagus. Ptyalin has the power of converting starch into maltose and dextrin, but only when the starch is fully cooked. In any case with most people food is generally swallowed almost as soon as eaten, and ptyalin has practically no opportunity of effecting any chemical change in the mouth. The action of ptyalin however continues awhile in the stomach, for it can proceed in the neutral or even slightly acid medium. It soon becomes too acid due to secretion of hydrochloric acid by the oxyntic cells in the cardiac end of the stomach.

9.4 DIGESTION IN THE STOMACH

The stomach acts as a reservoir for food so that feeding can be confined to a few relatively short meal times while the lengthy digestive processes continue.

9.4.1 Functions of the stomach

(i) The food is thoroughly churned and mixed with water producing chyme (from the Latin *chymus* meaning juice-like) the consistency of which favours enzyme action and passage through the long convoluted intestines.

(ii) The food is brought to the internal temperature of the body (40° C) at which fats change to oils and digestive enzymes are most active.

(iii) The pH is lowered sufficiently to destroy many bacteria introduced with food, a safeguard against much food poisoning.

(iv) Digestion of protein is commenced.

9.4.2 Composition and secretion of gastric juice

Gastric juice contains about 99 per cent water, sufficient hydrochloric acid to bring the pH of stomach contents down to 2, mucin and the proteolytic enzyme pepsin. Secretion of the milk clotting enzyme, rennin, is probably confined to infancy and although a lipase (fat-splitting enzyme) has been detected, it is considered to be ineffective.

The walls of the stomach are served by branches of the vagus nerve but secretion of gastric juice is not continuous. It is stimulated by the taste, the smell and even the thought of food so that some is likely to be present before food reaches the stomach. Much has been written about the benefits to digestion of attractive surroundings, pleasing service and relaxed feelings in addition to the more obvious advantage of good cooking.

Pepsin is secreted as pepsinogen, a zymogen or enzyme precursor which is inactive until brought into contact with hydrochloric acid. The gastric mucous membrane of the fundus contains both acid-secreting cells (called parietal or oxyntic) and pepsinogen secreting cells (called chief or zymogenic). The former are stimulated by the hormone gastrin, released when the stomach is distended by the entry of food, and this stimulation continues while food remains there. Certain components are particularly effective, notably extractives from meat; for this reason, soup is much employed as a 'starter' to a large meal. Another hormone, enterogastrone, is released by the walls of the duodenum when the stomach contents are emptied therein, with the effect on the parietal cells of stemming acid secretion. Thus acid secretion is under dual hormonal control and, in normal health, this is efficient. Where there is hyperacidity (excess of acid), with symptoms of 'heartburn' or 'indigestion', there may be disorders such as gastric or duodenal ulcers or even gall bladder inflammation.

9.4.3 Action of pepsin
Pepsin catalyses the hydrolysis of proteins, attacking peptide links at points within the protein molecule so that smaller fragments result. The names given to these fragments are, in order of decreasing size:

$$\text{Proteins} \rightarrow \text{proteoses} \rightarrow \text{peptones} \rightarrow \text{polypeptides}$$

Few if any amino-acids result from pepsin digestion so that further proteolytic action is needed.

9.4.4 The role of mucin
The stomach wall protects itself from self-digestion by producing a viscous fluid, mucus, from a third type of secreting cell. Mucus contains the glycoprotein mucin which adheres to the lining of the stomach keeping the pepsin away from the stomach walls. Normally mucin is only slowly digested and adequately replenished. In conditions of hyperacidity, the mucin is more rapidly digested and its protective action nullified with consequent dangers of tissue perforation.

9.4.5 Retention of food in the stomach
The entry to the stomach is controlled by the cardiac sphincter, the exit by the pyloric sphincter; both are muscular valves allowing, normally, only 'one-way' travel for the food. For periods varying between two and five hours following a meal, there will be periodic discharges of chyme from the stomach through the pylorus into the duodenum. The time of retention will vary with the composition of the meal. Wholly carbohydrate meals are held for shorter periods than mixtures. In particular, lipids slow down the emptying of the stomach, possibly by inhibiting muscular contractions, and fatty foods give longer sensations of satiety. Greasy foods are also associated with 'indigestion' and attempted explanations refer to the 'coating of protein with fat' which 'prevents contact with pepsin'. In the absence of irrefutable evidence, these need to be examined. Certainly lipids are not digested in the stomach because they have not by then been emulsified, but even if they succeed in preventing gastric digestion of proteins, this should not be detrimental. There

is much evidence to show that elimination of pepsin digestion by surgery does not prejudice the complete digestion of proteins within the small intestine. If 'indigestion' is understood to imply 'discomfort following food intake' rather than 'incomplete digestion', the sensations which follow consumption of greasy food may be due to excessive gastric secretion, caused by long retention of stomach contents with continued production of gastrin (see 9.4.2). Also many of the secretion-stimulating food flavours are fat-soluble and are only 'drawn-out' when fat is a component of the meal. These will vapourize from the stomach contents reaching the mouth and nose and reminding the diner of recently consumed fried onions, herrings, toasted cheese, etc. If this is accompanied by discomfort, these foods will be branded 'indigestible'. Another after-effect is 'biliousness', which usually follows a particular excess of greasy foods. This may be the result of a mild ketosis (see 10.5.3).

9.5   DIGESTION IN THE SMALL INTESTINE

When acid chyme leaves the stomach and enters the duodenum, the first loop of the small intestine, three digestive juices are poured in from the pancreas, the liver and the mucosal glands in the duodenum wall.

9.5.1   Pancreatic juice composition

The pancreatic juice is composed of:

(i) Water and inorganic ions, Na^+, K^+, Ca^{2+}, Cl^-, HCO_3^-, HPO_4^{2-}.

(ii) Enzymes—pancreatic lipase, amylase and maltose.

(iii) Zymogens—trypsinogen, chymotrypsinogen and procarboxy-peptidase.

The pH of the chyme is adjusted from strongly acid to slightly alkaline, mainly due to the secretions of bicarbonate ions (HCO_3^-). The potential enzyme activity of pancreatic juice cannot be achieved until the zymogens have been activated by contact with components of intestinal juice and until lipids have been emulsified by bile. Doubtless production of zymogens rather than active proteolytic enzymes serves to protect the tissues of the pancreas from self-digestion.

9.5.2   Intestinal juice composition (succus entericus)

In addition to water and inorganic ions (as in pancreatic juice), intestinal juice contains a wide range of enzymes whose names signify the substrate upon which each is effective. They include, among others:

> maltase
> sucrase
> lactase
> aminopeptidase $\Big\}$ formerly called erepsin
> dipeptidase
> lipase
> lecithinase

In addition the enzyme enterokinase is secreted, capable of converting trypsinogen to trypsin and thereby enabling the activation of all the zymogens in pancreatic juice:

ZYMOGEN		ENZYME
	enterokinase	
trypsinogen	$\longrightarrow$	trypsin
	trypsin	
chymotrypsinogen	$\longrightarrow$	chymotrypsin
	trypsin	
procarboxypeptidase	$\longrightarrow$	carboxypeptidase

9.5.3 Composition of bile

Bile contains no enzymes. Its contribution to digestion is emulsification of fats, thereby ensuring a large enough surface area for effective contact with the fat-splitting enzyme lipase. The emulsifying agents in bile are bile salts which show the dual properties, hydrophilic and hydrophobic, common to all emulsifying agents (see 6.2.3).

Also present are bile pigments (break-down products of haemoglobin from red blood cells) and cholesterol. Before it is ejected into the duodenum, bile is stored and concentrated in the gall bladder. Too high concentrations of cholesterol and bile salts can produce gall stones. If this necessitates removal of the gall bladder, the supply of bile will not be available in concentration at the time of entry of chyme into the duodenum. Curtailment of the dietary intake of fats will be needed, at least until there is adjustment to the effects of the operation.

9.5.4 Enzyme action in the small intestine

(i) *Proteolytic* A sufficient variety of proteolytic enzymes are present in the small intestines to degrade all sizes of protein fragments. Trypsin and chymotrypsin are endopeptidases attacking the larger fragments at peptide links within the chains. Aminopeptidase and carboxypeptidase are exopeptidases attacking the respective terminal ends of small polypeptide chains and removing single amino-acids. Consequently there is considerable chance of ingested protein being fully degraded to amino-acids which can be absorbed.

(ii) *Carbohydrate digestion* Any starch which has escaped ptyalin digestion in the mouth will be converted to maltose by pancreatic amylase. Then maltose will become glucose under the influence of maltase from either pancreatic or intestinal juices. The other disaccharides will be degraded to monosaccharides: sucrose to glucose and fructose, lactose to glucose and galactose.

(iii) *Lipid digestion* Triglycerides, the major components of dietary lipids, are not completely hydrolysed to fatty acids and glycerol during digestion. It is only a proportion of triglyceride molecules which is affected by the lipases present in the small intestine. Hydrolysis provides fatty acids and glycerol and also intermediate products, diglycerides and monoglycerides (see 4.2.3). These are effective emulsifying agents, especially the monoglycerides which together with the bile salts reduce the remainder of the fats into a very fine state of emulsion, with oil droplets small enough to pass through the cell walls of the mucous membrane lining the intestines.

Digestion reactions are summarized in Fig. 9.3.

	MOUTH	STOMACH	SMALL INTESTINE
CARBOHYDRATES	starch $\xrightarrow{\text{ptyalin}}$ maltose		starch $\xrightarrow{\text{amylase}}$ maltose maltose $\xrightarrow{\text{maltase}}$ glucose lactose $\xrightarrow{\text{lactase}}$ $\begin{cases}\text{glucose}\\\text{and}\\\text{galactose}\end{cases}$ sucrose $\xrightarrow{\text{sucrase}}$ $\begin{cases}\text{glucose}\\\text{and}\\\text{fructose}\end{cases}$
PROTEINS		protein $\xrightarrow{\text{pepsin}}$ $\begin{cases}\text{peptones}\\\text{and}\\\text{polypeptides}\end{cases}$	$\left.\begin{array}{l}\text{protein}\\\text{and}\\\text{peptones}\end{array}\right\}$ $\xrightarrow[\text{peptidases}]{\text{endo-}}$ polypeptides polypeptides $\xrightarrow[\text{peptidases}]{\text{exo-}}$ amino acids
LIPIDS			triglycerides $\xrightarrow{\text{lipase}}$ $\begin{cases}\text{fatty acids}\\\text{glycerol}\\\text{di- and}\\\text{mono-}\\\text{glycerides}\end{cases}$

FIG. 9.3. Summary of Digestion Reactions

9.6   ABSORPTION AND TRANSPORT

9.6.1   **Absorption**

The internal surface area of the small intestine is enormously extended by projecting villi. Absorption of the end products of digestion involves transporting monosaccharides, amino-acids, fatty acids and glycerides through the layer of epithelial cells which covers the villi and into the circulating fluids. Within each villus is a blood capillary network and a lacteal of the lymphatic system (see Fig. 9.4). Monosaccharides, amino-acids and lower molecular weight fatty acids enter the blood and are carried via the hepatic portal vein to the liver. The triglycerides and long chain fatty acids, in a fine state of emulsification, enter the lacteals and proceed in lymph via the thoracic duct to enter the blood stream in the left jugular vein. In the processes of digestion and absorption there is some re-arrangement of fatty acid residues about the glycerol framework so that the triglycerides in the circulation are not necessarily those which entered the body with the food.

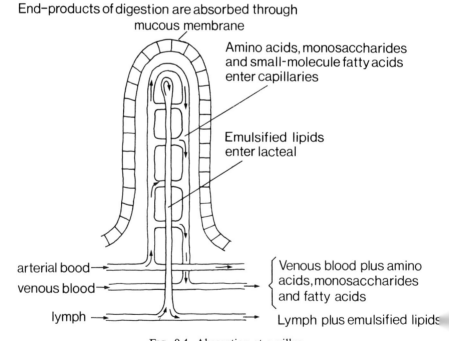

End-products of digestion are absorbed through mucous membrane

Amino acids, monosaccharides and small-molecule fatty acids enter capillaries

Emulsified lipids enter lacteal

arterial blood

venous blood

Venous blood plus amino acids, monosaccharides and fatty acids

lymph

Lymph plus emulsified lipids

FIG. 9.4. Absorption at a villus

9.6.2 Transport

Most of the carbohydrate circulating in the body is in the form of glucose which is readily soluble in water and diffusible through cell walls. Amino-acids are similarly mobile. On the other hand, lipids are insoluble in water and have to be 'carried' in the circulation. Chylomicrons are the structures used for this purpose. The triglyceride is complexed with protein and small amounts of phospholipid and cholesterol giving a particle which remains dispersed in water.

9.7 THE LARGE INTESTINE

Digestion is usually considered to be over by the time intestinal contents reach the colon; likewise absorption, apart from water which is withdrawn to concentrate the faeces. But the colon is a large organ and the material remains within it for many hours. During this time the bacterial population may well play a significant digestive role, although not on the scale of that in the caecum of a herbivore. It is certain that intestinal bacteria contribute appreciable amounts of the B group vitamins required by their host.

9.7.1 Efficiency of digestion

The digestive system is singularly effective. Unless there is impairment of organs or accelerated peristalsis, due to inflammation or irritation, it is likely that 90–95 per cent of ingested protein and fat will be absorbed and possibly more. Proteolytic enzymes appear to be capable of dealing even with over-baked and under-chewed meats, provided they do not pass too quickly through the intestines. Soluble and slightly coagulated dietary proteins are likely to be digested more quickly but not more completely. A slight impediment to protein digestion comes with the operation of the Maillard reaction. When reducing sugars and proteins are together in a food which is subjected to heat, a brown substance is formed due to polymerization between the reducing groups from the sugar and the amino groups from certain amino-acid residues in the protein. The amino-acid, lysine, is chiefly concerned and is rendered unavailable because the polymer is not broken down in digestion. The Maillard or non-enzymic browning reaction occurs on the surface of baked goods and roast meats, improving the appearance and the flavour.

Of the carbohydrates, cellulose is not hydrolysed in the digestive tract and passes unchanged from the small intestine into the colon. Other carbohydrates are readily digested and absorbed unless they are eaten as components of raw fruits or vegetables, especially unripe fruit or under-chewed raw vegetable. In these circumstances, cellulose cell walls may remain intact through to the large intestine where undigested starch and disaccharides contained therein can be fermented by bacteria, giving rise to flatulence, abdominal pain and watery stools.

9.7.2   Formation of faeces

The water which has poured from glands on to the food giving chyme its fluid consistency, is reabsorbed by the cells lining the large intestine so that faeces achieve a semi-solid form. Cellulose or 'fibre' is the major component remaining from the food. The rest is largely debris from the mucous membrane and dead remains of the large bacterial population. An adequate amount of fibre helps to prevent over-absorption of water and the formation of hard stools which can result in constipation. Lately diets lacking fibre have been associated with a number of affections of the bowel.

When diarrhoea occurs due to excessive peristalsis in the colon, there will be no time for water absorption and considerable quantities of fluid will be lost from the body. Whatever treatment is prescribed for this condition, this loss must be made good by increased water intake.

PRACTICAL EXERCISES

All experiments require standard precautions

Expt. 9.1   SALIVARY DIGESTION

Prepare a dilute solution of starch by dispersing a pinch of starch in half a test tube of cold water and stirring it into about $50cm^3$ boiling water. Allow to cool.

Rinse the mouth thoroughly to ensure removal of food debris. Obtain a solution of saliva by holding in the mouth for one minute some dilute salt solution and then transferring it to a beaker. Divide it into two portions and boil one of them. Set up two test tubes labelled A and B with the following contents:

A—$2cm^3$ starch solution + $2cm^3$ fresh saliva solution
B—$2cm^3$ starch solution + $2cm^3$ boiled saliva solution

Place both A and B in a water bath maintained at 37° C. Meanwhile prepare, on a tile, 9 or more spots of iodine solution. At 2 minute intervals, withdraw from A a drop of mixture with a clean glass rod and transfer to one of the iodine spots. When there is no longer any blue/black colour production (i.e. the achromatic point), all starch has been digested. Test the contents of A for reducing sugar (Fehling's or Benedict's test—Expt. 3.1 (iii) and (iv)) and the contents of B for starch.

Conclude concerning the action of saliva on starch and the effect of heat on salivary activity.

Expt. 9.2 GASTRIC DIGESTION

Prepare three test tubes, labelled A, B and C with the following contents:

A—2cm³ 1% pepsin solution + 2cm³ deionized water
B—2cm³ 1% pepsin solution + 2cm³ M/10 hydrochloric acid
C—2cm³ M/10 hydrochloric acid + 2cm³ deionized water

Drop into each a small strip of fully exposed photographic film. This consists of a plastic sheet coated with gelatin in which black particles of silver are embedded. Place tubes A, B and C in a water bath maintained at 40° C. Leave for 30 minutes at least. From time to time agitate the tubes slightly and look for evidence of digestion of gelatin, indicated by loosening of black particles from the film. Draw conclusions concerning the part in protein digestion by gastric juice of (i) pepsin and (ii) hydrochloric acid.

FURTHER READING

McNaught, A. B. and Callander, R. (1977). *Illustrated physiology*, Churchill-Livingstone.
Mackean, D. and Jones, B. (1975). *Introduction to human and social biology*, John Murray.

CHAPTER X

METABOLISM

10.1 CELL CHEMISTRY

Metabolism may be defined as the sum total of all chemical reactions within the cells. This is a useful statement as far as it goes but it hardly does justice to the organization within cells by which the many different chemical changes are integrated. The digestive changes take place outside the cells and are usually considered separately from the topic of metabolism.

10.1.1 Ends served by metabolism

(i) Respiration or energy production. The energy from nutrients, particularly carbohydrates and fats, must be made available to do work as and when required.

(ii) Synthesis of essential materials for structures, secretions and stores. Structural materials in the body are largely protein, and, to make them, amino-acids need to be strung together in precise formations. Secretions contain complex materials such as enzymes and hormones. Stores amount to glycogen in liver and muscles, synthesized from glucose, and triglycerides in adipose tissue, formed from fatty acids and glycerol.

(iii) Disposal of waste materials. Substances which have to be removed because their retention would lead to toxic concentrations have to be transformed into excretable materials. The nitrogen content of amino-acids, not required for protein synthesis, is such a substance. It is changed to urea which leaves the body in urine.

Before examining the means employed to serve these ends, attention will be paid to some particular aspects of cell chemistry.

10.1.2 Catabolism and anabolism

Break-down of relatively large molecules, from food or from the body's storage depots, into smaller simpler molecules such as carbon dioxide, water, urea and lactic acid, is termed catabolism. It is accompanied by energy release. Conversely anabolism is the synthesis of large complex molecules, e.g. glycogen, proteins, triglycerides, and requires an input of energy. Both processes are accomplished in the cells in step-by-step sequences of chemical changes, each controlled by an appropriate enzyme.

10.1.3 High-energy bonds and ATP

Adenosine, a nucleotide, formed from adenine (a carbon–nitrogen cyclic compound) and ribose (a pentose sugar) can be phosphorylated by reaction with inorganic phosphates, giving in sequence, adenosine monophosphate (AMP), adenosine diphosphate (ADP) and adenosine triphosphate (ATP). This is anabolism and energy must be available for such phosphorylations. Symbolically, ATP can be shown as A—$\circled{P}$~$\circled{P}$~$\circled{P}$ where A stands for adenosine, $\circled{P}$ for a phosphate group and ~ a particular kind of bond described as being 'energy-rich'. A relatively large amount of energy has to be supplied to make such a bond and an equal amount of energy is released when the bond is broken by hydrolysis. For present purposes, only the following changes will be considered.

(i) Energy input
$$\text{ADP} + \text{Pi (inorganic phosphate)} \quad + \text{energy} \xrightarrow{} \text{ATP} + H_2O$$

(ii) Energy output
$$\text{ATP} + H_2O \quad - \text{energy} \xrightarrow{} \text{ADP} + \text{Pi}$$

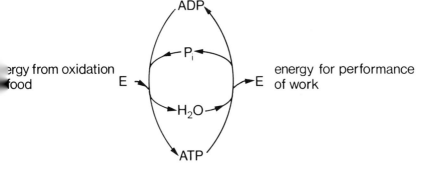

The amount of energy involved each time a molecule of ATP is produced or broken down is a precise quantity. When catabolism is occurring in cells, the energy released is not immediately used for purposes of mechanical work or synthesis but for building up molecules of ATP. This energy can be released 'on demand' by the rapid break-down of high energy bonds with the formation of ADP which can be re-converted to more ATP as energy becomes available from catabolism. The rate of production of ATP will depend on current needs in that a build-up of ATP in a cell will slow down the rate of catabolism and vice versa.

When describing a catabolic sequence, e.g. the oxidation of glucose (see 10.4.1,2,3,4 and 5), it is helpful to follow ATP formation. This is a good method of 'scoring' the useful energy produced during respiration. Some energy is wasted, for only whole multiples of the amount required to produce one ATP molecule can be stored and then released for performance of useful work. Calculations give the maximum amount which can be tapped by ATP as being in the region of 50 per cent of the amount which is released when food is burned in a bomb calorimeter (see 2.7.1). Further wastage occurs and brings the actual efficiency of the body, in converting the chemical energy of food into useful work, down to about 25 per cent. But even this is high compared with mechanical devices generally and points to the effectiveness of the ATP–ADP system.

In skeletal muscle, ATP is linked to muscle fibre protein. Hydrolysis to ADP, occurs with contraction.

$$\text{relaxed muscle–ATP} \xrightarrow{\text{hydrolysis}} \text{contracted muscle–ADP} + P_i$$

The body uses, to a lesser extent, some other energy-rich compounds, notably creatine phosphate in muscles where the very high demands on energy call for supplementary systems. However, discussion here will be confined to ATP.

10.2 ENZYMES

Virtually all chemical changes occurring within living organisms are controlled by enzymes. Reference has already been made to digestive enzymes which are produced by gland cells and affect reactions outside those cells, i.e. within the alimentary canal. Very many more enzymes are required by the body and every cell produces a large number of enzymes to control the chemical changes within its own cytoplasm.

10.2.1 Some characteristics of enzyme activity

(i) Enzymes act as organic catalysts, accelerating chemical changes so that they operate at rates appropriate for the needs of the organism, under tolerable conditions of temperature and pH.

(ii) Chemical changes catalysed by enzymes are all 'possible' reactions such as could be carried out in a laboratory given the necessary skills, although they would probably involve temperatures, pressures and pH levels incompatible with life.

(iii) Whether or not it takes part in the chemical reaction, an enzyme is unchanged at the end.

(iv) Enzymes are required in very low concentrations compared with that of the substrate (i.e. substance or substances undergoing chemical change). Presumably the enzyme is used again and again.

(v) For each enzyme there is a set of optimum conditions of temperature, pH, etc. for maximum activity. These correspond with conditions at the normal site of activity, i.e. body temperature and near neutral pH for those in the mammalian body. Pepsin's low pH requirement is exceptional (see 9.4.2). Activity rates fall off on each side of the optimum. Low temperatures inactivate enzymes and high temperatures destroy them.

(vi) All enzymes show some specificity. Each enzyme will influence one specific chemical change or a group of closely related chemical changes.

10.2.2 The chemical nature of enzymes

All enzymes so far investigated have proved to consist largely of a protein portion, the apoenzyme. This agrees well with expectations, proteins being large-molecule compounds with elaborate surface shapes and many polar and ionized groups likely to attract substrate molecules. Also their reactions to temperatures and pH changes explain the optimum conditions for enzyme activity (see 5.4.2).

Associated with the apoenzyme is a co-factor. This is known to take a variety of forms in different enzymes, e.g.

(i) Divalent metallic ions, especially Mg^{2+} or Mn^{2+}, useful for linking a negative point on the enzyme to another on the substrate.

(ii) A non-protein organic substance such as a nucleotide which is likely to activate substrate molecules. If such a co-factor is firmly bound to the apoenzyme, it is known as the prosthetic group (see 5.2), but if the co-factor only associates with the apoenzyme during its catalytic activity, it is called a co-enzyme. Several of the vitamins function in this way (see 10.2.3,4 and 5).

In the absence of its co-factor, an apoenzyme is inactive.

ACTIVE ENZYME = APOENZYME　　+　　CO-FACTOR
protein　　　　　　　divalent metallic ion
or
prosthetic group
or
co-enzyme

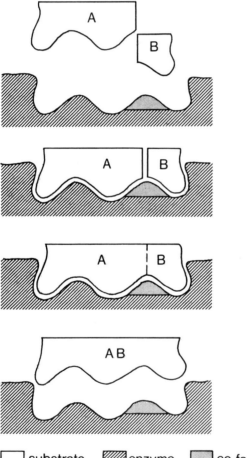

Substrate molecules A and B approach the vacant enzyme site

Initially polarity favours association between substrate and enzyme

Once in position, influenced by the co-factor, chemical links unite A and B forming AB, possibly producing less favourable polar conditions along the substrate/enzyme interface

The product of the reaction leaves the enzyme site which is available for further catalytic activity

☐ substrate　▨ enzyme　▨ co-factor

Fig. 10.1 Diagrammatic representation of postulated theory of enzyme catalysis of reaction A + B→AB

10.2.3 Explaining enzyme action
A 'lock and key' analogy is often suggested to explain enzyme action. An active site on the enzyme surface is the 'lock' into which fit the substrate molecules. During this momentary association, activation of the substrate seems to occur so that chemical change is facilitated. Unlike the reactants the products are not bound to the enzyme and they leave the active site vacant for further substrate molecules (see Fig. 10.1).

10.2.4 Inhibition of enzymes
Not only is enzyme activity prevented by unfavourable conditions of temperature and pH but by the presence of certain other substances with the substrate. These include any of the materials likely to denature proteins (see 5.4.1), as well as molecules with shapes similar to the substrate which, according to the 'lock and key' theory, jam the active sites on the enzyme surface.

10.2.5 Reversible reactions
Many metabolic reactions are reversible and for some of these, the same enzyme is effective for both the forward and the backward reactions. In the system $A + B \rightleftharpoons AB$, it is necessary to consider both reactions going on at the same. time. When the rate of $A + B \rightarrow AB$ equals the rate of $AB \rightarrow A + B$, the concentrations of A, B and AB will remain constant and equilibrium will have been reached. The effect of an enzyme will be to hasten the achievement of. equilibrium.

10.2.6 Names and categories of enzymes
Enzymes are usually named after their substrates and classified according to the type of reaction they influence. The ending 'ase' is used for the name, except in the case of some of the first to be extracted and these retain the older form of name, ending with 'in': pepsin, trypsin and ptyalin. Thus the enzyme which catalyses the hydrolysis of sucrose is a hydrolase called sucrase. At the same time, it could be classified as an invertase because sucrose is inverted on hydrolysis (see 3.3.4). Note that an oxidase catalyses the transfer of hydrogen from an organic molecule to oxygen, making water, while a dehydrogenase catalyses the transfer of hydrogen from one organic molecule to another.

10.3 OXIDATION, REDUCTION AND HYDROLYSIS

Many of the chemical changes of metabolism come within the

categories of oxidation, reduction and hydrolysis.

10.3.1 **Oxidation**

It is useful to consider three statements concerning oxidation.

(i) The most straightforward example of an oxidation is a chemical change in which oxygen is added to a substance, e.g. when carbon is burned forming carbon dioxide.

$$C + O_2 \rightarrow CO_2$$

(ii) Removal of hydrogen also counts as oxidation, e.g. when ascorbic acid is converted to dehydroascorbic acid:

ascorbic acid   dehydroascorbic acid

(iii) Removal of an atom of hydrogen can be thought of as removal of both a hydrogen ion and an electron

one atom of hydrogen (H)	=	one hydrogen ion (H^+)	+	one electron (e^-)

In an aqueous dispersion, hydrogen ions are mobile; it is the removal of electrons which is significant and which counts as oxidation, e.g. when iron II (ferrous) compounds are converted to iron III (ferric) compounds, an electron is removed from each iron II ion.

$$Fe^{2+} - e^- \rightarrow Fe^{3+}$$

Therefore whenever electrons are removed leaving a substance more electropositive, that substance can be said to have been oxidized, i.e. oxidation is an increase in electro-positivity. This is the most useful of the three statements as it embodies them all.

10.3.2 **Reduction**

This is the converse of oxidation and again, three statements are possible:

(i) Reduction is the removal of oxygen from a substance.
(ii) Reduction is the addition of hydrogen to a substance.
(iii) Reduction is a decrease in the electropositivity of a substance.

10.3.3 **Hydrolysis**

Translated literally from the Greek, this means 'loosening by water'. Applied to a category of chemical reactions, this is better defined as 'break-down by reaction with water'. All chemical changes in digestion are examples of hydrolysis and many more take place within the cells. Often word equations, or those employing biochemical abbreviations, neglect to show the involvement of water.

$$\text{e.g. starch} \xrightarrow{\text{amylase}} \text{maltose}$$

$$\text{ATP} \xrightarrow{\text{– energy}} \text{ADP}$$

The presence of water can be anticipated for all reactions occurring within living tissues but this universality of water is an indication of its relatively low reactivity. It is more likely to be the product of a reaction than to enter into one. For this reason, hydrolysis requires the presence of the appropriate hydrolase.

10.4 CARBOHYDRATE METABOLISM

Absorbed monosaccharides are transported in the blood via the hepatic portal vein to the liver. Here conversions occur of monosaccharides into the polysaccharide glycogen, with only sufficient of the monosaccharide glucose passing out from the liver to maintain the concentration in the blood at a fairly steady level, 60 to 100mg per 100cm^3 blood. Liver stores of glycogen are at a maximum following the absorption of the digestion products of a meal and are sufficient to last for some eight hours before the body needs to draw upon its long-term store of lipid in the adipose tissue. Muscle cells also take glucose from the blood and convert it into glycogen, stored in readiness for the high demands which arise when strenuous physical exercise commences.

When glycogen stores are at capacity, any additional carbohydrate from the diet will be converted by the liver into fatty acids and then to triglycerides which accumulate in adipose tissue. Because civilized man has learned to eliminate many of the emergencies which jeopardize food supplies, this mechanism can lead to excess weight gains.

The control of blood sugar level is hormonal, several of the endocrine glands being involved. One such is the pancreas which, as well as producing a digestive juice, secrets the hormone insulin *into the blood stream*. By influencing the permeability of certain cells to glucose, insulin is concerned with taking glucose out of circulation and putting it in cells where it is needed, notably in muscle cells. Absence or deficiency of insulin, such as occurs in the disease diabetes mellitus, will therefore cause glucose to accumulate in the blood especially as in this condition the liver is stimulated to convert glycogen into glucose. One of the symptoms is loss of glucose from the body in the urine. Treatment is by controlled carbohydrate diet and administration of insulin. Diabetes is sometimes present in patients without insulin deficiency. Usually they are obese and elderly and appear to have difficulty in dealing with excess carbohydrate by fatty acid synthesis. Obviously, for them, reduced dietary intakes of carbohydrate are indicated.

The importance of blood sugar level or, more precisely, blood glucose level, is highlighted by the fact that cells of the central nervous system can only metabolize glucose for energy production. A fall in blood glucose will deprive brain cells and coma results. Other nutrients, notably lipids, can be used instead by other cells but glucose remains the prime source of energy and its oxidation will be considered in the following sections. Bioenergetics, the study of energy provision and utilization in the body, amounts to a labyrinth of chemistry, of which only an outline can be attempted here. The reader is referred to texts listed at the end of this chapter for fuller treatments and the whole topic is commended for its relevance to the understanding of nutritional needs in general and of the biochemical roles of a number of vitamins in particular.

10.4.1 Glucose oxidation

The body works at constant temperature. This precludes combustion reactions which release energy in the form of heat. Instead, transfer of chemical energy from glucose molecules must be by a sequence of chemical changes geared to ATP production. Summarized rather crudely, this amounts to the 'picking to pieces' of the 6C glucose molecule, by splitting it into two 3C fragments, transferring hydrogen atoms two at a time to hydrogen acceptors and removing the carbons in turn as molecules of carbon dioxide. The stages in which this occurs will be dealt with in the sequence: glycolysis; formation of acetyl co-enzyme A; citric acid cycle; and electron transport chain.

10.4.2 Glycolysis

As a result of a sequence of nine enzyme-controlled steps, the 6-carbon glucose molecule is split so that two 3C pyruvic acid molecules are formed. This requires removal of four atoms of hydrogen.

$$C_6H_{12}O_6 \xrightarrow{\;-4\,H\;} 2\;CH_3CO.COOH$$

$$\text{glucose} \qquad\qquad\qquad \text{pyruvic acid}$$

Unless hydrogen acceptors are available to remove the hydrogen, this sequence cannot proceed. Nicotinamide adenine dinucleotide (NAD) is an enzyme co-factor, employed as a hydrogen acceptor. The B group vitamin, nicotinic acid, is necessary to ensure provision of NAD. ADP and inorganic phosphate (Pi) are also needed so that the energy released can be bound up in ATP.

$$C_6H_{12}O_6+2NAD+2ADP+2P_i \rightarrow 2CH_3CO.COOH+2NADH_2+2ATP$$

Glycolysis provides, from each glucose molecule, two molecules of $NADH_2$ to feed into the electron transport chain (ETC) and sufficient energy to give two ATP molecules.

In anaerobic conditions, pyruvic acid is converted to lactic acid. This will be considered later (see 10.4.7).

10.4.3 Formation of acetyl co-enzyme A (acetyl coA)

As a result of oxidation (removal of hydrogen) and decarboxylation (removal of carbon dioxide) a pyruvic acid molecule can be degraded to an acetyl group (CH_3CO-). Together with co-enzyme A, a complex molecule of which pantothenic acid forms a part, the 2C acetyl group forms acetyl coA, a key metabolite which can be fed into the citric acid cycle for energy production or be used for synthesis of fatty acids for lipid storage in adipose tissue.

Several enzymes, with their co-factors, are involved. One co-enzyme is thiamin pyrophosphate (TPP), a cocarboxylase, indicating the role of the B group vitamin thiamin, needed for the formation of TPP (see 8. 9. 2 and 3). A deficiency of thiamin leads to an accumulation of pyruvic acid which cannot be metabolized further and this results in the disease beri-beri.

As acetyl coA feeds its 2C acetyl group into the citric acid cycle, co-enzyme A is released to be used again.

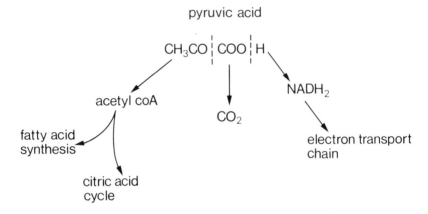

10.4.4 The citric acid cycle

The citric acid cycle is frequently called Krebs cycle acknowledging the contribution of Krebs to its elucidation, and in some texts referred to as the 'tricarboxylic acid cycle' (TCA cycle).

A 4C carrier molecule, oxaloacetic acid, picks up the 2C acetyl fragment from acetyl coA making citric acid, a 6C molecule. In the series of reactions which follows, the 6C molecule is degraded first to a 5C molecule and then to a 4C molecule by the discharge of two molecules of carbon dioxide (see Fig. 10.2). One of these

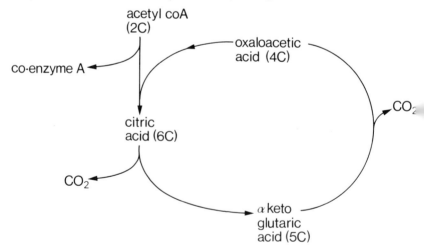

FIG. 10.2. Simplified diagram showing the fate of the two carbons of an acetyl group entering the citric acid cycle

reactions provides enough energy for the formation of a molecule of ATP. At each of four points in the cycle, a pair of hydrogen atoms is removed and transferred to the hydrogen acceptors NAD and an enzyme from the group of flavoproteins (FP). Yet another B group vitamin, riboflavin, is needed to form the prosthetic group of flavo-proteins (see 10.2.2(ii)).

The oxaloacetic acid molecule is restored with the completion of the cycle and is ready to pick up another acetyl fragment from more acetyl coA. So commences another 'turn' of the cycle. Every turn yields one ATP, one FPH_2 and three $NADH_2$ molecules. The reader is reminded that each molecule of glucose provides two acetyl fragments for acetyl coA formation and thus gives rise to two turns of the citric acid cycle.

10.4.5 The electron transport chain

For convenience the electron transport chain will sometimes be abbreviated to ETC in the text; elsewhere it may be called the 'respiratory chain'.

With the completion of a turn of the citric acid cycle, the glucose molecule is thoroughly broken down, but as yet the whole of the energy is not conveniently packaged in ATP molecules. Most is with the hydrogen acceptors, $NADH_2$ and FPH_2. To get at this, the hydrogen is transferred from one enzyme to the next in the electron transport chain until finally it is combined with oxygen forming water. The postulated sequence is:

(i) $NADH_2$ is oxidized by losing its hydrogen to flavoprotein $FP + H_2 \rightarrow FPH_2$. Energy is released with ATP formation.

(ii) The FPH_2 from (i) and that produced by the citric acid cycle, is oxidized by losing hydrogen to co-enzyme Q.

$$coQ + H_2 \rightarrow coQH_2$$

(iii) $CoQH_2$ loses its two hydrogen atoms in the form of two hydrogen ions and two electrons. The hydrogen ions should be thought of as being 'parked' in the surrounding water. The two electrons are transferred to a cytochrome, an enzyme having iron in its prosthetic group. The electrons convert the iron from the iron III (ferric) form to the iron II (ferrous) form:

$$2 Fe^{3+} + 2e^- \rightarrow 2 Fe^{2+}$$

Again energy is released and an ATP molecule is formed.

(iv) Three more cytochromes are considered to participate in the chain. Each in turn serves as the enzyme for the oxidation of its predecessor and electrons are transported to the end of the chain. Yet another ATP molecule is formed with the energy which is released.

(v) Finally the two electrons are united with two hydrogen ions (from the surrounding water) and with oxygen (obtained by breathing) so that water is formed.

$$2e^- \; + \; 2H^+ \; + \; \tfrac{1}{2}O_2 \; \rightarrow \; H_2O$$

For every $NADH_2$ fed into the ETC, three ATP molecules are produced. Each FPH_2 produces two ATP molecules.

10.4.6 ATP scoring
Table 10.1 gives an example of ATP scoring.

Table 10.1
ATP Scoring: Oxidation of one Glucose Molecule

During	Molecules of		
	$NADH_2$	FPH_2	ATP
Glycolysis	2		2
Acetyl coA formation (two molecules)	2		
Citric acid cycle (two turns)	6	2	2
totals	10	2	4
Electron transport chain—ATP conversion factors	$\times 3$	$\times 2$	
Total ATP formation	$10 \times 3 + 2 \times 2 + 4 = 38$ molecules		

10.4.7 More about glycolysis
Under certain circumstances, glycolysis operates not merely as the initial stage of respiration, as just described, but as an alternative means of energy provision. The sequence is taken a stage further with pyruvic acid being converted to lactic acid. The ATP formation is very limited, only two ATP molecules being produced from one molecule of glucose. But glycolysis has the advantage of being able to operate in anaerobic conditions such as occur in skeletal muscle with the onset of vigorous exercise when the demand for

ATP is not matched by the oxygen transport. Much of the lactic acid diffuses out of the muscles into the blood and, in the liver, is converted to glycogen. The rest is converted back to pyruvic acid to follow the aerobic respiratory sequence when oxygen becomes available. Everyone will have experienced the increased rate and depth of breathing which continues for some time after exercise has stopped. Its purpose is to provide the oxygen needed to metabolize the lactic acid produced by glycolysis.

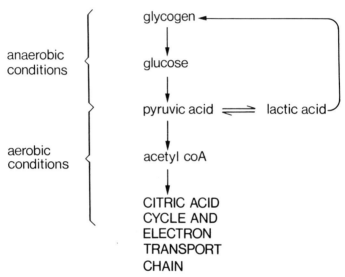

A build-up of lactic acid in skeletal muscles is associated with fatigue and the painful sensations which signal that exercise should cease. Lactic acid formation in carcass muscles after slaughter is significant to the quality of meat (see 15.1.5).

There is evidence that glycolysis occurs in the cells of intestinal walls. Probably, where glucose is abundant, as during absorption, there is advantage in merely degrading large quantities to lactic acid rather than taking a small proportion through complete oxidation. From the intestines lactic acid will pass into the blood and serve as a transportable source of energy.

10.5 LIPID METABOLISM

The body is able to store lipids in sufficient quantity to provide energy during a fast of some 20 days. This is a necessary safeguard for life under primitive conditions. For the affluent, the tendency to lay down adipose tissue is likely to become an embarrassment. The lipids in adipose tissue are mainly neutral fats, i.e. triglycerides, which have been synthesized to suit the human species from fatty acids and glycerol supplied by food sources derived variously from plants and animals. This involves the break-down by oxidation of the fatty acid into 2-carbon fragments which, together with co-enzymes A, form acetyl coA, the key metabolite which enables either (i) the synthesis of 'new' fatty acids or (ii) energy production via the citric acid cycle and ETC.

10.5.1 Fatty acid oxidation

The hydrocarbon chains of fatty acids are reduced in length two carbons at a time with formation of acetyl coA. For example, stearic acid, an 18-carbon fatty acid ($C_{17}H_{35}COOH$) in a series of reactions involving co-enzyme A forms a 2-carbon acetyl coA (CH_3COcoA) and a 16-carbon palmityl coA ($C_{15}H_{31}COcoA$). This in turn is degraded to acetyl coA and a 14-carbon fragment and the spiral sequence continues until the whole is converted to acetyl coA, nine 2-carbon molecules in all.

$$\begin{array}{ccccccc} & +\,coA & & +\,coA & & +\,coA & \\ C_{17}H_{35}COcoA & \longrightarrow & C_{15}H_{31}COcoA & \longrightarrow & C_{13}H_{27}COcoA & \ldots\ldots & C_3H_7COcoA & \longrightarrow & CH_3COcoA \\ \downarrow & & \downarrow & & & & & & \downarrow \\ CH_3COcoA & & CH_3COcoA & & & & & & CH_3COcoA \end{array}$$

The abundant acetyl coA formed provides a rich source of energy if fed into the citric acid cycle. The requirement for co-enzyme A and therefore for pantothenic acid, a B group vitamin, should be noted (see 10.4.3 and 8.8). In addition, with each turn of the spiral $NADH_2$ and FPH_2 are produced for feeding into the electron transport chain.

10.5.2 Fatty acid synthesis

Fatty acid synthesis is not a mere reversal of the oxidative break-down and the means will not be considered here. The relevance for food and nutrition studies lies in dietary implications. The body is capable of utilizing fatty acids from dietary fats and oils to make its own brands of lipids to lay down in adipose tissue for storage, protection and insulation as well as to be used for lipo-protein, the material of cell membranes and nerve tissue sheaths. A few fatty acids are termed 'essential', indicating that they are necessary for incorporation in neutral fats or lipo-proteins. These are listed as:

linoleic $C_{17}H_{31}COOH$ (2 double bonds)
linolenic $C_{17}H_{29}COOH$ (3 double bonds)
arachidonic $C_{19}H_{31}COOH$ (4 double bonds)

It is noteworthy that all are polyunsaturated (see 4.2.2). Deficiency symptoms have been observed in laboratory animals deprived of these and there is a measure of acceptance that they are necessary for children, although supporting evidence is not substantial. The only one with physiological activity may well be arachidonic. However, its representation in the diet is not crucial as it can be made from linoleic, by a process in which pyridoxine (vitamin B_6) appears to be implicated. As yet there is no clear evidence of a role for linolenic acid.

Fatty acids are not only made from other fatty acids but from excess glucose or from the break-down of certain deaminated amino-acids. In the course of their oxidations all form acetyl coA, the intersecting point of several metabolic pathways. Glucose can also be used to produce glycerol, needed to combine with fatty acids to produce neutral fats (triglycerides).

10.5.3   Energy from lipids

Attention is usually focused on energy release from glucose because all cells can utilize it, but some tissues, notably liver, kidneys, heart muscle and resting skeletal muscle, probably obtain 50 per cent of their energy from lipids. Weight for weight, lipids supply more 'useful' energy in the form of ATP than glucose.

During fasting and in diabetes, the body turns to adipose stores. Although this meets energy needs, albeit with body weight losses, a clinical condition known as ketosis is liable to occur. Ketone bodies, namely acetoacetic acid, betahydroxybutyric acid and acetone, are present in the blood in higher than normal concentrations and they can be detected in the urine. The breath smells of acetone, a sickly sweet odour. If the condition continues unchecked it will prove serious, even lethal, due to acidosis—a drop in blood pH below the level which can be corrected by buffering. Discomfort and nausea following an excessive and unaccustomed intake of dietary fats is also accompanied by an increase in blood ketone bodies. It appears that when the body has to cope with extra lipids, acetyl coA is produced in amounts in excess of that which can be fed into the citric acid cycle or used for fatty acid synthesis. This excess acetyl coA is changed in the liver into acetoacetic acid, itself a ketone body and the precursor of the other two. Ketone bodies leave the liver for surrounding tissues, there to be used for energy production, but in the interval before they are dispersed, ketosis conditions operate. Doses of sugar will alleviate the nausea produced by an ill-advised excess of fatty foods. Possibly this works by providing pyruvic acid (by glycolysis) which can be converted to oxaloacetic acid, the carrier molecule of the citric acid cycle, thus enabling the cycle to turn faster and use up more of the acetyl coA. In diabetes, dosing by insulin would be necessary to enable glucose to be absorbed by the cells and used for energy production, thus ending the body's dependence on its lipid stores. If fasting is enforced by food shortage, a more fundamental remedy is indicated.

10.6   PROTEIN METABOLISM

Within every cell there operates a mechanism whereby proteins can be made from amino-acids. The whole character of the cell is determined by the types of proteins which it produces for its own structure, its enzymes and, in the case of a gland cell, its secretions. The operation involves structures (organelles) within the cell, especially the nucleus (which contains nucleic acid, deoxyribonucleic acid—DNA) and the ribosomes. According to current theories of inheritance and cell replication, the DNA structures contain 'information' which enables a cell to go on producing its own kinds of proteins throughout its existence. When cell division occurs, the DNA ensures that this 'information' is passed on to both daughter cells.

Another type of organelle, present within every cell, is the lysosome. In most cells this only becomes effective when useful existence is over. Then enzymes are released from the lysosome which bring about the destruction of the cell's substance, notably hydrolysis of protein into amino-acids. There is a constant 'turnover' of tissue substance so that amino-acids enter the bloodstream from this source as well as from digested foods. Amino-acids circulating in the body fluids constitute a metabolic pool, from which cells can obtain their needs for protein synthesis. This serves as a reservoir but should not be thought of as a store against a possible food shortage for, as the blood circulates through the liver, amino-acids present in excess are removed and deaminated.

10.6.1   Deamination of amino-acids

Within the liver cells, amino-acids are deprived of their amino groups ($—NH_2$) and the remnants are utilized either in the ways described for carbohydrate (see 10.4) or for lipids (see 10.5). The nitrogen fragments are converted into urea which circulates in the blood until, on reaching the kidneys, it is excreted as urine.

10.6.2 Energy from amino-acids

If the energy content of the carbohydrates and lipids in the diet is inadequate, the body will use the protein component as an energy source, to the detriment of the needs for growth and tissue maintenance. Under starvation conditions, after exhaustion of adipose tissue stores, protein will be deliberately withdrawn from tissues in an attempt to keep up supplies of vital energy but to the detriment of the body substance. At the other extreme, when the diet is high in protein, there will be an overall excess of amino-acids. Likewise, consumption of a protein mixture, whose biological value falls short of 100, will leave some particular amino-acids which cannot be used for protein synthesis. The best the body can make of these excess amino-acids is energy provision and, following deamination, they are fed into the catabolic sequences.

10.6.3 Synthesis of non-essential amino-acids

The essential amino-acids are defined as those which must be supplied by dietary proteins because they cannot be made in the body (see 5.9.2). Non-essential acids are no less important to the cells for protein synthesis but since they can be made in the body it is not essential for them to be provided by the diet. Synthesis of non-essential amino-acids utilizes parts of molecules from both carbohydrate and lipid sources but the amino groups must be donated by other abundant amino-acids. The one usually employed is glutamic acid. The transfer of an amino group from one amino-acid to another is referred to as transamination.

10.6.4 Protein synthesis

Amino-acids are taken into the cell from the circulation and strung together in patterns dictated by the DNA in the cell nucleus. This is polypeptide chain formation (see 5.3.2) and it occurs, not in the nucleus, but in the cytoplasm on the ribosomes. Information from the DNA is carried from nucleus to ribosome by another nucleic acid, ribonucleic acid, called messenger-RNA. Small molecule forms of RNA, called transfer-RNA, collect appropriate amino-acids and bring them to the ribosome where they link to form polypeptide chains. Further linkages result in the secondary and tertiary structural features required for complete synthesis of protein molecules (see 5.3.5 and 5.3.6).

10.7 SUMMARIES OF METABOLIC SEQUENCES

Figs. 10.3 and 10.4 are diagrammatic summaries of the metabolic sequences.

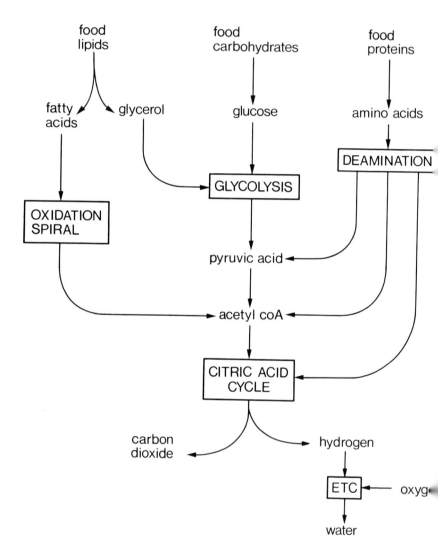

FIG. 10.3. Summary of catabolic sequences releasing energy from foodstuffs

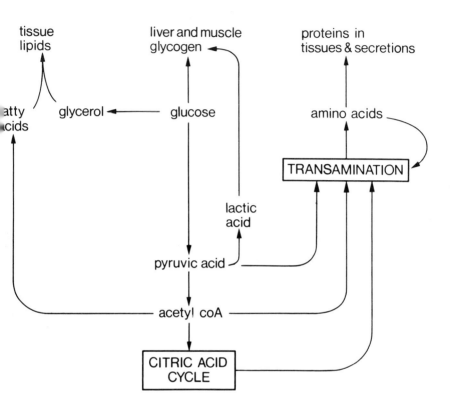

Fig. 10.4. Summary of anabolic sequences producing materials for structures secretions and stores

FURTHER READING

Holum, J. R. (1969). *Introduction to organic and biological chemistry*, Wiley.

Lehninger, A. L. (1975). *Biochemistry*, 2nd edit., Worth Publishing Co.

Conn, E. E., and Stumpf, P. K. (1976). *Outlines of biochemistry*, 4th edit., Wiley.

Rose, S. (1970). *The chemistry of life*, Penguin.

SECTION B.—COMMON FOOD MATERIALS

CHAPTER XI

CEREALS AND CEREAL PRODUCTS

Cereals are gramineous plants, i.e. members of the family Gramineae or cultivated grasses and they are one of the chief foods of mankind. Cultivation of crops for food and for production of some kind of bread has developed with the growth of civilization. Little is known as to the origin of cereals but bread is mentioned in several instances in the Bible; there is evidence to show that bread was known in Egypt at least as far back as 2000 BC; and archaeological discoveries show that milling equipment existed 75 000 years ago. Cereal crops include wheat, maize, rice, barley, oats, rye, sorghum and millet, and of these wheat is the most important crop.

11.1 WHEAT AND FLOUR

Wheat can be cultivated throughout the temperate regions of the world which include the greatest land areas. There are many varieties of wheat but these can be roughly divided into two main types, winter and spring wheat, and there are three distinct colours —white, red and yellow. Winter wheat is sown in the autumn and though the winters may be cold they should not be so severe as to cause excessive freezing of the soil. Winter wheat is cultivated in the UK. In other countries where the winters are extremely cold, like Canada, parts of the USA and Russia, the climate is too severe for winter wheat and spring wheat is grown. This is seeded in the early spring and has a fairly quick growing period so that it can be harvested before autumn frosts can damage the crops. Both winter and spring wheats are grown in the USA, and North America as a whole is the world's largest exporting area. It is because of these differences that flours from different types of wheat are so frequently blended to give a product suitable for the particular purpose for which it is intended—bread, pastries, cakes and biscuits. Thus flours may be derived from wheats from almost any of the principal wheat-growing countries of the world. Durum wheat is a special type of wheat known as *Triticum durum*, and is grown in Canada, USA, Italy, Russia and many other European countries. It constitutes about four per cent of the world's total wheat crop. Flour and semolina from durum wheat are required for the manufacture of macaroni, spaghetti and other pasta products. Not surprisingly Italy, with its high level of pasta in the diet, is the largest producer in Western Europe. The yield per acre is much lower than that of soft wheat. Flour from durum wheat is yellow and the sugar content is high; it is not normally considered to be a bread flour.

11.2 STRUCTURE OF THE WHEAT GRAIN

A spike of ripe wheat consists of a stalk to which the wheat grains or berries are attached, and each grain is covered by a protective yellow leaf or glume. When the wheat is threshed the grain is separated from the stalk and glumes, which form straw and chaff respectively. The berries themselves are roughly barrel-shaped and are more pointed at one end than the other. At the pointed end is a small tuft of hairs known as the beard and at the blunt end which was originally attached to the stalk of the wheat plant is a small rough protuberance. This is the germ embryo—the living part of the grain from which on germination the seedling develops. On the opposite side is a deep furrow which passes along the whole length of the grain. It is here that dust and bacteria are liable to collect and prove a source of trouble to the miller in his cleaning of the wheat before milling.

The wheat grain is the fruit of the plant. Fruits in general contain a seed or seeds surrounded by a protective covering known as the seed coat or testa and the whole is contained in an outer coat or pericarp formed from the wall of the ovary. The fruit of the wheat plant consists of a single seed with both seed coat and fruit wall— testa and pericarp—closely attached to one another. If a transverse section of a wheat grain is closely examined with a good lens it is possible to pick out these two outside skins of separate origin which in the milling of the wheat constitute the bran. Underneath comes a single layer of cells known as the aleurone or cerealin layer. These aleurone cells are almost square in section and are packed with protein granules and fats—with little or no starch. The rest of the berry is seen to be packed with starch cells of varying sizes. Each cell is filled with starch granules which vary in size and are supported by a protein matrix containing gluten particles. The starch is made up of two large molecules, amylopectin and amylose, in the ratio 4:1. This central part is the largest and, to the baker, the most important part of the wheat grain. It is known as the endosperm and contains a store of food materials

for the embryo when it germinates. This is the part of the wheat
berry which the miller makes into white flour.

When the wheat grain is cut longitudinally down the crease the
outside testa and pericarp can again be observed as well as the

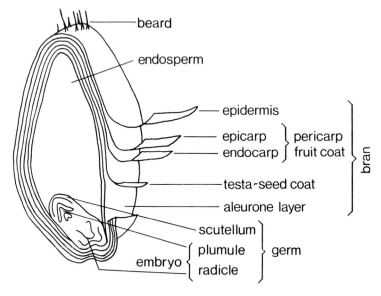

FIG. 11.1. Structure of a Wheat Grain

aleurone layer. In this section a much better idea is obtained of
the endosperm, which forms 85 per cent of the wheat berry (see
Fig. 11.1). The embryo or germ can also be clearly seen. It consists
of three parts—plumule, radicle and scutellum. The plumule is the
undeveloped shoot and contains the first shoots of the future wheat
plant. The radicle is the root centre and contains the root bulb.
The scutellum or cotyledon is a modified seed-leaf and consists of
several distinct tissues, the most important of which, the outermost epithelial layer, secretes the various enzymes required to bring
the food stores in the endosperm into a soluble and diffusible state
for the use of the developing embryo or seedling. The starch is
disintegrated and digested by diastase to maltose, which is converted
into glucose or grape sugar by another enzyme, maltase. The insoluble gluten and other proteins are converted into the soluble
peptones and amino-acids by appropriate proteolytic enzymes; these
are absorbed by the scutellum and with the sugar pass inwards to
the embryo.

11.2.1 Pericarp and testa

The outer covering of the wheat grain consists of the pericarp and testa, and is hard and indigestible being largely cellulose. It also contains small amounts of protein, fat, minerals and B group vitamins but these are not of any great significance as the outer layers of the grain are removed during milling and are only found in wholemeal and wheatmeal flours.

The pericarp consists of three layers, the epidermis, the hypoderm and the inner layer. The inner layer becomes torn during ripening and consists of branching cells known as tube cells. The testa or seed coat lies under the pericarp; the inner layer is often highly pigmented giving the grain its colour whilst the hyaline layer lying next to it is colourless.

11.2.2 Aleurone layer

The aleurone layer of the wheat berry (8 per cent) consists of a single layer of thick-walled cube-shaped cells, and surrounds the endosperm except where the endosperm and scutellum meet. It is rich in fat and protein; the nicotinic acid of the wheat berry is concentrated in this area as is the pyridoxin; and riboflavin and thiamin are present in significant amounts. The aleurone layer is discarded during milling as bran or offals.

11.2.3 Endosperm

This part of the wheat berry (85 per cent) constitutes the largest supply of food materials for the embryo. The thin-walled cells of the endosperm vary in shape, size and composition in different parts of the grain. The contents of the cells consist of starch granules packed together tightly with protein filling the intergranular spaces. Small amounts of fats and sugars are present as well as small amounts of the B vitamins.

11.2.4 Embryo and scutellum

The embryo is the young plant and associated with it is the scutellum lying between the embryo and the endosperm. The scutellum is capable of absorbing the food reserves in the endosperm and passing them to the embryo when the seed germinates. The embryo and scutellum are rich in protein and fat. Most of the thiamin in the grain is concentrated in the scutellum.

11.3 GERMINATION OF WHEAT

When wheat grains are soaked in water and kept at a temperature of about 20° C, germination quickly takes place. The water soaks into the cells of the grain, and the protoplasm present in the embryo acts upon the pro-ferments, or zymogens, in the epithelium of the scutellum and changes them into active ferments. These ferments or enzymes are of several types and each acts on one particular food material. The insoluble starch and proteins stored up in the endosperm are converted into sugars and soluble proteins, peptones and amino-acids. These are easily assimilated by the embryo, which increases in bulk. As a consequence the radicle or root centre emerges, shortly followed by the plumule or young shoot. If the wheat grain has not been planted in soil, growth continues until the food supply in the endosperm is used up, when the little plant withers and dies. If wheat which has begun to germinate is ground into flour, the flour and the bread baked from it are always of poor quality because of the active enzymes and the amount of soluble matter present, including some enzyme precursors. Hence the importance of careful storage of wheat before milling. This is generally done in silos in which precautions are taken to prevent sweating of the grain and the access of sufficient moisture to cause germination.

In normal wheat, beta-amylase is the only enzyme responsible for supplying the yeast with food when it is added to the dough. This enzyme can only attack broken granules. From these it produces 60 per cent maltose and dextrins of high molecular weight. With flour from sprouted grain alpha-amylase is present. It can attack a much greater proportion of the starch and produce dextrins of lower molecular weight. Beta-amylase can attack these and produce much more maltose. This can cause sticky crumb and the loaf may collapse completely.

When the grains are planted in soil the young roots are able to suck up moisture and mineral salts from the soil and the young shoot forces its way steadily upwards and emerges into the open to form leaves which derive food from the atmosphere. Autumn-sown wheat appears above ground while the weather is still cold and makes little apparent progress until the warm days of spring arrive. Rapid growth is then made, the plant increases in height and strength and the stem becomes hollow except at the nodes where the leaves appear. In early June the uppermost leaf begins to swell and shortly afterwards a flower spike emerges. The wheat plant is self-pollinated, i.e. male and female parts are found in the same flower. Pollen is also carried from one wheat plant to another by insects and wind. After fertilization the fruits or grains begin to form. When they reach a fairly good size they are plump and soft, and filled with a milky fluid. Later they become solid and gradually the plant changes its green colouring to a pale yellow shade. Later it turns to a golden colour which indicates that the wheat is ready for harvest.

At all stages of its growth wheat reveals itself as a grass, but by careful cultivation and seed selection a modern wheat plant produces an average of 6–12 stalks, although some specially fine plants have as many as 3–4 dozen, all bearing fine heads of grain. Each head yields from 30–50 grains, so that a single grain of wheat may contribute 300–400 grains to the harvest.

Hybrid wheats have been produced by cross-fertilization of different varieties, which not only give increased grain yield but are more resistant to wheat diseases such as rust, smut, mildew and ergot, and produce shorter and stiffer straw. Straw is not considered a desirable product these days. It does not suit the combine harvester to collect it.

11.4 THE MILLING OF WHEAT

11.4.1 Historical

Early man probably ate grain without any preliminary grinding to flour, but even in prehistoric times wheat was ground between stones. Two stones were commonly used, one being held in the hands and the other resting on the floor and more or less hollowed to hold the grain. With advance in civilization the lower stone was artificially hollowed and the upper one shaped to fit it. The next stage was the use of hand stones or querns in which the upper stone was rotated over the stationary bottom stone. This primitive type of mill is still in use among uncivilized races and in remote districts generally. Further improvements came with the use of larger stones driven by slaves or cattle. This was followed by the use of water wheels as motive power and subsequently windmills. Later still, steam power was utilized. All of these methods are the same in principle. Originally the whole of the grain was ground between stones and the coarse particles of bran afterwards removed in the dressing by hand sifting of the flour. Such stone milled flours were dark in colour because much of the bran was so finely divided as to pass through the silk sieves, and the quality of a flour was largely judged by its whiteness. The early white bread would be available only to the miller and his richer customers, but as long ago as the middle of the seventeenth century bran was separated for the use of cattle. Towards the end of the eighteenth century an Austrian, Parr, introduced the practice of high milling, a system of gradual reduction and purification. Roller milling dates from about 1820 but it was about 1867 that the first complete roller mill was built, and this at Pesth, Hungary. Roller milling did not start in England until 1887, before which time the meal from the millstones was sifted to remove the bran and germ. Later developments have been in improved methods of grain handling, storage, cleaning, conditioning, reduction and artificial bleaching and treating of flour. Recently there has been an increase in popularity of flours containing all or some of the bran and in some cases the germ, but white flour prepared by the roller milling process still constitutes by far the greater part of our supply of flour.

11.4.2 Roller milling process

The methods by which the miller separates the endosperm from the pericarp, testa, aleurone layer and embryo to produce flour may be divided into the following stages: cleaning, conditioning, break-rolling, reduction, bleaching. Each of these is considered briefly.

Cleaning The cleaning of the wheat is obviously necessary when it is realized that the grains of all plants growing in the wheat fields are taken up with the wheat. Wheat which is combine harvested is not as clean as wheat harvested by older methods. The first cleaning process is carried out by passing through a rubble separator, which removes foreign matter—sticks, stones, dirt and soil—and fans blow off the dust. The grain then passes through a disc separator. This machine is fitted with slots which retain the wheat grains and allow seeds of oats, barley, rye, poppy and other foreign seeds to pass through. The wheat is then passed over a magnetic separator to remove pieces of iron such as nails. Removal of metal will avoid damage to the machinery and is also desirable for reasons of safety. Dust clouds of flour are very explosive and could be set on fire by particles of metal striking a spark during processing.

After treatment in the scourer which removes surface impurities and the fine hairs at the pointed end of the grain known as the beard, the wheat reaches the washer and whizzer. It is carried into the machine in a stream of water and revolved rapidly at high speed. The grains being lighter than water float to the surface and remaining impurities sink to the bottom, the wheat is carried upwards out of the water and in this machine the grain can take up the correct amount of water for conditioning.

Conditioning   The wetting of the grain serves another purpose than that of washing. It conditions the wheat for break-rolling by making the bran tough without affecting the brittle character of the endosperm, so that the starchy endosperm can easily be powdered while the bran will not easily be reduced. Great care is necessary in this process, since hard wheats require long soaking, and medium and soft wheats require much less. The conditioning is completed in stone bins and the different samples of wheat blended to make up the particular grist for the mill. The next process is the break-rolling, but the wheat is given a dry brushing to remove any loose particles and a slight steaming before being milled. Conditioning also improves flour for baking purposes.

Great credit is due to the modern miller for the skill and ingenuity he displays in this very effective cleaning of the wheat, without which dirty flours of poor keeping qualities would be the general rule instead of the exception.

Break-Rolling   The actual milling begins with the passage of the grain through a series of three or more break-rolls. These consist of a pair of steel rollers with finely-fluted surfaces which rotate at different speeds. The rollers are about 250mm in diameter and the spaces between the flutes and ribs about 2·5mm. It is possible to adjust the distance between the rollers for fine or coarse 'breaking'.

The grain is split open at the crease in its passage through the first break-roll and the contents of the grain set free. This separation of the starchy endosperm, known as semolinas or middlings, from the bran or offals is made more complete by passage through several more break-rolls. Some of the endosperm is unavoidably reduced to flour at each break and is removed by sieving through woven wire sieves before the coarse 'overtails' are passed on to the next break. The flour formed at this early stage contains dirt from the furrow of the grain that has not been removed by the previous cleaning of the wheat.

After each break the endosperm is more and more completely separated from the bran, and the semolinas and middlings are made to travel in the opposite direction to a current of air in purifiers or separators, which blows away fine fluffy particles of husk which are collected and removed.

Reduction   The starchy, gritty semolinas and middlings are now ground to flour by passing through reduction or grinding rollers. These are not fluted like the break-rollers but quite smooth and set close together. The flour is then 'dressed' by sifting through fine sieves. Any particles which do not pass through the silk sieves are again passed through the rollers to grind them finer.

As regards the germ, part of it is removed with the bran or offal, a very small amount of it passes through the sieves along with the flour, but most of it is removed after reduction. This is because the high fat content of the germ causes it to be pressed flat between the reduction rollers instead of being crushed to powder. It is thus too large to pass through the sieves and is actually the last thing to be separated in the milling of flour.

Flour is produced at many different points in the milling system. These are called 'streams'. In the average mill up to two dozen flour streams are blended together to form what is called 'straight-run' flour.

Air Classification Air classification is a process designed to separate flour more completely. Sieving is not a suitable method for separating very fine particles, i.e. below 80μ. The flour passes into a circular chamber, where a stream of air is revolving rapidly like a whirlwind. The smaller particles are sucked into the centre of this vortex and drawn out of the machine. The larger particles are thrown towards the outside of the chamber.

11.5 Extraction rates

The extraction rate of flour is the ratio of the weight of grain used expressed as a percentage. Mechanical limitations of the milling processes make 75 per cent about the limit for white flour which has normally an extraction rate of between 70 and 72 per cent. Patent flour is the whitest flour derived from reduction of the best purified semolinas. It represents 20–40 per cent and would be referred to by the millers as a high grade flour. Patent flours are used in proprietary cake mix preparations. The fact that white flours are termed high grade does not mean that they should be used in preference to flours of higher extraction rates. During the Second World War the extraction rate was increased to 85% to utilize more of the available grain. The nutritional benefits from this procedure were reflected in the health of the nation.

Wheatmeal (brown) flours have an extraction rate of about 85 per cent and consist of a blend of wheat flours with added bran. Wholemeal flour is required to contain the whole of the product obtained from milling clean wheat. As the extraction rate increases flours contain proportionally less carbohydrate and more of all other nutrients especially vitamins of the B group. The proportions of thiamin rise steeply between 75 per cent and 85 per cent extraction rates due to high concentration of thiamin in the scutellum, whilst proportions of nicotinic acid, which is concentrated in the aleurone layer, rise steeply in extraction rates between 85–100 per cent.

The increased nutritive value of high extraction flours is offset by the increased percentage of dietary fibre in the form of bran. The presence of phytic acid, which is associated with the fibre of cereal grains, forms an insoluble compound with calcium and iron and prevents absorption. This is largely overcome by fortification of flour and offset by changes in breadmaking due to fermentation. If high extraction rate flours are used for staple foods, e.g. flour for chapatis, this could well be hazardous. The fortification of chapati flour has been advocated. It is generally accepted that the diet of developed countries is lacking in total fibre content. Lack of fibre certainly contributes to constipation, claims are made that it might well have some significance in diseases of the colon, coronary heart disease, diabetes and obesity but these cannot be proved conclusively. Whilst white flour is in itself a source of fibre the fibre content is much more significant in wholemeal flour.

11.6. BLEACHING AND IMPROVING

Bleaching of the pigment of wheat endosperm known as xanthophyll occurs rapidly as flour is exposed to air but less rapidly when flour is stored in bulk. This process can be speeded up by the use of permitted bleaching agents. In addition to bleaching, flour can also reach its optimum baking quality after about six months storage. Like bleaching this maturation or 'ageing' can be accelerated by the use of improvers. These modify the physical properties of the gluten, the tolerance of the dough is increased so that it can be made under a wider range of conditions, and it is also easier to handle. The finished loaf is larger in volume and has a fine crumb. Over-bleaching lowers the quality and gives a smaller loaf.

Some chemical agents added to flour both bleach and improve whilst others either bleach or improve. Bread and Flour Regulations control the use of bleaching and improving agents and these are under constant review. At the present time flour, other than wholemeal flour, may be treated with ascorbic acid, potassium bromate, potassium persulphate, ammonium persulphate, monocalcium phosphate, all of which act as improvers, and chlorine dioxide (DYOX) which both bleaches and improves. Benzoyl peroxide (a bleaching agent) is also permitted, as are chlorine (a bleacher and improver for use in flour intended for cake-making) and sulphur dioxide (for use in flour intended for biscuit-making).

The amounts permitted for each of these agents is also subject to legislation. Azodicarbonamide and L-cysteine hydrochloride are likely to be added to the permitted list. Controlled heat treatment can improve the quality of flour but this method of improving is not as widely used as that of improving by chemical agents.

The improving is generally thought to be due to oxidation of cysteine sulphydryl or thiol (—SH) groups which are present in wheat gluten. The complex reactions resulting from the oxidation process give a firmer, tighter dough with better bread-making qualities.

European Economic Community Legislation   At the time of writing none of the bleaching or improving agents, with the exception of ascorbic acid, would be permitted for flour which would go to make a standard 'EUR' bread. This bread could be sold freely in any member country. However, in addition, each member state could allow the sale in its own territory of bread conforming to national legislation. A similar proposal would cover nutrients added to flour for bread-making.

11.7   FORTIFICATION

The addition of iron, thiamin and nicotinic acid to all wheat flours, except wholemeal, is required by the Bread and Flour Regulations. The amounts are intended to restore the levels of these nutrients to those equivalent to an 80 per cent extraction rate. They are:

thiamin	0·24mg/100g flour
nicotinic acid	1·60mg/100g flour
iron	1·65mg/100g flour

In addition chalk, to give an average of not less than 235mg and not more than 390mg of calcium per 100g, is used to fortify flour. Changes in fortification and restoration of flour have been recommended and may well be adopted. It is likely that restoration of the nicotinic acid will be discontinued.

11.8   SPECIAL TYPES OF FLOURS

Most of the flour produced today is roller milled white flour. Some stone ground flour is available in health food stores and some supermarkets and grocers, and is rather more expensive than ordinary flour. Most of the stone ground flours are either wheatmeal or wholemeal (see 11.6). There is a variety of flour called wheat malt flour obtained from wheat malt, i.e. wheat which has been steeped in water, allowed to germinate and then treated to stop germination.

11.8.1 Self-raising flour

Self-raising flour is a flour which has raising agents added to it. The British housewife uses self-raising flour extensively, largely because it is so convenient. It is seldom used on the Continent. The moisture content of the flour should not exceed 13·5 per cent as this could cause premature reaction of the raising agents. The raising agents added are such that would allow carbon dioxide production to continue throughout mixing and baking (see 12.3.2). The Food Standards (Self-raising Flour) order requires self-raising flour to give not less than 0·40 per cent of available carbon dioxide. (Ministry of Agriculture, Fisheries and Food, 1974). A list of raising agents likely to be permitted for use in self-raising flours are:

> sodium bicarbonate (sodium hydrogen carbonate)
> monocalcium phosphate (ACP)
> acid sodium pyrophosphate (ASP)
> acid sodium aluminium phosphate
> glucono delta lactone (GDL)

Self-raising flours are marketed under a variety of brand names and are usually white, although self-raising wholemeal flours are available.

11.8.2 Other proprietary branded flours

Other proprietary branded flours include most flour for household purposes, both plain and self-raising. Flours of particular interest are those labelled 'strong', i.e. with high gluten-forming potential (e.g. McDougalls Country Life). These are of special significance for making yeast mixtures and flaky and puff pastries.

Types of Flour available for the Food Manufacturing Trade Flour can be processed in a variety of ways to suit specific requirements. Amongst these are:

(i) Agglomerated flour
Agglomerated flour is used for soups and as a thickening agent. It is obtained by allowing flour to fall through jets of steam; this produces a flour which is easily wetted and does not go into lumps when added to water.

(ii) Enzyme-inactivated flour
If the alpha-amylase content of flour is relatively high considerable

break-down of the starch present can occur resulting in either a sticky dough, or a gravy or soup where the flour cannot act as a thickening agent. Enzyme inactivated flour which has been treated with steam to reach 100° C is used for thickening soups and sauces, etc, but not for bread-making. In the latter case it would be unsuitable because the elastic properties of gluten are destroyed by steam treatment.

(iii) High-ratio flour.

This is a weak soft flour with very finely divided particles, much finer than ordinary cake flour. The gluten characteristics have been partially destroyed by treatment with chlorine which under ordinary circumstances would be deemed excessive. Treatment of flour by chlorine is permitted for cake-making. The flour thus produced enables successful manufacture of cakes with a high proportion of sugar to flour and a high total liquid content. The proportion of fat may correspond with that of the sugar but this is not essential. The demand for this type of flour is greater in the USA than in the UK, although demand is increasing in this country. Cakes made in this way are said to be very light with 'melt in the mouth' characteristics and the property of retaining freshness for several days.

11.9   PROPERTIES OF FLOUR CONSTITUENTS

11.9.1   Starch

Starch forms about 70 per cent of the total constituents of flour. Wheat starch, like most other starches, contains 2 polysaccharide components—amylose and amylopectin. Amylose is slightly soluble in water, giving a typical blue colour with iodine. It consists of straight unbranched chains of glucose units forming large molecules with a molecular weight between 40 000 and 340 000. Amylopectin is much less soluble than amylose, gives a more reddish colour with iodine and consists of highly branched glucose chains forming a molecule with a higher molecular weight than amylose. These two components react differently to enzyme action. Beta-amylase will convert amylose to maltose but cannot attack amylopectin beyond its branch points; alpha-amylase can attack the linkages at these branch points leaving them exposed for attack by beta-amylase. The results of these complex enzyme actions give rise to poor quality bread with a sticky crumb. However there is only a limited time during bread-making when these reactions can take place and the action would appear to be confined to starch granules damaged in the milling process. Wheat starch is hygroscopic and is the chief of the moisture absorbing qualities of flour on keeping. Large proportions of starch in flour give it a white colour and lead to the production of smaller closer loaves.

11.9.2 Gluten

The gluten-forming proteins of the flour are highly complex and known to be made up of many components. For convenience, one group of components comprising prolamins is referred to as gliadin whilst the remainder, known to be glutelins, are called glutenin. It should be noted that it is the quality of the gluten present which is significant for bread-making purposes rather than the quantity.

11.9.3 Soluble proteins

There are three other types of protein present in flour—albumins, globulins and proteoses. The albumins and globulins are known as the soluble proteins. Their function is not precisely known but it is considered that albumin proteins may be the reason for some of the baking characteristics among flours.

11.9.4 Water

Although flour ordinarily seems an extremely dry substance it always contains a certain amount of water absorbed from the atmosphere by the hygroscopic starch as well as that carried over from the endosperm. The amount of the absorbed moisture varies considerably according to the conditions under which the flour is stored; it is usually between 11 and 14 per cent. When stored for some time in a moist atmosphere flour actually gains in weight, and loses in weight when stored in a dry atmosphere. These variations may amount to several pounds per sack. If the water content of a flour rises above 14 per cent there is a danger of bacterial action and mould growth, and such flour will keep badly and develop acidity. It should be noted that the amount of absorbed moisture in flour has no connection with the water necessary for dough formation, which depends upon the gluten and not upon the starch of the flour.

11.9.5 Sugar

Simple sugars including sucrose, maltose, glucose and fructose are present in the endosperm up to 1 per cent. This helps to feed the yeast. The quantity of sugar in flour varies with the type and grade of flour between 1 and 2 per cent. The sugar of flour has a considerable effect on the bloom of the crust of the loaf owing to its caramelization during baking.

11.9.6   Fats

Flours with an extraction rate of 85 per cent contain about 1·5 per cent fat, flours with a low extraction rate of 70 per cent contain less fat, about 1·2 per cent. Wholemeal flours are very rich in fat because the germ is included which in itself contains 6–11 per cent fat. The fat consists of glycerides of fatty acids—mainly palmitic of the saturated fatty acids and oleic, linoleic and linolenic of the unsaturated fatty acids. Phospholids (see 4.4.1) are also present to the extent of about 4 per cent of the total content.

11.9.7   Enzymes

In addition to the diastatic enzymes alpha- and beta-amylase (see 11.9.1) flour contains proteolytic enzymes given the name of pro-tease. These split the proteins into simpler bodies such as peptones and polypeptides (see 5.3.4). Excessive protease action on gluten impairs its elastic qualities and is not desirable in bread-making. Also present are lipases and lipoxidases. The former hydrolyse fat and the latter are associated with rancidity in fat and the liberation of free fatty acids and oxidizing enzymes considered to be important in bread-making.

Phytase does not affect the baking qualities of the flour but hydrolyses the phytic acid present to phosphoric acid and inositol. Phytic acid inhibits the body's absorption of calcium and iron from foodstuffs. The effect of flour products on calcium and iron absorption will depend on the initial phytic acid content of the flour and the extent to which it has been acted on by phytase during food preparation. It has been estimated that 60 per cent of the phytic acid is hydrolysed during bread-making.

11.9.8   Vitamins

The vitamins of the B group are distributed in varying proportions throughout the wheat grain. This group includes thiamin, nicotinic acid, riboflavin, pantothenic acid and pyridoxin. The vitamin content of the flour increases as the extraction rate increases. Riboflavin is more evenly distributed throughout the grain than the other vitamins and therefore the riboflavin content is not so affected by the extraction rate as other flours. Flour also contains vitamin E although it is not considered to be a good source.

11.9.9   Mineral salts

The mineral salts present in flour are left behind as a fine white ash when the organic constituents are completely burnt away. They consist chiefly of phosphates of calcium, magnesium and potassium with traces of iron and manganese sulphates. Those mineral salts of flour that are soluble act as yeast foods and buffers during fermentation of dough and help in the stabilization of the gluten.

11.10 COLOUR

It is generally taken for granted that flour is white, but actually its colour may vary from dead white to greyish white, brownish grey and creamy yellow. These variations in colour are due to a variety of causes such as the presence or absence of bran particles, the species and variety of wheat, and the use of bleaching agents. Valuable indications of the character of a flour can be obtained from examination of its colour. Broadly speaking whiteness is an indication of large percentages of starch, greyness indicates poor quality, yellowness suggests high gluten percentage, brownness is probably due to bran particles, while dead-whiteness is an almost certain sign of bleaching. The usual method of judging the quality of a sample of flour is by comparison with a standard sample by the Pekar method. The two samples are placed side by side in small heaps on an oblong piece of plate glass and pressed down flat so that they are touching. The colours of the two samples are then compared. The glass is then very carefully lowered under water, starting with one corner and gradually sliding in the whole glass without allowing any flour to slip or any air bubbles to form in the flour. The glass is withdrawn and the colours of the two samples compared once more. Previous slight differences are now more distinct and become still more marked when the flours are dried.

11.11 BREAD-MAKING

Bread is made of four essential ingredients: flour, water, yeast and salt. Other optional ingredients are sugar, milk and fat which improve the quality of bread. The use of a 'strong' flour with a high proportion of good quality gluten-forming proteins is desirable. The correct proportion of water is important; too much or too little water will reduce the volume of the bread. Salt not only improves the flavour of the bread but it strengthens the gluten and controls fermentation. Excess salt will reduce yeast activity. Soft flours require a shorter fermentation period than strong flours and the speed of fermentation can be increased within limits by increasing the amount of yeast, the fermentation temperature and the supply of nutrients to the yeast. Increasing the fermentation temperature can result in growth of undesirable micro-organisms; too much yeast can give an undesirable yeasty flavour. It can be seen that the whole question of bread-making is of a highly complex nature. In this text we will consider the effect of optional ingredients on bread-making, household bread-making and large-scale bread-making.

Optional Ingredients   Sugar is not obligatory in bread-making although many recipes include it. Sugar as food for the yeast is supplied by the small amounts present in flour and by the action of amylases on starch. Extra sugar will speed up fermentation time and is said to give a browner crust and improve flavour.

Milk improves nutritional value, flavour and gives a brown crust. The milk should be heated before use otherwise a soft dough is produced and bread with a small volume and poor texture. This is caused by the active constituent of the whey proteins which is inactivated when heat denatures the proteins. Commercial bakers use a skimmed milk product which has been heat treated.

The inclusion of fat improves the quality of the bread. The volume and texture improve with additions of fat up to 4 per cent. Above 6 per cent the texture gets heavier and the volume of the loaf decreases. Most people prefer the flavour of bread with added fat, and the crust and crumb are more tender. This is sometimes attributed to the lubricating effect of fat on the gluten strands although this is by no means certain. Sweet doughs have a higher percentage of fat than ordinary bread dough.

Other Optional Ingredients   Malt is sometimes added to malt loaves and fruit loaves. As well as giving a distinctive colour and flavour to the loaf the proteolytic enzymes present reduce the strength of the gluten and give a smaller loaf with a closer texture.

Ascorbic acid is frequently used as an ingredient in household yeast mixtures, as it has the ability to shorten the fermentation time. It is necessary to increase the amounts of fat, yeast and water in the dough. Ascorbic acid is used in the Chorleywood process (see 11.11.2). It is by no means certain that the ascorbic acid acts in the same way in household baking.

11.11.1 Home bread-making

Straight dough method   All the recipe ingredients are mixed together and the dough allowed to rise. The order in which they are added does not matter but the dough should have a temperature of about 28° C. Excessive heat will destroy the yeast. The yeast is best added by rubbing in the flour or blending with the liquid.

Creaming yeast with sugar is not now advised, it is considered to give an excessive yeasty flavour to bread. The ingredients are mixed and kneaded together and then the dough is set on one side for fermentation (see 12.4.2) to take place. Good kneading is essential to develop the gluten framework in the dough. Insufficient kneading gives a dough that does not hold the carbon dioxide well. Ten minutes is the average kneading time figure given for household breads but strong flours need more kneading than soft flours. Over-mixing by hand is unlikely but it is easy in bakery processing—overmixing weakens the gluten and the dough does not retain the gas well in rising and baking.

When the dough has doubled in size it is 'knocked-back', i.e. lightly kneaded and then formed into the required shape (loaves, rolls, cobs, etc.) and put to rise again before being baked. The knocking-back process serves the purpose of reducing the size of the carbon dioxide bubbles and of introducing more oxygen into the mixture for the yeasts.

Fermentation has a beneficial effect on the gluten framework of the dough. During both fermentation periods the dough should be covered to prevent a crust forming on the surface. Clean greased polythene bags are ideal for this purpose. It is sometimes convenient to store dough in a refrigerator or in a home freezer but it must be remembered that dough will continue to rise in a refrigerator, although at a much reduced rate. Some rising will take place initially in a freezer until the dough is frozen. If the dough is put into the refrigerator after mixing the subsequent rising time will obviously be longer than for ordinary doughs. Likewise frozen doughs in the unrisen state will have to thaw before rising can start. The heat of the oven will inactivate the yeast so that no further fermentation takes place. The dough will, however, rise due to the expansion of gas and the production of water vapour (see 12.2.2). This is commonly referred to as oven spring.

11.11.2 Commercial bread-making
About 75 per cent of bread in the UK is made by the Chorleywood process. The rest is made by bulk fermentation.

Bulk Fermentation The basic ingredients for breadmaking, i.e. flour, yeast, salt and water together with other optional additions are mixed to form a smooth dough. This is set aside for several hours to ferment. During this period carbon dioxide is produced, fermentation products formed, which contribute to the flavour, and changes take place in the physical properties of the gluten framework produced in the initial mixing so that the ability to hold gas is improved.

After this fermentation period is concluded the dough is knocked-back, given a further rising period and then divided and roughly shaped. The dough is rested for a short period of 10–15 minutes and then moulded into the final shape. This moulding process tightens the dough improving its gas retention properties. The dough is rested for a final proving of 40–45 minutes before baking at a temperature of about 230–260° C for about 45 minutes. Steam is injected into the oven during baking to give a glaze to the crust.

In small bakeries mixing, moulding and movement of loaves are carried out by hand. In large bakeries these processes are carried out mechanically, and temperatures and relative humidity are automatically controlled. The actual baking is carried out in 'travelling ovens'. The loaves are placed on continuous bands and are cooked as they pass through the ovens which can be 30m or more in length.

Chorleywood Bread Process   The Chorleywood process is a batch process in which the bulk fermentation is replaced by a short period, about 5 minutes, of intense mechanical activity together with oxidation by the addition of ascorbic acid. Extra fat, water and a larger amount of yeast are used. This process is economically attractive, it saves time and space in the bakery, enables the baker to get more bread from a given quantity of flour and allows him to use a blend of flour which contains flour from a higher proportion of home grown wheat. Home grown wheats are cheaper than imported strong wheats. It is claimed that bread made from this process is similar in flavour and texture to bread made by the bulk fermentation process and stales less rapidly. A possible explanation of the effect of the intense mixing activity could be that the physical force involved smashes the disulphide bonds in the amino-acids which hold the proteins in their configurations. The breakage could speed up the uncoiling and reforming of the protein chains to form the gluten network. Similar changes are thought to take place slowly during dough fermentation.

11.12   WHEAT PRODUCTS

11.12.1   Semolina and pastas

Semolina is produced from hard wheat. Flour is the by-product amounting to about 10 per cent of the production, whilst semolina amounts to 65 per cent. The wheat is ground lightly in the early stages. Six or seven breaks are used in the grinding system. The semolina is carefully graded and purified to remove as much bran from the system as possible.

Pasta, e.g. macaroni, vermicelli, lasagne, spaghetti and noodles, is made from semolina. A hard wheat is essential and best quality pastas are made only from durum wheat. To make macaroni the semolina is made into a stiff dough and then extruded under heavy pressure through a die to make the required shape—tube or ribbon-like. In Italy the drying may be done outdoors but otherwise it is carried out in drying cabinets where the air temperature and relative humidity can be controlled.

11.12.2 Breakfast cereals
A number of breakfast cereals are made from wheat. There are three main types available—flakes, puffed and shredded. All of these require different treatment although the whole grain is used for each product and the manufacturing processes cause dextrinization of the starch rather than gelatinization. They have additional ingredients, such as sugar, honey, malt extract, to give colour and flavour.

11.12.3 Chapatis
These are made from wholemeal flour and form the staple wheat product in India, Pakistan and Iran. They are becoming increasingly popular in the United Kingdom. Coarse sieves remove some of the bran, usually between 5 and 7 per cent of the total weight. Thus the flour has an extraction rate of between 93 and 95 per cent. The flour, which may have added salt and oil, is mixed with water and kneaded. A piece of dough is rolled flat and thin on a wooden board and then cooked slowly on a flat iron pan over an open fire, being turned once during the cooking process. It is a skilled operation and results in a soft, well-flavoured product.

11.13 OTHER CEREALS

11.13.1 Barley—genus *Hordeum*
Barley is grown in temperate climates and has a geographic distribution similar to wheat. Bread made from barley and rye was the staple diet of the English peasant in the fifteenth century. Nowadays barley is used for animal feeds, mainly for pigs and beef. Barley meal is used for malting, brewing beer and making whisky. In the home it is used mainly as pearl barley in which the kernel is freed from the husk and polished and in Scotch barley which retains

some of the husk. Patent barley is the finest ground and purest form of barley meal available for domestic use.

11.13.2 Maize or Indian corn—*Zea mays*

Maize was originally grown in the USA but it is now grown in Africa, India, Australia and parts of Europe; hardy varieties are now being cultivated in the UK. It is used for human consumption, for animal foodstuff and for manufacturing a variety of products including cornflour, which is the principal ingredient of custard powder and blancmanges; corn syrup and glucose syrup used in confectionery; breakfast cereals such as corn flakes made from maize grits; corn oil, salad oil and cooking oils; and industrial spirit and whisky. The USA is the biggest domestic user of maize whilst the UK is probably the world's biggest importer of maize. The nutritive value of maize compares unfavourably with that of wheat, it is a relatively poor source of nicotinic acid and protein. The protein is deficient in lysine, like wheat, and also in tryptophan.

11.13.3 Oats—genus *Avena*

Oats are widely cultivated in temperate regions and are a more successful crop than wheat or barley in a wet climate. In the UK oats are grown extensively in the North of England and in Scotland. Most of the crop is used as animal feed although a proportion is processed for human consumption. Oatmeal is traditionally a food of the Scots and oatbread, parkin and haver cake are still made in the Lake District and the Yorkshire Dales.

Oatmeal is milled first to pinhead oatmeal, the coarsest form available, which in turn is ground and sifted to produce two finer meals, medium and fine. Rolled oats for quick cooking porridge are made from pinhead oatmeal or sometimes from whole groats. The oatmeal is cooked by steaming and the cooked meal passed between heavy rollers to dry and flake the product. Ready-cooked porridge is a type of porridge which can be made by stirring hot or boiling water in the bowl. These use oatflakes of a special type; they are thinner and stronger and contain a high proportion of starch which gelatinizes more readily. Another type of mix is made up of ordinary rolled oats mixed with thin flakes of a roller dried mixture of oatflour and water. The latter form a smooth paste when boiling water is added. Other oatmeal products include oatflour for baby foods and white groats for making haggis and black puddings.

Oats are rich in protein and contain mineral matter, calcium, iron, phosphorus and the B vitamins and fat. The presence of phytic acid can inhibit calcium and iron absorption but there is evidence that the body can adapt to this situation if a food containing phytic acid is eaten regularly. In addition oatmeal, when eaten as porridge, is usually taken with considerable quantities of milk which in itself is a good source of calcium.

11.13.4   Rice—*Oryza sativa*

Rice is cultivated in swampy fields in most eastern tropical countries. In India, China and Japan rice is the most important cereal crop. It is also grown in the USA which is the world's largest exporter and to a certain limited extent in Spain, Italy and Egypt. Rice is used mainly for human food. Many distinct varieties and qualities of rice are available and they may be named according to the country of origin or to the region where cultivated. The two main varieties are: Patna type (long grain rice) and Carolina type (short grain rice). In this country long grain rice is generally used for savoury dishes and the short grain for sweet dishes. Threshed rice has a thick fibrous husk, and is known as 'paddy' or rough rice. The processing of rice involves cleaning, shelling or hulling, and milling whereby the bran and germ are partially or wholly removed. Whole kernels with only the hulls removed are called brown rice. The outer bran layers of brown rice are removed to give unpolished milled rice and when this in turn is polished to remove the aleurone layer the resulting product is polished rice. Polished rice lacks the vitamin content of unpolished rice; milling and polishing can cause losses of 76 per cent of the thiamin content, 50 per cent of the riboflavin and 63 per cent of the nicotinic acid. This loss causes concern in countries where rice is the staple diet. Parboiling rice can reduce these losses but parboiled rice is not always acceptable. In some areas, e.g. Puerto Rico and the USA, rice fortified with thiamin and nicotonic acid is available. Riboflavin is not added because it causes discoloration. Rice is largely composed of carbohydrate, polished rice having a carbohydrate content of about 79 per cent, as against 6–8 per cent protein. The fat content of polished rice is less than 1 per cent.

Rice products include rice starch, rice flour used in baking, ground rice and breakfast cereals. Quick cooking rice is available, as is 'boil-in-the-bag' rice, 'curry type' packaged 'ready-to-fry', and similar partially prepared rice.

11.13.5   Rye—*Secale cereale*

Rye can be used for bread-making and is the main bread grain of Scandinavia and Eastern European countries. In the UK it is grown mostly in East Anglia and Yorkshire. It is more resistant than wheat to pests, diseases and the cold and will grow in poorer sandy soils. The cleaning, conditioning and milling of rye resembles that of wheat but in milling the endosperm is more difficult to separate from the bran and although the endosperm reduces to flour more easily the flour is hard to sift. Rye is used for making rye bread and is usually mixed with wheaten flour to make crispbreads such as Ryvita. Pumpernickel bread is a soft rye bread made from coarse rye meal. Rye dough lacks elasticity and bread is usually made with sour dough or leaven, not yeast. Rye is also used for making malt, distilling rye whisky. Rye flour is used in soups and sauces in the USA.

11.14   OTHER FARINACEOUS PRODUCTS

11.14.1   True sago

True sago is produced from the pith of the sago palm growing in Malaya, the Philippines, Borneo and India. The pith after being scooped out of the planks of the tree is pulped with water and then strained. The starch which settles is washed, drained clear of water and then dried in the sun. The flour is granulated by being passed through a sieve and shaken. The grains are roasted for a few minutes, being changed into a nearly transparent and glutinous substance. After a further roasting on hot metal plates they become smaller and harder and take on the characteristic dark greyish colour. The dried grains are sifted into the three grades, large, medium and small sago. By far the greater proportion of what is sold as sago is not true sago, being prepared from tapioca.

11.14.2   Tapioca

Tapioca is a food starch prepared from the underground stem of cassava or manihot, which is grown in the tropics of America, Africa and Asia (Java, Penang and Singapore). The rhizomes are dug up, washed, scraped and pulped. Juice, pressed out of the pulp, is boiled down to a thick black fluid. The pulp is washed with water, and so freed from a poisonous constituent; the starch is left to settle and the water drawn off. The starch after drying in the sun is made into tapioca by partial roasting on hot plates, during which process the granules burst their cellulose coatings and liberate the inner gelatinous contents, which sticking together form nodules. These are kept small by constant stirring during heating, and form flake tapioca. After sun drying the starch is powdered, made into paste and granulated by being passed through a sieve. It is finally roasted. Tapioca starch is largely soluble starch and consequently dissolves to a certain extent in water, as well as taking up water to form a jelly, when warmed with water or milk, and this much more quickly than rice.

11.14.3 Arrowroot

Arrowroot like tapioca, is a starch derived from underground stems, in this case of maranta, a plant grown in various parts of the two Indies, tropical Africa and America. St Vincent is the only important exporting source. It is manufactured largely on the lines of tapioca as far as the stage of precipitating the starch, which is then dried in copper pans with a gentle heat. It is sold in two forms: granular and pulverised. Like tapioca it dissolves slightly in water, and quickly swells up in warm water or milk, and is consequently, easily digested—hence its use as an invalid food.

PRACTICAL EXERCISES

All experiments require standard precautions

WHEAT FLOUR TESTING

Most of the following tests are designed for use with white flours and are likely to require some modifications for application to brown flours. Several tests are aimed at judging the quality of a flour for a particular purpose, usually bread-making. The results of several tests taken together and interpreted by experienced workers enable decisions regarding flour mixing, recipe balance, inclusion of improvers, etc. to be taken, aimed at uniformity of the end product, a prime consideration for commercial bakeries. In their laboratories, testing involves complex instruments which improve upon the methods given here.

Expt. 11.1 MOISTURE CONTENT

For analytical purposes, it is often necessary to determine moisture content first so that the aliquot portions, taken for other determinations, can be adjusted. For large-scale baking, some knowledge of moisture content of flour is needed so that the volume of water or other fluids in the recipes can be corrected.

Oven-drying method. Preheat a steam oven and use to dry petri dishes (three for each flour sample). Cool in a desiccator and weigh both bases and lids. Weigh out exactly 5g flour into each base, tap to give a uniform layer and return to the oven with lids off. Heat 3–4 hours. Cool in a desiccator, each dish covered with its own lid. Re-weigh, return to the oven and repeat the heating–cooling–weighing sequence until constant weight is achieved.

$$\% \text{ moisture content} = \frac{\text{loss of weight in grams}}{5} \times 100$$

More rapid, albeit less accurate, methods exist, employing specialist apparatus such as the infra-red moisture tester.

Expt. 11.2   WATER ABSORPTION

This depends on the worker's skill at judging consistency and at replicating results. Weigh 25g flour into an evaporating dish and add tap water from a burette a few cm^3 at a time, mixing flour and water with a spatula. Continue until the mixture achieves the consistency judged to correspond with that of bread dough. Read off the volume of water used and express water absorbed as a percentage of the flour used.

$$\text{water absorption} = \frac{\text{volume of water (cm}^3\text{)}}{\text{weight of flour (g)}} \times 100$$

Repeat until satisfied that results are being reproduced.

Expt. 11.3   GLUTEN CONTENT

Gluten separation   Weigh (to nearest gram) 20g flour and place in a large evaporating basin. From a burette, add 11cm^3 tap water and make a dough using a small spatula. Standardize the time taken (not exceeding 8 minutes) and the effort used, counting the number of 'figure-of-eight' spatula movements required for dough formation, and applying these in subsequent determinations. Cover the ball of dough in the basin with tap water at room temperature and leave to stand 30–40 minutes, allowing maximum water absorption. Transfer to a basin lined with butter muslin and cover with tap water at 30° C. Work with the fingers to separate out the starch. Change the water, using the muslin to avoid loss of gluten fragments. Continue washing until all starch is removed. The final washing water should be clear and ideally should give a negative result to an iodine test. Gather all fragments of gluten together in the palm of one hand and mould with fingers into a coherent mass. Lay aside for 10 minutes to allow surplus water to drain away, squeezing slightly to assist in this. This is the yield of 'wet gluten' from 20g flour which should be weighed to determine % wet gluten.

$$\% \text{ wet gluten} = \text{weight in grams wet gluten} \times 5$$

Percentage dry gluten   Gluten tends to absorb twice its own weight of water. An approximate value for % dry gluten is given by dividing % wet gluten by three. A more accurate value is obtained by the steam oven-drying method, as given for flour in Expt. 11.1.

Expt. 11.4 · PREPARATION OF GLUTEN BALLS

Repeat the procedure for Expt. 11.3 but use 50g flour and about 30cm^3 water, adjusted to give dough consistency. Knead the gluten thoroughly to form a smooth ball and bake in a preheated oven (220° C), reducing the heat once the ball has expanded due to pressure of water vapour. This illustrates the role of gluten within aerated baked goods.

Expt. 11.5   MICROSCOPIC EXAMINATION OF DOUGH

Prepare a small amount of fairly stiff flour and water dough, kneading very thoroughly to develop the gluten. Take great care to avoid contamination from dust and lint which could draw misleading interpretations. Press a minute amount of dough between a slide and a coverslip, so that a very thin layer of dough is formed. Place one drop of dilute iodine solution at the edge of the coverslip and allow it to penetrate the dough. Examine under low and high power magnifications. Starch granules stain blue–black, while gluten strands colour amber.

Expt. 11.6 ZELENY'S SEDIMENTATION VALUE

This test compares the swelling of gluten in lactic acid solution; the greater the swelling, the stronger the flour. Weigh out 4g of each sample of flour under test. (NB. For accurate determinations, this should be corrected for moisture content variations from 14%.) Place in a stoppered 100cm³ measuring cylinder and add 50cm³ acid fuchsin reagent (2·5g acid fuchsin per litre deionized water). Shake for 30 seconds and stand for 5 minutes. Add 25cm³ lactic acid (diluted to 20% and matured for three weeks or refluxed for six hours) and mix by inversion precisely ten times. DO NOT SHAKE. At the end of the tenth inversion replace on the bench and start a stop clock.

When sedimentation has proceeded for EXACTLY FIVE MINUTES, read the volume of the solid phase in cm³. This is the SEDIMENTATION VALUE for the flour. Values range from 20 for low strength flours to 50 and over for flour of high breadmaking quality, such as is used in commercial bakeries. Most flours available on the retail market will rate 30 or under.

Expt. 11.7 CYLINDER TEST FOR STABILITY OF FLOUR

This provides a means of comparing the ability of a flour dough to extend during fermentation and to hold gas—two important qualities in flour for bread-making. Three or four samples of different flours can be used simultaneously and comparisons made. For each sample of flour under test, make a batter from 20g flour, 30cm³ tap water at room temperature and 2g fresh yeast. If dried yeast has to be used, use less (1g) and pre-mix it with the water to which glucose has been added (5g per 100cm³) and stand for 10 minutes before using to make the batters.

Pour each batter into a 250cm³ measuring cylinder, taking care that none adheres to the sides. Note the initial level in each. Stand together in a warm draught-free position or else in a water bath maintained at 30° C. At 5 minute intervals, read off the level of each ferment. Continue until maximum height has been reached and the mixture has collapsed. Sometimes there is a second extension.

For each, plot a graph of 'increase in height' against time from which comparisons can be made regarding a flour's ability to extend during fermentation and to retain aerating gases.

Expt. 11.8 PEKAR'S TEST FOR COLOUR OF FLOURS

White flour, devoid of pigmented bran layers, is not dead white but slightly coloured by xanthophylls and carotenoids in minute quantities. Although of little concern to the domestic user, commercial bakers, aiming to produce uniformly white bread, investigate flour colours and then choose accordingly.

To compare the colours of a number of samples of white flours, place on a Pekar board (a rectangular plank or piece of plate glass about 250mm × 75mm) a heaped teaspoonful of each flour under test. Press each firmly with a palette knife to give a flat rectangular cake in which each sample meets one or two others, providing boundaries which aid in the discrimination between colours. To heighten differences, convert the cake of flours into a 'wet slick'. Take care to straighten the edges of the rectangle, compacting the flours thoroughly with the palette knife. Immerse the Pekar board into a capacious bowl of water at an angle of 30° to the horizontal. One steady gentle sweep should allow the flours to become wetted without dislodging flour or forming air bubbles. Withdraw in a similar manner allowing excess water to drain away. In this form colour differences are most apparent, especially at the 'demarcation lines'.

Expt. 11.9   DETECTION OF FLOUR IMPROVERS

Improving agents, defined as being substances capable of simulating the effects produced by the natural ageing of flour, are added to flours to improve their breadmaking qualities. Those permitted in the UK are ascorbic acid, potassium bromate, ammonium persulphate, potassium persulphate, monocalcium phosphate (ACP) and chlorine dioxide, with chlorine for cake flours and sulphur dioxide for biscuit flours. Chlorine dioxide, chlorine and sulphur dioxide serve also to bleach flour. The only additive permitted which serves solely as a bleach is benzoyl peroxide. Bleached flour has a noticeably white colour (see Expt. 11.8) and provides grey-looking gluten (see Expt. 11.3).

Test available samples of flour, including self-raising and wholemeal for the following:

(i) Potassium Bromate

To a flour and water paste, add some 0·5% potassium iodide in 2M hydrochloric acid. Mix thoroughly.

Positive result   Black specks, indicate bromate present.

(ii) Ascorbic Acid

Disperse a little flour in a test tube with 2cm³ dilute acetic acid and 1cm³ acetone. Add one drop of an aqueous solution of 2:6 dichlorophenol-indophenol.

Positive result   Immediate decolouration, indicates ascorbic acid present.

(iii) Monocalcium Phosphate

Detect as in Expt. 11.10.

Expt. 11.10   MINERAL MATTER IN FLOURS

In addition to the natural mineral content of flours, white flours in the UK are fortified with chalk (to between 235 and 390mg per 100 g) and iron (to not less than 1·65mg per 100g). Self-raising flours contain chemical raising agents. Mineral matter may be determined as a percentage by ashing (see Expt. 7.1) and individual mineral elements identified (see Expt. 7.2). Alternatively mineral matter may be separated intact as follows:

Shake 50g flour with 200cm³ dry carbon tetrachloride in a separating funnel with a wide-bore tap. On standing the flour floats to the surface while the mineral matter sinks and should be run into an evaporating dish. After allowing the carbon tetrachloride to evaporate, test the residue for mineral elements (see Expt. 7.2) and also for monocalcium phosphate (also called acid calcium phosphate), present as an improver or, in self-raising flour, as an acidic salt. Residues from self-raising flours should be investigated as in Expt. 12.2.

REFERENCES

Ministry of Agriculture, Fisheries and Food (1974). *Food standards committee second report on bread and flour*, HMSO.

FURTHER READING

Kent-Jones, D. W. and Amos, A. J. (1967). *Modern Cereal Chemistry*, Food Trade Press.
Harrison, S. G. *et al.* (1969). *Oxford book of food plants*, Oxford University Press.

CHAPTER XII

RAISING AGENTS

12.1 AERATED TEXTURES

Aeration may be defined as the process by which prepared foods achieve various open textures: spongy, flaky, crumbling or a foam. This involves the introduction of suitable gases and, where the preparation includes the application of heat, aeration will be aided by expansion of the gases. A certain elasticity will be necessary in the mixture, allowing stretching in response to expansion, while successfully trapping the gas. The final consistency of the food must have sufficient solidity to maintain the aerated structure. Whichever gases operate the aeration, diffusion will ensure that air occupies the cavities within the final product.

12.2 SUITABLE GASES

The gases and any materials used to generate them, must of necessity be harmless. In addition they must not introduce any undesirable taste, colour or odour. The three suitable gases and the means by which they are introduced into foods are summarized as:

   (i) AIR—introduced mechanically

   (ii) CARBON DIOXIDE—generated $\begin{cases} \text{either chemically} \\ \text{or biologically} \end{cases}$

   (iii) WATER VAPOUR—produced by heat on water

Each will be considered in turn, although it should be appreciated that usually two, if not all three, of the gases operate together.

12.2.1 Air

Mechanical methods of introducing air include whisking, beating, sifting and folding. So that appreciable amounts of air will be held, a mixture with a slack consistency, due to water content, must possess foaming properties. Substances which, dissolved in water, allow foam formation within foods are mainly soluble proteins. These are effective because they lower the surface tension of water and allow it to be drawn out to form the films which enclose air bubbles. The effect is similar to that of soap in water. Protein foams may well have the advantage of greater permanence due to denaturing effects of heat or mechanical action as in meringues. Gelatin foams are supported by the gel structure which forms on cooling.

Other types of mixtures which can be manipulated so that they will hold air, are creamed plastic fats (see 4.3.6) and elastic doughs which are rolled out and folded repeatedly in the making of flaky and puff pastries. The multiple layers are prevented from sticking together by fat, and small, though significant, amounts of air are trapped.

In jelly foams, cold soufflés, whipped cream and meringues, air alone serves to aerate the mixtures. Elsewhere it operates together with other aerating gases, water vapour or carbon dioxide. In fact, air fulfils the minor role of creating the spaces into which these other gases are given off in greater quantity during the baking. The techniques used for introducing air into soufflés and puff pastry are not concerned so much with providing the means of expanding the mixtures but rather with creating the typical textures, spongy and flaky respectively. Thus there are rounded bubbles in the soufflé mixture and very thin air layers within the pastry, both of which expand appreciably as the oven heat produces water vapour.

In some mixtures, more than one air-trapping technique is employed. The creaming method for cake-making utilizes the ability of soft plastic fats to cream when thoroughly beaten. The effect of the sugar is merely mechanical, serving the same role as rotor blades. The usual preference for caster sugar indicates an optimum crystal size for this purpose. When the eggs are beaten in, a fat-in-water emulsion is formed with the particles of the disperse phase consisting of fat still containing the air from creaming. In addition some air will be whisked into the continuous phase of water from beaten egg.

12.2.2 Water vapour

It is possible to estimate the air content of a batter by vacuum extraction. If then the coefficient of expansion of air is applied for the temperature rise expected in the baking of a Yorkshire pudding, some idea of the aeration due to air can be obtained. Studies have shown this to be well below the actual expansion, even allowing for the expansion of the materials of the batter. The major influence is the water vapour which is produced during the baking. Water vapour is also very significant in expansion of flaky pastries.

Indeed water vapour will feature in the aeration of all wet mixtures which are subjected to strong heating.

12.2.3 Carbon dioxide

Carbon dioxide is a normal constituent of the atmosphere, albeit only about 0·04 per cent at the most. It is a harmless colourless gas, almost odourless and tasteless. For it to feature as a raising agent it must be deliberately introduced into mixtures. One method is to use supersaturated solutions of carbon dioxide, formed under pressure, for mixing bread doughs. Just as bubbles of gas appear in soda water when the pressure is released, so the carbon dioxide would come out of solution within the dough and effect aeration. However this has had very limited application and exclusively in the commercial field. Far more important is the production of carbon dioxide within mixtures either by chemical action or biological activity.

12.3   CHEMICAL PRODUCTION OF CARBON DIOXIDE

The origin of the carbon dioxide produced by chemical reaction, is always a carbonate and, with one exception, the carbonate employed will be sodium hydrogen carbonate, better known as sodium bicarbonate or baking soda. The means used to liberate the carbon dioxide are either by reaction with acid or by thermal decomposition.

12.3.1 Acids and carbonates

All carbonates react with acids according to the general equation:

$$\text{acid} + \text{carbonate} \longrightarrow \text{salt} + \text{water} + \text{carbon dioxide}$$

It is important to realize that reactions of acids are essentially those of hydrogen ions which only form when the acid is dissolved in water. The presence of water will ensure that the sodium bicarbonate dissolves, providing bicarbonate ions (HCO_3^-), and thus the production of carbon dioxide can be explained by reference to the following:

$$\underset{\substack{\text{hydrogen ion} \\ \text{from the acid}}}{H^+} \;+\; \underset{\substack{\text{bicarbonate} \\ \text{ion from} \\ \text{baking soda}}}{HCO_3^-} \;\rightarrow\; H_2O \;+\; \underset{\text{carbon dioxide}}{CO_2 \uparrow}$$

This equation summarizes the effective chemistry of acid–bicarbonate reactions, whichever acid happens to be employed. Some traditional recipes require measured amounts of sodium bicarbonate to be used together with acidic ingredients such as sour milk, vinegar, fruit juice and treacle. All are likely to vary in their acidities, the last named having, at times, an insignificant content. Therefore the amount of carbon dioxide liberated is not constant. A better method employs an acidic powder such as cream of tartar, which can be measured to correspond with the sodium bicarbonate. Alternatively a baking powder may be employed, obviating the need for meticulous measurement of two ingredients.

12.3.2 **Baking powders**

All commercial brands of baking powder consist of three ingredients: sodium bicarbonate, an acidic component and a filler. The sodium bicarbonate is the source of the carbon dioxide. Dissolved in water, it provides the bicarbonate ions for the reaction shown in 12.3.1. All brands of baking powder also contain a filler, usually corn or rice flour and therefore mainly starch. The purpose is to separate particles of carbonate and acidic component and thereby avoid premature reaction. Water is needed to bring the two reactants into ionic contact and the starch, by effectively absorbing atmospheric moisture, succeeds in preventing this. Nevertheless the ordinary precautions of storing in dry conditions in an airtight container ought to be observed for an extended shelf life. Starch also acts as a filler, diluting the active ingredients and making less critical the precise measurement of the recipe inclusion.

It is the choice of the acid component that distinguishes the various brands of baking powder. Manufacturers choose between a number of possible compounds, all being powders which are harmless and unlikely to affect the colour and flavour of the food significantly. The advantages and disadvantages of each are set down below; the principal criteria for choice being cost and rate of reaction with sodium bicarbonate from the time mixing commences. An acid or acid salt which dissolves in cold water gives a 'quick-acting' baking powder; one which is only appreciably soluble in hot water gives a 'delayed-action' baking powder, only producing significant amounts of carbon dioxide during the cooking process. The advantage of the latter is that carbon dioxide is not lost from the mixture before the heat-setting changes can occur. There is a danger, however, that a firm outer crust will form on a large cake before heat has penetrated sufficiently to begin the reaction internally. The result would be either a close texture or a crack through which unbaked mixture erupts.

In consequence, there is a demand for 'double-action' baking powders which commence the opening up of the texture from the point of mixing and continue through the baking until setting changes are well advanced. The acid components employed can be a mixture of cold-water soluble and hot-water soluble compounds, or else substances whose acidity increases as rising temperatures advance their hydrolysis.

A manufacturer makes his choice from the following:

(i) *Tartaric acid*   Tartaric acid is the only suitable true acid which fulfils all requirements. In water, it ionizes giving hydrogen ions as the only positive ions—the criterion of a true acid.

$$(CHOHCOOH)_2 \rightarrow (CHOHCOO)^{2-} + 2H^+$$

$$\underset{\substack{\text{1 molecule} \\ \text{tartaric acid}}}{} \qquad \underset{\substack{\text{1 tartrate} \\ \text{ion}}}{} \qquad \underset{\substack{\text{2 hydrogen} \\ \text{ions}}}{}$$

Being readily soluble in cold water, tartaric acid would be included to give quick-action type powders or, if used with other acid components, it contributes to double-action. Its disadvantages are cost and relatively poor keeping qualities.

(ii) *Cream of tartar*   Cream of tartar is the acid potassium salt of tartaric acid with the chemical name potassium hydrogen tartrate. In water, once dissolved, it ionizes giving both hydrogen and potassium ions as positive ions (hence not a true acid).

$$\begin{array}{l} CHOHCOOH \\ | \\ CHOHCOOK \end{array} \longrightarrow \begin{array}{l} CHOHCOO^- \\ | \\ CHOHCOO^- \end{array} + H^+ + K^+$$

$$\underset{\substack{\text{1 molecule potassium} \\ \text{hydrogen tartrate}}}{} \qquad \underset{\substack{\text{1 tartrate} \\ \text{ion}}}{} \qquad \underset{\substack{\text{1 hydrogen} \\ \text{ion}}}{} \quad \underset{\substack{\text{1 potassium} \\ \text{ion}}}{}$$

Only one hydrogen ion from each relatively high weight molecule means that an appreciably greater bulk of cream of tartar is needed than of tartaric acid to give the same acidity. This makes cream of tartar an expensive ingredient but it has the advantage of being only sparingly soluble in cold water, giving a delayed-action property to a powder.

(iii) *Acid phosphates*   Much use is made of acid calcium phosphate and acid sodium pyro-phosphate not only in baking powders but also in cake/pudding mixes which incorporate their own chemical raising agents and in self-raising flour (see 11.8.1). Cost is certainly an influence towards phosphates and away from tartrates.

Acid calcium phosphate (ACP) is an acid salt giving moderate activity in cold water. Ionization of phosphates varies with conditions prevailing but that of ACP can be considered as:

$$3CaH_4(PO_4)_2 \rightarrow Ca_3(PO_4)_2 \downarrow + 4HPO_4{}^{2-} + 8H^+$$

3 molecule ACP   8 hydrogen ions

The precipitation of calcium phosphate complicates the investigation of the solubility of ACP. The moderate reactivity in cold water makes ACP useful in a double-action powder but it limits keeping qualities. Where there is abundant filler as in self-raising flour, this tendency is overcome and the fact that the calcium, introduced as ACP, serves as a flour improver, influences its selection as an acid component in these circumstances.

Acid sodium pyro-phosphate (ASP) has little reactivity below baking temperatures and on this account is often used together with ACP. Again its ionization in water can vary but may be expected to include:

$$Na_2H_2P_2O_7 \rightarrow 2Na^+ + P_2O_7{}^{4-} + 2H^+$$

1 molecule ASP   2 hydrogen ions

If used exclusively as the acid component in a baking powder, ASP imparts a slightly bitter flavour to baked goods.

(iv) *Compounds which hydrolyze to acids* Compounds which hydrolyze to acids include an inorganic salt, soda alum (sodium aluminium sulphate, SAS) and lactones, which are organic compounds with some similarity to sugars. They react with water and, in consequence, hydrogen from the water is made available as ions to enter into the reaction with sodium bicarbonate. The advantage of these compounds is that hydrolysis rates adjust to the temperature and allow carbon dioxide production to continue throughout mixing and baking. At present alums are not permitted food additives in this country and lactones are newcomers on the market.

With so many available acid components, it is important to remember that the significant chemistry of baking powders is encapsulated in the reaction between bicarbonate ions and hydrogen ions (as stated in 12.3.1). It is also useful to know that manufacturers agree to standardize their products according to the amount of carbon dioxide which a given measure of baking powder will produce. This is in the region of 12 per cent by weight, enabling the baking powder inclusion in a recipe to be stated irrespective of brand. Formulation of the product aims at calculating the amount of acid component capable of reacting completely with the sodium bicarbonate. On this basis, the equivalent of the above named acid components is given by:

1 part by weight	Parts by weight	
Sodium bicarbonate	0·89	tartaric acid
	2·24	cream of tartar
	1·25	ACP
	1·36	ASP

Some slight excess of sodium bicarbonate is allowed to insure against the presence of other acidic ingredients and a possible acidic end-point in a flour mixture which could weaken the gluten structure.

12.3.3   Thermal decomposition of sodium bicarbonate

On heating dry, or in solution, sodium bicarbonate decomposes with evolution of carbon dioxide. This proves a second method of generating this gas chemically for aeration. The reaction is given by

$$\underset{\substack{\text{sodium} \\ \text{bicarbonate}}}{2NaHCO_3} \xrightarrow{\text{heat}} \underset{\substack{\text{sodium} \\ \text{carbonate}}}{Na_2CO_3} + H_2O \uparrow + CO_2 \uparrow$$

Traditional use of this method derives from times before reliable branded baking powders were available. Certainly it is cheaper but the outlay is very marginal and unlikely to influence present day choice. Where it is recommended, it is for the characteristics which it bestows on cakes and biscuits. The residue, sodium carbonate, is an alkaline salt which, heated with sugars, gives a strong yellow to brown colour, reminiscent of very rich cakes subjected to long slow cooking. In alkaline conditions, the gluten structure also alters, giving interesting crumb characteristics (without a high proportion of fat for shortening); sticky when moist, brittle when dried out. By using sodium bicarbonate alone as the leavening agent, cheaper cakes can be made which emulate somewhat the richer varieties. The incidental bitter taste of sodium carbonate (chemically equivalent to washing soda) has to be countered and thus this method is usually reserved for strongly flavoured products: chocolate and spiced fruit cakes, gingerbread and parkin.

12.3.4   Ammonium bicarbonate

Ammonium bicarbonate is the one exception to the rule that all chemical raising agents are based on sodium bicarbonate. On heating it decomposes into wholly volatile products: ammonia, water vapour and carbon dioxide.

$$NH_4HCO_3 \xrightarrow{\text{heat}} NH_3 \uparrow + H_2O \uparrow + CO_2 \uparrow$$

Its use is limited to biscuits made commercially, it being necessary to ensure thorough heat penetration and then complete decomposition.

12.3.5 Nutritional considerations

The alkaline residues from both baking powders and sodium bicarbonate (baking soda) are responsible for diminishing the thiamin content of baked goods. Thiamin is more heat-labile in alkaline than in neutral or acidic media (see 8.9.1). This is a consideration in favour of biological leavening agents, especially in the light of deliberate fortification of this country's white flour with thiamin (see 8.9.5) which could bring flour products into the ranks of 'good dietary sources' of this vitamin.

12.4 BIOLOGICAL PRODUCTION OF CARBON DIOXIDE

Carbon dioxide is a product of the energy-providing catabolic reactions which occur within the cells of all living organisms. Yeasts are the only living organisms extensively utilized for carbon dioxide production within foods. Their advantages include the ability to grow and reproduce readily at temperatures which can be achieved in the kitchen, the palatability of the intermediate products of their metabolism and, pre-eminently, the fact that carbon dioxide is produced during both the anaerobic and the aerobic sequences of glucose metabolism. Thus it is that yeasts, incorporated within doughs where available oxygen is strictly limited, will serve as leavening agents, producing carbon dioxide by the anaerobic processes of fermentation. The accompanying product is ethanol, the most familiar and sought after of the alcohols. Of no consequence in bread-making, ethanol production is the desirable end of brewing and wine-making and in these pursuits, air is deliberately excluded to ensure anaerobic respiration. Another aspect of yeast cultivation, which likewise has no deserved place in a chapter on aeration, is the preparation of nutritional supplements from yeast concentrates. Wild yeasts, especially in spore-form, are air-borne and can contaminate certain foodstuffs. The resulting fermentation is a form of food spoilage (see 19.2).

12.4.1 Growth characteristics of yeasts

The familiar yeast plant is a microscopic organism consisting of a single cell, round or oval, averaging 0·1–0·75mm across; the size and shape of the cell vary with the species and the variety. Each cell is bounded by a transparent wall and contents include a well marked and comparatively large vacuole, associated with a granular network of chromatin, the nuclear apparatus. When conditions of life are favourable, the yeast cell increases in size and reproduces rapidly by a process of budding (gemmation). Such conditions are a satisfactory temperature (10–35° C); a sufficient supply of food material in solution comprising sugars, proteins or other utilizable forms of nitrogen; such mineral matter as the phosphates of magnesium, potassium and calcium; and, if they are top yeasts, a supply of oxygen. Bottom yeasts grow deep down in the medium and acquire their oxygen indirectly.

Spore formation is regarded as part of the normal life cycle of some forms of yeasts. The cells must be young and well nourished. The culture must be well aerated and there must be abundant moisture. The yeast cell becomes spherical and its content divides equally within four spherical spores, in a case called an ascus. The spores are called ascospores. *Saccharomyces cerevisiae* used in bread- and beer-making belongs to this group; and so does *Saccharomyces ellipsoideus*, the yeast used in the making of wines. Other yeasts form spores but no ascus; they include the type used in the making of sauerkraut. Still other yeasts produce no spores. Spores will survive a period of starvation, drought, heat or cold and are easily dispersed in the atmosphere. If, by chance, they reach spots where conditions are more favourable, they pass into the ordinary form of yeast plant and quickly start up fermentation in any sugar medium available to them. Yeast spores can withstand a temperature up to 60° C and even higher when dehydrated.

12.4.2 Metabolism in yeasts

The yeast plant absorbs glucose and converts it to ethanol and carbon dioxide without the incorporation of oxygen. Fermentation is now known to be glycolysis (see 10.4.2) whereby pyruvic acid is produced, followed by its decarboxylation (carbon dioxide removal) giving acetaldehyde which is reduced to ethanol.

$$\text{glucose} \xrightarrow{\text{glycolysis}} \text{pyruvic acid} \quad (1)$$

$$C_6H_{12}O_6 \xrightarrow{-4H} 2\ CH_3CO.COOH$$

$$\text{pyruvic acid} \xrightarrow{\text{decarboxylation}} \text{acetaldehyde} \quad (2)$$

$$CH_3CO.COOH \xrightarrow{-CO_2} CH_3CHO$$

$$\text{acetaldehyde} \xrightarrow{\text{reduction}} \text{ethanol} \quad (3)$$

$$\text{CH}_3\text{CHO} \xrightarrow{+2H} \text{C}_2\text{H}_5\text{OH}$$

Reactions (1), (2) and (3) may be conveniently summarized as follows:

$$\underset{\text{C}_6\text{H}_{12}\text{O}_6}{\text{glucose}} \xrightarrow{\text{fermentation}} \underset{2\text{C}_2\text{H}_5\text{OH}}{\text{ethanol}} + \underset{2\text{ CO}_2}{\text{carbon dioxide}} \quad (4)$$

It must be stressed that even the detail expressed in reactions (1), (2) and (3) is a mere summary of the complex series of reactions known to comprise fermentation. Many enzymes are involved; some of them require B group vitamins, notably thiamin, riboflavin and nicotinic acid, to function as co-enzymes. The name zymase has long been applied to the complex of enzymes which operate fermentation reactions within yeast cells.

In the presence of oxygen, the energy potential of glucose is more fully utilized with the oxidation changes carried beyond glycolysis to full break-down resulting in the formation of carbon dioxide and water. Aerobic respiration may be summarized by:

$$\underset{\text{C}_6\text{H}_{12}\text{O}_6}{\text{glucose}} + \underset{6\text{ O}_2}{\text{oxygen}} \longrightarrow \underset{6\text{ CO}_2}{\text{carbon dioxide}} + \underset{6\text{ H}_2\text{O}}{\text{water}}$$

This form of respiration is more profitable to the organism because of the greater energy yield and when the aim is growth of yeast cells, a plentiful supply of oxygen should be available.

The familiar forms of yeast will be found capable of utilizing not only the monosaccharide glucose but also the disaccharides, maltose and sucrose. These must first be hydrolysed to monosaccharides by digestive enzymes, maltase and sucrase respectively, secreted by yeast cells on to the substrate.

$$\text{maltose} + \text{water} \xrightarrow{\text{maltase}} \text{glucose}$$

$$\text{sucrose} + \text{water} \xrightarrow{\text{sucrase}} \text{glucose} + \text{fructose}$$

Thereafter the monosaccharides are absorbed into the yeast cells.

The yeasts used in baking will not digest starch. The presence of a diastatic enzyme in wheat flour ensures that, in the warm moist conditions which operate in a dough, a small amount of starch will be hydrolysed to maltose which serves as the food for the yeast. Thus it is not necessary to include sugar (sucrose) in a bread dough recipe, although this is often the practice (see 11.11).

$$\text{starch} \; + \; \text{water} \; \xrightarrow[\text{(wheat)}]{\text{diastase}} \; \text{maltose}$$

12.4.3 Yeast production

The yeast employed in bread-making is a traditional by-product of beer brewing. *Saccharomyces cerevisiae* has two distinct strains, both found within the 'wort' or mash of malt and hops from which beer is made: 'bottom yeasts' and 'top yeasts.' The former has significance in the production of beverages such as lager which have a carbon dioxide content. The latter forms the creamy froth on top of the beer vat and in times past, the practice was to skim some off and use it in home bread-making. Nowadays the bitter flavour and aroma of hops and the dark colour are unacceptable in bread and the only outlet for brewers' yeast is as a nutritional supplement, with an appreciable content of thiamin, riboflavin and nicotinic acid.

Distillers' yeast is the equivalent by-product from the manufacture of whisky. Because there is greater concern for the yeast cultures used in production of spirits, the surface yeasts were considered worth collecting carefully, washing and compressing. This set a standard which bakers came to demand for their leavening.

Nowadays, bakers' yeast is the result of deliberate production on sugary wastes from the distilleries (malt mash) or from sugar refineries (cane or beet molasses). These are inoculated with selected strains of *S. cerevisiae* and also with a lactic bacillus 'starter'. The resulting acidity limits bacterial contamination, safeguarding the yeasts not only during culturing but also after marketing. Alcoholic fermentation is depressed and reproductivity encouraged by vigorous aeration. The appreciable energy liberation, consequent upon aerobic respiration, is evident as heat, and cooling is necessary to maintain the temperature between 22 and 26° C. As the culturing proceeds, abundant froth is produced on the surface and this is repeatedly skimmed off and centrifuged to separate the yeast cells. Following washing, the yeast is compressed into cakes. In this form, yeast has a limited shelf-life which can be prolonged by refrigerator storage. Spoilage takes the form of liquefaction, brought on by autolysis (self-digestion). The alternative form of dried yeast pellets has better keeping qualities, making it useful to the housewife.

12.5 WILD YEASTS

The bloom on grapes is a coating of cells of the wild yeast, *Saccharomyces ellipsoideus*, which will ferment the sugar content when the fruit is crushed. The resulting wines owe many of their distinctive qualities to the varieties of *S. ellipsoideus* which flourish in particular vineyards. The yeast found on cider apples is *S. pasteuranus*. Other fruits are likely to culture yeasts on their surfaces and, although these may be insufficient or unsuitable to operate 'home-brew' fermentations, they should be regarded when the fruits are being preserved (see 19.4.3).

12.6 INDUSTRIAL USES FOR YEASTS

In addition to those already mentioned, several species of yeasts, including some from genera other than *Saccharomyces*, are cultivated for their industrial applications.

12.6.1 Yeast extracts

When heated and concentrated under reduced pressure, yeast forms a viscous fluid, brown in colour and strongly flavoured by the products of protein hydrolysis. In this form (viz. Marmite), it resembles meat extract and has similar uses. Richness in B group vitamins, notably riboflavin and nicotinic acid, makes yeast products valuable supplementary foodstuffs.

12.6.2 Novel protein foods

A major contribution to food supplies of the future could result from growth of yeasts not only on industrial carbohydrate wastes but also on mineral oils, enriched with mineral matter and inorganic nitrogenous compounds. The masses of yeast cells produced are valued for their protein content which has human food potential, whether used to feed stock or subjected to sophisticated processing in the production of meat analogues (see 15.6 & 7).

12.6.3 Enzymes

The original investigations into enzymes were carried out on yeast extracts, and yeasts continue as sources of enzymes for many industrial purposes. One such is the introduction of yeast enzymes into egg prior to drying; the zymase ferments, and thereby removes, the small glucose content so that keeping quality is improved, and the proteases degrade protein structures giving a more homogeneous slurry for spray drying.

PRACTICAL EXERCISES

All experiments require standard precautions

Expt. 12.1 DEMONSTRATION OF CARBON DIOXIDE PRODUCTION BY REACTION BETWEEN CARBONATES AND ACIDIC SUBSTANCES

Obtain samples of the following, dissolving in water where necessary:

> vinegar
> fruit juice
> sour milk
> cream of tartar
> acid calcium phosphate
> acid sodium pyrophosphate
and, if possible,
> delta glucono lactone
> sodium aluminium sulphate.

Using pH papers, wide and then narrow range, determine the pH of each solution and classify accordingly.

Add each in turn to a little sodium bicarbonate in a test tube. Note evidence of gas production and test for carbon dioxide. Withdraw gases from the mouth of the test tube with a small syringe, taking care not to allow the nozzle to touch the liquid. Eject contents of the syringe into a small pool of clear limewater in a watch glass on a dark ground (Fig. 12.1). Take care to empty all carbon dioxide from syringe before re-using it.

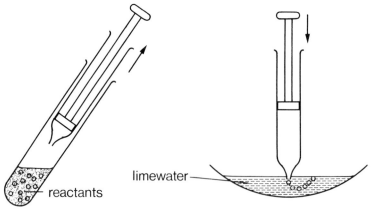

limewater

reactants

FIG. 12.1. Test for carbon dioxide

Positive result Milky appearance indicates carbon dioxide.

Expt. 12.2 INVESTIGATION INTO THE COMPOSITION OF BAKING POWDERS

Apply to a selection of branded baking powders (presence of sodium bicarbonate can be assumed).

(i) Carbon Dioxide Production

To a sample in a test tube, add a little cold water. Note any effervescence and test for carbon dioxide production (Expt. 12.1). Allow any reaction to subside and apply heat. Look for renewed reactivity. Apply the results to classifying the powder as 'quick-action', 'delayed-action' or 'double-action'.

(ii) Presence of a Filler

To a little powder on a white tile, add a few drops of iodine solution.

Positive result Blue–black colour, indicates the presence of a starch filler.

(iii) Identification of Acid Components

Separation of mineral matter from filler Shake about 4g of the baking powder under test with 60cm³ dry carbon tetrachloride in a separating funnel with a wide-bore tap. When allowed to settle, the starch floats to the top and the mineral matter sinks. The layer containing the mineral matter can be run out through the tap. Allow the carbon tetrachloride to evaporate over a water bath, leaving a dry sample of the active ingredients, still unreacted, to be tested for the following:

(*a*) *Phosphates* To a portion, add 1cm³ dilute nitric acid and 2cm³ ammonium molybdate solution. Heat in a water bath.

Positive result Yellow colour indicates phosphate present. If positive, go on to distinguish between ortho- and pyrophosphates.

(*b*) *Ortho- and pyrophosphates* Shake a further portion with water and filter. Check neutrality of filtrate and add silver nitrate solution.

Positive result Yellow precipitate indicates orthophosphate (ACP). White cloud indicates pyrophosphate (ASP).

(*c*) *Calcium* Dissolve a portion in dilute hydrochloric acid, neutralize with dilute ammonium hydroxide solution, then make just acid with acetic acid and add ammonium oxalate solution.

Positive result Cloudy white precipitate, possibly slow to form, indicating calcium present, probably as orthophosphate.

(*d*) *Tartrate* Acidify a portion with dilute acetic acid; add a drop of freshly made iron II sulphate solution, a few drops 10% hydrogen peroxide solution and an excess of sodium hydroxide.

Positive result Violet colour, indicates tartrate present, either tartaric acid or cream of tartar. If positive, go on to distinguish as in (*e*) and (*f*).

(e) *Potassium*   Use a platinum wire or silica rod, heated in a flame until it gives no colour change. Dip into hydrochloric acid and then into a little of the test material. Return to the flame and observe through cobalt glass which absorbs the coloured light from sodium and possibly from calcium.

Positive result   Lilac-coloured flame, seen through the blue glass, indicates potassium present, probably as potassium hydrogen tartrate.

(f) *Tartaric acid*   Work throughout with DRY APPARATUS and ANHYDROUS MATERIALS. Shake a portion of the test material in absolute alcohol. Filter through dry filter paper into a test tube containing a dry strip of blue litmus paper.

Positive result   Litmus paper turned red, indicates tartaric acid present.

Expt. 12.3   QUANTITATIVE ANALYSIS OF A BAKING POWDER FOR AVAILABLE CARBON DIOXIDE—Chittick method

The Chittick apparatus (Fig. 12.2) is constructed to give % composition by an almost direct reading. A detachable $250cm^3$ decomposition flask (A) and a $25cm^3$ dispensing burette (B) are connected by a manifold (C) fitted with a 3-way stopcock (D) to a gas measuring burette (E) leading by a flexible tube to a $300cm^3$ levelling bulb (F) mounted on a sliding carriage. The displacement solution in E and F is effectively a saturated solution of carbon dioxide, preventing dissolution of evolved carbon dioxide. The acid in B is dilute sulphuric acid $(1+5)$.

Outline of procedure   (Full details are supplied by manufacturers together with correction factors for variations in temperature and atmospheric pressure.) A 1·7g sample of baking powder is weighed into a decomposition flask which is connected to the apparatus. With D open to the air, the level in E is brought to the $10cm^3$ mark above zero; then D is closed. The pressure within the apparatus is reduced below atmospheric by lowering F. This ensures that there is no impediment to the passage into E of the carbon dioxide evolved when $10cm^3$ of acid is added to A from B. As the level in E falls, that in F must be kept even lower. Agitate A to ensure complete reaction between the baking powder and the excess acid. Allow 5 minutes for the apparatus to attain equilibrium and bring the pressure to atmospheric by equalizing levels in E and F. The level in E gives a direct reading of the volume of gas evolved—$V cm^3$. This is used to calculate.

$$\% \text{ total carbon dioxide} = \frac{V \times \text{correction factor}}{10}$$

In normal use, baking powders leave a carbonate residue so that some of the carbon dioxide is unavailable for aeration. The % residual carbon dioxide is determined by allowing a second 1·7g sample of baking powder to react with $20cm^3$ water and, after standing for 20 minutes, heating on a boiling water bath for one minute. After cooling, this flask is attached to the apparatus and the procedure repeated.

$$\% \text{ available } CO_2 = \% \text{ total } CO_2 - \% \text{ residual } CO_2$$

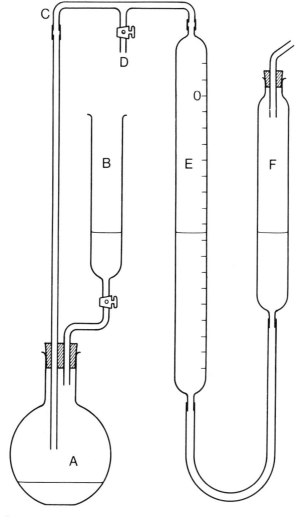

FIG. 12.2. Chittick apparatus

Expt. 12.4 THERMAL DECOMPOSITION OF BAKING SODA (SODIUM BICARBONATE)

(i) Heat a little baking soda in a hard glass tube held by tongs horizontally (to prevent condensed water vapour running back on to hot glass). Test gases from the mouth of the tube for carbon dioxide. Allow the tube to cool and use for (ii).

(ii) To cooled tube from (i) add some water to dissolve the residue. Determine the pH of the solution; then add a pinch of glucose and heat in a water bath. Apply results to an explanation of appropriate uses for sodium bicarbonate as a sole raising agent.

Expt. 12.5   MICROSCOPIC EXAMINATION OF YEAST CELLS

Make a very dilute suspension of fresh yeast in water and spread one drop on a microscope slide. Cover with a coverslip and examine under low power magnification.

Remove the slide from the microscope. Add a small drop methylene blue stain at the edge of the coverslip. Allow this to spread through the suspension and re-examine under high power. Note that the stain is taken up more fully by the nuclear apparatus than by the cytoplasm in active cells. Dead cells stain completely blue; effete cells show intermediate colouring.

Expt. 12.6   SIMPLE DEMONSTRATION OF THE EFFECTS OF VARIOUS TEMPERATURES ON YEAST ACTIVITY

Crumble a level teaspoonful of bakers' yeast into a test tube and add 10% sucrose solution, almost filling the tube. Invert repeatedly to form a uniform dispersion. Divide evenly between three test tubes labelled A, B and C.

Leave A to stand at room temperature; place B in a beaker of boiling water for 5 minutes then allow to cool; and place C in the coldest compartment of the refrigerator for 10 minutes.

Reassemble tubes A, B and C and place a balloon over the mouth of each. Make sure each balloon flops loosely to one side at the outset. Stand all three in a beaker of luke-warm water (35° C). Observe and record signs of gas production and apply results to proper procedures for using yeast in aeration.

Check that the gas produced is carbon dioxide by passing the contents of inflated balloons into clear limewater.

Expt. 12.7   SIMPLE INVESTIGATION INTO THE NUTRIENT REQUIREMENTS OF YEAST

Crumble a level teaspoonful of fresh bakers' yeast (not dried) into a test tube nearly filled with water. Invert to mix thoroughly and divide equally between four test tubes labelled W, X, Y and Z.

To W add sufficient	water	to double the contents
To X add sufficient	20% sugar solution	to double the contents
To Y add sufficient	10% salt solution	to double the contents
To Z add sufficient	water, plus a pinch of starch	to double the contents

Invert each tube to mix contents. Fit a balloon over the mouth of each and stand all together in a beaker of water maintained at 35° C. Observe for signs of gas production and conclude which of the nutrients supplied are utilized by yeast.

Expt. 12.8 CYLINDER TEST FOR COMPARING GAS-PRODUCING QUALITIES OF YEAST SAMPLES

Weigh out 2g of each sample of yeast and disperse in $30cm^3$ tap water at room temperature. Make each into a batter with 20g strong plain flour. Pour each batter into a $250cm^3$ measuring cylinder, taking care not to allow it to trickle down the inside surface. Read and record the initial level of each. Leave all cylinders to stand together in a warm draught-free position or in a thermostatic water bath at $30°$ C. At 5 minute intervals, read off the level in each cylinder. Plot a graph of 'rise in level' (not actual level) against time for each cylinder and draw comparisons between the yeast samples under test.

REFERENCE

Pearson, D. (1970). *The chemical analysis of foods*, 6th edition, Churchill.

FURTHER READING

Fox, B., and Cameron, A. (1977). *Food science—a chemical approach*, 3rd rev. edn, Hodder & Stoughton.

Brown, M. A., Cameron, A. G. (1977). *Experimental Cooking*, Edward Arnold.

CHAPTER XIII

MILK AND MILK PRODUCTS

13.1 Characteristics of Fresh Milk

Milk is the creamy white liquid formed by all female mammals for feeding their young. Cow's milk is the one most commonly used and is regarded as nature's most perfect food. It contains every type of nutrient: protein, carbohydrate, fat, mineral salts, water and most vitamins. For infants milk is by nature a complete food, but for adults as well as for children there is too much water in milk for it to be used as the sole article of diet. It is not only valuable by itself but it greatly increases the food value of cereals and bread when these are mixed with it. It should always be remembered that milk is a food and not merely a beverage.

The creamy tint of milk is due to tiny globules of fat, tinted by carotene and a small amount of xanthophyll. These are soluble in the fat phase of the milk. Another pigment, lactochrome, is present in the water phase.

When milk is allowed to stand the globules of fat, each surrounded by a protein wall, being lighter than the rest of the milk, rise to the surface of the milk and form a layer of cream. When this cream is removed by skimming or by a separator the remaining portion is known as 'skimmed milk' or 'separated milk'. This skimmed or separated milk contains all the dissolved food materials of milk and is a valuable article of food with many uses.

If milk is allowed to stand for a few days it separates out into two different parts—a coagulum at the surface known as 'curd' and a watery liquid underneath known as 'whey'. This change is brought about by lactic acid bacteria which feed upon the sugar in milk (lactose) and change it into an acid (lactic acid), which then curdles the chief soluble protein of milk, caseinogen. This takes place when the isoelectric point is reached. This is at a definite pH when the particles no longer carry an electric charge and therefore do not repel each other (see 5.5). Clotting, as distinct from curdling, is brought about by the rennet used by cheese-makers for clotting milk. This contains an enzyme, rennin, obtained from the fourth division of a calf's stomach in which it is secreted to coagulate the milk which the calf drinks as its food. Junket is made by adding rennet in solution to warm milk at blood heat and then adding some flavouring material. The rennet is inactivated if heated beyond 60° C.

The specific gravity of good milk is between 1·028 and 1·034. If cream is taken out of milk the specific gravity of the milk is raised. Measurement of the specific gravity of milk is made by means of a lactometer. It is possible to take cream out of milk and, by putting in water, still to keep the specific gravity between 1·028 and 1·034. A lowering of the concentration of the milk sugar below the normal value indicates adulteration of this kind. The only entirely reliable test is an analysis of the milk for fat content together with a lactometer reading (see Expt. 13.6). When milk is heated it easily 'boils over'. This is because the heat has denatured and coagulated another protein substance dissolved in milk known as lactalbumin, which forms a skin on the surface of the milk, and the collection of steam underneath it causes the milk to 'boil over'. Caseinogen is coagulated by acids and rennet but not by heat.

13.2 COMPOSITION OF MILK

The composition of cow's milk varies with the breed of animal, the stage of lactation and the character of the food, i.e. whether it is hay and oil cake, or fresh pasture grass, and this young or old, rich or poor in staple. On the average, good cow's milk as marketed has a composition which varies little from the following:

Composition of Cow's Milk (per cent)

Water		87·55
Protein	3·40 ⎫	
Fat	3·60 ⎪ solids	12·45
Milk sugar	4·70 ⎬	
Ash	0·75 ⎭	

Human milk differs from cow's milk most evidently in two respects: it contains more milk sugar and less protein—1·5 per cent total protein as compared with 3·5 per cent in cow's milk. Accordingly when cow's milk is used for the rearing of infants it is usually diluted with water, and a little sugar, preferably milk sugar or glucose, added to it, but without correcting for the difference in kind of the proteins.

Composition of Human Milk (per cent)

Water		87·40
Protein	2·29	
Fat	3·81	solids 12·60
Milk sugar	6·20	
Ash	0·30	

13.2.1 **Milk proteins**

Milk proteins consist of caseinogen, lactalbumin and lactoglobulin, the first being relatively more abundant in cow's than in human milk. Caseinogen is a complex phosphoprotein closely associated with calcium ions. Calcium caseinogenate is readily hydrolysed by lactic acid to give calcium lactate and casein in the form of a curd. The enzyme rennet throws down a clot of casein in combination with calcium ions; cheese is prepared on this principle. Heat does not coagulate caseinogen at temperatures up to boiling, but lactalbumin and lactoglobulin coagulate round 70° C. The fat globules in milk are enveloped by the proteins which serve to stabilize the emulsion.

13.2.2 **Milk fats**

Milk fat separating as cream is a mixture of many fats, some simple and others mixed glycerides of quite a long series of fatty acids. It contains branch chain fatty acids and odd number straight chain fatty acids, carbons 11–19, as well as short chain fatty acids (butyric, caproic, caprylic, myristic, etc.). There are some 60 identifiable fatty acids in milk. The chief fatty acid is oleic acid, but the most characteristic is butyric acid (see 4.3.2). Oleic acid being unsaturated is liable to take up oxygen and give rise to a variety of derivatives, some of which give substances with unpleasant odours and flavours. Other unsaturated fatty acids react in the same way to give this oxidative rancidity. Bacterial decomposition by *Bacillus coli* of the butyrates can give ordinary rancidity with the liberation of butyric acid. The natural flavour of cream and its chief product, butter, is due to the lower volatile acids and their esters, and not to the higher members of the series. When freshly drawn the fatty globules of milk are microscopic in dimensions ranging between 1×10^1mm and $2·2 \times 10^{-2}$mm in diameter. The fat globules have the property of adsorbing proteins out of their water solution to form layers of these on their surface, which function as continuous films or coatings, and tend to keep the globules from coalescing.

In addition to ordinary fats milk contains small quantities of two other important substances—lecithin and cholesterol. Lecithin belongs to the group of phosphatides. It is relatively more abundant in human milk than in cow's milk, and contributes one-third its total phosphoric acid. Lecithin is a phosphorylated fat (see 4.3.9). The fatty acids in lecithin are more unsaturated than in ordinary fat, and tend to give oxidative rancidity. Lecithin along with protein seems to be the covering of the fat globules, serving as an emulsifier.

Cholesterol varies between amounts of 0·07 and 0·4 per cent. It is usually found in animal fats; its isomer, phytosterol, is found in vegetable fats. Butterfat also contains carotenoids which influence the colour. Tocopherols are also found. They can influence the keeping qualities by preventing oxidative rancidity (see 4.3.7 and 8,6).

13.2.3 Milk sugar

Milk sugar or lactose in cow's milk amounts to about 4·7 per cent, and in human milk about 6·2 per cent. It may be recognized as a reducing sugar in milk that has been both skimmed of cream and cleared of casein clotted by rennet. It is a disaccharide, and is hydrolysed by the ferment lactase to form an equimolecular mixture of glucose and galactose (see 3.4.5). When heated it caramelizes, hence the flavour of milk puddings. It is readily acted upon by lactic acid organisms and yields lactic acid, which makes buttermilk and whey sour.

13.2.4 Minerals of milk

The mineral elements represented in the final dried and incinerated residue of whey are sodium, potassium, calcium, magnesium and iron, as phosphates, chlorides, sulphates and carbonates. The abundance and availability of the calcium salts and phosphates have the further advantage of increasing the effect of any vitamin D in other articles of food. The percentage of iron is very low, and altogether inadequate to meet the needs of a developing infant. Cow's milk is even more deficient in iron than human milk; in the case of the young animal it can, however, eke out its supply by nibbling grass. Iron in some form or other should be added to cow's milk, all the more when it is diluted as usually supplied to young children. For a while only, a young baby can draw on its own stores of iron in the liver.

13.2.5 Vitamins in milk

Milk contains all the commonly recognized vitamins; it is particularly rich in riboflavin—38 per cent of that consumed in the ordinary diet comes from milk. Milk is a good but not wholly sufficient source of thiamin. Ascorbic acid is quickly oxidized in milk and is absent from pasteurized milk. Milk fat is an excellent source of vitamin A and a variable source of calciferol. Cow's milk has received an extraordinary amount of attention, so far as its vitamin content goes, perhaps more so than any other substance, and inevitably the assessments of the values of the several vitamins by many observers throughout the world vary somewhat. It is now recognized that the amounts of vitamins in milk vary not only with the breed of the cow and its physiological state, but also with the character of its food. The vitamins as a whole, and particularly A and D, are higher in summer when cows are out to grass and in the sunshine, than in winter and early spring when they are kept in the byres on hay and oilcake. The composition of the herbage and its age, for instance whether it is short and freshly grown or mature and fibrous, affects the vitamin content of the milk. The amount of ascorbic acid in milk also varies as between the winter and the summer feeding and exposure of the cows to sunlight. This vitamin is very appreciably diminished in value on heating in the air, and on exposure to sunlight, as in dairy bottles. For this reason therefore a whole milk or partial milk diet of young children should be reinforced by reasonable doses of fruit or vegetable juices rich in ascorbic acid, e.g. citrus fruits.

The riboflavin content of milk is also reduced by exposure to sunlight and as milk is such a good source of riboflavin the loss of this vitamin is more significant than the loss of ascorbic acid. In addition riboflavin is yellow in colour and absorbs blue light, this acts as a sensitizer bringing about the photochemical oxidation of ascorbic acid (see 8.10.5).

13.3   SPOILAGE OF MILK

Milk is not only a splendid food for animals and human beings but also for bacteria. Some of the bacteria are harmless and turn milk sour, while others are disease germs, as of diphtheria, typhoid and tuberculosis. Every care should therefore be taken to prevent the entrance of bacteria, and pathogenic organisms in particular, at every stage from the cow to the consumer—in the farm, in transit by road or rail, in delivery by the roundsman and not least in storage in the home. Too great care cannot possibly be taken in obtaining clean milk and in keeping it meticulously clean throughout, otherwise it may become positively dangerous.

The best milk is that which reaches the consumer as nearly as possible in the state in which it leaves the cow's udder. The odour, taste, keeping quality and health value of the milk depend entirely upon the bacterial content. Milk alters at first slowly and later rapidly; partly because it absorbs taints and odours from its neighbourhood, and partly because of bacterial action. Very great care is required if milk is to keep its normal condition for any length of time.

13.3.1 Bacterial action

Bacterial contamination of milk enters at various stages, which may be briefly indicated in order. (i) The cow's udder: even in healthy cows the milk produced is not absolutely sterile; milk from diseased animals teems with bacteria and should never be used for human food of any kind. (ii) The cow's body: where cattle are not kept clean and groomed, and open pail milking is practised, there is every opportunity for vast numbers of micro-organisms to get into the milk. (iii) The atmosphere of the byre: dust is always full of micro-organisms, derived from the hay and fodder, dried dung, cobwebs, etc. (iv) The milker: the utmost cleanliness of person and methods of milking, and the sterilization of all utensils, are plainly indicated. When the transit from the milk producer to the consumer is short, as in the country or medium-sized towns, the chance of contamination is much reduced if the milk is in sealed bottles filled at the dairy and deposited on the doorstep or window sill of the consumer. In the vastly more considerable industry of getting milk from thousands of farms over dozens of counties, often many hundreds of miles from the final centre of distribution, the chances of contamination are now largely reduced by elaborate methods of pasteurization. But all the care of the producers and transporters of milk may be easily brought to nought by the householder if she fails to observe reasonable precautions against exposure to contamination. Milk should be kept cool, in the dark, and sealed. It should not be left for any length of time in open basins or jugs. In summer time if not in a refrigerator these should be kept cool and protected from flies and dust by close muslin covers—a single fly can carry several hundred thousand bacteria. Milk should never be placed near a sink or any food substance with a strong odour.

The main types of micro-organisms found in milk are as follows:

1 (i) True lactic bacteria—*Streptococcus lactis*
  (ii) *Bacillus coli communis* and groups
     These ferment milk sugar
2 (i) Casein-digesting bacteria

(ii) Bacteria causing colour changes
These do not ferment milk sugar
3   Pathogenic bacteria
(i) Accidentally introduced food poisoning bacteria
As typhoid, diphtheria, etc
(ii) Derived from the cow
As tuberculosis, cow pox, brucellosis

Lactic bacteria, chiefly *S. lactis* grow best in milk at 25°C giving about 1 per cent lactic acid which is mild in taste and coagulates the milk, no whey forming. Aciduric bacteria of the genus *Lactobacillus*, *L. bulgaricus*, *L. acidophilus* and *L. bifidus* also ferment lactose to lactic acid. They can tolerate more acidity, and their optimum temperature is 35° C. They are important in cheese making. *Bacillus coli communis* and other groups ferment milk sugar to give acids and gas. The milk so soured has an offensive odour and a disagreeable taste. Acids other than lactic acid are formed, such as butyric acid, acetic and formic acids. The clot often encloses gas bubbles and in time shrinks, and may be liquefied if any peptonizing bacteria are present. The presence of this group of bacteria indicates careless handling. Their growth is favoured by an appreciably higher temperature (30°–40° C) than that suitable to lactic acid bacteria.

Casein-digesting bacteria give alkaline products with unpleasant odours and flavours and are encouraged by the reduction of the acidity of ordinary sour milk. Quite a variety of bacteria produce, on occasion, alarming changes in the colour of milk: generally red, but some blue (*Pseudomonas cyano-fluorescens*); these bacteria are seldom dangerous and seldom seen.

13.3.2   Protection against milk-borne infections

Tuberculosis and brucellosis (undulant fever) can be transmitted by milk but the milk is usually contaminated by direct transmission of the pathogenic organisms from either a cow with tuberculosis of the udder or, in the case of brucellosis, a cow suffering from abortus fever. All milk sold in the UK comes from attested herds. A farmer can only obtain a licence to sell milk after all his cows have been individually tested and certified free from tuberculosis.

Tuberculin Test   Each animal is injected with a specially prepared reagent, tuberculin. If a swelling appears round the point of injection the test is positive and the cow is slaughtered. If an animal is found to be infected the buildings are disinfected and the remainder of the herd tested again at intervals of not less than 60 days, until there are no 'reactors'. Tests are then made after six months and then every year unless more reactors are found.

Occasionally contamination with *Bacillus tuberculosis* can be caused by a tuberculous person handling the milk. The risk of tuberculosis from milk is now very slight and there is also some evidence to support the claim that no cases of brucellosis are caused by drinking heat-treated milk. Milk-borne diseases were once a serious hazard in the UK but their incidence has declined rapidly since the late 1930s. In addition to tuberculosis and brucellosis, milk-borne diseases have included scarlet fever, septic sore throat, diphtheria, typhoid and paratyphoid fever, dysentery, gastro-enteritis and possibly infective hepatitis. Excluding the first two infections, most cases have been caused through contaminated water, or utensils, or a careless milk handler. Unfortunately many patho-genic organisms causing the diseases mentioned thrive in milk.

13.3.3 Stages in spoilage of milk
Four fairly definite periods in the decomposition of milk may be recognized:

(i) For the first four to six hours after milk is drawn there is an apparent decrease in the number of micro-organisms, due probably to the clumping of the bacteria and to the presence of the antibiotic nisin.

(ii) The second period is that of normal souring due to the enor-mous development of *Streptococcus lactis*, which makes 99 per cent of the total flora by the time the milk becomes sour and curdles. Before the milk can curdle sufficient lactic acid must be formed to react with the calcium caseinogenate to form calcium lactate, and thus little free acid is available for a while. The characteristic odour and taste of sour milk is not due to lactic acid, but to the presence of undetermined volatile compounds. Such sour milk, though spoiled for ordinary use, is in the first stage for cheese making.

(iii) When coagulation of the casein has taken place, free lactic acid is in sufficient strength (about 1 per cent) to stop the further development of the lactic organisms, and their num-bers diminish more or less rapidly. The aciduric bacteria now grow, since they can tolerate the higher acidity. Or-ganisms now develop which have hitherto been dormant (*Oidium lactis* and other moulds, and yeasts), and as they grow the acidity is lowered until the proteolytic bacteria can grow, the milk becomes alkaline and the final stage is reached.

(iv) In the fourth stage the liquefying and peptonizing bacteria rapidly decompose the various proteins and thus alkaline whey is formed with an unpleasant odour.

Abnormal fermentation of milk occasionally takes place, generally as a result of insanitary dairy conditions. *B. coli communis* produces disagreeable odours and flavours. One of the commonest forms of bacterial spoilage is ropy or slimy fermentation due to *B. lactis viscosus*, a form resistant to heat and only removed from dairy utensils by drastic scalding and disinfection. Bitter milk, due to bacterial changes, is occasionally met within the cold storage of milk. Yeasts very occasionally cause alcoholic fermentation of milk sugar.

13.4 TREATMENT OF MILK

In these days when large quantities of milk are transported often considerable distances from the producer to the consumer—many hours elapsing between drawing in the dairy and using in the home —it has become necessary to have as long a period as is reasonable in which the milk will keep sweet. It is further recognized that raw untreated milk may be a medium for the transmission of infections. Various methods have been adopted with a view to inhibit the growth of organisms, or to bring about a substantial reduction in their numbers. Purely mechanical treatment, such as straining milk through wire or cloth sieves, or centrifugalizing it, with a view to the removal of the gross particles of dirt, and with them some proportion at any rate of bacteria, fail in the main purpose of improving the bacterial content of milk. In any case in any clean dairy practice there should be no dirt to remove.

Various chemical preservatives have been used, the chief among them being calcium hypochlorite, formalin, boric acid, borax, benzoic and salicylic acids, acid potassium fluoride, hydrogen peroxide, sodium carbonate and bicarbonate. The use of all such preservatives in milk and cream is now prohibited.

It is by the use of certain temperatures that the life of milk microorganisms is best regulated. Very few can increase in numbers at 10° C or below, even though none of them is destroyed. 10° C is the most favourable temperature for the storage of milk, for at this point the lactic bacteria can grow and produce lactic acid sufficiently to check the action of the proteolytic organisms. Cooling milk as soon as drawn is both efficient and harmless as a method of preservation.

Ninety per cent of milk sold in Great Britain today is heat-treated, i.e. pasteurized, ultra heat-treated or sterilized.

13.4.1 Pasteurization

The commonest form of preservation of milk by heat treatment is by pasteurization, the object being to destroy the pathogenic and spoilage organisms without affecting the milk. There are two methods of pasteurization. The Holder method whereby the milk is heated to 63–65° C and maintained at this temperature for half an hour, and flash pasteurization when the milk is heated to 72° C for 15 seconds. The milk is then cooled rapidly to not more than 10° C using an apparatus called a heat exchanger. Immediate rapid cooling of the milk is a vital part of the treatment; high or warm temperatures would encourage the growth of heat resistant organisms, reduce the riboflavin content and affect the cream line of non-homogenized milk and may give a cooked flavour to the milk. The efficiency of industrial pasteurization is very largely a matter of the competent exercise of thermal and bacterial control. If any portion of the milk is insufficiently heated, pathogenic organisms may escape destruction and are afterwards free to develop. If the temperature as a whole rises above the limit the cream line can be changed, the lactalbumin coagulated, the ribo-flavin content will be reduced and an excessive proportion of lactic acid bacteria destroyed so that the milk does not sour normally on keeping and is liable to undesirable changes not immediately apparent to the consumer.

13.4.2 Ultra Heat Treatment

Ultra heat treatment of milk is commonly referred to as UHT. It is carried out in an apparatus similar to that used for pasteuriza-tion but in this case the milk is heated to 132° C for one second. It will keep for two to three weeks without refrigeration if it has been packed under sterile conditions. The flavour is similar to pasteurized homogenized milk.

13.4.3 Sterilized milk

Sterilization destroys bacteria and other micro-organisms more completely than pasteurization. The milk is first pre-heated, homo-genized and filled into bottles which are then hermetically sealed. The 'sterilization' may then be carried out by either of two methods. In the batch process the filled bottles are heated for 30–40 minutes at a temperature of 104–110° C in an autoclave, removed and allowed to cool in the atmosphere. In the continuous process the bottles pass on a conveyor belt through hot water tanks to a pressure steam chamber for 30–40 minutes at 107–110° C and then into a series of water cooling tanks. The higher temperature causes slight caramelization of the lactose and produces a cooked flavour and creamy appearance. Milk thus treated will keep for two to three months without refrigeration if it is unopened.

13.4.4 Homogenization
In the process of homogenization the milk is forced through a tiny valve under pressure. The fat globules are broken down to a uniform size 2μ to 1μ in diameter). The milk as the name implies has been 'made uniform' and the cream does not rise to the top because the fat globules are so small they remain in homogeneous suspension. Homogenized milk is said to have a creamier taste and to be more easily digested, partly because the fat globules are smaller and partly because the curd tension has been lowered and a softer curd is formed during digestion.

13.4.5 Effect of heat treatments on nutritional value

Pasteurization   Up to 10 per cent of the thiamin and vitamin B_{12} are destroyed and 10–20 per cent of the ascorbic acid. Effect of UHT is somewhat similar.

Sterilization   About 50 per cent of the ascorbic acid is lost, 30 per cent of the thiamin and nearly all the riboflavin. There is a slight reduction in the biological value of the protein.

13.5 GRADES OF MILK

Milk may bought in various grades and full details of the complex conditions governing the issue of licences are to be found in the Milk (Special Designations) Regulations, 1963 (see Bell and O'Keefe). The main grades indicated on the bottle tops are:

Untreated Channel Islands or South Devon milk
Pasteurized milk
Pasteurized Channel Islands or South Devon milk
Pasteurized homogenized milk
Pasteurized kosher milk

In addition farm-bottled milk is available. This is raw milk which has been bottled on the farm on which it is produced. Stock conditions on the farm must comply with government regulations.

13.6   MILK PRODUCTS

Milk is remarkable among natural foods because of the great variety of processed foods prepared from it, most of them having a great advantage over the original substance in their properties of preservation. Chief among the different forms of milk products are the following:

> Cream
> Ice cream and dairy ice cream
> Separated and skimmed milks
> Buttermilk
> Condensed milk—sweetened and unsweetened
> Milk powders
> Butter
> Cheese
> Yoghurt and fermented milks

13.6.1   Cream

When milk is allowed to stand the globules of fat, being lighter than the rest of the milk, gradually rise to the surface, clump together and form a distinct layer of cream, the volume of which is about one-tenth that of the milk. This cream can be separated by skimming it off or by the use of a separator, which is a specially constructed centrifugal machine. The former method is nothing like so efficient as the latter. Skimmed milk contains about one per cent of fat whereas the amount of fat left in separated milk is almost negligible. Separated cream also contains less bacteria than skimmed cream, for this is not taken off the milk until it has stood for some considerable time (up to 24 hours). This gives time for the multiplication of micro-organisms. Skimmed cream will not keep fresh anything like so long as separated cream.

Legislation   In the past many preservatives have been used in cream but their use is now illegal. It was also a common practice to add thickening materials to cream, such as starch, mucilage, gelatine or sucrate of lime, but the use of thickening agents of any type is now prohibited under the Public Health (Preservatives, etc., in Food) Regulations.

13.6.2   Ice cream

Food Standards (Ice Cream) Regulations lay down composition requirements for ice cream, dairy ice cream and milk ice. Dairy ice cream, which is usually more expensive than ordinary ice cream, contains milk, cream products, sugar, flavourings and a stabilizer. The stabilizing agent is necessary to prevent separation of ice crystals—gelatine is often used. Ordinary ice cream is usually made from skimmed milk and vegetable fat. The best ice cream is made from the cream of milk partially ripened at 15–20° C and then frozen. Regulations as to the use of stale milk are very strict. If stale milk is used the bacterial content could be high and may not be caused by lactic acid bacteria; excessive growth of putrefactive bacteria could result in food poisoning.

13.6.3 Separated and skimmed milk

These are milks from which the fat has been removed either by a separator or by hand skimming. As a food for infants such forms of milk are to be condemned on account of their deficiency in fat, but as ingredients in articles of food which contain fats their use is to be commended on account of the protein, sugar and mineral constituents. Such milks are frequently employed in making bread, cakes, biscuits and ices.

A typical analysis (per cent) of skimmed milk is:

Water	90·2
Fat	0·2
Protein	3·5
Carbohydrate	5·0
Minerals	0·6
Other matter	0·5

13.6.4 Buttermilk

Buttermilk is the by-product of butter manufacture. It contains all the constituents of the original milk except fat. This acidity is due to the activity of lactic acid bacteria in forming lactic acid from the milk sugar. Buttermilk is used to a very limited extent in baking scones and buns; its acid liberates carbon dioxide from the bicarbonate of soda (sodium hydrogen carbonate), used as an aerating agent. It is not often used in diets in the UK although it is becoming increasingly available in selected supermarkets and health food stores.

13.6.5 Evaporated and condensed milks

Both evaporated and condensed milks may be produced from whole milk, partially skimmed or skimmed milk. Evaporated milk is usually unsweetened condensed full cream or half cream milk, whilst the term condensed milk is generally used for sweetened milk. The milk is first pasteurized and then evaporated at reduced pressure in steam heated vacuum pans at a temperature between

50–55° C. When the volume has been reduced to almost 60 per cent the milk is homogenized, cooled and transferred to cans which are then sterilized at 115° C for 20 minutes. This product is evaporated unsweetened milk. Condensed milk has about 15 per cent of sugar added before evaporation, acting as a preservative because sugar has a greater affinity for water than bacteria and prevents access of bacteria to the reduced amount of water in the milk. Sterilization at a high temperature is therefore unnecessary. The composition and labelling of condensed milk is governed by the Condensed Milk Regulations 1959. The cans must indicate the suitability or otherwise of the contents in relation to feeding babies. The volume of full cream or skimmed milk to which the contents can be diluted must be declared.

Whilst condensed and evaporated milks are useful as emergency supplies their pronounced flavours are not always acceptable, and their use for infants is open to certain objections. Condensed skimmed milk is deficient in fat and sweetened condensed milk contains excess sugar which is liable to affect digestion. It gives too high a kilojoule value for the protein content and tends to produce an over-fat flabby baby. The dilution of such milk with water to give a more correct sugar content gives a product even more deficient in protein and fat.

13.6.6 Milk powders or dried milks

These are produced by removal of water from milk at such a temperature that the constituents are as little altered as possible and the solids produced will have a moisture content of 5 per cent or less. The milk is homogenized, heat-treated and condensed until its moisture content has been reduced to about 60 per cent before drying. It can be dried by either of two methods—roller drying and spray drying.

In roller drying the milk is spread on to a heated revolving roller and the milk is automatically scraped off as it dries. This method is used for most baby foods because the higher temperatures used promote sterility. Due to partial denaturing of the proteins, the milk powder does not reconstitute very easily. Spray drying is considered to be a better method. The milk is pumped as a fine spray into a chamber where hot air is circulated. The droplets of milk dry immediately and fall to the floor of the chamber as a fine powder. This method has an advantage over roller dried milk as its solubility has not been impaired and it therefore reconstitutes more easily, also the protein has a slightly higher nutritional value. The Dried Milk Regulations prescribe the description and composition of dried milk and set out requirements for labelling. As in the case of condensed milk its suitability as to feeding of infants must be shown, as must the equivalent contents of liquid milk of appropriate standard composition. Dried whole milk powder contains all the nutrients of milk in a concentrated form with the exception of ascorbic acid, thiamin and riboflavin, which are partially destroyed during the manufacturing process. Dried skimmed milk contains protein, calcium and riboflavin but virtually no fat or fat-soluble vitamins.

13.6.7 Filled milk
This is partly skimmed or completely skimmed milk to which a non-milk fat has been added to replace the butter fat. The non-milk fat is usually a vegetable oil which may be enriched with vitamin concentrate to compensate for a lack of vitamins A and D which would be removed with the butter fat. The manufacture of filled milk in the UK is limited and advertising and labelling are controlled by Skimmed Milk with Non-Milk Fat Regulations. The term 'filled milk' has itself no meaning in the law of this country. It has its use in countries where supplies of whole milk and butter are insufficient and possibly in some diets where large amounts of 'saturated' fats are considered to be less desirable than 'unsaturated fat' (see 4.2.2).

13.6.8 Cheese
This important milk product is dealt with in detail under 13.7.

13.6.9 Fermented milks
The most primitive method of preserving milk is by fermentation, a practice still followed by nomads or peasants in many parts of the world, according to details peculiar to the district, or to the source of milk, whether from cow, sheep, goat, camel, mare, reindeer, etc.

Two main types of milk beverage may be distinguished: the effervescent and the non-effervescent.

Effervescent Fermented Milks   Examples of effervescent fermented milks are Kefir, as made in South Russia and the Balkans, and Koumiss, as made from mare's milk in Russia.

Kefir is made in skins by the addition of 'kefir grains' to the milk of cows, goats or sheep, so that this is fermented to a drink containing 1 per cent alcohol and 0·8 per cent lactic acid. The grains are yellow nodules composed of bacterial filaments entangling yeast cells; the former consist of different organisms, decomposing lactose with the evolution of gas and not curdling milk, and the latter of a special yeast fermenting malt and cane sugars but not milk sugar. Koumiss is fermented from mare's milk by a starter carried over from the last brew, consisting of a yeast of the lactose fermenting type and lactic acid bacilli. A simultaneous alcoholic and acid fermentation results in about 2·0 per cent of alcohol and 1·0 per cent of acid. Similar fermented milks are prepared in Egypt and Norway by other yeasts and bacteria in symbiosis.

Non-Effervescent Milks Examples of non-effervescent milk are Yoghurt (Turkish), Kindo Mleko (Balkans), Matzoon (Armenia), etc. These are all thick curdled milks containing lactic acid and a very little alcohol. They are made from the milk common in the various regions, fermented by *Lactobacillus bulgaricus*. The milk is first boiled and, while still warm, is heavily charged with a portion of previously fermented milk. The milk clots in a few minutes, forming a creamy mass. It is eaten next day with bread, rice or fruit. Yoghurt has now become a popular protein food in the British Isles. The coagulated milk does not separate into curd and whey, even on standing, and may become decidedly acid to taste due to the activity of the micro-organisms present, and may become too acid to be palatable although other bacteria as well as yeasts are present and modify the flavour. The high acidity inhibits the growth of pathogenic and putrefactive bacteria, so that these milk beverages may be safely kept for a long time.

Commercial Manufacture of Yoghurt Yoghurt can be made from whole, partially skimmed, evaporated or dried milk or any mixture of these. The milk is homogenized, heated to a temperature between 88–105° C and then cooled to 41–45·5° C. It is then inoculated with a culture containing *Lactobacillus bulgaricus*, *Streptococcus thermophilus* and some *Lactobacillus acidophilus*. The yoghurt is incubated for $2\frac{1}{2}$–$3\frac{1}{2}$ hours at a temperature of 40° C. This can take place either in the air or in a water bath. When the acidity reaches 75 per cent and clotting takes place the yoghurt is cooled and kept at a temperature of 4·5° C until it is required. Apart from lactose which is used up during the production of lactic acid by the bacteria, yoghurt contains all the nutrients of milk. In addition it is very easily digestible and can therefore serve a useful purpose in the diet not only as a constituent of sweet and savoury dishes but also on its own account. It is available in a wide range of flavours and frequently has pieces of fruit or sometimes nuts added. The increase in acidity which may make the yoghurt unacceptable will occur more slowly if the yoghurt is kept cool. The curd may break if the container is shaken and a small amount of whey will then be released. This may affect the appearance but will not spoil the flavour or impair the nutritive value.

13.6.10 **Butter**

Although technically a milk product, butter, as a fat, is considered in Chapter XIV.

13.7 CHEESE

Cheese is made from milk by curdling the protein which is only soluble under certain conditions. When the acidity of the milk rises it curdles, this is most complete at the iso-electric point (see 5.5) and success in cheesemaking is dependent on attaining this level of acidity. This is brought about by inoculating fresh pasteurized milk with strains of lactic acid producing bacteria. The enzyme rennin contained in rennet, an extract of the digestive stomach of the cow, is also added which assists coagulation.

The differences in cheeses produced in different places are due to varying compositions and types of milk used, variations in the processes and differences in types of bacteria used. These different varieties of cheese can largely be classified into two main groups— hard and soft. Hard cheeses have most of the whey removed while in soft cheeses a considerable amount remains.

For the making of Cheddar cheese a prepared culture of lactic acid bacteria known as the starter is added to pasteurized milk in a cheese vat. The milk is brought to about 30° C and its lactic acid concentration allowed to reach 0·2 per cent. Rennet is added at this stage and, ideally, complete coagulation is reached in about 20 minutes, giving a curd-like solid junket. The curd is ready for cutting when it is solid enough to break clearly over one's finger. Cutting is carried out using two 'American' knives, horizontal and vertical bladed. These are passed through the curd, cutting it into pea-sized cubes. The curd consists of casein and milk fat, while the soluble mineral salts, lactose and lactic acid are largely in the whey. The curd is then stirred continuously during a scalding period of one hour. The contents of the vat reach a temperature of between 36–40·5° C. This scalding helps to expel the whey from the curd and to obtain the required texture. The acid content of the curd also increases. If this is developing rapidly the scalding takes place more rapidly and to a higher temperature. Stirring continues for about 20 minutes after the heat is turned off. The whey is then run off and the curd cut into blocks, 20cm square, which are piled on each side of the vat and completely drained. The blocks of curd are then milled or cut into chips about the size of a walnut and salt is added at this stage. The salted curd is packed into moulds lined with cloth which are traditionally cylindrical although square cheeses are now made which require less storage space and need no turning, during ripening. The moulded cheeses are pressed for a short time at about two atmospheres to drive out the remaining whey. They are then sprayed with hot water and left under pressure for 24 hours. The hot water sprayed on gives rise to a thin hard rind necessary if the cheese is to keep satisfactorily.

The next process is that of ripening in which profound changes take place. This occurs in well-aired rooms at temperatures of 15–25° C. The flavouring substances are developed and the digestibility improved—the 'soluble nitrogen' being increased to a large extent by the rennet enzymes. The development of flavour is entirely due to bacteria (almost entirely aciduric bacteria) over which the maker has very little control. The pepsin found in the rennet, in the presence of acid, acts on the casein, partially converting it into soluble albumoses and peptones. It is possible that the enzyme lactase may also play a part in the ripening. As the ripening process goes on the cheeses are turned daily at first, and then less frequently, and rubbed well with oil. The bacteria which effect the ripening may find their way into the cheese naturally through the milk or from the atmosphere of the dairy. In large modern cheese factories they are introduced into the cheese as pure cultures. The ripening of the cheese is the most important part of its preparation and requires skill and care if the cheese is not to be spoilt. The Cheese Regulations 1965 give details of fat and moisture standards of all types of cheese including processed cheese and cheese spread and prescribe appropriate labelling requirement.

13.7.1 Food value

The food value of cheese is particularly high; indeed there is no foodstuff ordinarily available which approaches it in respect both of concentration and of variety of food principles. An average whole milk cheese consists of protein, fat and water in the approximate proportion 2:3:3; there are also appreciable quantities of minerals, among which calcium is most abundant. The proteins consist mainly of casein and its soluble derivatives—albumoses, peptones and amino-acids. Casein itself is a protein of high biological value, and yields in useful proportions all the amino-acids that are required for the synthesis of the proteins of the different tissues. As a source of organic phosphorus it is particularly valuable in the building up of the cell nuclei of nervous and glandular tissues. The fat, being butter fat and having a low melting point, is easily dealt with in the intestine if not in too large a quantity. As a ready and cheap source of energy a hard full milk cheese is much superior to raw beef, yielding some 1726kJ per 100g as against 888kJ from stewing beef. In the matter of vitamins, cheese contains those found in the milk from which it is produced, chiefly vitamin A and riboflavin.

13.7.2 Types of cheese

There are hundreds of varieties of cheese which can be classified in many different ways but they can be divided roughly into two main groups: hard and soft cheeses. In hard cheeses the whey is allowed to drain away slowly, consequently the moisture content of soft cheese is much higher than the moisture content of hard cheese. Within these two groups there are other factors which account for the distinctive properties of each cheese—differences in type and quality of the milk used and variations in the methods of manufacturing and maturing processes. Cow's milk is commonly associated with cheese manufacture but milk from any mammal could be used; cheeses from goat's or ewe's milk are by no means uncommon. The milk itself may be used whole (Cheddar and Cheshire), skimmed or separated (Edam and Gouda) or milk to which cream has been added (some Stilton and Gorgonzola). In this country most cheese-making is carried out in creameries, although some is still farmhouse made. These cheeses which enjoy considerable reputation attribute their distinction to the quality of the pasture grazed by selected herds and not least to the expertise of their individual cheese-makers. Milk Marketing Boards are responsible for grading English Cheddar, Scottish Cheddar, Cheshire and Lancashire cheeses made on farms under contract. Some well-known varieties of cheese can be classified as follows:

(i) *Hard Cheeses*
United Kingdom: Caerphilly, Cheddar, Cheshire, Derby, Double Gloucester; Lancashire, Leicester, Wensleydale. Blue veined: Dorset, Stilton, Blue Wensleydale.
Commonwealth: Australian, Canadian, New Zealand.
European: Dutch cheddar, Edam, Emmental, Gouda, Gruyère, Parmesan. Blue-veined: Bresse Bleu, Danish Blue, Gorgonzola, Roquefort.

(ii) *Soft Cheeses*
United Kingdom: Cottage cheese, Lactic cheese, Wiltshire.
European: Bel Paese, Brie, Camembert, Demi-sel, Mozzarella.

Cream cheeses are often classified as soft cheeses but strictly speaking they are not true cheeses because they are not made from any basic curd. Single cream cheese has a butter fat content of between 20–30 per cent and will keep about a week in a refrigerator. Double cream cheeses do not keep quite so long and have a butter fat content between 50–60 per cent.

Processed Cheeses Processed cheeses are usually made from cheddar cheeses and other hard pressed cheeses. The natural cheese is finely ground and then emulsified with special salts, usually sodium citrate and disodium hydrogen phosphate, some water and whey powder or paste. It is heated and thoroughly mixed to produce a homogeneous pliable mass, colourings and flavourings are added and sometimes chopped meat or fish. Processed cheeses are available in slices, individual portions, blocks or as cheese spread. These products are more expensive than real cheeses, they have a mild flavour and keep well.

13.7.3   Characteristics of well-known cheeses

BRITISH CHEESES
Caerphilly. Originally a Welsh cheese but it is also made in Devon, Somerset, Wiltshire and Dorset. Creamy and white; close textured; mild and slightly salty in flavour. Not a good cooking cheese.
Cheddar. The most widely used cheese in the country. Farmhouse cheddar is more expensive; most of it is made in Somerset. Close texture; mellow nutty flavour; both texture and flavour improve with keeping.
Cheshire. Commonly a white cheese; the flavour is said to be due to Cheshire soil which is rich in salt. Available also as Red Cheshire when it is coloured with annatto, a vegetable dye, and Blue Cheshire which has artificially introduced blue veining; this has the fullest flavour.
Derby. Open textured; pale honey colour. The flavour develops during maturing and changes from a mild to a tangy flavour. Should be eaten about six months old. Has sage leaves added to it when it is sold as Sage Derby.
Dorset or 'Blue Vinny'. Very seldom made these days; hand skimmed milk is used. A Dorset farmhouse cheese, said to improve if

mouldy harness is left in the room during the making.

Double Gloucester. A pale orange colour; open texture; mild flavour; resembles Cheshire cheese; should be allowed to mature for three months before eating. Single Gloucester is rarely made now. It was a pale yellow in colour.

Lancashire. A white crumbly cheese; very good for cooking; the flavour is stronger than either Cheshire or Cheddar and is available as Lancashire mild or Lancashire tasty. The latter can have a very strong flavour.

Leicester. An orange coloured cheese; flaky texture; tangy flavour; both a good cooking and table cheese.

Stilton. Made from rich milk or milk with cream added; rich creamy flavour; blue veins due to mould *Penicillium roqueforti*; veining may be encouraged by piercing with skewers or wires dipped in mould; the aeration also assists mould growth. Ripens in three to six months. White Stilton is also available, a distinctive cheese with a less pronounced flavour.

Wensleydale. Resembles Caerphilly in flavour when young; mild; slightly salt flavour; fairly close texture. Better for the table than for cooking.

Blue Wensleydale. Similar to Stilton; soft curds are drained on tacks; a lightly pressed cheese; flavour said to be due to the limestone in the soil of the Ure Valley in Yorkshire.

FOREIGN CHEESES   A selection of widely known cheeses, many of which are available in this country:

Bel Paese. A soft and creamy Italian cheese; good for the table. As it melts easily, used for pizzas.

Bresse Bleu. A small-sized blue-veined French cheese with a strong flavour, creamy texture, said to resemble Gorgonzola.

Brie. A soft French cheese; should be eaten quickly when ripe, distinctive flavour; white crust; smooth creamy pale yellow curd.

Camembert. A popular soft French cheese; matures more quickly than Brie and has a stronger flavour; creamy texture; white crust.

Danish Blue. A strong rich-flavoured cheese with blue/green veins. Two types available. Danablu, white with blue/green veins and Mycella, a milder cheese, pale yellow with greener veins.

Demi-sel. A mild flavoured slightly salted cream cheese made in France, originally in the Normandy region.

Edam. A Dutch cheese made from partly skimmed milk; has a distinctive bright red rind; not good for cooking.

Emmental. A Swiss cheese with large holes due to generation of gas by bacteria in the making; has a strong flavour; commonly used in Switzerland for making cheese fondues.

Gorgonzola. A well-known 'blue veined' Italian cheese; a good table cheese; veining is pale green rather than the blue caused by *Penicillium roqueforti.*

Gouda. A Dutch cheese made from whole milk; softer than Edam. Yellow rind and pale in colour.

Gruyère. A Swiss cheese not unlike Emmental but with smaller holes and a darker rind; good for cooking.

Parmesan. A well known Italian cheese; it has a very good flavour; very dry and hard with a black rind; used grated for soups and pastas and often sold in this form.

Port Salut. Takes its name from the monastery where it was first made; a creamy smooth texture; yellow curd; a bright orange rind; mild flavour.

Roquefort. A blue-veined French cheese made from ewe's milk. The blue veining is due to *Penicillium roqueforti*; during ripening it is pierced with needles to let air get to the mould in the interior. Distinction of this cheese said to be due to ripening in caves in the region around Roquefort in France. Danish Roquefort is produced these days.

PRACTICAL EXERCISES

*All experiments require standard precautions; those marked * involve particular hazards and should be supervised*

Expt. 13.1 MICROSCOPIC EXAMINATION OF MILK

Dilute a small quantity of whole milk with an equal volume of water and place ONE DROP of this mixture on a microscope slide. Cover with a cover-slip, avoiding the formation of air bubbles. Examine under low and high power magnification, keeping the microscope platform horizontal.

When under high power, vary the light intensity and also the focus. Globular droplets of oil will be seen dispersed in the continuous water phase, shining brightly. Brownian movement (erratic jostling) of the droplets is evidence of their colloidal dimensions.

Repeat with cream and with skimmed milk and note differences in oil droplet concentrations.

Expt. 13.2 SEPARATION OF CREAM AND FORMATION OF BUTTER

Remove the cream from a bottle of milk which has been kept for 24 hours. Separation is most effectively carried out by siphoning away the lower layer, reserving the skimmed milk for Expt. 13.4. Put the cream in a wide-necked jar with a stopper. The cream should about half fill the jar, leaving an adequate head space of air. Agitate gently and continuously for what might be quite a protracted period, until separation into butter and buttermilk. Pour off the buttermilk and wash the butter by shaking in some ice-cold water. Empty through butter muslin and compact the butter pressing gently to express water. Taste and flavour with a little salt.

Expt. 13.3   DETECTION OF NUTRIENTS IN MILK

*(i) **Lipid**

The grease spot test (Expt. 4.1 (i)) is not readily given by milk, except the cream layer. The following extraction is recommended for detecting lipid in whole or skimmed milk.

To 4cm³ milk in a boiling tube, add a few drops of concentrated ammonia solution and heat to break the protein envelopes around oil droplets. EXTINGUISH FLAME and add first 2cm³ alcohol, then 2cm³ ether shaking between additions. Allow to settle so that an upper ethereal layer forms. Dip into this a strip of filter paper and allow to evaporate.

Positive result   A grease spot which stains bright orange–red in Sudan III indicates lipid extracted from milk.

(ii) **Proteins**

The tests for protein (Expt. 5.3) are best applied to the coagulum separated by the action of acid and heat together. This will leave a protein-free filtrate which can be tested for carbohydrate and mineral elements.

In a beaker dilute 25cm³ milk with an equal volume of water and add dilute acetic acid dropwise to bring the pH down to about 4·5 when precipitation will be maximal. Heat the mixture to about 80° C to ensure heat coagulation and filter. Reserve the filtrate for (iii) and (iv) below. To the coagulum, apply the full range of tests given in Expt. 5.3 together with a phosphate test (Expt. 7.2 (iv)).

(iii) **Carbohydrates**

Using half the filtrate from (ii) test for the presence of soluble carbo-hydrates using Expt. 3.1.

(iv) **Mineral Elements**

Using the other half of the filtrate (ii) test for mineral elements present in the form of soluble ions (see Expt. 7.2). Dried milk ash is another suitable medium for testing for mineral elements.

Expt. 13.4   RENNET COAGULATION

Use the skim milk from Expt. 13.2 warmed to 37° C in a shallow dish over a water bath. Do not allow to overheat. Stir in the rennet, the amount depending upon the volume of milk and the concentration of the rennet available. That produced for cheese-making is much stronger than junket rennet. As the latter is more likely to be available the amount recommended is 20cm³ rennet to 500cm³ skimmed milk unless the information on the label gives contra-indication.

Allow the dish to stand for 30 minutes or more in a warm place. When the junket has formed, examine the gel and then make criss-cross cuts through it to facilitate separation of curds and whey. Return the dish to the water bath and warm slightly while stirring to coalesce the curds. Strain through cheese cloth or filter paper, retaining both the residue (curds) and filtrate (whey).

(i) **Curds**

Add a little salt and taste, making comparisons in flavour and texture with cheese.

(ii) **Whey**

Note greenish colour and green fluorescence under ultra-violet light due to riboflavin content. Also test for lactose (Expt. 3.2).

Expt. 13.5   ISO-ELECTRIC POINT OF CASEIN

Dilute 5cm³ fresh milk in a test tube with an equal volume of deionized water. Mix and determine pH using wide range and then narrow range papers. Record this as pH value of fresh milk.

Now add dilute acetic acid one drop at a time, inverting the tube between each addition. Continue until the precipitation (mainly of casein) is maximal. Find the pH; this is the iso-electric point of casein. It will be necessary to repeat this, probably more than once, to ensure that the pH for least solubility is detected.

Expt. 13.6   QUANTITATIVE ANALYSIS OF MILK FOR PERCENTAGE FAT CONTENT AND PERCENTAGE SOLIDS NOT FAT (SNF)

*(i) **Gerber's Method** for percentage Fat Content

10cm³ concentrated sulphuric acid (specific gravity 1·815) is pipetted into a special tube called a butyrometer and the 11cm³ of the milk being sampled and 1cm³ amyl alcohol are added (see Fig. 13.1). The butyrometer is

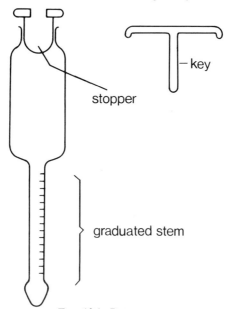

FIG. 13.1. Butyrometer

securely stoppered and shaken until the acid has first curdled then dissolved the whole of the protein, freeing the fat from emulsification. Separation is facilitated by 4 minutes centrifuging at 1100 rpm which brings the fat into a layer in the graduated stem of the butyrometer. This allows for a direct percentage reading, provided the butyrometer and contents are brought to 65° C by immersion in a thermostatic water bath.

Specialist Equipment   Butyrometers with adjustable stoppers and a key. Special pipettes for:
    10cm³ sulphuric acid (safety).
    10·94cm³ milk.
    1cm³ amyl alcohol (safety).
Rack for holding butyrometers (optional).

Gerber centrifuge.
Thermostatic water bath.

Points on Procedure   THROUGHOUT HAVE REGARD FOR THE HIGHLY CORROSIVE NATURE OF CONCENTRATED SULPHURIC ACID

(*a*) Carry out four determinations simultaneously on each sample of milk.
(*b*) Allow milk to adjust to room temperature (20° C) and mix to disperse cream.
(*c*) Keep neck of butyrometer dry when filling.
(*d*) Add milk to acid gently, forming a top layer.
(*e*) Insert stopper well into butyrometer.
(*f*) EITHER use a butyrometer rack while shaking OR wrap each individually in a dry cloth and invert gently and repeatedly until all curd disappears.
(*g*) Transfer butyrometers to centrifuge in multiples of four, taking care to balance the head.
(*h*) Immerse butyrometers in water bath with stems uppermost.

Result   The whole of the fat should be within the graduated stem of the butyrometer. If not, apply pressure with the stopper key. Read as soon as possible after taking from water bath. The graduation units are a direct reading of the percentage fat content.
    For homogenized milk, a second and third 4 minute spell in the centrifuge, each separated by 4 minutes in the water bath, will aid separation.

(ii) Lactometer Determination of Specific Gravity of Milk

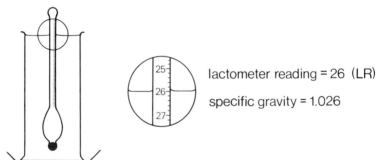

lactometer reading = 26 (LR)

specific gravity = 1.026

FIG. 13.2. Lactometer

The specific gravity of milk can range from 1·025 to 1·035. Graduations on the stem of the lactometer (a special purpose hydrometer—see Fig. 13.2) are marked from 25 (near the top) to 35. The float and sinker ensure upright floating in a liquid.

Points on Procedure

(a) Bring the milk to the temperature stated on the hydrometer, usually 15·5° C.

(b) Pour into a suitable cylindrical container standing in a dish.

(c) Immerse the lactometer in the milk so that it just overflows.

(d) Allow the instrument to achieve a steady level and read off the stem (lactometer reading—LR).

(iii) Calculation of Percentage of 'Solids not Fat' (SNF)

The specific gravity of milk is a function of that of water (unity), that of fat ($<$ 1) and that of the other solids, protein, lactose and mineral matter ($>$ 1). The proportion of each has a bearing on the final result. The Richmond formula uses knowledge of the specific gravity of milk (lactometer reading—LR) and percentage fat content to calculate percentage solids not fat (SNF).

$$\% \text{ SNF} = 0·25 \text{ LR} + 0·2\text{F} + 0·4$$
$$\text{where F} = \% \text{ fat}$$

(iv) Presumptive Minimum Standards

The presumptive minimum standards for milk on sale to the public are:

% fat content—3 (Channel Islands and S. Devon milks—4)
% SNF content—8·5

Expt. 13.7   TESTS FOR EFFECTIVE PASTEURIZATION

Pasteurization achieves a marked reduction in the numbers of microorganisms present in milk without achieving complete sterility. Several tests are available for checking the effectiveness of the heat treatment, including the two which follow. In principle, these allow pasteurized milk to be held at a temperature which promotes multiplication of any bacteria remaining viable. Then a dye is added which decolorizes when reduced, as when bacteria are present. Extent of decoloration in a given time is an index of the numbers of bacteria present.

(i) Methylene Blue Test

Samples of milk are stored overnight at 18·5° C (judged to be atmospheric shade temperature in summer). To 10cm³ milk, 1cm³ methylene blue solution is added and the sample is incubated in a water bath at 37° C for 30 minutes. Meanwhile a control tube is set up and sterilized by immersion in boiling water for 3 minutes.

Provided the pasteurization was efficient and no undue contamination followed, there will be no colour change (compared with the control). Bacteria present will exhaust the dissolved oxygen and then proceed to reduce the methylene blue, with resultant bleaching. Thus the extent of decoloration is an index of the bacterial population.

If possible, repeat the procedure using untreated milk.

(ii) **Reazurin Test**

The Reazurin test works on the same principle as methylene blue. Reazurin is violet dye which, on reduction, turns through pink to colourless. Tablets are sold with instructions for use. When dissolved and added to milk in the concentration stated, followed by incubation at 37° C for 10 minutes, the colour produced gives an indication of the keeping quality of the milk. Colour charts are available for comparison. This is a useful test for milk producers and caterers and is often called the 'ten minute test'.

Expt. 13.8   NUTRIENT ANALYSIS OF CHEESE

A sample of cheese, such as cheddar, provides a profitable material on which to practise both quantitative and qualitative food analysis procedures.

(i) **Qualitative Analysis**—detection of nutrients present

Original material
(*a*) Water, see Expt. 6.1
(*b*) Lipid, see Expt. 4.1
(*c*) Starch, see Expt. 3.1 (ii)
(*d*) Salt, see Expt. 19.3

Cold water extract   This is obtained by shaking grated cheese in deionized water and filtering.
(*a*) Soluble carbohydrate, see Expt. 3.1
(*b*) Soluble protein, see Expt. 5.3
(*c*) Mineral ions, see Expt. 7.2

Residue from filtration
(*a*) Insoluble protein, see Expt. 5.3

Ash   Ash is obtained as described in Expt. 7.1
(*a*) **Mineral elements, see Expt. 7.2**

(ii) **Quantitative Analysis**—percentage composition

(*a*) Water: Thoroughly heat a weighted sample of well-grated cheese in a shallow dish in a steam heated oven. Cool in a desiccator and re-weigh. Repeat procedure until weight becomes constant.

$$\% \text{ water} = \frac{\text{loss in weight}}{\text{original weight of sample}} \times 100$$

(*b*) Protein Kjeldahl determination, (Expt. 5.5)
(*c*) Lipids Soxhlet determination, (Expt. 4.7)
(*d*) Salt, see Expt. 19.3

REFERENCE

Bell, W. J., and O'Keefe, J. A. (1968). *Sales of food and drugs*, Butterworth.

FURTHER READING

Vanstone, E., and Dougall, B. M. (1960). *Principles of dairy science*, Cleaver-Hume Press Ltd., and Macmillan.

EEC Dairy Facts & Figures (1978). Milk Marketing Board.

United Kingdom Dairy Facts & Figures (1978). Federation of the U.K. Milk Marketing Boards.

CHAPTER XIV

FATS AND OILS

14.1 ORIGINS

Edible fats and oils can be divided into two main groups: those derived from animal sources, and this group should include marine oils; and those from vegetable sources. The two main animal fats used are butter and lard, but beef and mutton fat also belong in this group—they may be sold to the housewife as dripping or they may be processed and sold under trade names for frying purposes. Ghee is an animal fat in general use in India and other tropical countries. It is often made from buffalo milk and is somewhat similar to clarified butter. The oil produced is sold as ghee and is almost completely free from water and water-soluble proteins. It keeps much better than butter, a decided advantage in a hot climate.

Marine oils contain a high proportion of unsaturated fatty acids in their triglyceride molecules. Sources of marine oils are oily fish, e.g. herring and pilchard; when refined and hydrogenated they are included in some brands of margarine and cooking fats. Although hydrogenated whale oil was at one time used extensively in margarine manufacture, it is used no longer. Due to over culling the whale population has been drastically reduced to the point where some species face extinction; stocks of herring have also been seriously depleted and marine oils in general are likely to be in short supply. The most important plant sources are soya bean, cottonseed, groundnut, sunflower, coconut, palm, palm kernel, olive, sesame, maize and rapeseed. Blends of these oils are used in margarine, oil and cooking fat manufacture.

14.2 EXTRACTION OF VEGETABLE OILS

Oils in plants are contained in the cells of the seeds. There are thousands of cells in each seed. There are two methods of extracting the oil: mechanical extraction, the oil being forced out by extreme pressure; and solvent extraction, the oil being dissolved out using a solvent of low boiling point in which the oil is soluble. In practice neither process is as simple as it sounds and in an oil mill the two processes are often combined.

The seeds are first cleaned and sifted, and ferrous metals removed by electro-magnets at various points throughout the plant. The seed is broken up by passing through heavy fluted rollers in the case of hard tough seeds such as palm kernels or plain rollers in the case of less tough seeds. If very high quality oil is required which has a mild flavour and a pale colour the meal is then passed to a press. To obtain the maximum yield the seeds are cooked, passing through a series of kettles around each of which is a steam-heated jacket. The seeds are stirred inside the kettles and the temperature rises to between 71–110° C depending on the type of seed being processed. The heating of the seed facilitates extraction but tends to give the oil a stronger flavour and darkens its colour. The oil can be expressed by means of a hydraulic press but most modern oil mills use an expeller presser. The principle is similar to that of a kitchen mincing machine, a powerful screw forces the mixture forward against a restricted opening and as the squashed seed is pushed to the end of the machine the oil escapes through slots in the barrel housing the screw. The expressed oil is collected, filtered, automatically weighed and pumped to storage tanks. There are two main types of expellers: a low pressure expeller which gives a very high quality oil, as only the oil is expressed; and a high pressure expeller with a much higher squeezing efficiency. The quality of this oil is not so good, as other substances can be squeezed out at the same time.

After low pressure expelling the residue is usually subjected to solvent extraction. This process is dependent on the fact that oils are soluble in a number of organic liquids. The seed is broken up on cracking rollers, dried and then passed through rollers which flatten it into thin flakes, so that the solvent can soak into them more readily. The oil is washed out by the solvent using the counter current principle, i.e. the seed passes in one direction and is washed by the solvent moving in the opposite direction. This ensures that the seed with the lowest oil concentration is finally washed with new solvent which removes practically all the remaining oil and the solvent with the highest concentration of oil dissolved in it finally washes fresh seed with a high oil content. The solvent is then distilled, the vapour is condensed for re-use and the residual oil is sent for refining. The remaining seed is usually processed for animal fodder, unless, as with soya bean residue, it can be processed for human consumption (see 15.6). The solvents used vary according to the exact method used but both petroleum spirit and trichlorethylene are used.

14.3 REFINING

Crude oil needs refining to improve its taste and smell, to lighten its colour and to remove free fatty acids and other impurities. The impurities in suspension form gums in the presence of water and the first stage in refining is known as degumming which takes place when warm oil and hot water are mixed together and then transferred to a centrifugal separator. The gum particles having a higher density than the oil are thrown to the bottom of the separator leaving the clarified oil at the top. The oil is neutralized by the addition of caustic soda solution which converts free fatty acids into insoluble soap which is allowed to settle to the bottom of the neutralizing tanks where it is run off. The remaining oil is washed several times with hot water to remove all traces of soap. The oil is then bleached with fuller's earth or activated carbon. The heated oil is dried under vacuum and the bleaching material mixed into it. Both fuller's earth and activated carbon have a great capacity for absorbing colouring material. After mixing for about 15 minutes the oil is pumped through filters and is deodorized by passing steam through the hot oil under vacuum.

The oil is ready for blending and is frequently stored in an inert atmosphere of nitrogen to avoid oxidation. Hydrogenation may take place at this stage (see 4.3.5).

14.4 RANCIDITY

All oils and fats are liable to spoilage, commonly described as rancidity, which gives the fat or oil an unpleasant odour and flavour. Different types of oils and fats deteriorate at different rates: vegetable oils are the most resistant to spoilage, animal fats are more susceptible, whilst marine oils deteriorate more rapidly still. There are two main types of rancidity: oxidative rancidity, which is the commonest, and hydrolytic rancidity. Oxidative rancidity, as its name implies, is caused by the reaction with oxygen of unsaturated oils and is not dependent on impurities in the oil; this reaction produces a rancid flavour (see 4.3.7). Hydrolytic rancidity is caused by the presence of moisture in the fats and oils resulting in hydrolysis of the triglyceride molecules to glycerol and free fatty acids. The presence of enzymes and micro-organisms speeds up the reaction considerably and hence hydrolysis is more rapid in fats and oils which have not been heat treated.

14.5 MARGARINE

A wide range of oils are used in the manufacture of margarine, most of which are imported. These include palm oil, groundnut, coconut, sunflower, cottonseed, soya bean, rapeseed, sesame seed, beef and mutton tallow, herring and pilchard oil. Specific brands of margarine are made from a blend of several of those listed. The blends will vary according to supply and cost of oils at the time of manufacture. In the USA soya bean and cottonseed are mainly used as large crops of these plants are grown there.

Each particular brand of margarine is designed for a particular market, thus there are brands designed for the table which will spread even when refrigerated, margarines for baking which have plastic properties and good creaming qualities (see 4.3.6 and 6.2.3), margarines for the Jewish community, brands which are manufactured from purely vegetable sources and some which have a high proportion of polyunsaturated fatty acids in the triglyceride molecule (see 4.2.2).

A report on 'The Prevention of Coronary Heart Disease' issued in 1976 by the Royal College of Physicians and the British Cardiac Society recommended a reduction in the amount of saturated fats and a partial substitution by polyunsaturated fats. Whilst this measure has received support from other quarters the DHSS document 'Eating for Health' endorses the advice given by the Committee on Medical Aspects of Food Policy to reduce the total amount of fat in the diet but has reservations about recommending consumption of large quantities of polyunsaturated fats. They state that there is no new evidence which would suggest that their inclusion would reduce the incidence of coronary heart disease and add that many doctors are uneasy about the introduction of large quantities of polyunsaturated fatty acids in foods such as vegetable oils.

14.5.1 Margarine manufacture

The characteristics of the finished product, melting point, plasticity, consistency, etc. of margarine depend on the particular blend of oils chosen. In the UK between 15–30 per cent of the fat phase will be solid fat. Within these limits there will be considerable variation —a soft table margarine will have a large proportion of liquid oils, a harder fat designed for flaky or puff pastry will have a relatively high solid content to withstand rolling between layers of dough.

Margarine is a water-in-oil emulsion; this is achieved by emulsifying water with added milk solids and the blended fats. Before the aqueous phase and the fats are mixed the other ingredients are added. These are salt, originally added to inhibit the growth of micro-organisms as well as to improve flavour, at the rate of 1–2 per cent; vitamins A and D; colouring materials, usually annatto (a yellow/red vegetable colouring) and beta-carotene; emulsifiers, to help stabilize the emulsion, in the form of monoglycerides and lecithin (see 4.3.9); and flavouring agents. The flavouring agents are intended to give a palatable acceptable flavour and are some of the constituents known to be present in butter, e.g. butyric acid, caproic acid and delta lactones.

The manufacture is nowadays almost entirely carried out by a continuous process using a machine called a votator. The fats, water and other ingredients are pumped to the votator which is a series of chromium-plated steel tubes cooled on the outside. Each tube has a rotating blade fitted and the mixture is forced through the tubes under pressure. The mixture cools rapidly, crystals form along the inner surface of the tube and are scraped off by the rotating blades and mixed with the rest of the ingredients. The process is rather more complicated than this and includes pre-crystallizing systems, at least one chilling system and a post-crystallization section where the cooled emulsion completes its crystallization and can be worked to give the desired texture. Margarines containing a high proportion of polyunsaturated fatty acids are more difficult to handle than harder margarine; they have to be cooled to lower temperatures and require more working. The softer margarines are usually packed in PVC tubs. For harder margarines, vegetable parchment and aluminium foil are used. Some margarines, destined for export, are canned and nitrogen is added to the mixture to enhance keeping qualities. All packs should form a barrier to light, moisture, oxygen and micro-organisms.

14.6 COOKING FATS

Cooking fats resemble lard more closely than margarine as they are a pure fat and not a solid emulsion. They are usually a mixture of vegetable, animal and marine oils. The proportion of the various types of oil used and the individual varieties used vary with the current economic conditions. The oils are partially hydrogenated so that the required degree of plasticity is obtained, the refined oils are blended and cooled using machines rather like those used for margarine manufacture. Some brands of cooking fat have an inert gas incorporated into the mixture and this improves its creaming qualities.

14.7 High Ratio Fats or Super-glycerinated Fats

High ratio fats are specially manufactured for commercial baking, the term 'high ratio' being the trade mark of the producers Procter and Gamble. Such fats have glyceryl monostearate (GMS) added which is an emulsifier enabling the use of a high proportion of sugar and water in flour mixtures and making the fat go further. The addition of GMS improves the creaming and shortening qualities of the fat.

14.8 Vegetable Oils

14.8.1 Olive oil

Olive oil has been used for cooking purposes in Mediterranean countries for centuries. In the UK it is mainly used in mayonnaise and salad dressings. It has a distinctive and, to many people, a highly acceptable flavour although it is an expensive oil. It contains a high proportion of unsaturated fatty acids, notably the mono-unsaturated oleic acid (see 4.3.2). The best quality olive oil can be used without purification.

14.8.2 Cooking oils

Blended vegetable oils are widely available and are used mainly for frying and to some extent for salad dressings and mayonnaises, although the average housewife tends to use ready-made salad creams and dressings. The blended oils are cheaper than olive oil and cheaper than individual oils such as sesame and sunflower seed oils which are also on the market. Cooking oils have competed very favourably with animal fats for frying in recent years and, before the development of margarines with a high polyunsaturated content, were used for making cakes and pastries for diets recommending the use of vegetable oils in preference to animal fats.

14.9 Butter Manufacture

For the purposes of butter manufacture cream is separated from large quantities of milk using a cream separator. The cream is placed in large glass or stainless steel lined holding tanks which are well insulated and often equipped with agitators so that the cream can be subjected to slight agitation. The cream is held at about 4·5° C for a sufficiently long period to ensure uniform hardening of fat globules. During this period the cream is sometimes ripened by the addition of acid-producing bacteria. This gives a butter with a fuller flavour but shorter keeping qualities than that made from sweet cream. The flavour required depends on the time allowed for acid production and the temperature at which it is held. Conditions vary from 10–13° C overnight to 15·5–18·5° C for 3–4 hours.

Churning takes place at about 7° C and results in separation of granules of butter about the size of wheat grains. The effect of churning breaks the film of solids-not-fat round the small fat globules in the cream so that granular formation of butterfat can take place. This 'breaking' is seen through a glass panel in the front of the churn. The temperature control of the cream is important as otherwise the 'break' may be delayed.

The buttermilk is drawn off and used for animal feeding or for inclusion in powdered milk manufacture. The butter grains are then washed to remove any remaining buttermilk which might adversely affect the keeping qualities of the butter; it also helps to harden the fat. Excess water is then drained off to meet the legal maximum moisture content, which is 16 per cent in the UK. Salt is added at this stage if required. Many consumers prefer salted butter and it improves the keeping qualities of the butter by inhibiting growth of yeasts, moulds and proteolytic and lipolytic bacteria; amounts vary between 1 and 1·5 per cent. The butter is 'worked' into a smooth solid mass and is then ready for packing. It is forced through a shaping machine and divided into individual blocks by an automatic weight controlled packing machine and packed in either vegetable parchment or aluminium foil. A small amount of butter is made by a continuous process. This requires the use of special machines which have been developed specifically for that purpose. The butter produced is usually extruded from the machine in a continuous ribbon ready for the packing machines.

14.10 LARD

Lard is prepared from pig's fat and is 98–100 per cent lipid. The melted fat is refined and usually mixed with an antioxidant before being packed in vegetable parchment wrappers. It has a low melting point, good shortening properties; an acceptable colour and a bland flavour. The process of interesterification (see 4.3.6) has improved the creaming qualities of lard. It is suitable for frying and for pastry-making, when it is frequently used in conjunction with margarine. It is not usually used for cake-making but if used would be more suitable for cakes which have ingredients with a distinct flavour such as chocolate or ginger cakes as the lard itself lacks a distinct flavour.

14.11 LOW-ENERGY SPREADS

To meet the demand for a fatty spread for bread which has a lower energy value than butter or margarine, some manufacturers market a product with a very high water content, possibly approaching 50 per cent. Obviously this will have an appreciable inclusion of emulsifier and it will be unsuitable for uses such as frying and baking. Slimmers would fare equally well by eating less of the normal table fats. Another approach by food technologists is to employ interesterification (see 4.3.6) whereby fatty acids are exchanged to the end that triglycerides are formed with mainly short chain fatty acids giving, weight-for-weight, lower energy yields. Obviously such sophisticated processing will add to the cost of the final product.

PRACTICAL EXERCISES

*All experiments require standard precautions; those marked * involve particular hazards and should be supervised*

Expt. 14.1 MELTING TEMPERATURES OF FATS

(i) **Capillary Tube Method**
(Apply to any solid fat)
Melt a little fat and draw it into a short length of capillary tubing. Cool to solidify. Attach to the bulb of a thermometer with an elastic band. Support in a beaker of water and heat gently. Observe the temperature at which the fat runs together and forms a clear liquid. This is called the melting point of the fat, although softening will have occurred over a range of temperatures.

(ii) **Boiling Tube Method**
(Apply to butter, margarines (various), lard, cooking fat, dripping and 'low-energy' spreads)
Pack about 20g of fat into a boiling tube. Support this in a beaker of water and heat gently, using a stirrer to spread the heat. At the first sign of softening, insert a thermometer into the fat and take the temperature. This is the 'temperature of incipient fusion'. Continue heating until the fat is just molten and take the temperature. The difference between the lower and upper temperatures is the 'temperature range of softening' for the fat.
    NB. Reserve the tube and contents for Expt. 14.3.

*Expt. 14.2 VAPORIZATION OF FATS AND OILS (Apply to fats and oils recommended for frying)

WORK SHOULD BE CARRIED OUT IN A FUME CUPBOARD, WITH AN ASBESTOS MAT AT HAND IN CASE OF IGNITION
Support a crucible, containing sufficient fat or oil to cover a thermometer bulb, in a sand tray. Heat from below until the fat melts and continue gently until a faint blue haze is seen—TURN OFF HEAT. Take this temperature with

a wide range or a frying thermometer (250° C or over). Vaporization temperatures should not be lower than temperatures recommended for frying. A depressed vapour point is an indication of presence of impurities.

Expt. 14.3 CONSTITUENTS OF PLASTIC FATS

(Work with samples of butter, margarines (various), lard, cooking fats, drippings (various), 'low-energy' spreads)

(i) Presence of Non-lipid Constituents

Obtain boiling tubes containing molten fats (as from Expt. 14.1 (ii)). Describe the appearance of the molten fat in each. Turbidity indicates non-lipid constituents; in this circumstance, return the tubes to the water bath and heat thoroughly to facilitate separation into layers. Water and solids will settle below molten fat.

Allow fats in all the tubes to solidify. Attempt to estimate the proportion of lipid layer to total content in the tube. Compare the evidence for non-lipid constituents, noting separated water and solids.

For all the tubes of re-solidified fats, compare the colours and the textures with those of the original products. An increase in depth of colour is associated with breaking of emulsions, whether water in oil or air in oil. A more granular texture indicates formation of larger crystals.

(ii) Microscopic Examination

Choose a fat with a water content (as shown by (i) above) and compress a very small amount of the original material (not re-solidified) between a slide and coverslip. Examine microscopically, first with lower power and then high power with a darkened field. Look for rounded droplets of water dispersed in the continuous phase of oil. Repeat with the same fat, re-solidified after melting. Look for evidence of loss of the emulsion and altered crystal size.

Repeat with other fats available including vegetable cooking fats, advertised as being 'pre-creamed'. Look for rounded air cells dispersed in the continuous phase.

*Expt. 14.4 DETECTION OF PEROXIDES, INDICATING INCIPIENT RANCIDITY

(Apply to butter, olive oil etc, available in both fresh and stale conditions.)

Dissolve about 1cm³ of the fat/oil under test in an approximately equal volume of chloroform (or the minimum volume necessary). Add 2cm³ glacial acetic acid and 1 drop 10% potassium iodide. Shake to mix and leave to stand.

Positive result Iodine liberated, giving a brown colour and confirmed by added starch solution, indicates peroxides present which are likely to precede oxidative rancidity.

Expt. 14.5 DETECTION OF ADDED COLOURING MATTER IN BUTTER/ MARGARINE

Melt a little of the butter or margarine and strain to remove solids. Dissolve 2–3cm³ in a little ether and divide between two test tubes:

(*a*) Add 1–2cm³ hydrochloric acid (1+1), i.e. concentrated acid diluted with an equal volume of water. Allow to stand.
   Positive result   Red colour indicates an azo dye present.
(*b*) Add 1–2cm³ 10% sodium hydroxide solution
   Positive result   Yellow colour indicates vegetable colouring, probably annatto, present.

See also Chapter IV for general experiments on lipids.

FURTHER READING

Fox, B. and Cameron, A. (1977). *Food science—a chemical approach*, 3rd rev. edn., Hodder & Stoughton.
Royal College of Physicians of London & British Cardiac Society (1976). *Prevention of Coronary Heart Disease*, The Society.
DHSS (1974). *Diet & Coronary Heart Disease*, HMSO.

CHAPTER XV

MEAT, FISH AND SIMULATED MEATS

15.1 MEAT STRUCTURE AND COMPOSITION

Meat consists primarily of muscular tissue with amounts of fatty (adipose) tissue varying not only with the cut or joint but also with the animal, its species, age and feed. It is low in lean and young meat and high in the flesh of animals intensively fed for the market. In addition meat invariably contains connective tissue which binds the individual muscle fibres together and, in places, is massed into gristle or tendons, linking muscle with bone or cartilage. Nerves and blood vessels, capillaries, small veins and arteries, are dispersed throughout the flesh. Chops and some joints as bought and cooked have, in addition, a fair proportion of bone or cartilage. These several tissues, other than fat, are composed in the main of various proteins in water.

15.1.1 Chemical composition of 'lean'

Muscle, without bone and with adipose tissue layers removed, contains about 75 per cent water and 18–25 per cent protein. The most abundant protein is myosin which, with actin, forms the myofibrils within the muscle fibres. Water-soluble proteins, albumins and globulins, are also present in muscle fibres, dispersed in the water of the sarcoplasm, i.e. the fluid within the muscle fibres. They give heat-coagulation properties to muscle fibres. Myoglobin is another water-soluble protein which is the pigment in meat: purple–red or bright red in raw; brown in well-done; and bright red in medium-rare meats. The function of myoglobin in living tissue is carriage of oxygen between blood within the capillaries and the sites of metabolic oxidation, i.e. the mitochondria which cluster against the myofibrils.

Connective tissue proteins form fibrous structures; collagen fibres are tough, white, inextensible and often gathered into wavy bundles, while elastin fibres are elastic and branching. Collagen fibres are the more common, being present in all connective tissues. Elastin fibres are less widely distributed and are only present in appreciable amounts in certain well-developed and exercised muscles. Amounts of connective tissue generally increase with animal age and muscle activity.

Intramuscular fat, which shows up in meat from fattened cattle as 'marbling', is evidence of good quality meat. Such deposits are only laid down in young animals of good nutritional status.

Non-protein water-soluble constituents in and around the muscle fibres include intermediate products of metabolic cycles, both respiratory and excretory: creatin, lactic acid and ions of mineral elements. Among these are the substances which contribute the flavour to meat and are collectively referred to as extractives, being the principal constituents of meat extract concentrates. Stimulation of gastric secretion results from their presence in the stomach.

15.1.2 Chemical composition of 'fat'

Adipose tissue consists of massed cells, so filled with lipid material that nuclei and other cellular inclusions are compressed against the boundary membranes. Connective tissue fibres permeate the whole. The lipids are mainly true fats (triglycerides) in which residues of stearic, oleic and palmitic acid predominate. Fat-soluble vitamins are distributed throughout but not in sufficient amounts for meat fat to be listed among their major dietary sources.

15.1.3 Muscle fibres

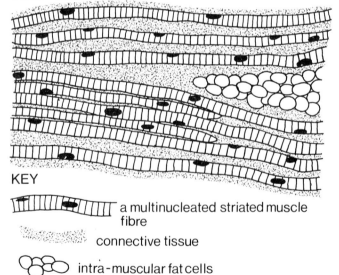

KEY

a multinucleated striated muscle fibre

connective tissue

intra-muscular fat cells

FIG. 15.1. Diagrammatic representation of tissue structures in meat

An individual muscle fibre is a long cylindrical structure with the sort of dimensions associated with a hair. When viewed under a microscope cross-striations are apparent (see Fig. 15.1). They arise from the orderly formation of two types of filament which, lying parallel to the axis of the fibre, make up the myofibrils. The cross striations are formed by alternate ranks of myosin and actin filaments. The myosin filaments, being thicker, form the dark bands with fine actin filaments giving the light bands. Actin filaments extend into the dark bands overlapping the myosin filaments. With contraction, this overlapping increases, resulting in an overall shortening of the muscle fibre (Fig. 15.2).

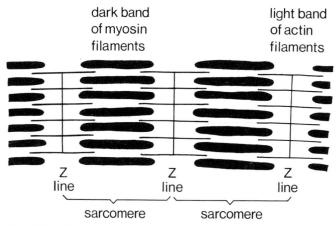

FIG. 15.2. Diagrammatic representation of striations in a muscle fibre

15.1.4 Biochemical aspects of contraction

A number of explanations have been postulated regarding the chemical changes which cause actin filaments to be pulled into the dark bands. There is general acceptance that between the myosin and actin filaments, oblique cross-links form, shorten, break and re-make, repeatedly while contraction proceeds. Thus the sarcomere length (Z–Z) is reduced. Within muscle fibres, as in other living cells, phosphates, both inorganic (P_i) and organic (notably adenosine diphosphate, ADP), are present. Energy liberated by nutrient oxidation is used to unite them, producing adenosine triphosphate, ATP (see 10.1.3).

In relaxed muscle, ATP is associated with myosin filaments and serves as a plasticizer, preventing cross-linking with actin filaments. The effect of ATP is similar to that of plasticizing side groups, deliberately added to synthetic polymers in pliable plastics which prevent cross-linking into rigid structures. With nervous stimulation to the muscle to contract, calcium ions are flooded into the fibres with the effect of activating myosin to become an enzyme, ATP-ase, which breaks down ATP, releasing energy needed for the mechanical work of contraction. With the loss of ATP, cross-links form between myosin and actin. It is probable that calcium ions are involved in these cross-links. Meanwhile continuing respiratory oxidation allows for ATP replenishment, resulting in the breaking of cross-links. Thus the sequence of making and breaking of cross-links continues, increasing and maintaining contraction (Fig. 15.3).

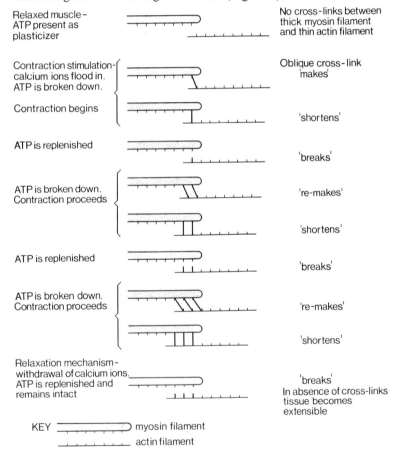

FIG. 15.3. Diagrammatic representation of the contraction–relaxation sequence in striated muscle

Relaxation comes with the withdrawal of calcium ions. The muscle tissue becomes extensible due to the plasticizing effect of the ATP which, in the absence of ATP-ase activating calcium ions, remains intact.

15.1.5 Meat conditioning

During life, with the energy released for muscle contraction, there is evolution of heat, which serves to maintain body temperature. After slaughter, temperature begins to fall and in a reflex effort to restore it, all available ATP is broken down, including that produced by the metabolism of any glycogen in the muscles. In the absence of oxygen (due to bleeding of the carcass), this is limited to anaerobic glycolysis with its meagre yield of ATP. The consequence is that, with all ATP broken down and no further replenishment, the plasticizing effect is gone and myosin filaments cross-link with actin giving inextensible acto-myosin. The muscles become hard, the condition being rigor mortis. Carcasses are 'hung', i.e. stored until rigor has passed and muscles have softened. This must have occurred before cooking otherwise the meat would be unacceptably tough when eaten. Enzymes called cathepsins, released from cellular inclusions known as lysosomes, break down protein complexes in dead tissue and are undoubtedly implicated in the tenderization process. In spite of expectation there is no conclusive evidence that connective tissue proteins are hydrolyzed by cathepsins or that their proteolytic action reverses the acto-myosin formation. Possibly they promote fracturing of muscle fibres at Z lines.

Anaerobic glycolysis results in lactic acid production (see 10.4.7). The amount will depend upon the glycogen content of the muscle at slaughter and, in turn, this will relate to the animal's condition, rested or agitated, at the time. Measures are taken at slaughter houses to ensure that glycogen stores will not have been unduly depleted by alarm or struggling and in consequence the lactic acid production will be sufficient to bring the pH level to 5·5 or thereabouts. This is low enough to limit bacterial spoilage during hanging, but not to prevent it. To do this, carcases need to be cooled; EEC legislation requires cooling to 7°C as soon as possible following slaughter. This causes muscle tissue to exhibit a phenomenon known as cold-shortening which is irreversible and results in tough meat. Production of carcase meat which is sufficiently 'aged' to be tender and not unduly contaminated by bacteria requires a careful balance between length of hanging time and temperature storage.

15.2 THE COOKING OF MEAT

Tradition among civilized communities demands that meat should be cooked and much of interest and enjoyment can be achieved by way of flavour and consistency in meat dishes. At the same time keeping quality is increased and incidence of disease transmission is lessened although not eliminated. Because cooked meat is more readily masticated, digestion is hastened by cooking; enzymes being more effective on a substrate with a large surface area.

15.2.1 Texture changes

Heat coagulation of proteins extracted from meat begins at about 45° C and continues as the temperature rises with different proteins coming out of solution at distinct temperatures until, at about 80° C, all separation will have occurred. The pigment myoglobin is one of the last to denature (see Expt. 15.2). Further rises in temperature bring shrinkage of the coagulum with loss of bound water. This indicates that, for the cooking of the muscle fibres in meat, temperatures below 80° C are all that are needed. In contrast, collagen fibres are only converted to gelatin by prolonged exposure to water at 80° C or above. Consequently when faced with meat containing an appreciable proportion of connective tissue, the cook is in something of a dilemma. The application of simmering-water temperatures, as in the 'moist' methods of cooking, for lengths of time required to hydrate the collagen sufficiently to give a tender bite, will inevitably cause overcooking of the muscle fibres. The proteins therein first coagulate and then shrink, exuding water and water-soluble constituents into the cooking liquor. Obviously cooking skill will involve appreciable discrimination with regard for times and temperatures to avoid, on the one hand, under-done tough meat and, on the other, a shrunken, stringy and tasteless product.

The protein elastin is in no way altered by cooking and, if present in appreciable amounts in the connective tissue, no amount of cooking will eliminate its toughening effect. Grinding the meat is one solution, for it is only within the mouth that the texture is appreciated. Once swallowed, elastin is digested along with other proteins.

The expensive cuts are those with little connective tissue in proportion to muscle fibre. For these, the 'dry' methods of cooking are appropriate: grilling, frying and roasting counting as dry in that no water is added, although the appreciable water content of all meats will serve to hydrate internal collagen to some extent. Baking of joints of meat in covered receptacles or within foil wraps or so-called roasting bags, all of which retain moisture, amounts to a moist method of cooking and the eating quality will be that of steamed meat. True roasting produces an outer pellicle of coagulated protein and residues of water-soluble constituents including the flavoursome extractives, left as water evaporates from the surface. Again judgement is required of the cook to produce the desired result, be it 'rare' or 'medium' or 'well-done', while avoiding the dried and shrunken over-done joint which, although it may give tender eating, will have lost much in quality and substance.

Heat applied to the adipose tissue layers melts the fat which drains out of cells compressed by the shrinking of connective tissue fibres.

15.2.2 Colour of meat

The pigment in muscle is myoglobin which is purple–red in colour. Like haemoglobin, which it resembles chemically in possessing an iron-containing prosthetic group, myoglobin can 'pick-up' atmospheric oxygen, forming an unstable compound, bright red in colour. Oxy-myoglobin will dissociate in a region where oxygen is scarce and thus it is a means of transporting oxygen. The bright red of the exposed cut surface of raw meat is due to oxy-myoglobin. During cooking, oxy-myoglobin forms and is retained within 'rare-done' joints, giving the familiar bright red colour, while on the outside (and throughout a well-done joint) there is a change to brown globin-haemochrome. This lacks the added oxygen but, as shown in Fig. 15.4, the iron within the porphyrin group has been oxidized, by electron removal, from iron II (Fe^{2+}) to iron III Fe^{3+}), while the major part of the molecule, the globin, suffers denaturation.

The brown colour on the outside of cooked meat is due in part to the concentration of dried denatured globin-haemochrome and in part to non-enzymic browning, the Maillard reaction (see 9.7.1). Meat turns brown on staling due to formation of yet another oxidation product of myoglobin. Metmyoglobin is the result of conversion of iron II to iron III in conditions of low oxygen tension due to bacterial activity; presence of air favouring 'oxygenation' rather than 'oxidation'. Metmyoglobin formation can be reversed by reducing agents such as ascorbic acid, which is added to ground beef in some countries, although prohibited in the UK.

Pickled meats, especially ham and bacon, are treated with concentrated solutions of salts, these being mainly sodium chloride (common salt) together with a nitrite source. Traditionally this is potassium nitrate (saltpetre) which under anaerobic conditions is converted by bacteria to the nitrite. In bacon factories, nitrites are added directly. The pink colour of such meats is nitroso-myoglobin formed by reaction between nitrite ions and the porphyrin groups of myoglobin.

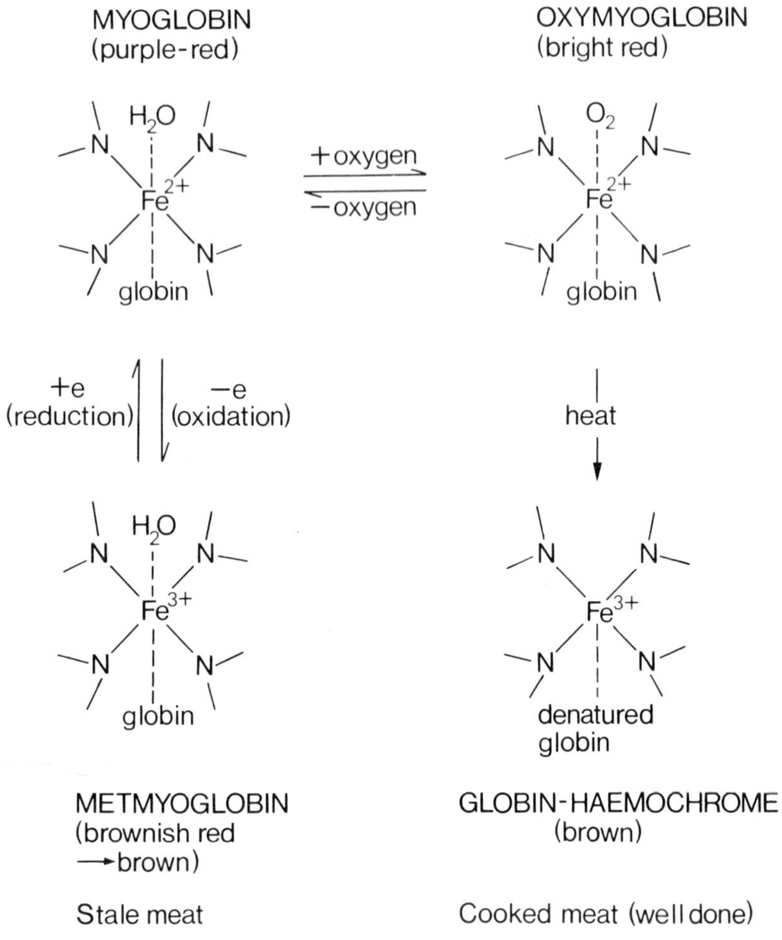

FIG. 15.4. Pigments in meats

15.3 THE FOOD VALUE OF MEAT

The primary importance of meat as a food lies in the fact that when digested its protein is reduced to its ultimate amino-acids, which when assimilated by the system suffice as building units for the repairs of all types of cells and tissues and the formation of new growth. Muscle protein is of high biological value, containing all essential amino-acids in proportions approaching those required for production of human body tissue. This is a reasonable expectation considering the similarities between our body structures and those of the mammalian species from which meat is obtained. Gelatin, which is derived from the collagen of various types of connective tissue, has, in contrast, a zero biological value, being low in methionine and phenylalanine and wholly lacking in tryptophan. It is incapable by itself of tissue building although, being a moderate source of both lysine and arginine, it can supplement other proteins, such as that in wheat, which are limited by these amino-acids.

The proteins in meat are readily digested, in a matter of three to four hours depending upon the character of the meat, and almost completely absorbed from the intestines, little being rejected in the faeces.

The fat generally associated with flesh may be regarded as secondary to the protein, only in so far as it suffices as a supply of energy and not as a tissue former. None-the-less it is an important ingredient in meat foods supplying, in a well balanced diet, a large portion of the fuel energy required by the body. The amount depends on the consumer's custom and taste. Because it fixes flavour, it promotes consumption of other foods such as rice, pasta and vegetables.

The flavouring extractives of meat play an evident role in giving palatability to cooked meats and soups. They do not contribute materially to tissue building and have a negligible energy content. Claims formerly made concerning the growth and health promoting properties of patented meat extract concentrates are no longer urged, although they do have notable contents of the B group vitamins, nicotinic acid and riboflavin.

The mineral elements supplied by meat include appreciable amounts of potassium and phosphorus, as could be expected from the metabolic roles of the ions of these elements. The iron content of meat is low and yet, when compared with other food sources and set against the daily requirements, it is found to be among the more important dietary sources. In contrast, the calcium in meat makes a very minor contribution to the whole intake.

The vitamin contributions of meats are only of significance with respect to the B group, of which riboflavin and nicotinic acid are the most abundant. Thiamin is present but only in appreciable amounts in pork.

Cooking affects the food value of meat in that water soluble constituents pass out into the cooking water or drain out with the juices. These include mineral elements in the form of ions, water-soluble proteins prior to coagulation and B group vitamins. Provided use is made of the stock or gravy, there is retrieval of losses except in the case of heat-labile substances. Of the vitamins, thiamin is the most susceptible and losses of up to 60 per cent have been recorded. Cuts of meat and cooking procedures will affect the degree of retention. With roasting, larger joints cooked to 'rare-done' or 'medium' give better results for retention than small and/or 'well done' joints. Small and possibly insignificant losses of certain amino-acids (e.g. lysine) which enter into the Maillard reaction occur where there is surface browning during cooking. The draining of melted fat out from meat tissue is another 'nutrient loss' which, strictly speaking, could be attributed to cooking but consumer taste will differ markedly over the amounts of fat eaten with lean; amounts which are acceptable as nourishment by some would be rejected as excessive by others.

15.4 OFFAL

The various forms of offal include many different cell structures and their inclusion in the diet will increase the range of proteins contributing to the metabolic pool of amino-acids. In consequence a protein mixture of a higher biological value is obtained than from the consumption of muscle protein only. The most popular forms of offal—liver and kidney—have particular nutritional significance in providing certain of the vitamins and iron. All forms of liver are excellent sources of retinol (vitamin A) and valuable sources of ribo-flavin, nicotinic acid and vitamin B_{12}. While not rating as high as liver, kidney from various sources provides useful amounts of these vitamins.

Raw liver and kidney are the only animal foods with a significant ascorbic acid content. If they are served lightly grilled or fried, it is likely that some of this most labile of vitamins will be conserved. The coincidence of ascorbic acid and the iron, which is present in higher amounts in liver and kidney than in any other commonly eaten foodstuff, could be advantageous for absorption.

15.5 FISH

The edible parts of fish resemble meat in being composed of muscle fibres held by connective tissue. While there are marked differences in the muscle shapes, with those of fish forming the familiar flakes, both types of fibre are formed of similar contractile tissue. In fish there is less connective tissue and it is entirely collagenous with no elastin. Cooking is only required to coagulate the protein and moderate temperatures and short cooking times are all that is re-quired. Toughness is not a problem but excess exposure to heat will cause over-coagulation of fibres with much loss of bound water; the result being shrunken and hardened material.

The edible part of fish will contain something in the region of 20 per cent protein. In demersal fish (often called white fish) which swim close to the sea bed, the remainder is mainly water with a very little oil distributed through the tissues: less than 1 per cent in cod and haddock, as much as 2 per cent in plaice and sole and 3–5 per cent in hake and halibut. Pelagic varieties which swim nearer the surface, of which the most notable examples are herring and mackerel, have appreciably higher oil contents. The percentage varies with the season but can be as high as 20 per cent.

The smell of fish is due to the presence of an unstable substance, trimethylamine oxide, which under the influence of bacteria, is converted to the odorous trimethylamine. Fish are particularly susceptible to bacterial activity once caught, there being no build-up of lactic acid following death which is invariably accompanied by struggling and the depletion of glycogen (see 15.1.5).

15.6 SIMULATED MEAT PRODUCTS

Artificial 'meats' are not really anything new. The first meat substitute was made by Dr John Harvey Kellogg of cornflake fame as early as 1866. He believed that a wholly vegetarian diet was preferable to a diet based on meats and he developed his product with this in mind rather than as a cheap substitute for meat. Since then many artificial 'meats' and 'sausages' have been prepared for the vegetarian market. However in recent years due to the increased cost of protein foods from animal sources (especially meat and fish) a whole new range of simulated meat foods has come onto the market. Simulated fish products are available as 'fish' cake mixes. These are not artificial proteins but the protein is from vegetable rather than animal sources.

The soya bean provides the main supply of protein for the simulated meats, but wheat and yeast proteins and other oilseed proteins such as peanut and cottonseed may be used. Soya beans have been prized for their culinary value for many years in the Far East, and in other parts of the world pulse vegetables have been recognized as good sources of protein and used extensively by vegetarians. Soya bean products were used to supply protein in the German diet prior to the Second World War. Soya beans in the raw state have certain drawbacks, notably a trypsin inhibiter which could be expected to affect digestion and certain haemagglutinins. However there is reason to believe that the moist heat employed in processing will eliminate both of these agencies.

Some attempt has been made in the UK to utilize field beans, a type of broad bean, as a source of protein but on the whole manufacturers of simulated meat foods rely on the soya bean. The use of field beans would have been advantageous in that they can be cultivated in a temperate climate, thus avoiding the need to import soya beans, though research is being done to develop a strain of soya bean that will grow in temperate climates. There are two main types of simulated meats on the market, an extruded product and a spun product. The latter is the more expensive.

15.6.1 Spun Proteins

This spun proteins process was patented by Robert Boyer about 1957. Proteins are extracted from the de-fatted vegetable material with a mild alkali. This is refined and yields a protein isolate of between 95–98 per cent purity: this isolate, as an alkaline dispersion at pH 12, is spun through spinnerets, similar to those used in the rayon industry, into a coagulating bath of food grade acid and sodium chloride, which is adjusted for acidity, where the fibre formation occurs. The acid bath is at a pH below the iso-electric point to ensure precipitation and the fairly high concentration of salt dehydrates the protein fibres and affects their tensile strength. By changing the composition and treatment of the spinning mix, the size of the spinneret holes, the conditions in the acid bath and the treatment of the fibres after formation the product can vary from tender fibres to tough strands. The spun fibres are stretched by passing over rollers of increasing diameter and washed to remove the acid. Colourings and flavourings are added at this stage. Additional nutrients may also be added; fat is injected into the fibres and a protein binder such as egg albumen is used. Then the fibres are heat processed to coagulate the product.

Products can be sliced, diced or ground (minced), and in this state, as they have been cooked during manufacture, they resemble cooked meat and in most cases can be handled in the same way as conventional cooked meat. They are usually sold as dehydrated product and have a shelf life of about twelve months. Tinned and frozen forms are available in the USA. In many spun products the texture-producing fibrils only constitute about 40 per cent of the dry weight. Bland protein concentrates from algae yeasts or fish can be added in the blender cooker although at present this is not practised in products manufactured in the UK. The addition of low-cost animal products, i.e. pork fat, generally improves the flavour of the product.

15.6.2 Extruded proteins

Extruded proteins are often referred to as textured vegetable protein (TVP) which is the brand name of one particular firm. These products are derived directly from defatted soya flour. The moisture content of the flour is increased and the temperature of the mixture raised. The hot liquid is forced under pressure through nozzles at a controlled temperature (120° C). As pressure reduces, it froths up and sets with a fibrous texture. It can be obtained in chunks, granules or strips. Flavourings and colourings to resemble chicken, ham, pork, beef and bacon can be added before extrusion. An extruded product will contain about 50 per cent protein and is a dry porous material, the residue being largely carbohydrate. It needs rehydrating before use and has the ability to soak up oils and two to three times its own weight of water. This ability to absorb fat makes it a useful addition to meat pies and sausages.

15.6.3 Nutritional value and uses of simulated meats

When rehydrated, the protein content of both the spun and the extruded products will approach that of lean meat. The extruded products will differ, largely in containing carbohydrate and in lacking fat. The quality of protein from soya and field beans is lower than that of meat. All essential amino-acids are represented but methionine with cystine is even more limited than in meat protein. As the textured product is used mainly as a meat extender, in products whose minimum meat content is safeguarded by law, this is not a serious drawback. It has been used in some canned foods and in various dehydrated foods intended for vegetarians. The use of these to the exclusion of meats could conceivably be hazardous. The spun product is used as a meat substitute and as an extender, it is available to the catering trade and in certain canned foods when its inclusion will be stated on the list of contents. It is used by School Meals Services and in many canteens. It should not be confused with reformed dehydrated meat used in some commercial products. To safeguard nutritional standards, a Food Standards Committee has recommended, at the time of writing, the supplementation of all simulated meats with methionine and also, if necessary, with iron, thiamin, riboflavin and B_{12} to levels comparable with those in meat. In recognition of lack of precise knowledge of the significance of other discrepancies, there is also a recommendation to limit substitution in institutional catering to 10 per cent for the time being.

Whatever the type of simulated meat used it should be incorporated into well-flavoured dishes and if appropriate accompanied by a sauce with a distinctive flavour; dishes like curry are ideal. If these products are used to supplement the meat content of sausages, hamburgers, meat pies, etc, the protein cannot count towards the minimum specified meat content as laid down by the Food and Drugs Act, 1955. This act and the Trade Descriptions Act, 1968 should protect the consumer from being sold simulated meats as genuine meat products. If vegetable proteins are contained in a prepacked food this should be stated on the container.

Simulated meats are unlikely to become popular in the Third World if they have not been readily accepted in the Western World. One school of thought encourages the use of a variety of legumes in the diet as an addition to stews and soups rather than the use of simulated meat foods. At present these products are certainly cheaper than conventional meat products although the cost has risen due to increased production costs and is likely to rise further as the cost of soya beans increases. Spun and extruded proteins have had a wider acceptance in the USA than the UK, and it may be that in future they will be accepted as readily as margarine is accepted as a butter substitute today.

15.7 OTHER METHODS OF SUPPLEMENTING PROTEIN FOODS

Some varieties of fish are becoming scarce and certainly more expensive to buy. To increase supplies of fish various methods of fish farming are being tried out in different parts of the world. Trout farming has proved to be quite a successful commercial proposition. The average consumer is a very conservative person and will only buy foods with which he is familiar. It may be that we must learn to accept fish in our diet that are not so aesthetically pleasing to look at, e.g. ink fish and monk fish—the latter has quite an attractive scampi-like flavour and is used readily in parts of Scotland. Fish which can be caught in deeper waters and other fish which have not a ready market could be processed into fish products like fish fingers or perhaps into fish meal.

Developed countries rely on fish meal for animal feeding stuffs, the demand rising from two to five million tonnes between 1960 and 1970. It is forecast that the demand will reach eight or nine million tonnes by 1985, probably exceeding supply by at least one million tonnes. Developed countries use large amounts of vegetable protein in animal feeds to produce animal protein. This is not a very efficient use of protein. Cattle eat about twelve times as much protein weight for weight as they produce in the form of beef. Milk production is rather better, being 38 per cent efficient, whilst egg production and broiler chicken production are about 31 per cent efficient. The process can also be time-consuming. Various methods of producing protein more efficiently have been developed in many parts of the world. The processes involve fermentation using yeasts, bacteria and fungi and there is microbial oxidation of carbonaceous biodegradable substrates and the raw materials used are petroleum products and industrial and agricultural waste. The microbial proteins produced are used for animal feeding. It has not been possible to assess the toxic effects, if any, of long-term use to enable them to be used for human foodstuffs at present but research is being directed to this end.

PRACTICAL EXERCISES

All experiments require standard precautions

Expt. 15.1   MICROSCOPIC EXAMINATION OF MUSCLE TISSUE

Obtain a very small fragment of raw lean meat and spread it on a microscope slide, attempting to separate fibre from fibre with a pair of mounted dissecting needles. Add a drop of water and lower a coverslip over the fibres, taking care to avoid formation of air bubbles.

Examine with low and high power magnifications, darkening the field to identify the features mentioned in the text (see 15.1.3). As the material is in the form of fibres or bundles of fibres and not a cut section, it is not possible to get a uniform view and it will be necessary to vary the focus for different features. Do not expect to see cross-striations throughout the whole of one view, as might be expected from the diagrammatic representation in Fig. 15.1.

The myoglobin shows in the fibres as an amber colour. Any intramuscular fat (only seen in meat from choice cuts) will glisten when viewed in a darkened field. It is difficult to see connective tissue with any degree of definition in such unstained preparations.

Expt. 15.2   COAGULATION TEMPERATURES OF SOLUBLE PROTEINS IN MEAT

The 'drip' which runs from frozen meat as it thaws is an aqueous dispersion of the soluble proteins from within and around the muscle fibres and it provides a suitable material for examining the coagulation of meat proteins. Alternatively such proteins can be extracted by soaking minced meat (raw) in cold water, containing a little salt, for several hours and filtering.

Describe the colour and consistency of the meat protein dispersion. Pour about 50cm³ into a boiling tube and support in a water bath fitted with a stirrer and heated gently. Keep both the water in the water bath and the contents of the boiling tube well stirred to spread the heat. For the latter, a thermometer may be used, with due care, as it will be needed for temperature readings.

Bring the temperature to about 50° C when the fluid will begin to cloud. Stop heating and wait until light-coloured flecks of coagulated protein form. Filter, collecting the filtrate in another boiling tube. Label residue, on the filter paper, 'coagulum 1'. Note the colour of the filtrate and return it to the water bath. Continue heating so that further coagulation occurs. At about 65° C, remove from the water bath and filter as before. Label the residue 'coagulum 2'. Describe the filtrate and return to the water bath. Heat until no red colour remains and a brown coagulum separates from a clear fluid. Note the temperature at which this change occurs. Filter to obtain 'coagulum 3'.

Compare the colours and textures of coagula 1, 2 and 3, and test to verify the protein nature of each. Also test the final filtrate to determine whether any of the proteins in meat are not subject to heat coagulation.

Finally take about 20cm³ of the original meat protein dispersion in another boiling tube and heat thoroughly in a boiling water bath for about 10 minutes. Compare the texture of this coagulum with 1, 2 and 3.

Attempt to relate results to likely textures of meat cooked at different temperatures.

REFERENCE

Ministry of Agriculture, Fisheries and Food (1974). *Food standards committee report on novel protein foods*, HMSO.

FURTHER READING

Griswold, R. M. (1962). *The Experimental study of foods*, Constable.
Lawrie, R. A. (1979). *Meat science*, 3rd rev. edn., Pergamon.
Watkin, Gerald (1976). *British Food Fish*, Pub: Witherby & Co., Ltd., for The Worshipful Company of Fishmongers.
Pirie, N. W. (editor) (1975). *Food Protein Sources*.
Unilever, Ltd. (1976). *Plant protein foods*.

CHAPTER XVI

EGGS

16.1 ORIGINS

By the term eggs we ordinarily mean the eggs of the domestic fowl, but these are not the only edible eggs. The eggs of ducks, geese and turkeys as well as those of such wild birds as the plover, gull and heron have all been used as human food; other eggs used as food are those of the turtle and many varieties of fish, e.g. sturgeon (caviar), and herring (roe). For our purpose we shall confine ourselves to the hen's egg, which constitutes the chief source of our supply of eggs.

16.2 STRUCTURE

It will materially assist our understanding of the structure of an egg if we realize at the outset that it is a living organism consisting of an embryo or germ and its store of food enclosed in the protective shell. Everything about an egg is wonderfully designed by nature to ensure the safe development of its living embryo into a young chick, able to step out of the shell into the outside world and capable of very largely fending for itself.

One end of a hen's egg is narrow and the other broad and blunt. This shape has several advantages. It prevents the egg from rolling far from the nest, since it rolls in a circle if accidentally moved. This is particularly important in the case of eggs laid on the ground or on narrow cliff ledges as those of sea fowl. The ovoid shape also helps the close packing of the eggs in the nest and materially increases the resistance of the shell to external pressure.

The shell consists chiefly of chalk (calcium carbonate) with small quantities of calcium phosphate and organic matter. The shell is porous to allow the passage of air into the interior of the egg; it is through these pores that the living embryo and the developing chick obtain the necessary oxygen for respiration and that surplus carbon dioxide escapes. Unfortunately also this porous character of the shell allows the entry of bacteria into the egg, which cause the putrefaction of the contents. A freshly laid egg has a mucous covering which prevents this. Hence the higher price asked in some countries for clean unwashed eggs since this coating is removed by washing. Underneath the shell is a thin parchment-like membrane, called the keratin membrane, which at the broad end of the egg divides into two layers to form an air chamber. Inside the shell membrane are the 'white' and the 'yolk' (see Fig. 16.1).

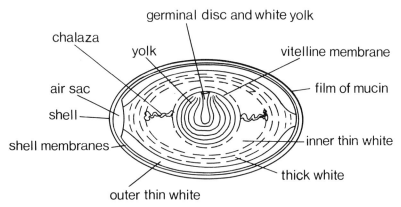

FIG. 16.1. Diagram of a fowl's egg

The white is divided into three layers: thin white, thick white, thin white. The thick white contains more carbon dioxide, which alters its pH and causes the colloid to become more viscous than in the thin white.

The yolk is a golden yellow fluid mass enclosed in a thin elastic membrane, and spherical in shape. It contains the germinal disc or living embryo, which can be seen in a fertile egg as a small circular speck underneath the yolk membrane (the vitelline membrane). The yolk is not of the same consistency throughout, but consists of layers, laid down during development within the oviduct. There is a very light yolk, the white yolk, passing from the embryo to the centre of the yolk. Attached to the vitelline membrane of the yolk are two thick fibrous bands, the chalazae or balancers. The other ends are attached to the thick white. As the egg gets older the thick white gives up its carbon dioxide and becomes thinner. It can no longer hold the yolk in position, so the latter floats upwards and rests against the keratin membrane. Also the yolk receives water by means of osmosis from the thick white and accordingly increases in volume. This stretches the vitelline membrane so that it tends to break. It is for such reasons that it becomes impossible to break an old egg without breaking the yolk. It also accounts for the spread of an egg in poaching and frying. The fact of the yolk being lighter in the region of the embryo ensures that the embryo will be upper-most and nearest to the heat of the hen's body. Should the egg be moved, the fibrous balancers allow the yolk to revolve slowly inside the egg until the embryo is again uppermost.

16.3   WEIGHT AND COMPOSITION OF EGGS

The average weight of a hen's egg is about 55g and its approximate composition is as follows: Shell and membrane, 10·1 per cent; white, 59·7 per cent; yolk, 30·2 per cent. Without the shell the proportions of white and yolk are: white, 66·4 per cent and yolk, 33·6 per cent, so that there is almost exactly twice as much white as yolk. It is obvious from Table 16.1 that the yolk is greatly superior in food value to the white.

Table 16.1   Composition of Hen's Egg

	Water %	Protein %	Fat %	Ash %	Undeter-mined %	kJ (per 100g)
Whole egg (without shell)	73·7	12·3	11·26	1·1	1·64	662
White	87·2	10·7	0·1	0·6	1·4	155
Yolk	47·1	15·5	33·3	2·0	2·1	1470

The white of egg or egg albumen is essentially protein in charac-ter. Almost 70 per cent of egg white protein is ovalbumin. The yolk is much richer and more complex in character. It contains much less water, more protein and a high proportion of fats. In addition to ovalbumin, egg yolk contains the phosphorized protein, vitellin, the phosphorized fat, lecithin, and the sterol, cholesterol. Lecithin is a phosphorylated fat. It is an excellent emulsifying agent (see 4.3.9 and 6.2.3). This makes yolk of egg use-ful in linking up oil with watery substances, e.g. olive oil and vinegar in making mayonnaise. It often softens the crumb in baking. The fats of yolk consist of olein and stearin with small amounts of palmitin. The mineral salts contain valuable calcium and iron com-pounds. The characteristic colour is due to the presence in it of the colouring material xanthophyll.

Eggs are fairly rich in all the vitamins except nicotinic acid and ascorbic acid. Thiamin, riboflavin and vitamins A and D are found in the egg yolk.

In spite of the greater food value of egg yolk it does not command so high a price as egg white when the two are sold separately. This is because of the foaming powers of egg white in which the egg yolk is deficient. It should be remembered however that egg yolk is a valuable ingredient in baked goods on account of the rich colour it imparts and its enriching, flavouring and shortening action, apart from its emulsifying effects. The best results are obtained when the whole egg is used for confectionery purposes. Generally speaking, whole eggs are capable of aerating an equal weight of flour. They set around the raising agent, and a low gluten flour can then be used in baking. They also form additive colloids with milk, giving a set as in scrambled eggs and baked custards.

16.4   COOKING OF EGGS

The digestion of raw eggs begins in the stomach and is completed in the small intestine. Rennin will not precipitate egg protein as it will casein of milk. This gives time for egg to be digested. New laid eggs are more easily digested than eggs which are several days old, but the most easily digested form of egg is one which has been lightly boiled. A hard-boiled egg is slower to digest than either a raw egg or a lightly boiled one. The same applies to other methods of cooking, e.g. frying, scrambling, poaching, etc. By whatever method an egg is cooked the result is always the same—the coagulation of the proteins. This coagulation begins at 62° C, so that fully boiling water is not essential to the 'boiling' of an egg. Raw egg white contains a protein avidin which renders biotin unavailable. Cooking prevents this by denaturing the avidin.

16.4.1   Uses of eggs in food preparation

In addition to their use directly as food and as aerating and enriching agents in sponge and cake mixtures, eggs are used in omelettes, custards, Yorkshire and other puddings, etc. Whites are used separately in such items as meringues, macaroons, royal icing and certain types of biscuits. Egg yolks are used in pouring custards and in choux pastry. They are also used in mayonnaise for their lecithin content.

16.5 STORAGE OF EGGS

When eggs are to be kept for some time they should be placed in a suitable tray with the blunt end containing the air chamber uppermost so that it does not bear the weight of the egg. In this way the yolk is kept in its proper position, surrounded by the white; the white is less likely to deteriorate into the condition known as 'watery' white. The white has a bactericidal action, strongly putrefactive bacteria disappearing from it on incubation; the yolk on the other hand is favourable to the growth of bacteria. About 10 per cent of ordinary eggs are infected in the yolk.

The ideal storage temperature for eggs is 10° C and they should not be in close contact with other strong smelling foods and household goods as they tend to absorb the odour.

16.6 TESTING OF EGGS

On account of their high nutritive qualities eggs are an excellent medium for the rapid multiplication of bacteria which rapidly putrefy the food contents. The sulphur compounds of the albumin yield sulphuretted hydrogen as a decomposition product, and it is this gas which gives the distinctive smell to a rotten egg. Another cause which renders eggs unsuitable for human food is the partial development of the embryo owing to irregular collection or accidental incubation. Since the egg is enclosed in a mineral shell it is impossible to know by ordinary visual examination whether the contents of the egg are good or bad until the shell is broken when it is sometimes forcibly apparent that things are not as they should be. Some simple method of testing the quality and freshness of a whole egg is obviously desirable, and two methods are in common use. These tests are the brine test and the candling test.

16.6.1 **Brine test**

The brine test consists in placing the egg in a 10 per cent salt solution—100g salt per litre of water in a tall jar—and is a simple and infallible test. A newly laid egg will sink in such a solution and lie flat at the bottom of the jar. An older egg has lost weight by evaporation of water through its porous shell, while the shrinkage and drying of the contents enlarge the air chamber. As a result, the egg becomes lighter and more buoyant with age. A two-day-old egg will float near the bottom of the solution with its broad end upwards. A three-day-old egg will float about half way up the solution and one five days old or more will float on the surface.

Thus the older the egg the nearer the surface it floats. While it is not always possible to judge the exact age of an egg by this method, it is easy to decide whether the egg is fresh or not.

16.6.2 Candling test

The candling test is dependent upon the transparency of eggs to light and not upon their buoyancy. It is a quicker method and more suitable for large-scale work than the brine test but requires skill and experience to obtain reliable results. The apparatus consists of a lamp surrounded by a metal shade bored with a hole. The egg to be tested is placed against the hole, slowly turned between finger and thumb, and the transparency of the egg observed. For home use a simple form of candling lamp can be improvized by cutting a hole in a sheet of stiff cardboard, placing the egg against the hole and holding the cardboard up to some source of light. Alternatively an electric bulb can be placed in a cardboard box and the egg placed in a hole in the lid.

It is not sufficient merely to hold an egg near some source of light, since light can pass round the egg and obscure the test. Only light actually passing through the egg must reach the eye of the observer. When a new laid egg is tested by this method the white appears dense and homogeneous, the air chamber is small and the yolk is dimly seen in the middle of the egg. In an older egg the white appears cloudy, the air chamber is enlarged and the yolk is displaced to the top of the egg, because the chalazae can no longer hold it in place. A rotten egg is opaque.

16.7 SPOILAGE

'Spots' in eggs are due to bacteria, blood or mould growth. The term 'spot rot' is applied to eggs in which the germ is dead and decomposing. Moulds often develop in eggs, old eggs being more susceptible to their growth than fresh eggs. Bacteria also cause decomposition. 'White rot' shown in sour or addled eggs is in the first stage pale yellow and watery. 'Mixed rots' are in a more advanced stage, and then the yolk is rarely intact, the contents are thin and sour, and sulphur odours are given off. 'Black rot' marks the last stage of decomposition, when the contents are very dark and appear mixed with water, with a strong smell of sulphuretted hydrogen. Fishy and musty flavours are also caused by micro-organisms. Hens can pass on *Salmonella* infection to man through their eggs and could therefore be a cause of food poisoning. Cases from this source are however comparatively rare, cases of food poisoning due to eating duck eggs are far more common and consequently all duck eggs should be thoroughly cooked before being eaten.

16.8 PRESERVATION OF EGGS

Egg supplies have greatly improved as regards numbers due to the new methods of production by battery and deep litter. Fresh eggs are now available all the year round.

The three methods used for the preservation of eggs are freezing, drying and pickling.

16.8.1 Freezing

Whole eggs cannot be successfully frozen in a home freezer and neither can cooked eggs. Separated eggs however will freeze satisfactorily. Egg yolks should have sugar or salt added before packing in a suitable container. This will prevent the yolks thickening. Egg whites, for freezing, can be packed without additives and both whites and yolks will keep up to ten months in a home freezer. Eggs which are not first quality are processed into frozen egg. The eggs are washed, broken and then carefully examined. Any unsatisfactory eggs are discarded as they could contaminate the whole batch. The eggs can be pasteurized by heating to 63° C for one minute. They are thoroughly mixed, sieved and then put into large cans and frozen by being left at −16° C for 72 hours. Cans can be stored frozen for some considerable time and transported in refrigerated ships and vehicles.

16.8.2 Dried Egg

This is a convenient form of preserved egg used by the catering industry and not generally available to the housewife. Eggs which are as fresh as possible are mixed to a homogeneous liquid, pasteurized and then spray dried. This limits the growth of undesirable bacteria. The method used is similar to that used for processing spray dried milk (see 13.6.6). A too high temperature during the drying process must be avoided if the dried egg is to have an acceptable flavour. The moisture content of the finished product should not exceed 5 per cent; sometimes the pH of the liquid egg is adjusted to 6·5 and then dried to 1 per cent moisture. The addition of sugar to liquid egg before drying gives a product which reconstitutes more readily and which is quite acceptable for cake-making. Dried egg should not be reconstituted for any length of time before use as micro-organisms present multiply in the liquid egg.

16.8.3 Pickling

This is the common method used in the domestic preservation of eggs so that the eggs can be bought when they are plentiful and cheap, and used when they are scarce and dear. The new laid eggs are placed in a solution of water-glass (sodium silicate) or lime water. The pores in the shell are hermetically sealed and bacteria are prevented from entering the egg. It must be remembered however that there are bacteria in the egg even before it is laid, so that some decomposition will take place. This decomposition will be very slow since the supply of air is cut off, and only the anaerobic bacteria can multiply in the absence of oxygen. A 'pickled' egg will remain fit for use 9 or 12 months. When a 'pickled' egg is boiled the shell almost invariably cracks, because the pores of the shell are sealed, and the expansion of the air chamber during heating causes a sufficient internal pressure to break the shell. The breaking of the shell can be prevented by making a small hole through the broad end of the egg into the air chamber by means of a pin or needle.

16.9 THE EGG TRADE AND THE EEC

Marketing standards for eggs are controlled by Regulation (EEC) No. 1619/68 of the Council, 1968.

Egg Weight Grading	per egg
Grade 1	70g or over
Grade 2	65g and under 70g
Grade 3	60g and under 65g
Grade 4	55g and under 60g
Grade 5	50g and under 55g
Grade 6	45g and under 50g
Grade 7	under 45g

A tolerance of 10 per cent is allowed on weight grading: out of 100 eggs purporting to be, say grade 3, there may be up to 10 eggs from grades 2 and 4, but not more than 6 of these may be grade 4.

Egg quality classes
  Class A   fresh eggs
  Class B   second quality or preserved eggs
  Class C   non-graded eggs intended for the manufacture of food-stuffs for human consumption

Class A eggs may be described as 'extra' if they meet certain fairly stringent conditions. Packers intending to market eggs under the description extra must be separately registered. Eggs which are to be marketed as extras must be collected from producers twice weekly, once weekly is sufficient for all other eggs.

Stamping

Eggs in class A may be, but do not have to be stamped.

Eggs in classes B and C must be stamped, except for those broken out on the premises and eggs in class C which are so cracked that they cannot be stamped.

Regulations regarding labelling are also laid down. In addition to quality and weight grading marks egg packs should have a number indicating the country of packing (9 stands for the UK).

PRACTICAL EXERCISES

*All experiments require standard precautions; those marked * involve particular hazards and should be supervised*

Expt. 16.1 GENERAL EXAMINATION

Note the shape of the egg and the porous character of the shell. Break the shell and gently tip the contents on to a glass plate on a dark ground. Look for features referred to in the text (see 16.2) including distribution of thick and thin white, chalazae, vitelline membrane, germinal disc. Examine the inside of the shell with the double membrane and the air sac at the blunt end.

Test the white with pH papers (wide range at first, then narrow range) and note the alkalinity, exceptional in foodstuffs.

Separate the yolk from the white as completely as possible. Weigh each part including the shell and derive an approximate percentage composition in terms of white, yolk and shell.

Reserve material for the tests below.

Expt. 16.2 DEMONSTRATION OF FOAMING PROPERTIES OF EGG WHITE

Into one test tube place 2cm³ water and 2cm³ egg white. Into another place 4cm³ water and a few drops of washing-up detergent. Shake vigorously and simultaneously. Compare the foam produced in each. Allow to stand and compare stability, also the effect of renewed shaking.

Fill each tube with water, as in washing out the tube. Look for evidence of loss of solubility in one or both foams.

Expt. 16.3 DEMONSTRATION OF EMULSIFYING PROPERTIES OF EGG YOLK

Into each of three test tubes put 1cm³ cooking oil and 1cm³ water. Add to one 1cm³ washing-up detergent diluted 1 in 4, to the second 1cm³ egg yolk and to the third 1cm³ water. Shake each test tube equally and compare for evidence of emulsification, allowing each to stand in order to observe the stability of any emulsion formed.

Expt. 16.4 COAGULATION TEMPERATURES

(i) **Egg White**
Put some egg white into a small ignition tube (use of a Pasteur pipette (teat pipette) will assist in this). Fasten to the bulb of a thermometer with an elastic band. Hold the thermometer in some water which is being gently heated and move the thermometer about to distribute the heat. Observe closely for evidence of coagulation—opacity—and note the temperature at which it begins and is completed.

Record the coagulation temperature range.

(ii) **Egg Yolk**
Repeat (i) with yolk. Evidence of coagulation is harder to discern. The use of a fine glass rod inserted into the ignition tube and moved to detect viscosity changes will help.

Record coagulation temperature range and compare with that for yolk.

(iii) **Whole egg (beaten)**
Repeat (i) for whole egg and then for another sample whose pH has been lowered to 5·5 with dilute acetic acid. Sweeten a third sample with a little sugar and make yet another determination.

Relate results to effects on the coagulation of eggs from other ingredients with which they are combined during cooking.

Expt. 16.5 CONSTITUENTS OF EGG WHITE

Dilute about 3cm³ egg white with 10cm³ deionized water and mix. Look for slight precipitation of ovo-globulin. To a 2cm³ sample add salt, a few grains at a time, inverting between additions, with the intention of re-dissolving the globulin. (See text references to protein classification according to solubility and to 'salting-in'—5.2.1 and 5.6.)

To the remainder add dilute acetic acid dropwise to bring pH to 5·5 (use narrow range pH paper). This precipitates ovo-mucin and most of the globulin. Filter and verify the protein nature of the precipitate (see Expt. 5.3, Biuret or Sakaguchi). Boil the filtrate to coagulate the albumin (and any remaining globulin). Again verify the protein nature of the precipitate. Any protein remaining in the filtrate will be ovo-mucoid, a carbohydrate–protein complex, giving positive both for soluble protein and for soluble carbohydrate tests.

*Expt. 16.6 CONSTITUENTS OF EGG YOLK

Extract triglycerides and lecithin from about 3cm³ yolk by shaking well with 1cm³ alcohol followed by 10cm³ ether (CARE).
(*a*) Filter (residue)
    Wash with a little ether. Test for protein and for phosphate. Positive results for each confirm the presence of the phospho-protein, vitellin.
(*b*) Filtrate
    Concentrate by allowing it to evaporate in a shallow dish. Dip in a strip of filter paper. When the ether evaporates, look for a grease spot. To the remnant of filtrate add a slight excess of acetone and look for precipitation of lecithin (see Expt. 4.5).

Expt. 16.7 SHELL

Place a piece of shell in a test tube and add dilute hydrochloric acid. Warm slightly and test any gas given off for carbon dioxide (see Expt. 12.1). Continue warming, adding extra acid if required until mineral matter is dissolved. Remove the shell membrane and verify its protein nature (see Expt. 5.3, Xanthoproteic).

Neutralize the shell solution with dilute ammonium hydroxide and test for calcium ions (see Expt. 7.2).

Expt. 16.8 STORAGE CHANGES

A collection of eggs of different ages will prove instructive. If dated on receipt and stored in a refrigerator, changes due to evaporation will proceed, together with structural changes in the proteins, but bacterial activity will be impeded and there will be no offensive smell when the eggs are opened. If it is necessary to demonstrate this, storage in dry conditions at room temperature is necessary.

Apply the following procedures to a selection of eggs of different 'ages' which have been stored in comparable conditions.

(i) **Candling**

Examine eggs with a candling lamp which is hooded so that all the light received has passed through the egg and not around it. This enables the position of the yolk to be viewed and also gives an indication of the size of the air sac. Experienced workers are able to distinguish blemishes, e.g. 'meat spots', 'blood spots', a developing embryo in a fertilized egg, all of which are causes for rejection of eggs, although, in fact, there is no real loss of wholesomeness.

(ii) **Brine Test for Density**

The density of an egg falls during storage due to the escape of water as vapour and replacement by air which is less dense and which expands the air sac.

Nearly fill a tall cylindrical glass jar with 10% brine and lower each egg into it in turn. Note the position taken up by each and record this against the age of the egg.

(iii) **Contents**

Carefully break each egg on to a glass plate on a dark ground and compare for (1) proportion of thick to thin white and (2) doming of the yolk.

Ageing affects secondary and tertiary structures in the protein, interfering with water binding properties. Viscosity of white is reduced and osmosis causes water to pass from the white into the yolk. In turn this loses viscosity and the vitelline membrane becomes strained and may burst.

If the eggs have aged in the refrigerator, there will be no typical smell of bad eggs and if held for a protracted period, dehydration will alter the nature of the contents of the egg.

Violet–blue fluorescence increases with ageing. This can be checked if an ultraviolet lamp is available.

FURTHER READING

Griswold, R. M. (1962). *The experimental study of foods*, Constable.
Newall, Venetia. *An Egg at Easter*, Routledge & Kegan Paul.

CHAPTER XVII

FRUITS AND VEGETABLES

17.1 Types of Fruits

Botanically considered, a fruit is the modified pistil of a flower or more strictly the ovary and its contents, the ovules, as developed after fertilization of the egg cells by pollen. The pistil consists in all of the following: the stigma on which the pollen grains alight, the style down which the pollen tubes grow, and the ovary, an enclosure in many instances partitioned, in which are contained one or more ovules. After fertilization the ovule develops as a seed, its integuments becoming the seed coat (testa) within which is contained the embryo, either filling the whole of the space, or being enclosed still further in food stores or endosperm. Meanwhile the ovary containing the seeds increases considerably in size and is often much modified in structure, its wall becoming the pericarp.

Fruits are conveniently divided into two main classes according to the character of the pericarp; dry fruits and succulent fruits. In the former class the pericarp is on the whole dry and tough, and not such as would normally be eaten, either as a fruit or vegetable; examples are the husks of hazel nuts and the peascods of peas. In succulent fruits the pericarp is often pulpy, and when it contains sugar and substances of flavour and aroma may be both attractive and edible; this would appear to be their significance in nature, attracting animals so that they might disperse the seeds. Succulent fruits are usually further divided into five main groups:

Berries: grapes, tomatoes, bananas, gooseberries, blackcurrants, redcurrants.

Pepos: melons, cucumbers, squashes, vegetable marrows.

Hesperidia: citrus fruits—oranges, lemons, limes, grapefruit.

Drupes: stone fruits—plums, apricots, peaches, cherries.

Pomes: apples, pears and quinces.

Aggregate fruits are strawberries and raspberries. Collective fruits are mulberry, fig and pineapple.

In stone fruits the pericarp is formed of three distinct layers or tissues: the outer skin, rind or epicarp; the pulp or mesocarp, often edible; and the stone or endocarp within which is the kernel or seed containing the embryo. In the case of berries the innermost layer of the pericarp is not stony or in any way toughened, and is usually scarcely different from the pulpy mesocarp; the epicarp is the skin or peel. Among berry fruits are gooseberry, grape (including raisin and currant), black- and redcurrants, banana and tomato.

Common examples of drupes are apricot, peach, plum, sloe and cherry. The almond, coconut and walnut are examples of drupes; but as usually marketed the two outer layers (skin and pulp) have been stripped, and only the endocarp or stone left with the kernel inside.

Besides the drupes and berries, there are other types of succulent fruits which are distinguished botanically from these in some important respect or other. The blackberry, dewberry, raspberry and loganberry are aggregate fruits consisting of several small drupes and not, as their names would suggest, berries. The mulberry is a collective fruit formed by the fusion of the fruit forms of several originally separate flowers. The apple, pear and medlar are botanically falsefruits or pseudocarps, because in their cases the greater part of the pulp is formed from the hollow receptacle of the flowers; the core with the pips being the representative of the original ovary. The pulp of the strawberry is formed by the much enlarged and fleshy receptacle on which are carried scattered dry achenes. The pineapple is another pseudocarp; in its case the whole inflorescence stalk bearing many flowers becomes more or less succulent. The fig is formed from a deeply hollowed inflorescence axis, within which are scattered a large number of separate small flowers.

In many fruits, especially if freshly plucked, the more or less withered remnants of the other floral parts, the stalk, sepals, petals and stamens, and in some cases also the style or its scar at the pole of the fruit may be made out. This is where decay begins. In cleaning small fruits for domestic use or for canning or jamming it is these fragments that are removed by riddling and sieving, along with fragments of soil, etc.

17.2 TISSUE STRUCTURES, RIPENING AND SPOILAGE CHANGES

During the formation of a succulent fruit, the ovary walls become considerably enlarged by the rapid development of new tissue, and juicy by the absorption of water. Food reserve material is passed into the developing fruit from the main plant and is laid down in various forms including sugars, starches and organic acids. Cellulose fibres embedded in an amorphous hemicellulose matrix form the cell walls. Pectic substances, which are made up of chains of galacturonic residues (see 3.5.3), form the intercellular cement layer, known as the middle lamella. The firm structure of under-ripe fruit is probably due to the presence of pectic substances in the form of insoluble calcium salts of pectic acid which are decomposed during the ripening process into water-soluble pectin. Enzymes called pectinases are involved. Pectin may be extracted from near-ripe and just-ripe fruit by simmering in water. The colloidal solution forms gels with sugar in correct concentration, aided by the presence of acid. Only those fruits which yield abundant pectin on boiling form a well-set jam; among these are apple, gooseberry and currants, both black and red. Other fruits may be mixed with pectin-rich fruits, as strawberry with gooseberry, or alternatively with prepared pectin, in order to obtain a firm set. Over-ripe fruits give poor yields of pectin due to enzyme activity breaking down the pectin polymers into fragments too small to support a gel.

Another change involved in ripening is hydrolysis of starch by specific enzymes to give sugars, chiefly glucose, with lesser amounts of fructose, which produce sweetness. The tartaric, malic, citric and succinic acids which make unripe fruit particularly sour are either largely converted when the fruit is fully ripe into other substances, including sugars, or their taste is masked by the excess of sugar. The particular flavour of a fruit is due to small quantities of esters (compounds of alcohols with acids) and essential oils, distributed throughout the pulp, and in some cases, as in the citrus fruits, particularly abundant in the rind. Fruit is usually in its most edible condition when the proportions of sugar and acid are so balanced as to be most agreeable to the palate. As fruit ripens it gives off carbon dioxide and water. Ethylene seems to be involved in the ripening and must be produced in the process. Its presence accelerates the ripening of apples, pears, citrus fruit and bananas (see 19.9). Tannic acid is important in flavour development. It gives tang to a flavour, particularly in apples. When fruit is over-ripe some of the sugar and acid are oxidized and the essential oils and esters are destroyed with a consequent loss of aroma and flavour. At the same time the fruit becomes less firmly attached to the plant and presently falls to the ground or bursts and ejects the seeds.

Following harvesting, fruits remain 'alive', in as much as tissue respiration continues, for periods which vary with kind and with storage conditions. There will be some loss of substance and possibly some shrivelling, but no decay until 'death point' is reached. Thereafter, autolysis (self-digestion) will proceed apace, with loss of structure and degradation to a pulpy mass. Fungal spores can now germinate giving mould growths or yeast ferments. In consequence, the once solid structure is transformed into gaseous and soluble matter, suitable for re-cycling in new plant growth.

17.2.1 Enzymic browning

Bruising damages fruit, precipitating spoilage changes. Enzymic browning occurs in bruised or cut tissues of many fruits and some vegetables. Oxidases (see 10.2.6) bring about the conversion of phenolic compounds, notably catechol, to quinones which polymerize to dark brown pigments. Air exclusion and introduction of reducing agents such as ascorbic acid and sulphur dioxide are means of preventing such oxidation changes. Lowering the pH by adding acids or adding soluble salts, two measures which reduce the solubility of the effective enzymes, are other means of inhibiting enzymic browning. Heating destroys enzymes by causing protein denaturation (see 5.4.2); hence the blanching of fruits and vegetables prior to preservation.

17.3 FOOD VALUE OF FRUIT

In most fresh pulpy fruits proteins and carbohydrates form a comparatively small part of their mass, which is usually made up largely of water and of seeds that are rejected in eating. Apart from the dissolved sugars and pectins their value as foodstuffs lies mainly in their minerals and vitamins. It is as protective foods and incidentally as providing a certain amount of suitable roughage rather than as flesh building or energy foods that dessert fruits are to be most valued, and their proper role in a balanced dietary ascribed. The minerals of fruits, organic acid salts or salts of potassium, calcium and iron, when finally oxidized, yield alkaline ash, and consequently in the course of metabolism within the system serve not only to neutralize the acidity due to oxidation of proteins and carbohydrates, but also to maintain the alkalinity of the blood at its normal value. Some fruits contain only traces of the vitamins, but it is the antiscorbutic vitamin, ascorbic acid, that is commonest in fresh fruits, particularly the citrus fruits, oranges, lemons and grapefruit; blackcurrants, redcurrants, strawberries, gooseberries and tomatoes are also good sources. It is for this reason that their consumption is to be most commended. Yet the distribution of vitamins among common fruits varies considerably. While oranges and lemons are particularly rich in ascorbic acid, limes are comparatively deficient. Apples differ considerably in ascorbic acid but a few varieties are fair sources. Tomatoes are more varied than most fruits in their vitamins. The yellow fruits, apricots and peaches and tomatoes, are good sources of carotene, pro-vitamin A.

17.4 VEGETABLES

A great variety of plants and of different parts of them are eaten as vegetables. A rough botanical classification of vegetables commonly used in this country is as follows:

  (i) Green leaves—lettuce, watercress, cabbage, sprouts, spinach, broccoli, mustard and cress, turnip tops and kale.
 (ii) Leaf-stalks—celery and rhubarb.
(iii) Stems—asparagus, sea-kale.
 (iv) Roots—carrot, parsnip, beetroot, swede, turnip, radish.
  (v) Tubers—potato, artichoke.
 (vi) Bulbs—onion, leek, garlic.
(vii) Inflorescences—cauliflower, broccoli.
(viii) Fruits and seeds—cucumber, vegetable marrow, tomato, pulses (peas, beans, etc.), mushroom, pepper, aubergine.

17.4.1 Dietary functions

Apart from those vegetables consisting essentially of reserve organs, such as tubers and bulbs, their chief function as foodstuffs is to provide the protective substances—minerals, vitamins and roughage. In ordinary vegetative structures the amounts of available proteins and carbohydrates are practically negligible; the cellulose of such foods as cabbage and celery, though considerable in bulk, is not digestible, but yet serves a useful purpose in the intestines as roughage. It is only in the reserve organs (e.g. the tubers of potato and artichoke, the roots of carrot and beet, and the bulbs of onion and the like) that there is a considerable proportion of available carbohydrates, as starch or sugar, and in the seeds of the pulses (e.g. pea, bean, etc.) in addition good proportions of protein and fat. This last group of vegetables is consequently of first importance as a source of energy and to a scarcely less extent also of flesh building material. It is upon the potato that the greater part of the population of this country depends for supplementing bread as their chief supply of energy by way of carbohydrates. The potato also contains a small amount of available protein of good grade; it has the further advantage of containing many minerals and most water-soluble vitamins, and particularly it is admirable as a medium for admixture with a great variety of other foodstuffs such as milk, meat, fish, eggs, etc. Onions and leeks are especially rich in sugars, which are also fairly abundant in turnips and parsnips.

The percentage of proteins in leaves is low, but what is present is of the highest grade. A good supply of enzymes has been found among the proteins of the leaves, including the various respiratory enzymes and the enzymes of phosphorylation. The proteins in the leaves function mainly in this way. The chloroplasts in the leaves consist of small green bodies (the grana) in a clear stroma. The chlorophyll and the yellow carotenoid pigments of the leaf are bound to the granum protein. Also bound to the granum proteins are fatty materials and traces of minerals, calcium, iron, copper and zinc. Each cell contains a thousand different enzyme proteins. Many are present in the cytoplasm of the cell, thus accounting for the small amount of protein found there.

Greens are especially rich in ascorbic acid and carotene, so closely related to vitamin A. Most of the vitamins of the B group are well represented: thiamin, riboflavin, nicotinic acid among the commonest, and in addition pyridoxine, pantothenic acid, folic acid and vitamin K.

17.4.2 Cooking

Greens when cooked, especially in an open container or with baking soda—to keep the colour unchanged—lose much of their ascorbic acid. The cooking of vegetables also allows the passage from the tissues of cell sap and its contained mineral salts. If vegetables are boiled in much water the salts pass into the water and are often thrown away with it as waste. It is no better to cook vegetables by steaming, for then ascorbic acid tends to be oxidized. Green vegetables should be plunged into boiling water in small amount to destroy the enzyme oxidase which causes the oxidation of ascorbic acid. They should not be chopped too finely since this allows the cell sap which contains the oxidase to contact the intercellular substance which contains the vitamin. The same contact is induced when vegetables are wilted. Greens should be cooked as short a time as possible. This preserves the texture, and the ascorbic acid and minerals are not leached out to the same extent. Because of this leaching out the cooking water should be used in stocks for soups and for sauces wherever possible.

Chlorophyll, the green pigment in plants, resembles the pigment myoglobin in meat (see Fig. 15.4), but instead of iron, there is magnesium at the centre of the nitrogen ring. When green vegetables are cooked, chlorophyll is broken down with loss of magnesium; the residual pigments being yellowish-green to brown. In acidic conditions, these changes are accelerated and accomplished within normal cooking times. In alkaline conditions, some chlorophyll decomposition occurs but the resulting pigment still contains the magnesium and has a definite green colour; for this reason baking soda used to be added during cooking before its detrimental effect on ascorbic acid content was appreciated. Alkalinity also affects the texture of vegetables. Sodium salts of hemicelluloses and pectic substances (see 3.5.3) are formed and this increases the water-solubility of the inter-cellular cement substance. Consequently there is an increased tendency for cells to separate one from another with loss of firm texture.

17.5 PULSES

Pulses are the dried seeds of leguminous plants, such as peas, beans and lentils: the peanut or earth-nut is also a pulse. They are all particularly rich in proteins. They contain a fair amount of the essential amino-acids, and, in addition, they contain a large amount of indigestible material as cellulose. They are low in methionine, but higher in lysine than the cereals. The arginine and valine content in peanuts, and the arginine and lysine content of soya beans are high even in comparison with animal protein. They also contain a fair amount of starch and oil, particularly peanuts from which arachis oil is extracted for the manufacture of cold-water soap and margarine. Dried pulses require to be well soaked in water and to be cooked slowly—preferably in soft water—and for a prolonged time, to be made digestible. Fresh green pulses are fairly rich in vitamins A, C and E, thiamin and riboflavin, but vitamin D is missing. Dried pulses are seriously lacking in all except the B group vitamins. However, when legumes are germinated for five days ascorbic acid is generated in good value. Boiling legumes with soda with a view to improving their colour destroys thiamin, and any ascorbic acid present. During recent years the preservation of peas, as of other vegetables, has made tremendous strides, very largely the result of scientific research not only on the details of processing and the design of plant machinery, but also in the hybridization of varieties with desired features of size, colour, food contents and cooking qualities.

Soya bean, a legume of Manchurian origin, since 1918 has entered the world's markets as a particularly valuable foodstuff with a very wide range of uses. It contains a very high percentage of good quality protein (44.2) and some 20 per cent of fat, which when extracted can be used, among other purposes, for the manufacture of margarine.

An artificial milk made from soya beans has much the same

appearance and composition as ordinary milk, with the advantage that it is much less liable to spoilage by bacteria, and may therefore be kept sweet for long periods. It is suitable for those with lactose or milk protein intolerances. Meat analogues, currently available, are derived from soya protein (see 15.6).

17.6 NUTS

Nuts are various in origin and botanical character. Strictly, a nut is a fruit with a hard pericarp within which is a single seed, e.g. the cob or hazel nut and the sweet chestnut, but popularly the term covers any fruit or seed with a hard case, and so includes examples where the stone or endocarp of drupes has been stripped of the outer soft parts, as the walnut, shell almond and coconut, and where the outermost coat or testa of the seed is woody, as the Brazil nut.

Nuts generally are richly stored with protein, fat and carbohydrate, and contain the B vitamins and most mineral food salts. The proteins in the main are of good biological value, and the most perfect of any vegetable proteins to replace animal proteins in a balanced diet; almond and walnut are best in this respect. Nuts, including pine kernels and peanuts, are the mainstay of a complete vegetarian diet. Coconut shredding or copra, though rich in oil is, however, poor in most other food principles—proteins, salts and vitamins. The oil is used for many industrial purposes, including the manufacture of cold water and sea water soaps. Kernels of Brazil nuts are very rich in oil—some 70 per cent—and consequently are peculiarly liable to decay in transport and storage.

PRACTICAL EXERCISES

All experiments require standard precautions; those in which appreciation of results involves tasting should be carried out in hygienic conditions, free from chemical contamination

Expt. 17.1 MICROSCOPIC EXAMINATION
General Structures
Use the firm tissue of vegetables such as potato, carrot and beetroot, and such fruits as apples and pears. Cut sections as thinly as possible using a dissecting scalpel or razor. Spread out on a microscope slide, add a drop of water and lower a coverslip into position. Examine under low power magnification. If satisfied that the section is thin enough (which it may well be around the edges) to provide views of cell structures, go on to examine under high power. Look for features common to all, such as cellulosic cell walls. Also look for particular features such as pigmented cell sap (beetroot), cellular inclusions, especially starch granules (potatoes), and orange–

red angular carotenoid chromoplasts (carrots). Non-cellular granular structures, schleroids, can be seen scattered through the tissue of pear. With promising sections, proceed as follows:

Staining

Methylene blue is taken up by cellulose and will give greater definition. Iodine will likewise, in addition to identifying starch granules distinctly. Remove the slide from the microscope and add one drop of stain to one side of the coverslip. Draw the stain through the section by applying a strip of filter paper to the opposite side of the coverslip. Allow a few moments to elapse and then wash away excess stain with water, irrigating the section in the way described for staining.

Re-examine under the microscope, with the magnification found to be most suitable, and draw the features seen.

Expt. 17.2 MICROSCOPIC EVIDENCE OF COOKING CHANGES IN POTATOES

Cut a section from raw potato and another from cooked potato. Mount both sections in water, side by side, on the same microscope slide. Stain with iodine as above. Examine with low power. Look for (1) changes in cellular contents, and (2) changes in the adhesion of cell to cell.

By moving the slide from one section to the other, the two states of the tissue can readily be compared. In the raw tissue, discrete starch granules within cells should be discerned. By contrast, in the cooked tissues, masses of stained starch will be seen to fill the cells which tend to separate from each other due to dissolution of intercellular cement substances.

Expt. 17.3 ENZYMIC BROWNING, ITS INCIDENCE AND PREVENTION

(i) Susceptible Materials

Obtain a selection of pale-coloured fruits and vegetables, e.g. potato, turnip, celery, pear, apple, banana, grape. Cut thin slices from each and leave exposed to the atmosphere for about 30 minutes. Record the degree of browning which has occurred in each.

Select ONE which shows appreciable browning and use it in further trials.

(ii) Conditions Affecting Browning

Cut eight similar segments from the one fruit or vegetable, number 1–8 and pair them for treatment as shown:

1. Leave intact
2. Chop or grate

3. Cut into four fragments
4. Break into four fragments

5. Bruise slightly
6. Bruise heavily
   without breaking

7. Leave in warm room until
   some evidence of browning
8. Leave in refrigerator
   for same time

Relate findings to the theory that such browning it due to enzymes which operate in ruptured cells.

(iii) Preventive Measures

Cut eight similar segments from the same fruit or vegetable and number 1–8, and treat as follows:

1. Leave immersed in water
2. Immerse in water 30 seconds, then leave exposed
3. Immerse in 5% vinegar solution 30 seconds, then leave exposed
4. Immerse in 5% ascorbic acid solution 30 seconds, then leave exposed
5. Immerse in 5% Camden tablet (sulphite) solution 30 seconds, then leave exposed
6. Immerse in boiling water 30 seconds, then leave exposed
7. Leave exposed without any treatment.

Compare results and record in terms of evidence of browning and any success in preventing it.

Expt. 17.4   COOKING OF VEGETABLES

(i) pH Effects on Green Vegetables

Wash and thoroughly chop some cabbage. Mix to give uniform distribution of tissues and weigh out four 50g samples, A, B, C and D.

A   Cook in tap water (check pH), bringing $100cm^3$ to boiling in a small covered pan, adding cabbage and noting the time at which boiling recommences. Cook at boiling, with lid on until judged to have achieved an acceptable texture. Record time for this.
B   Cook exactly as for A but in $90cm^3$ tap water with $10cm^3$ vinegar added (check pH).
C   Cook exactly as for A but in $100cm^3$ tap water with 1g sodium bicarbonate added (check pH).

Compare results for colour and texture. If possible, obtain acceptability ratings from independent tasters.

NB. Vitamin C levels in green vegetables are influenced by pH. See Expt. 8.1 and 8.2 for methods which could be adapted to investigate this.

(ii) pH Effects on Dried Pulses

Use either dried marrowfat peas or haricot beans. Weight out four 20g samples, A, B, C and D.

A   Soak overnight (16 hours) in $100cm^3$ tap water with 1g sodium bicarbonate added, then cook in the same solution until the texture is considered acceptable. Note the time taken for cooking.
B   Soak overnight (16 hours) in $90cm^3$ tap water with $10cm^3$ vinegar added. Then cook in the same solution for the time taken for A.
C   Soak overnight (16 hours) in $100cm^3$ tap water. Then cook in the same water for the time taken for A.
D   Cook in $100cm^3$ tap water with 1g sodium bicarbonate added for the time taken in A but without soaking.

Compare the textures of the products and the evidence for procedures adopted for the cooking of pulses.

FURTHER READING

Duckworth, R. B. (1966). *Fruit and vegetables*, Pergamon.
Grigson, J. (1978). *Vegetable Book,* Michael Joseph.
Janick, Schery, Woods, Rullan (1974). *Plant Science*, Freeman & Co.

CHAPTER XVIII

SUGAR

18.1 GROWTH OF SUGAR INDUSTRY

The history of sugar as a source of food goes back to ancient times. Sugar cane was first cultivated in India, in the Ganges valley in what is now the State of Bihar. It spread slowly eastward to China and more rapidly westward into the Nile Valley. The Arabs carried its cultivation along the southern shores of the Mediterranean into Spain and Portugal and from here it was introduced to the New World. Columbus took sugar cane to Hispaniola on his second voyage in 1493. From the eleventh to the fifteenth century sugar was scarce and expensive. The lucrative sugar industry based on the slave trade made sugar more plentiful and cheap in North America and Europe. In England the consumption per head rose from about 2kg in 1700 to about 6kg in 1780.

Sugar was first extracted commercially from beet early in the nineteeth century during the Napoleonic Wars when supplies of cane sugar to France were cut off by the Royal Navy. It was not until after 1828 in France and 1836 in Germany that its manufacture was a commercial success. In the second half of the nineteenth century the quantity of beet sugar produced began to challenge the production of cane sugar. In 1970 the proportions of sugar produced were approximately 60 per cent cane sugar to 40 per cent beet sugar. Beet sugar is grown in a temperate climate, the USSR and the USA being the biggest producers. In the UK about 160 000 hectares, mostly confined to East Anglia, Lincolnshire and West Midlands, are under sugar beet cultivation. This produces rather less than 1 000 000 metric tonnes per annum. The sugar beet industry in this country was stimulated to a large extent by the drastic reduction in food supplies during the First World War. Nowadays about a third of the sugar in the UK is home produced. Sugar consumption, after a rapid rise up to the 1960s has reduced somewhat in the UK and the average consumption at the present is just under a kilogramme per head per week. Of this a little over half is as packeted sugar, the remainder is in the form of sweets, biscuits, cakes, ice cream, soft drinks, etc. Excess consumption of sugar is likely to give cause for concern as it can contribute to obesity and dental caries.

18.2 MANUFACTURE OF SUGAR

The manufacture of sugar from either cane or beet falls into three main stages: extraction of juice; concentration of the juice and crystallization; and refining of the sugar. The initial extraction and processing of cane and beet sugar varies somewhat in the processing factories. Cane sugar is initially processed in the country of origin but refining is carried out in the UK. There is no difference between the end products obtained. However raw sugar, i.e. unrefined sugar from beet, may have a less attractive taste and smell. The initial methods of extraction and processing at processing factories vary slightly.

18.2.1 Extraction of cane sugar

Sugar cane, an enormous grass rather like bamboo, is either mechanically harvested or cut by hand and taken to the processing factory as soon as possible. The cane is first shredded finely and then passed through sets of heavy rollers to extract the juice. Juice or water is sprayed over the partly crushed grain entering the last sets of rollers to increase extraction. The left over fibre, bagasse, is used for boiler fuel at the mill and for the manufacture of paper and hardboard. The solution obtained contains about 13 per cent sugar and 3 per cent impurities. This is then boiled and lime added; some impurities are precipitated, whilst others coagulate and form a scum on the surface. The impurities are removed by filtration and the solution is ready for concentration.

18.2.2 Extraction of beet sugar

Sugar beet is a biennial root crop. The beet is harvested mechanically by a combine that removes the top and lifts the beet from the soil. The tops are used for cattle food and the beet are taken to the factories, washed, sliced and put into large rotating cylinders full of hot water at 70° C. The sugar goes into solution due to osmotic interchange between the water and the sugary sap of the beet cells. Most of the non-sugar solids are left behind. The process is designed to ensure that the maximum amount of sugar is extracted by the minimum amount of water. The solution passes through a set of diffusers operated on a counter current system—concentrated juice passing into a diffuser which contains the unextracted beet, and fresh hot water passing over the exhausted beet pulp. Proportions of sugar and impurities in the solution obtained are similar to those found in the extraction of sugar from sugar cane. The beet sugar solution is treated with slaked lime and carbon dioxide. The calcium carbonate formed settles to the bottom with most of the impurities. The precipitate is removed by filtration from the solution which is ready for concentration.

18.2.3 Concentration and crystallization

The extracted juice is progressively concentrated by being evaporated with steam coils under several stages of reduced pressure and corresponding temperatures: the pressures range from 640mm of mercury for the fresh juice to 150mm for the most concentrated and the temperatures from 56° C to 94° C. When fully concentrated the dark brown liquor contains 50–55 per cent sugar. It is filtered and further evaporated to a concentration of some 85 per cent, at which point crystallization begins around the steam coils, and is allowed to complete in cooling tanks with stirrers. The crystals are separated from the molasses, or mother liquor, in centrifugal machines. The molasses is further evaporated and allowed to crystallize to give a 'second product sugar', leaving a second molasses, from which more crystal sugar may be obtained if required. Molasses from beet juice may contain 40 to 50 per cent sucrose and a little (1·5 per cent) invert sugar as a result of the action of acid. Sugar does not however crystallize from this molasses owing to the presence of 8–10 per cent mineral salts, notably calcium. Molasses are used for manufacturing rum and industrial alcohol.

18.2.4 Refining

Raw sugar still contains some molasses. Hot water is added to soften the molasses, it is then centrifuged and the separated syrup is boiled, this process extracting more sugar. The sugar is dissolved in fresh hot water and filtered and treated with lime once more. Carbon dioxide is passed through the liquid. This converts the lime to form calcium carbonate which traps any remaining impurities. The liquid is filtered once more and decolorized by the use of animal charcoal. The clear liquid is boiled in vacuum pans until a super-saturated solution is produced. Crystallization is initiated by seeding with a crystal of sugar. This is a complex skilled operation and careful timing is critical. Different timings will produce different sugars, e.g. ordinary granulated sugar, caster sugar with smaller crystals or preserving sugar with very large crystals. The sugar crystals are suspended in syrup and are removed by centrifuging.

18.3   VARIOUS GRADES OF SUGAR

All sugars are equally sweet if they are examined weight-for-weight. A fine sugar will dissolve more rapidly than a coarse sugar and it will give the impression of greater sweetness, icing sugar will therefore appear to be sweeter than granulated sugar. Types of sugar which are readily available can be listed as below.

Granulated Sugar   This is the cheapest and the most popular sugar. It is 99·9 per cent sucrose and has a sparkling white crystal.

Caster Sugar   Dissolves more quickly than granulated sugar and has a small crystal. It is used for creaming with fat in cake making and for dredging on cakes and pastries.

Icing Sugar   This dissolves very rapidly and is made by grinding down sugar crystals to a fine powder. It is used for all types of icing and may be flavoured or prepared as an instant icing which does not require the addition of egg white as required for royal icing.

Preserving Sugar   As its name indicates it is intended for making jams, marmalades, for preserving fruits and for pickling. Use of preserving sugar results in a better quality jam. The large crystals dissolve more slowly than granulated sugar, they do not settle at the bottom of the pan and consequently the jam or marmalade needs less stirring to prevent burning.

Cube Sugar   Granulated sugar is moistened and moulded into neat cubes. These are often wrapped with distinctive labels advertising hotels or catering establishments.

Soft Brown Sugar   Soft brown sugar is ideal for making rich fruit cakes. They are finely grained fine sugars which vary in colour from beige to dark brown.

Coffee Crystals   Coffee crystals are either white, brown or multicoloured. They have a large crystal which takes longer to dissolve than ordinary sugars and were originally intended for the coffee lover who liked his initial sip of coffee to be bitter, the coffee becoming sweeter as the crystals dissolved.

Demerara Sugar and Muscovado Sugar   Demerara sugar and Muscovado sugar used to be unrefined raw sugars put on the market straight from the plantation. Nowadays they are more likely to be a refined sugar with molasses added to restore the flavour to something approaching the original. However, four natural raw cane sugars are imported: Demerara, light Muscovado, Muscovado and Molasses sugar. They are generally more expensive but have a superior flavour and a higher mineral content. They can be identified easily because they carry the name of the country of origin on the packet.

18.4 GOLDEN SYRUP

Syrups vary in colour and in flavour according to the refinery where processing is carried out. Syrup is made from the liquor left at the end of the crystallization process. Most of the syrup is removed by spinning in centrifugal machines and then washing the sugar with hot water and centrifuging again. The syrup and washings still contain appreciable amounts of sugar which is extracted by recrystallization. When the sugar produced will no longer reach the required standards the syrup is concentrated to make golden syrup. In some cases it may be used to manufacture soft brown sugar.

Treacles, or black treacles as they are sometimes called, resemble cane molasses. They are darker in colour with a full flavour and are used in baking and sweet-making when a strong flavour is required. Syrup and treacle contain a high proportion of invert sugar which prevents crystallization.

18.5 SUGAR DERIVATIVES AND THEIR PREPARATION

Sugar Candy Sugar candy is prepared by suspending thin strings in a hot concentrated cane sugar solution. The sugar slowly crystallizes out on the string in the form of large cubic crystals.

Barley Sugar When cane sugar is heated it melts at 100° C. If a little water is previously added to the sugar it melts at a slightly lower temperature. The melted sugar becomes straw-coloured and on cooling sets to a brittle non-crystalline mass of barley sugar. When prepared by confectioners it is either cast into moulds or twisted into strips before it hardens.

Caramel or Black Jack On further heating sugar darkens in colour and at about 210° C is converted into a dark brown substance known as caramel. This has the smell and taste of burnt sugar, and is much used as a colouring and flavouring material in sauces, gravy browning, 'artificial' vinegar, rich cakes, soups, spirits, liqueurs, beers and stouts.

Fondants Fondants are really of two types—those used by sugar boilers as sweets and those used by confectioners for cake decoration. The principles underlying their preparation are, however, in both cases the same, and consist in the formation of a sugar syrup which does not crystallize out on cooling. It is a super-saturated solution. In other words it sets to a permanent solid mass instead of becoming 'crumbly' or 'sugary'. This 'cutting of the grain', as it is called, is accomplished by partial 'inversion' of the cane sugar, or the addition to it of a certain amount of glucose. The presence of even small amounts of glucose in a sugar syrup prevents the crystallization of the sugar on cooling or keeping until it is subjected to mechanical beating. Actually, crystallization does take place slowly, but the crystals formed are small. It is for this reason that all fondant and toffee recipes will be found to contain either glucose or small amounts of such acid substances as cream of tartar, tartaric acid, citric acid, lemon juice, acetic acid or vinegar. During the boiling of the sugar syrup the acid substance present inverts part of the sucrose to form sufficient glucose to prevent large crystals from forming.

Toffees and Sweets We have already seen that when sugar is heated with water—500g to 200ml—it first of all dissolves and on continued heating turns dark brown to caramel. On still further heating it turns black to form sugar charcoal or carbon, and finally burns completely away. In actual fact there are several gradual changes in the sugar between melting and caramelization which are not easy to distinguish except by the experienced eye. An experienced sugar-boiler can recognize ten different and distinct stages or 'degrees':

Syrup	104° C
Thread degree	108° C
Pearl degree	110° C
Blow degree	113° C
Feather degree	116° C
Soft ball degree	118° C
Hard ball degree	121° C
Soft crack degree	138° C
Hard crack degree	150° C
Caramel	177° C

These various degrees can be determined best by the use of a sugar-boiler's thermometer on which the various temperatures are marked, or in skilled hands by the shape and consistency of a sample poured into cold water. For ordinary purposes only four of these degrees are of any real importance. They are—thread degree for boiled icing, soft ball degree for fondants, crack degree for toffee, and caramel for colouring and flavouring. These correspond with temperatures of roughly 108° C, 118° C, 143° C and 177° C respectively, or can be less accurately determined by the following simple tests:

(i) THREAD DEGREE   A spoon is dipped first into cold water and then into the syrup and immediately back again into cold water. If a thread is formed when the syrup is squeezed between finger and thumb and they are separated the thread degree is reached.

(ii) SOFT BALL DEGREE   A sample is poured into cold water from a spoon and when worked between the finger and thumb forms a soft ball.

(iii) CRACK DEGREE   At this degree a sample poured into cold water will crack and when taken out will be found to be hard, dry and brittle.

(iv) CARAMEL   The sugar begins to darken rapidly in colour and the smell of burnt sugar becomes noticeable.

Other points of importance in sugar boiling are that the sides of the pan should be kept free from particles of sugar, and that once the sugar has begun to boil and the scum removed the sugar should be brought quickly to the required degree without stirring. The presence of sugar particles on the sides of the pan or stirring during boiling is liable to cause graining, i.e. the batch will become crumbly on setting.

18.6   HONEY

Honey is deposited by bees in the cells of wax combs, and is derived in the first instance by them from the nectar of the flowers they visit. While in the body of the insect the nectar sugar undergoes change, chiefly inversion, so that honey sugar is almost entirely invert sugar, making 75 per cent of the total mass. The flavour and aroma are due to the scents derived from the flowers; honey of different origins may thereby be distinguished, e.g. heather honey and clover honey. A ready means of distinguishing real honey from artificial honey is by use of the microscope, when abundant and distinctive pollen grains are evident in the case of the former.

During ancient and mediaeval times honey was the chief source of domestic sweetening materials. There are occasional references to bee-gardens in the Domesday Book. When allowed to ferment, a solution of honey or washings from combs produces mead, a popular drink among the Anglo-Saxons and the Vikings, and still available in certain country districts notably in North East England where it is produced for the tourist trade.

PRACTICAL EXERCISES

*All experiments require standard precautions; those marked * involve particular hazards and should be supervised*

*Expt. 18.1 SUGAR BOILING DEGREES AND TEMPERATURE EQUIVALENTS

Combine together in a heavy pan, 500g sugar, 1 cup (140cm³) water and ¼ level teaspoonful cream of tartar (2g). Heat gently, stirring until dissolved. Allow syrup to boil steadily without stirring, and with a mounted sugar boiling thermometer in the syrup hooked to the side of the pan. As the water content falls due to evaporation, the boiling point is elevated (see 6.2.1). EXERCISE CARE throughout, on account of the high temperatures achieved with sugar syrups. At temperature intervals of approximately three degrees C remove a small sample and drop into cold water. By finger touch, attempt to recognize 'thread', 'soft ball' and 'crack' degrees, registering for each the corresponding temperature. Stop heating IM-MEDIATELY a straw-colour develops (this should correspond with 'crack' degree). Allow to cool somewhat and pour half out into a shallow greased tin to be used for barley sugar preparation in Expt. 18.4 (ii).

Re-heat the remnant in the pan gently until golden brown. IMMEDIATELY remove from the heat and register the temperature for 'caramel'. Pour out a sample for tasting and put a little into a crucible or tin lid for further heating.

Caramel for flavouring should not taste of burnt sugar but the critical temperature can easily be missed. Caramel for colouring is further heated to give a dark brown soluble material (black jack) suitable for gravy browning. Heat the remnant in the crucible to this stage, noting the smell of burnt sugar followed by formation of a charred mass which ignites and burns away.

Expt. 18.2 SUGAR CRYSTALLIZATION AND 'CUTTING THE GRAIN'

Warm 30g sugar and 10cm³ water in an evaporating basin over a water bath until a clear solution is obtained. Pour half into a second evaporating dish, marking portions A and B. Add to A a pinch of tartaric acid (or ¼ tea-spoonful cream of tartar). Heat both A and B on boiling water baths for equal times (20–30 minutes). After heating, leave both solutions to stand for several hours observing for signs of crystallization. Interference with crystallization is referred to by confectioners as 'cutting the grain'.

Differences between A and B are attributable either to the presence of the acid itself or else to products of chemical change promoted by the acid. These considerations are pursued in Expt. 18.3, for which dishes A and B should be retained.

Expt. 18.3   INVERSION OF SUCROSE

Prepare a 10% solution of sucrose and test a sample with a Clinistix paper (see Expt. 3.1 vi). To a 10cm³ sample, add about 1cm³ dilute hydrochloric acid and boil thoroughly. Allow to cool and test again with Clinistix. If the result is positive, repeat with another sample of 10% sucrose solution substituting tartaric or citric acid for the mineral acid.

NB. Hydrolysis of sucrose yields a mixture of the two monosaccharides, glucose and fructose, but there is no 'instant' test for fructose.

In order to throw light on the effective agent in 'cutting the grain', repeat the procedure for Expt. 18.2 but using 10g sucrose, 5g glucose and 5cm³ water in an evaporating dish marked C, heated over boiling water for the same time applied to A and B. Make comparisons between signs of crystallization in C with those in A and B.

Expt. 18.4   PREPARATION OF VARIOUS SUGAR CONFECTIONERIES

(i) **Preparation of Sugar Candy**
Prepare a concentrated sugar solution in a beaker of water. Try to get as much sugar as possible dissolved without raising the temperature unduly. Suspend in the thick syrup a length of thread tied to a glass rod across the top of the beaker. Set the beaker aside for several days, covered with polythene film to hinder evaporation, and note the formation on the string of large cubic crystals.

(ii) **Preparation of Barley Sugar**
Use the 'crack' degree boiled sugar from Expt. 18.1 which has been poured into a shallow greased tin. While still pliable, cut into strips and twist into the form of traditional barley sugar and allow to harden. If already solidified, note the brittle texture of the non-crystallized mass, as well as the typical colour and taste.

(iii) **Preparation of Fondant**
Heat 100g sugar with 40cm³ water and 0·1g cream of tartar to 'feather' degree (116°C). Allow to cool somewhat, then pour into a glazed earthenware basin. Continue to cool to about 40° C. Now stir with a wooden spoon from sides to centre. The syrup becomes increasingly viscous and creamy. When stirring becomes difficult ✳, handle instead, kneading into a creamy mass of fondant which can be used in preparation of cake icing and other confections.

(iv) **Preparation of Pulled Sugar**
('Rock'). If the sugar preparation in (iii) is differently handled at ✳, it can be made into a hard shiny confection with a fibrous structure, familiar as 'rock'. The plastic mass is slung over a hook and, as it elongates under its own weight, it is folded back repeatedly over the hook until the desired texture is achieved.

Expt. 18.5   MICROSCOPIC EXAMINATION OF HONEY FOR POLLEN GRAINS

Dilute a little honey with an equal quantity of water in a test tube. Allow to sediment over night. Remove the sediment to a microscope slide by carefully introducing an elongated Pasteur pipette (rubber teat) into the honey solution and withdrawing the lowest layer. Examine under low and high power magnification. Comparisons with microphotographs of pollen grains of known origins can lead to the identification of the source of the honey. All honey will give some pollens.

Expt. 18.6   DETECTION OF ADDITIVES TO NATURAL HONEY

Natural honey may be 'extended' by the addition of invert sugar which has been produced by hydrolysis of sucrose (called 'technical' invert sugar). Crystallization properties of honey might possibly be modified by the addition of glucose syrup, prepared from starch by hydrolysis with sulphuric acid followed by neutralization with lime. This gives a residue of calcium sulphate.

(i) Invert Sugar

Fiehe's Test. Dissolve $5cm^3$ honey in $5cm^3$ water and add $5cm^3$ ether (FLAMMABLE). Shake thoroughly and pour into a stoppered separating funnel. Leave to stand and reject the lower aqueous layer. To the ethereal layer, add a few drops of freshly prepared 1% resorcinol solution in concentrated hydrochloric acid. Shake gently.

Positive result   Pink colour in acid layer, deepening to red at the interface, indicates presence of 'technical' invert sugar.

(ii) Glucose Syrup

Ash a sample of honey. Genuine honey should give only about 0·35% ash. Excess suggests adulteration. Test any discernible ash for sulphate and calcium (see Expt. 7.2).

Positive results for both   These indicate glucose syrup added to honey.

FURTHER READING

Brown, M. A., Cameron, A. G. (1977). *Experimental Cooking*, Edward Arnold.

CHAPTER XIX

FOOD PROCESSING

19.1 COOKING

The practice of cooking meat and other flesh foods has grown up with civilization and the general advance in refinement of taste. Raw meat is, if anything, more digestible than cooked meat, but to modern ideas it is not so presentable or palatable. Heat treatment of meat results in the removal of its raw appearance by the decomposition of myoglobin, the partial coagulation of the proteins of the meat fibres, the gelantinization of the collagen surrounding the muscle fibres and the loosening of these so that they become more accessible in digestion to digestive juices, and the melting away of fats from amongst the masses of muscle. Pork is usually slower to digest because in its case there is a super-abundance of fat.

Cooking is mainly practised because it results in food which is more appetizing to the taste, smell and eye than raw food. With the sick or convalescent, preparation and presentation of food are particularly important.

The heating of food in cooking is sometimes justified by the argument that parasites and pathogenic bacteria possibly contained in the raw food are wholly, or to a very large extent, killed by heat. With respect to this suggestion it need only be said that food known to contain such organisms should not be eaten under any circumstances. Unless meat inspection is thorough and the retailers well instructed in such matters and honest, it is nevertheless true that diseased meat may pass into consumption. In such cases it must not be forgotten that the temperatures reached in the ordinary process of cooking are quite insufficient to sterilize the meat throughout, all the more where the bacteria are in the spore form and parasites are encysted.

The following processes of cooking are usually distinguished: boiling, steaming, stewing, roasting (baking), frying, grilling (broiling), braising and microwave. During conventional cooking heat is transferred to the food by conduction, convection or radiation, or by a combination of one or more of these processes, employing either moist heat, dry heat or hot fat. In the case of microwave cooking heat is generated in food by the action of the microwaves; in addition some heat will be transferred within the food itself by conduction.

When food is cooked there is, inevitably, some reduction in the nutritive value of the food. Water-soluble nutrients will be leached out into cooking water and others will be lost due to the action of heat and oxidation. The pH of the cooking medium will also have some bearing on the nutrient loss. Ascorbic acid is the nutrient which is most easily destroyed during cooking, it is water-soluble and affected by heat, oxidation and alkalis. If there is little loss of ascorbic acid during cooking it can be taken that there will be little loss of other nutrients.

19.1.1 Boiling and steaming

Boiling and steaming have much in common. The temperature of the medium in which the food is cooked does not rise above 100° C at ordinary pressure. An increase in pressure will result in a higher cooking temperature and consequently a shorter cooking time. This is the principle behind pressure cooking which is really a variant of steaming. Pressure cooking can be considerably advantageous because not only is the cooking time shortened but loss of nutrients is likely to be less. Pressure cooking appears to result in a smaller loss of ascorbic acid than either boiling or steaming.

Steaming is a method commonly used for flour mixtures such as suet pastries, suet and sponge puddings, fish and occasionally smaller pieces of meat like chops, when cooking for invalids, as the finished product is thought to be more digestible than grilling or frying. Vegetables too can be cooked by steaming, although this is not a common practice and is really only suitable for jacket potatoes and root vegetables; these could be cooked when other foods are being steamed with a view to fuel economy.

Boiling is suitable for large joints of meat (especially beef, ham, tongue), for flour mixtures (as an alternative to steaming) and for vegetables. Vegetables are best cooked conservatively, i.e. in the minimum amount of water for the shortest time that will give satisfactory results. This ensures maximum retention of nutrients together with a good flavour. Water in which meat or vegetables have been boiled should be used as stock for soups, sauces and gravies to avoid wasting the soluble nutrients.

Cooking of meat by boiling does not require that the water should be actually at boiling point; a temperature well below this, say 75° C, will be actually better, for then there is little risk of the over-coagulation or hardening of the muscle fibres.

19.1.2 Stewing

Stewing is usually employed for meat cooked with or without added vegetables and for fruit. It is either carried out over heat, generally in a pan with a tightly fitting lid to reduce evaporation, or in an oven in a covered dish or casserole. Many cookery books refer to casseroling as a method of cooking; it is in fact, a variant of stewing. The liquid is kept at simmering point; in the case of meat for about two hours or more. Stewing has the advantage that soluble nutrients are utilized because the cooking liquor is eaten with the cooked food. It is particularly suitable for cooking tougher cuts of meat, the long slow cooking in the presence of water promotes hydrolysis of collagen (see 15.2.1). Stews can be classed as either white or brown; in the latter case the meat is first browned in oil or fat before the addition of stock, water and other ingredients.

19.1.3 Roasting and baking

True roasting is cooking by means of radiant heat, either as in the old practice when a joint was turned on a spit over a hot fire or the modern equivalent when turned on a rotisserie spit beneath the heated grill of a gas or an electric stove. Meat and potatoes cooked in an enclosed oven are often termed roast but should really be called baked.

Meat may be baked in an oven in either of two ways, in the open or in a closed tin, the difference being almost entirely one of the rate of evaporation. It has been found that in the covered roast, where evaporation is much diminished, there is a much greater loss of salts from the meat than in the open roast, and that owing to the large reduction of evaporation, which requires latent heat of evaporation, the closed meat cooks more quickly than the uncovered meat. The water runs out of the meat instead of evaporating from the surface. An enclosed roast loses more weight and water than the open roast as a result of its more rapid cooking and earlier shrinkage. The use of foil wrappings or roasting bags are a variant of the closed tin method.

Baking is the method generally used for flour mixtures, this includes all types of yeast mixtures, pastries, cakes, biscuits and scones. Alternatively varieties of scones, oat cakes, etc., are cooked by direct contact with a hot griddle or frying pan.

19.1.4 Frying

Frying is a method of cooking food in hot fat which can attain a much higher temperature than water. It is a rapid method of cooking and the end-product is generally very acceptable. There are two methods of frying—shallow and deep fat frying. Shallow frying is carried out in a shallow pan usually with a coating of fat on the bottom, but in the case of foods containing a lot of fat, e.g. bacon or sausages, additional fat is seldom required. Deep fat frying is carried out in a deep pan; food is lowered into the hot fat at a temperature of between 175° C and 200° C. There is considerable loss of water from the surface of the food which results in rapid bubbling of the fat. Certain foods such as croquettes and fish require coating with a batter or egg and crumb. This sets very rapidly in the hot fat and reduces loss of water and salts from the food. The temperature of the fat should be adjusted according to the food being fried and it is advisable to use a thermometer to check the temperature. There is a fire risk with over-heated fat and if the smoke point is reached the fat begins to decompose rapidly. Fats which contain impurities decompose at the high temperatures involved in frying and can give an unpleasant smell and taste to the food. This is one of the reasons why fat should be strained after use. Refined vegetable oils are very suitable for frying because they can be heated to a higher temperature than fats such as lard before the smoke point is reached. If a fat contains water it will spatter on heating with the danger of burning the cook and fat spattered outside the pan increases the risk of fire and also causes a dirty stove. Fried food has an increased energy value; losses due to leaching out of nutrients are reduced to a minimum.

19.1.5 Grilling

Grilling is used for cooking pieces of meat, bacon, sausages, fish and foods such as mushrooms and tomatoes by radiant heat under the grill of a gas or electric stove. The food is seasoned and usually brushed with oil or melted fat before grilling and needs frequent turning under the grill. The food should not be so thick that heat cannot penetrate and cook the inside of the food before the outside is burned. This method is called broiling in the USA. If an infrared grill is used the cooking time is considerably reduced. Grilling is a quick cooking method which produces highly acceptable results. Grilled food is generally considered to be more digestible than fried food and its comparative energy value is less. There may be some loss of nutrients through the drip in the grill pan and so this should be used when possible.

19.1.6 Braising

This usually refers to cooking meat by initial frying in hot fat for a short period followed by cooking by moist heat. The meat is cooked on vegetables immersed in the cooking liquid. This method is particularly suitable for cooking joints of meat which are likely to be tough if roasted or baked.

19.1.7 Microwave cooking

Microwave cookers are not used to any great extent in the home at present. This is partly due to the initial cost and partly due to the fact that use of the cooker is somewhat limited. Food cooked in a microwave oven does not brown or become crisp, this means that food needs browning at some stage by conventional grilling or frying. The short cooking time does not allow flavours to develop and this may make food unacceptable. In addition timing is critical and small errors in this respect will have very significant effects which may result in totally unacceptable food. Microwave cookers are used quite extensively in the catering trade, e.g. in hospitals and snack bars where they are used for rapid reheating of food rather than prime cooking. The initial cooking can be carried out by trained chefs and the reheating by less skilled operators, thus reducing labour costs. The big advantage in microwave cooking is the speed of the operation, which makes it invaluable for reheating cooked food and for rapid defrosting of frozen food.

In a domestic kitchen microwave ovens are very compact and a 13 amp plug is needed to operate the appliance but no other installation is required. Some sophisticated models have a browning element and other attachments. In this rapidly advancing field of cooking, the latest information can be obtained from literature supplied by distributors.

Emission of electro-magnetic waves would be highly dangerous and it is for this reason that the British Standards Institute is considering a safety requirement for commercial and domestic ovens. The electro-magnetic waves are generated by a magnetron and directed into the oven cavity. Microwaves have a very high frequency and a short wavelength, those used for microwave cooking usually have a frequency of 2450 megacycles per second. They can be absorbed, transmitted or reflected according to the nature of the material. Metals reflect microwaves; materials with a low dielectric constant such as china, earthenware, glass, polypropylene transmit microwaves. This makes them suitable materials for containers. Materials with a high dielectric constant absorb microwaves and foods come into this category. When food absorbs microwaves, molecules in the food begin to oscillate rapidly; this causes friction between the molecules and consequently heat is generated. Microwaves penetrate food to a depth of 2·5–4·0cm causing generation of heat which is transferred to other parts of the food by conduction. The rate of heating in the food will vary with the consistency; water has a high dielectric constant and foods which contain a lot of water will cook more rapidly than those with less water. Other factors which influence the cooking time are the initial temperature of the food and the quantity. The higher the initial temperature the faster it will cook, the greater the quantity of food the longer the cooking time.

Suitable containers are essential for microwave cooking and should transmit microwaves; they will remain cold at first but will become hot due to transference of heat from the hot food. Metal containers reflect microwaves and should be avoided; they can distort the patterns of the microwaves in the oven and cause 'arcing', when flashes of light can be seen. Arcing reduces the efficiency and the life of the magnetron. Arcing can also occur when the oven is switched on without food inside and this should be avoided on the grounds of efficiency and safety as there is nothing in the oven to absorb the microwaves.

The use of microwave baking in the manufacture of bread is being developed. Rapid internal heating of dough results in a faster generation of steam and carbon dioxide than is possible in conventional baking. This enables bread to be made with a higher proportion of soft flour, available from home grown wheat. The carbon dioxide and steam which are generated in this method exceed the amount that would be lost using the softer flour. In addition the rapid heating reduces the alpha-amylase activity with its associated ill-effects (see 11.8.2(ii)). Subsequent browning by conventional means is required to produce an acceptable loaf and development of suitable dual-purpose baking pans is essential. Metal would be unsuitable for a microwave cooker and plastic pans are unsuitable for a conventional cooker. Glass can be used for baking trials, but lacks the durability required for routine usage.

19.2 PRESERVATION

The end-products of food production, be they of animal or vegetable origin, will deteriorate during storage, and sometimes this will happen very rapidly, e.g. meat, fish, milk, salad vegetables, soft fruits etc. Food spoilage is due in part to the results of microbiological action by bacteria, yeasts or fungi (moulds). All raw foods will be contaminated with these micro-organisms and further contamination can take place by contact with human beings, pests (e.g. rats, mice, flies) and the equipment used to process and store food. In addition biochemical reactions occur within food; these are almost always catalyzed by some enzyme in the food. Not all biochemical and microbial changes are necessarily harmful, e.g. meat becomes more tender and has an improved flavour after such changes (15.1.5). Cheeses rely on microbial action to produce their distinctive flavour (13.7). The production of Indian tea and wine- and beer-making also use the effects of microbial action. Changes, which may be beneficial in the early stages, may make food totally unacceptable if allowed to proceed too far, e.g. meat may become uneatable and butter rancid.

Micro-organisms which cause food spoilage fall into three main categories: moulds, yeasts, bacteria. Moulds are the largest group; they are microscopic fungi consisting of filaments of cells which form a visible growth on the surface of foods and are more likely to occur in damp conditions. They are nearly always undesirable, moulds in certain cheeses being a notable exception, and although they may not actually cause disease they are indicative that other spoilage changes might have taken place. Yeasts also are fungi and are round or oval-shaped cells. Although they cause food spoilage, they have beneficial action in two main spheres due to their ability to convert sugars into alcohol and gaseous carbon dioxide, i.e. in production of alcoholic drinks and in production of carbon dioxide for leavening dough in bread-making. Bacteria form the smallest of the three categories. Two of the common types are *cocci*, which are spherical, and *bacilli*, which are rod-shaped. Undesirable bacteria are either pathogenic which cause illness or even death, or food spoilage organisms which make food unacceptable and which could affect the nutritive value but are not themselves a health hazard. *Salmonellae, Clostridium botulinum* and *Staphylococcus aureus* are typical food pathogens, whilst *Lactobacilli* which produce lactic acid and consequent souring in foods are typical food spoilage organisms.

Because food production is largely seasonal some sort of food preservation is necessary. To be successful any method of food preservation will either stop the changes which take place as the result of both enzyme action and the action of micro-organisms or slow down the rates at which they take place. At the same time the food itself should not be manifestly changed or rendered inedible by the processes.

Preservation can be achieved by freezing, removal of oxygen, removal of water, application of heat or adjusting the pH and the chemical environment. Removal of water by drying in the sun and wind was no doubt the first method primitive man used to preserve his food. Other simple methods include salting, smoking and pickling. Salt fish was one of the foods brought by the Romans when they invaded Britain. Smoked fish (a forerunner of the present-day kipper) is referred to in the Bible; pears, plums, onions, are known to have been soaked in vinegar as early as 1000 BC; whilst tribes in Arctic regions packed raw fish and meat into caches in the ice. Modern methods of food preservation such as dehydration and freezing are developments of these primitive techniques.

19.3 PRESERVATION WITH SUGAR

19.3.1 Jams

Fresh fruit contains fibre, water, sugars, fruit acids and a polysaccharide known as pectin. Jam is made by boiling fruit with the addition of sugar. When the sugar, pectin and pH of the whole reach certain desired limits a 'gel' will be formed on cooling. The amount of pectin in the jam will be small, probably less than 1 per cent of the whole, whilst the sugar content will probably be nearer 70 per cent. However, in spite of the small amount present, the quantity and quality of pectin in the fruit and amount of acid are very critical in successful gel formation. This explains why some fruits, e.g. strawberries, which have a low pectin content and also little acid, are difficult to convert into jam, whilst fruits containing a relatively high proportion of pectin, e.g. blackcurrants, are easily converted into jam.

It is possible to obtain commercial pectin preparations such as Certo. When these are used the time of boiling is very much reduced, the yield of jam is greater, the fresh fruit flavour and colour are more readily preserved, and a well-set jam is ensured. Such concentrated pectin preparations should, however, be used with care and the directions usually enclosed followed accurately, otherwise the jam will be too stiff or the delicate fruit flavour will not register, since it is no longer volatile.

Jam-making The conditions necessary for successful jam-making are briefly as follows. The first consideration is, of course, the fruit. This should be perfectly fresh and have attained full size without being over-ripe. It is at this stage that fruits are richest in pectin and acid, while over-ripe fruits contain a diminished amount of pectin and acid, and are liable to mould growth and to lose colour and flavour. After the removal of undesirable fragments such as stalks, leaves and calices, the fruit should be cooked for some time before the sugar is added. The length of time taken for this cooking varies according to the fruit used; from 10–15 minutes with such fruits as raspberries, to 30–45 minutes with addition of water in the case of plums, damsons and blackcurrants. During this preliminary cooking the cell walls of the fruit are broken down and pectin extracted, and some water is lost by evaporation. In the case of fruits deficient in fruit-acids some further acid, i.e. lemon juice or citric acid, should be added at this stage, for its assists in pectin extraction.

This preliminary cooking of the fruit is complete when a good pectin clot is obtained with the following test. A teaspoonful of juice free from seeds and skins is placed in a glass and three tea-spoonsful of methylated spirit added to it. The mixture is shaken gently and left for a minute. If the fruit contains sufficient pectin a transparent jelly-like clot of pectin will be formed and when poured from one glass into another remains in one piece. A poor clot may divide into two or three lumps, and a very poor clot into numerous small pieces.

Provided the fruit has given a good pectin clot in the tests just described it is now ready for the addition of sugar. The most suitable type of sugar is a good quality crystallized sugar. It makes no difference whether it is cane sugar or beet sugar, provided it is of good quality. Once the sugar has been added the jam should be stirred until all the sugar has dissolved, and then boiled as rapidly as possible. During boiling the stirring should be reduced to a mini-mum, otherwise air-bubbles and scum are liable to become mixed up with the jam and spoil its appearance. This boiling period will vary from about 3–20 minutes according to the kind and quantity of fruit, as well as the shape and size of the pan. The object is to reduce this period of boiling with sugar to a minimum in order to produce a jam with a fresh fruit flavour, good colour and firm set. If boiled for too long the setting qualities of the pectin will deter-iorate since it cannot withstand prolonged boiling with acid. In addition, too prolonged boiling may caramelize some of the sugar and consequently spoil both the flavour and colour of the finished jam. On the other hand, if the jam is not boiled long enough an insufficient amount of sugar will be inverted and the jam will 'grain', i.e. crystallize and become sugary on storing. Further, the pectin, acid and sugar in the jam must be in correct proportions if the jam is not to set to a thick sticky mass. The proportions are reached by the loss of moisture by evaporation during boiling.

While it is impossible to lay down any hard and fast rules as to the amount of sugar which should be used for every type of fruit it is generally true to say that the best results are obtained when added sugar is 60–65 per cent of jam in the final product. The actual percentage of total sugar will be higher than this on account of the natural fruit sugar present in the fruit and the loss in weight which takes place by evaporation. With less percentages than 60 the jam will be liable to ferment, while with more than 65 per cent of sugar the jam will be too sweet and liable to crystallize out.

Another point about sugar is that when added to the fruit it has a hardening effect upon it, due to absorption of water by osmosis. For this reason fruits with hard skins, such as damsons and blackcurrants, should be cooked until thoroughly soft before the addition of sugar, while soft fruits, such as strawberries, are better covered with sugar overnight as this toughens them and helps to keep them whole when made into jam.

The amount of sugar used will also depend on the pectin content of the fruit. A general guide is: equal quantities (weight-for-weight) of sugar and fruit for jams such as raspberry; less sugar than fruit for a low pectin fruit such as strawberries; and more sugar than fruit for fruits with a relatively high content of pectin such as blackcurrants. In the latter case the fruit will be cooked with additional water and in the case of strawberry jam no additional water will be added.

The following tests may be made to find when the jam has reached setting point.

(i) COLD PLATE TEST A sample of the jam is poured from a wooden spoon on to a cold plate. When the jam has reached setting point the surface of the sample should set quickly and crinkle when pushed with the finger.

(ii) FLAKE TEST A sample of the jam is taken out on a clean wooden spoon and turned horizontally until the sample is partly cooled. The jam is then allowed to drop from the edge of the spoon, and if the drops run together into flakes which break off cleanly setting point is reached.

(iii) TEMPERATURE TEST Provided a suitable thermometer, e.g. floating dairy thermometer or sugar boiler's thermometer, is available, this is the most reliable test. When the jam boils at 105° C the sugar has reached the correct proportion and the jam will set on cooling.

(iv) WEIGHT TEST This test consists in weighing the pan and its contents (without spoon) on a suitable spring balance, until the requisite weight is reached. The requisite weight is reached when the weight of added sugar forms 60 per cent of the weight of the jam. (It must be remembered, of course, that the weight of jam does not include the weight of the pan in which it is boiled.)

When setting point is reached the jam should be removed from the source of heat and any scum quickly removed. The jam should then be quickly poured into clean, dry, warm jars, which should be filled quite up to the top to allow for considerable shrinkage on cooling. After cooling, a small waxed disc should be placed on the surface of the jam in each jar, which should then be covered.

19.3.2 Fruit jellies

The preparation of jellies depends on the same principle as that of jam-making—it is essential that the pectin, fruit acid and sugar should be in correct proportions. All common fruits with the exception of those deficient in pectin and acid can be made into jellies. After preliminary preparation, the fruit is cooked slowly and thoroughly. The amount of water used is dependent on the type of fruit, 2kg soft fruit to $\frac{3}{4}$ litre water or 2kg hard fruit to $1\frac{1}{2}$ litres water. When cooked the fruit should be strained through either a jelly bag or several folds of butter-muslin which should have previously been scalded. Squeezing the jelly bag to speed up the draining will spoil the colour and clarity of the jelly and should be avoided.

The juice obtained should be measured, heated, skimmed and sugar added allowing 800g to 1 litre of juice. The sugar should be dissolved in the juice before heating. Boiling should continue without stirring until setting point is reached and further procedure should be as for jam-making.

19.3.3 Marmalade

The preparation of marmalade from such citrus fruits as oranges, lemons, grapefruit and limes, is so similar in method and principles to jams and jellies that the following details only need be mentioned.

The thick rinds of citrus fruits require boiling for at least two hours, and the addition of water is essential during the cooking. It is important that the white inner skin or pith of the citrus fruit should be soaked and cooked along with the rest of the fruit since the pectin is derived from it and not from the juice. If considered desirable, this white inner skin can be placed in a muslin bag along with seeds soaked and cooked with the marmalade, and then taken out before the sugar is added. The seeds are very high in pectin. The soaking should be 24–48 hours. This is not absolutely obligatory but is advisable. It may also be necessary to add a suitable acid such as tartaric acid to obtain a perfect set. In this way the valuable pectin is extracted without spoiling the appearance of the marmalade by the presence of white pith in it.

19.3.4 Commercial jam-making

Factories are dependent on a steady supply of fruit for jam manufacture; for this reason they use preserved fruits at certain times. If preserved fruit were not used the factories would be faced with a glut of fruit at harvest time and a closed plant during winter months. The fruits are preserved in a weak solution of sulphur dioxide. The fruit is submerged in the solution either in its raw state or after cooking. Soft fruits are usually preserved uncooked whilst fruits with skins, such as currants and plums, are cooked first. This is because sulphur dioxide has a tendency to toughen the skins. Sulphur dioxide bleaches the fruit but the colour is restored after cooking when nearly all the sulphur dioxide is driven off. Sulphur dioxide is a permitted preservative in jam and preserves, the maximum amount being limited to 100 ppm.

In commercial jam-making amounts of fruit, sugar and pH are carefully controlled. Cooking is usually carried out in large open pans, although certain new processes are carried out in closed vessels. The boiling time is limited to about ten minutes. The short boiling period avoids destruction of the gel forming properties of the pectin and in addition keeps the amount of invert sugar formed to suitable proportions, i.e. between 25–40 per cent. Sucrose may crystallize when the proportion of invert sugar is too low and too high a proportion can give a poor set or cause the invert sugar itself to crystallize out. The setting point can be judged by visual means as in home jam-making, by boiling to $105°$ C or more accurately by using a refractometer. This will measure the refractive index of the solution and from this the concentration of soluble solids can be calculated.

After the required concentration is reached the jam is cooled as quickly as possible to prevent further production of invert sugar. The waxed disc placed on the top of the jam when in jars prevents condensation on the surface. Water on the surface gives a layer of jam with low sugar concentration and which is therefore more prone to mould growth. Jars which are hermetically sealed do not require a waxed disc.

19.3.5 Candied peels

The chief candied peels are those of the lemon, orange, citron and lime. The methods of preparation are similar in each case, though there is some variation in the strength of sugar syrup used and the times taken for the various processes. It will be sufficient to describe the preparation of lemon peel, for this is typical of the others. A special variety of lemon with a thick rind grown in Italy and Sicily is most suitable. The fruits are cut in two transversely and the pulp extracted. The 'caps' are then soaked in brine for several days to remove undesirable matters and to open up the rind to render it more porous. The caps are next transferred to cold water to remove the salt, and then placed in tanks or tubs of weak sugar syrup. Here partial fermentation takes place and a certain amount of sugar is absorbed by the rind. The caps then pass successively into stronger and stronger syrups until saturated. They are then drained and air-dried and become the so-called 'drained caps'. The drained caps are candied by heating on wire trays to a high temperature for several hours. The heating sets the sugar, hardens the caps and partly sterilizes them. They are finally cooled in a cold dry room and packed in air-tight tins ready for use.

19.3.6 Glacé and crystallized fruits and flowers

Included under this heading are not only such fruits as cherries, currants, apricots, plums and pears but also the rhizome of ginger, the stem of angelica and the petals of sweet Parma violets or roses.

All fruits should be in perfect condition and just ripe. Stone fruits must have their stones removed. They are cooked in weak sugar syrup until soft, and then allowed to drain. The fruit is afterwards dipped or rolled in melted sugar. This gives a coating of sugar on the outside of the fruit, which is crystallized by subjecting it to dry heat.

The rhizome (underground stem) of ginger (*Zingiber officinale*) is first cleaned and then cooked in weak sugar syrup until soft. It is passed through rising strengths of syrup, 24 hours in each, and packed in strong syrup in stone jars. Ground ginger is prepared by cleaning and afterwards grinding the dried rhizome.

Angelica (*Angelica archangelica*) is a perennial umbelliferous plant which grows wild in swampy districts in this country and is also cultivated. The stem is candied in a similar way to candied peels, and used for similar decorative and flavouring purposes in confectionery.

Sweet Parma violets and rose petals are crystallized by placing them on wire frames placed one above the other in tiers. Under the lowest frame is a tray to catch excess syrup which is allowed to drip through the frames until the petals are saturated. Finally, the petals are dried by gentle heating or exposure to the sun.

19.4   HEAT STERILIZING WITH AIR EXCLUSION

19.4.1 Canning

Canning or bottling of food for the purpose of food preservation was started at the end of the eighteenth century. Nicolas Appert was supplying bottled food to the French Navy in 1806 and a little later factories in London were supplying the British Navy. Unfortunately canning techniques had not been perfected and some food, packed in large cans, had insufficient heat treatment and deteriorated. Successful canning or bottling requires careful selection of fresh food, suitable containers which can be sealed to exclude air and which will withstand the temperatures required for sterilization, a method of heat treatment to kill off micro-organisms in the food. Preparation of food prior to canning involves cleaning and removal of inedible material. This will vary according to the food being canned. Vegetables will need peeling, fish may have bones and some skin removed. In addition foods such as soups and stews will be cooked.

Fruits and vegetables are then blanched, either by steam or boiling water. This drives out air bubbles from the food and also causes shrinkage which makes the food easier to pack. Packing and filling are carried out automatically, air is drawn out and the cans sealed whilst under vacuum. They are subjected to heat treatment, the extent of which depends on the food being processed and the can size. Acid foods are given a short heat treatment since bacteria do not grow under these conditions, for this reason cans of fruit need only to be heated to boiling point. Foods such as fish, meat and vegetables require heating under pressure to kill off bacteria and heat resistant spores which would grow in non-acid conditions. They are usually processed at a temperature of 115° C, again the time is related to the type of food and size of can. Cans are cooled rapidly to avoid overcooking, this is carried out by immersion in cold water which should be sterile in case some is drawn into a faulty can. All cans of food should be stored under dry conditions. Any which become 'blown' i.e. bulging outwards at either or both ends, should be discarded. The bulging may be caused either by natural acids attacking the tin-plate and generating hydrogen, or by the growth of bacteria in the food which generate gases. To prevent acids attacking tin-plate, cans which are to be used for acid foods are lacquered on the inside.

19.4.2 Aseptic canning

Aseptic canning is a process used for liquid or semi-solid foods such as soups. Food is sterilized at about 120° C using equipment which gives a high rate of transference of heat. The sterilized food is sealed into sterilized cans. This method avoids over-processing and is eminently suitable for large-size catering cans because there are no problems about heat penetrating to the centre of the can.

19.4.3 Bottling

The same principles apply in bottling as in canning but the process is normally carried out in the home. It should be confined to preservation of fruit and tomatoes. The temperatures reached are not sufficient to prevent the growth of spore-forming bacteria which may be present in non-acid foods. A jar with a tight fitting lid is essential. This could be a bottling jar of a reputable make, a jam jar or an empty instant coffee jar with a lid designed for bottling purposes. In addition a 'Porosan' food preserving skin could be used. This is a non-toxic plastic film made to rigid specifications which will give an airtight seal to a jar when used according to the instructions. It is very useful for obtaining seals on jars or bottles which are not of standard size. Porosan skins and tops are obtainable from well-stocked hardware shops.

There are three main ways of bottling using different equipment: a pressure cooker, an oven, or a sterilizer (or water bath). When using the oven the fruit is packed into jars, heated in a moderate oven for $\frac{3}{4}$–1 hour. The jars are filled immediately with boiling water or syrup on withdrawal from the oven, and then sealed. When sterilizing in a water bath or sterilizer the clean jars are packed tightly with fruit and filled with water or sugar syrup and the lids placed on. The jars are placed under cold water so that there is no contact either with the bottom of the sterilizer or with each other. A false bottom of wood or a wire tray may have to be used. The use of a thermometer to judge the water temperature is advisable. The water should be raised to boiling point over the period of one hour, rising 8° C every five minutes. An alternative method involves placing the bottles in boiling water for a shorter time depending on the contents of the jar. This method is particularly suitable for apple pulp. Whichever method is adopted the fruit used should be sound and the jars clean. Fruit which is sliced or stoned takes up less space in the jar and is more economical. Use of a sugar syrup rather than water improves the flavour and improves the keeping quality; brine is often used for tomatoes. During cooling, screw top jars will need tightening, and after cooling is complete the seal should be tested. Food in jars which have not sealed should either be reprocessed or used up without delay.

19.5 DEHYDRATION

Dehydration is one of the time honoured methods of food preservation. It has the advantage of giving a product which takes up less storage space than the fresh food and which is, therefore, comparatively easy and economical to handle.

Dried fruits are a well-known example of the dehydration process which was originally confined to fruits with a high sugar content. In addition to sultanas, currants and raisins, fruits such as apples, apricots, peaches, dates and bananas are also dried. The traditional method was to dry fruit by exposing it to the sun and wind, and indeed this is still carried out in many areas. The process requires a hot dry climate free from rainfall at harvest time and the immediate period afterwards and it is not surprising that dried fruit industries have developed in areas where these conditions are found, notably in the USA (California), in the Mediterranean areas (Greece) the Middle East (Turkey, Iran), parts of Australia and South Africa. Of these areas, the USA is the world's largest exporter of dried fruit as a whole.

Sun drying, whilst relatively cheap, has its drawbacks. Labour costs can be high and the fruit can be contaminated by dust and dirt whilst exposed in the atmosphere; there is also danger of spoilage due to rainfall and insect pests. In Greece—the main currant-producing area—bunches of grapes are dried in the shadow of the vine, this protects the skins of the fruit which are more delicate than other grapes used for sultana and raisin production. Other methods of drying are by placing grapes on fibre mats or on wire netting trays arranged in tiers and protected from the sun and rain.

The fruit may be turned occasionally. Before drying fruit is often given some pre-treatment with a view to enhancing its appearance and keeping qualities. This treatment will vary according to the fruit but a common method is fumigation with burning sulphur. Raisins, sultanas and prunes are often treated with an emulsion of olive oil and lye (an alkaline substance made from sodium or potassium hydroxide, bicarbonate or carbonate). After drying, some dried fruits are treated with liquid paraffin, which prevents the fruit sticking together and improves its keeping qualities. This is one of the reasons for the need to wash dried fruit before using. The presence of a preservative (sulphur dioxide) and liquid paraffin should be stated on packaged dried fruit.

Artificial drying is carried out by passing hot dry air over the fruit. This can be performed in several ways, air can be passed over trays of dried fruit, the fruit placed in rotating drum driers or placed in a tunnel dryer where moist fruit enters at one end and emerges as dried fruit at the other end.

Other foods beside fruit are dried; dried vegetables have been on sale for about 100 years and many varieties are now available. Dried soups and dehydrated meats are also on the market. Vegetables are prepared according to their kind and then treated with steam to eliminate enzyme action. Some are treated with sulphite to preserve the colour and prevent loss of ascorbic acid. They are then dried in drying cabinets or tunnel dryers. Other products are subject to hot air drying which is often carried out under reduced pressure. Under low pressure water is evaporated at comparatively low temperatures and this avoids cooking the food and speeds up the process. The water vapour is dispersed by a current of air to avoid condensation. Food is usually divided into small pieces before drying, the larger surface area promotes more efficient drying so that minced meat and finely chopped or shredded vegetables are included in dehydrated meal packs. These usually only require a very short simmering time in water to rehydrate satisfactorily.

19.5.1 Freeze drying
Freeze drying relies on the principle of sublimation, i.e. moisture can pass from a solid state in the form of ice-crystals into a vapour without passing through the liquid phase. This is appreciated by the housewife who hangs out her washing on a frosty day and finds it will dry after freezing stiff. Food is prepared and quick frozen. It is then dried under vacuum which speeds up the sublimation process, in addition enough heat is supplied to provide the latent heat of sublimation of the ice without letting the temperature rise above freezing point. This process gives a product which is a brittle honeycomb-like structure which will not have materially shrunk and which is very friable with a tendency to disintegrate after drying. The process is an expensive one and is confined to certain products for which it is particularly suitable. Accelerated freeze drying (AFD) was commonly referred to at one time. The name was used after an improved method of heat transfer had been developed, but nowadays manufacturers refer mainly to freeze drying. In this country the process is largely confined to prawns, some soups, a particular brand of peas and instant coffee.

19.6 FREEZING

Freezing is a very popular method of food preservation. The product resembles its unpreserved equivalent more closely than most other methods, as freezing has little effect on colour, flavour and nutritive value.

To obtain high quality products food is frozen as soon after it is harvested as possible, factories are situated near agricultural areas and fishing ports and some fish is frozen at sea. The freezing is carried out as quickly as possible. Because of the salts and other soluble materials food begins to freeze at a temperature slightly lower than 0° C. This is the critical point in food freezing. If this process is carried out too slowly there are likely to be unfavourable changes, mixings of mineral salts may occur as they become concentrated in the unfrozen water. Large ice crystals are formed during slow freezing. This is particularly critical in freezing fruits and vegetables because the internal cell structure can be damaged resulting in a soggy thawed product. Cell membranes in meat are more elastic and therefore formation of large ice crystals is not so deleterious.

Before freezing, all foods are subject to preliminary preparation. Some foods are indeed cooked before freezing. Fruits and vegetables are blanched to prevent enzyme activity and destroy microorganisms. This is particularly important for vegetables.

There are three methods of quick freezing in use in the UK: air blast, plate and immersion freezing.

19.6.1 Air blast freezing
Cold air is forced into the freezing compartment between racks of food in containers lowering the temperature at a rate which precludes microbial spoilage. Effectiveness depends upon efficient removal of extracted heat. In some plants, a fluidized bed is incorporated to allow production of small items such as peas, sliced beans and berries to be frozen individually before packing.

19.6.2 Plate freezing
Plate freezing is used for products such as fish fillets, pastry or other foods which can be packed in flat cartons. The cartons are frozen by direct contact with metal shelves in which a very cold refrigerant is circulated.

19.6.3 Immersion freezing
Immersion freezing is sometimes referred to as cryogenic freezing. The product is either dipped into a refrigerant or sprayed with it. It is the fastest technique of all, and much lower temperatures are employed, i.e. $-30°$ C to $-200°$ C. Liquid nitrogen is the refrigerant used which has a temperature of $-196°$ C. Immersion in liquid nitrogen would allow a strawberry to be frozen in about 30 seconds. Freon, the trade name for a fluorinated hydrocarbon, has been approved by the USA Food and Drug Administration for direct

contact freezing. Freon has been used for some time as à refrigerant in refrigerating systems.

19.6.4 Thawing

Food passes through the freezing stages in reverse when thawing. Frozen food is liable to food spoilage as soon as it is completely thawed. Re-freezing of food which has thawed reduces the quality of the product and therefore, although not necessarily harmful, it is not recommended.

19.6.5 Home freezing

Freezing can be carried out by the housewife who has a home freezer and much advice is given upon this subject. A few important points are worth mentioning. The freezer should be kept at a temperature of -18° C and be lowered to a temperature of -29° C to freeze a fresh load of food. This can be done by depressing the fast freeze switch, if there is one, or by setting the regulator as low as possible for two to three hours before adding food. The switch can be turned back to normal after all the food is frozen. Not more than one-tenth of the freezer capacity should be frozen at a time. Any packaging material used should be able to withstand the low temperature involved and should be moisture vapour proof. It is advisable to keep a record of food in the freezer and to remember that certain foods have a limited life in the freezer, e.g. pork and shell fish. Certain foods are not at all suitable for freezing. These include: salad vegetables, e.g. lettuce, cucumber, whole tomatoes—due to high water content; whole eggs (see 16.8.1); bananas, due to blackening; and mayonnaise, milk and single cream—due to separation of fat and water, although homogenized milk and double cream will freeze successfully.

19.7 PRESERVATION BY IONIZING RADIATIONS

This is a comparatively new technique which can reduce enzyme activity and destroy micro-organisms. It can also kill food pests and inhibit sprouting of stored crops. Irradiation is rather an emotive subject; whilst there is no supportive evidence to indicate that foods which are subject to irradiation have toxic effects there is a possibility that they may be harmful. Irradiation of food intended for human consumption is not permitted in the UK. Although its use for sterilizing bacon was once permitted in the USA this permission was withdrawn.

19.8 CHEMICAL PRESERVATIVES

The addition of a so-called preservative to food results in the production of a chemical environment which is not conducive to the growth of micro-organisms. This is because their metabolic enzymes are ineffective and also because the autolytic enzymes in food are inactivated.

19.8.1 Traditional methods

Many traditional methods of food preservation involve the addition of certain chemicals. Long usage has absolved them from the caution, and indeed suspicion, which surrounds more recent introductions. There is no legislation affecting the use of the following:

(i) Sugar and salt (sodium chloride): Both these ingredients are employed in high concentrations as osmotic agents which make water unavailable for spoilage changes and cause plasmolysis of infecting organisms.

(ii) Acetic acid in vinegar: This inhibits bacterial activity by lowering the pH below the range tolerated for growth and metabolism.

(iii) Alcohol (ethanol) in the form of wine or spirits: Denatures proteins and therefore affects the activity of both autolytic and microbial enzymes.

(iv) Smoke: Phenols and aldehydes present in smoke have an effective bactericidal action but this is chiefly confined to surfaces of food on which tarry vapours condense.

19.8.2 Permitted preservatives

Legislation limits the use of other chemicals as food preservatives. The Preservatives in Food Regulations, 1962 (S1 1962 No. 1532) list the following as permitted preservatives:

(i) Sulphur dioxide in the form of sulphurous acid solution or as the sulphites of sodium potassium or calcium, is effective in inhibiting growth of moulds, yeasts and aerobic bacteria. It also prevents enzymic browning (17.2.1).

(ii) Benzoic acid and benzoates used to prevent the growth of yeasts and moulds in acidic foods in which the pH is low enough to inhibit bacterial action.

(iii) Sorbic acid—used as a sodium, potassium or calcium salt. It is most effective against the growth of yeasts and moulds in acid conditions.

(iv) Diphenyl. This is effective against moulds but not yeasts or bacteria. It is used on rinds of citrus fruits or their respective wrappers.

(v) Orthophenyl phenol. Used against yeasts and bacteria; it is applied as a dip or a spray for fruits.

(vi) Tetracyclines. These are antibiotics and permitted for use on raw fish to the extent of 5ppm.

(vii) Nisin. This substance is found naturally in cheeses; it controls thermophilic strains of *Bacillus* and *Clostridium*, and its use is permitted in processed cheese and other milk products.

(viii) Copper carbonate—controls rot and is allowed in wrappers used for pears.

19.9   CONTROLLED ATMOSPHERE STORAGE

Controlled atmosphere storage was originally termed 'gas storage'. It implies storage under carefully controlled conditions and is an adjunct to, rather than an alternative to, cold storage.

Fruits and vegetables are living structures and some metabolic activity continues after harvest, changing their composition and quality. They can lose water either by evaporation or by the process of transpiration, resulting in a dried out or wilted crop. Other changes in the organic constituents may be advantageous, i.e. ripening processes may be completed. Energy released by respiration is used by plant organs when these changes are taking place. Generally fruits and vegetables which have a low overall rate of respiration as measured by the rate of carbon dioxide production are stored reasonably well after harvest without noticeable deterioration. Rapid rates of respiration indicate changes are taking place which could have deleterious effects on the acceptability of the product.

Vegetables such as roots, tubers and bulbs can be stored for considerable periods with little change if they are harvested at a suitable stage. Some fruits, e.g. apples, pears and bananas, can be harvested before they are ripe and ripening regulated by controlling the storage conditions. Ripening of soft fruits cannot be controlled in this way. When fruits and vegetables are stored in a confined space the oxygen in the atmosphere is depleted and the carbon dioxide increased. Relative concentrations of oxygen and carbon dioxide and storage temperature are all factors which influence the rate of respiration and all these factors can be controlled during storage.

Generally, respiration rates rise with an increase in temperature and cool storage can delay related undesirable changes. In addition cooler atmospheres reduce water losses in transpiration resulting in a better product. Low temperatures also reduce microbiological activity and consequent deterioration. The actual temperature can damage plant tissue and the extent of damage varies between different products. Some varieties of apples and pears can stand up to storage for long periods at temperatures around freezing point whilst tropical fruits can be damaged at higher temperatures. Bananas, for example, are damaged by temperatures much below 11° C. A reduction in oxygen concentration or an increase in carbon dioxide concentration will generally slow down respiration, but if the carbon dioxide concentration rises too high tissue damage occurs whilst too low concentrations of oxygen result in anaerobic respiration and accumulation of acetaldehyde and ethanol. Another factor which influences the changes which take place in fruit is the presence of ethylene and other volatile substances in the atmosphere. They are produced as the fruit is ripening; if they are not removed they can cause premature ripening in other stored fruit. Ethylene can be introduced to promote the ripening of certain fruits, notably green citrus fruits.

After harvest of fruits and vegetables the immediate modification of environmental conditions is desirable. The produce should be cooled as soon as possible, particularly if long journeys or extended storage periods are involved. Potatoes and other root vegetables have traditionally been stored in clamps or pits on the farm but modern methods have more accurate control over conditions. The International Institute of Refrigeration (IIR) makes certain recommendations for land transport and cold storage. Usually the more mature the product the greater its susceptibility to chilling injury. Before storage fruit should be subject to air cooling and vegetables may be subject to water cooling although this is not always possible. A well-designed storage room will ensure rapid cooling of the produce. Heat generated by respiratory activity should be removed, as should heat which leaks into the room through the walls; ideally the walls should be gas-tight. A good circulation of air should be maintained and packaging and stacking should not interfere with air circulation. Drying effects can be avoided by having the cooling coils in the storage room cooler than the actual produce.

Conditions in the store will vary according to the produce and there will be significant differences between varieties of a similar crop, e.g. varieties of apple. The relative humidity of the atmosphere is important: too high a humidity will encourage microbiological growth and too low will promote wilting. Fruits require a relative humidity of 90 per cent; leafy vegetables up to 95 per cent; onions and sweet potatoes require a lower level of between 80–85 per cent. Ventilation is very important in controlling the atmosphere: 10 per cent carbon dioxide is considered to be the upper safe limit but short-term treatments are often administered in excess of this by the use of dry ice (solid carbon dioxide). This has the advantage of reducing the build-up of micro-organisms on soft fruit. Wherever possible mixtures of produce in one store should be avoided as respiration products of one can have deleterious effects on another. After storage the produce should be allowed to warm up in dry air. This is particularly important for items such as plums or cherries. Packaging with air-tight plastic film is not to be recommended. Perforation of the film or a fungicidal pre-treatment is desirable.

PRACTICAL EXERCISES

*All experiments require standard precautions; those marked * involve particular hazards and should be supervised*

Expt. 19.1   DETECTION OF SULPHUR DIOXIDE PRESERVATIVES

Sulphur dioxide is used as a preservative either in the form of sulphurous acid or one of the sulphites: sodium, potassium or calcium. All forms decompose readily giving sulphur dioxide which is driven out of food on heating.

*Lead Acetate Test
Include a sample of food under test in a small conical flask with a little granulated zinc and dilute hydrochloric acid. Cover the mouth of the flask with a piece of filter paper soaked in lead acetate solution (POISONOUS). Set up a control flask omitting the food sample.

Positive result Filter paper stained darkly with lead acetate indicates sulphur dioxide preservatives, the sulphur dioxide having been reduced by hydrogen gas.

Expt. 19.2   DETECTION OF NITRITE IN CURED MEATS

Prepare a cold water extract of the food under test by chopping or mashing thoroughly and shaking in water before filtering. To the filtrate add a few drops each of Griess–Ilosvay reagents I and II.

Positive result Pink coloration within a few minutes, indicates nitrite present.

Griess-Ilosvay reagent   I   0·5g sulphanilic acid ⎫
                              30cm³ glacial acetic acid ⎬ Mix and filter
                              120cm³ deionized water ⎭

    II Dissolve 0·1g 1-naphthylamine in 120cm³ deionized water by boiling. Add 30cm³ glacial acetic acid and filter.

Expt. 19.3 QUANTITATIVE DETERMINATION OF SALT IN A FOOD

Fragment the food by chopping or grinding. Weigh 25·0g and transfer to a 250cm³ standard flask. Make up the volume with deionized water to give a 10% aqueous dispersion. (If the food is known to be markedly salty, a 5% dispersion will suffice; if salt is present merely for flavouring and not as a preservative, a 20% dispersion should be made.) Mix thoroughly and allow to stand for 30 minutes or more to ensure complete extraction. Mix again, allow sedimentation and filter off supernatant liquid.

Pipette 25cm³ filtrate into a conical flask and add 10 drops fluorescein indicator (0·1% solution in alcohol). Fill burette with 0·1M silver nitrate solution and titrate against food extract until a pink colour is seen in the conical flask at the point of entry. Thereafter add silver nitrate dropwise until a pronounced pink colour is obtained. Repeat and average three replicating results.

Calculation   Let Tcm³ be average titration result.

$$AgNO_3 + NaCl \rightarrow AgCl + NaNO_3$$

1 litre M silver nitrate reacts with 58·5g sodium chloride
1cm³ 0·1M silver nitrate reacts with 0·00585g sodium chloride
Tcm³ 0·1M silver nitrate reacts with 0·00585g$\times T$ sodium chloride which is contained in 25cm³ food extract or 2·5g food

$$\therefore 100\text{g food contain } \frac{0\cdot00585T \times 100\text{g}}{2\cdot5} \text{ sodium chloride}$$

$$= 0\cdot0585T \times 4\text{g sodium chloride}$$

REFERENCES

Pearson, D. (1970). *The chemical analysis of foods*, 6th edition, Churchill.

FURTHER READING

Duckworth, R. B. (1966). *Fruit and vegetables*, Pergamon.
Nuffield Advanced Chemistry (1971). *Food science—a special study*, Penguin.
Allison, S. (1978). *The Book of Microwave Cookery*, David and Charles.
Webb, J.M. (1977). *Microwave: the cooking revolution*, Forbes Publications.
Glew, G. (editor). *Cook/freeze catering*, Faber.
Napleton, L. (1975). *A Guide to Microwave Catering, Catering Times*, Northwood Industrial Publications Ltd, 2nd rev. edition.
Leach, Margaret (editor) (1975). *Freezer Facts*, Forbes Publications.

CHAPTER XX

BEVERAGES, FLAVOURING AND COLOURINGS

20.1 TEA

Tea has been used as a beverage in China at least since 2700 BC. It was introduced into this country early in the Stuart period, but it was not until 1660 that it came to the notice of Pepys.

Tea consists of the dried leaves of a shrub, *Camellia thea*, grown in China, India, Sri Lanka, Java and Japan. Originally all tea on the London market came from China, but since 1833 it has come increasingly from India, and since 1877 from Sri Lanka also.

The tea plant is kept down by severe pruning to a low shrub, and its leaves are plucked at intervals during the season. The size of the leaf varies according to age and position on the twig and determines the grade of tea. The finest tea is the small top half of the twig and the bud—Flowery Orange Pekoe. Other grades are Orange Pekoe, the second leaf, long and wiry; Souchong, two or three larger leaves further down the twig and Congous, leaves below the Souchong. The different grades of leaves are plucked from the same bushes at the same time.

The process of manufacturing tea is briefly as follows:

(i) *Withering* Here about half of the water in the leaf is dried out by exposing the fresh leaves on mesh trays in a well ventilated shed.

(ii) *Rolling* The individual leaves are rolled either by hand as in China, or by machine as elsewhere. This breaks down the leaf texture and allows the enzymes to ferment the carbohydrate in the leaf.

(iii) *Fermenting* The rolled and bruised leaves are spread out in cool dark ventilated rooms and covered with damp cloths and allowed to ferment for several hours. The colour darkens and the aroma is developed. Lightly fermented tea gives a pale and pungent infusion; fully fermented tea gives one that is deep and flavoured. Green tea is not fermented. Green teas and Oolong teas (semifermented) come mainly from China. Even fully fermented teas from China are pale in colour.

(iv) *Firing* Currents of hot air dry the leaves, stop fermentation.

and make the final crisp and twisted tea.

Tea is generally imported into this country as 'originals' or unblended tea and is afterwards blended by wholesalers to suit the tastes of the retailers, or rather their customers, in different districts, to a very large extent dependent upon the character of the drinking water, whether it is hard or soft. Roughly, the grades of tea stocked in a grocer's shop follow the course of the prices; the so-called cheaper teas on the balance of flavour, aroma and colour of infusion are not the more economical. The British prefer teas which are very 'broken', whereas the continental housewife buys larger leaf teas. In order to make tea satisfactorily, the water should have just been brought to the boiling point; the pot, preferably one of earthenware, already hot; the leaves crushed and broken so as to expose the largest surface and as speedily as possible to the boiling water, and infusion should be allowed to continue for three minutes or so for Indian tea, and for five minutes for China tea. China teas lack tannin and body. An infusion that has been long standing has lost much of its quality by the excessive amount of tannin then extracted. Caffeine and tea oil, the characteristic ingredients of tea, are easily extracted by infusion, and are largely absent from any second infusion.

Tea as such has no nutritive value, other than perhaps in its riboflavin. At best, because of its caffeine ($C_8H_{10}N_4O_2$), 1·5 to 3 per cent by weight, it is a mild nervous stimulant, which is not followed by any depression; at the worst when drunk in excess, particularly in lower grades, or excessively infused, by reason of its tannin, it disturbs the digestive system generally. Caffeine, a stimulating drug, is a white flavourless solid. The flavorous substance in tea is theine, probably a group of substances. Tannin, if present in quantity, spoils the flavour of tea. It precipitates in hard water, staining teapots and cups. The chief undoubted advantage of the use of tea is that it ensures for most persons the imbibition into the system of fairly large quantities of warm water. Tea as usually served with cream or milk and sugar gains the food values of these substances. The percentage of drinkers taking sugar is much lower than it used to be.

At the present time tea bags are commonly used in this country. Acceptance by the public has been comparatively recent although they have been popular in the USA for some time. Their popularity is probably due more to their convenience in use than anything else as, weight-for-weight, the cost of tea bags exceeds that of similar quality packet tea and there is considerable difference of opinion regarding the respective flavours.

20.2   COFFEE

Coffee was introduced into England from the Levant in 1652 and quickly became the vogue in 'coffee-houses'. Coffee is the seed-leaf of *Coffea arabica* and allied species, an evergreen shrub or small tree growing in the moist tropics, chiefly, Arabia, Kenya, Ethiopia, India, Sri Lanka, Java, Jamaica and Brazil. The fruit or coffee cherry consists of an outer skin, a pulp and a parchment skin enclosing two seeds, called the berries. The berries must be roasted before use to oxidize some of the tannin and develop the flavour. This is effected by many types of roasters, commercial and domestic, which roast, not simply bake, the berries—a process taking from eight to twelve minutes. In the process caffeine is dissociated from tannin and the sugar is caramelized. As soon as roasted the berries should be quickly cooled and afterwards kept in an air-tight canister, otherwise the oils are oxidized to rancid products which spoil the flavour. Roasting should be done frequently, even daily, and preferably followed by grinding according to the immediate needs. The aroma quickly disappears after grinding and particularly if the ground coffee is not kept enclosed. To make coffee in the home the simplest plan is to use an earthenware jug with a lip for pouring and a lid. The jug should be first warmed and there should be put into it 100g if not more, of coffee for every litre of liquor required. Freshly boiling water should be poured in and stirred well with a wooden spoon. Infusion should be allowed to continue in a warm place for about six minutes, and the clear liquid then carefully poured out. Milk when used with coffee should be hot, but not boiling and nowadays single cream is being increasingly served as an alternative. A variety of coffee percolators and coffee-makers are on the market and like tea, coffee is also available in coffee bags. Unfortunately unlike tea the coffee made and served in this country compares very unfavourably with coffee served in other parts of the world and many visitors to the UK consider the coffee to be quite unacceptable. Coffee essence has been in use for many years but the advent of instant coffee powders is comparatively recent in the history of coffee consumption. Many people would argue that drinks made from such powders bear little resemblance to true coffee, however they are certainly very popular and palatable and their increased consumption is thought to have contributed to the diminished consumption of tea in this country.

20.2.1 Instant coffee

An extract is made of those parts of the coffee bean that dissolve in water; this retains much of the flavour and aroma of the roasted bean. A concentrated liquid extract of coffee is then spray dried. The most acceptable products are found to be those where a 20 per cent solution of coffee solids is dried at $-25°$ C. This results in a preparation where one teaspoonful of instant coffee powder is used for each cup of coffee. Low concentrates require comparatively high temperatures for drying. As the concentrations increase drying must be carried out at lower temperatures to avoid 'puffing' and poor solubility. Granular instant coffee is made by the accelerated freeze dry method (see 19.5.1).

20.3 Cocoa

Cocoa was introduced by the Spaniards into Europe from Mexico and Peru, and first came to this country about 1650. It is derived from the roasted seeds of a small evergreen tree, *Theobroma cacao*. The beans are roasted, then cracked and the several parts, cocoa-nibs, germ and shell separated. The nibs, after blending, are ground to a semi-liquid mass, from which part of the cocoa-butter or fat is pressed, and the cocoa-cake is left to be still further ground down and sifted to form cocoa powder or essence. Eating chocolate is made by adding sugar and cocoa-butter to cocoa-cake. Navy cocoa or pure block cocoa is the solidified ground nib and therefore contains much fat, in fact too much so for the ordinary consumer. Soluble cocoa is obtained by treating the cocoa at one stage or other of its manufacture with an alkali, so that the natural acidity is neutralized, the colour darkened, the aroma and flavour appreciably modified and the fine particles of the cocoa made more buoyant so that they do not settle quickly.

The characteristic nitrogenous ingredient of cocoa is the alkaloid theobromine $C_7H_8N_4O_2$ (2·2 per cent), a substance similar to caffeine in composition and in its action on the nervous system, though much milder. Cocoa beans when gathered are very rich in fat (cocoa-butter), but in the manufacture of cocoa powder for domestic uses the proportion is reduced to about 20 per cent. The energy value of cocoa powder is some 1869kJ per 100g, corresponding to the high contents of fat, of protein (18 per cent) and of carbohydrate (36 per cent)—some original, some added. Cocoa powder contains useful amounts of the vitamins A, riboflavin and nicotinic acid as well as of the minerals iron and calcium; but in the spoonful or so used for making a breakfast cup the amounts are of little significance, other than that of making an agreeable beverage of hot milk or water.

20.4 SPICES AND CONDIMENTS

Spices, condiments and similar flavouring materials, natural flavourings from plants, used in great variety in the preparation and serving of food though not for nourishment—providing as they do little that is a source of energy or of building material—have yet definite uses in giving relish to food, in arousing appetite and in promoting the secretion of saliva and gastric juice and so positively aiding digestion. Even ordinary healthy appetites appreciate the presence of an appropriate pungency by way of condiments in the various foods before them; all the more so jaded appetites where the palate or digestion is enfeebled by either sickness or abuse. · Particular flavourings are associated with various meats: mustard or horse-radish with roast beef; mint-sauce with lamb; caper sauce with mutton; sage and onions with pork or fowl; red currant jelly with hare; lemon juice with fillets of fish or oysters, and vinegar with oysters and molluscs generally, or crabs and other crustaceans. Pepper and salt have a universal application in the kitchen and at the table. Sauces and chutneys are real assistants in the eating of cold and insipid meats.

In mediaeval times, and even later until what may be called the agricultural revolution, fresh meat after September was rare, for then most of the herds had been slaughtered and their carcasses salted down to serve until well on into the new year. In comparison with our present-day fresh or refrigerated meat produced on far better pastures than were ever available in the old times, meat was then at best coarse, and at worst tough and unpalatable, if not repulsive because of decay. The use of spices and condiments was necessary to hide the unpleasant taste and flavour of imperfectly preserved and half-rotten flesh. The demands of Western Europe for these assistants to digestion resulted in a very considerable spice industry in the Orient and Levant, and on its transport and commerce the Venetians largely built up their empire of the seas. It is sometimes stated that the serious hindrance to the flow of spices into Europe, overland and by sea, from the East resulting upon the capture of Constantinople by the Ottoman Turks in 1453 was a primary factor in turning the attention of western navigators to the possibility of other routes to the spice islands of the East by way either of the southern route by the rounding of Africa which was discovered by Vasco da Gama in 1497, or westward across the Atlantic, found by

Columbus in 1492. Spices are less used today in this country, apart from pepper, mustard and prepared sauces, than in Asiatic countries, in America or on the Continent. Where spiced breads and sweets, and various kinds of sausage are consumed in quantity, as in Germany, the consumption of spices of all sorts is heavy.

The botanicals from which flavours can be separated include herbs, roots, seeds, leaves and flowers. The flavours are obtained by the processes of maceration, percolation and digestion.

Oleo-resins are extractions of seeds, roots, barks, leaves and fruits with alcohol or some other pure solvent of low boiling point. Oleo-resins supply taste to spices, but essential oils give the aroma.

Essential oils are volatile oils carrying the particular odour or flavour of the plant concerned. They are insoluble in water and are collected either by squeezing them out, or by steam distillation. Another method is the French enfleurage method, absorption in oil.

Essential 'oils' may be many different chemical substances, aldehydes, ketones, esters, alcohols and even hydrocarbons. The hydrocarbons are terpenes. Removal of terpenes gives terpene-less oils with very delicate characteristic flavours. Essences are flavorous substances dissolved in alcohol. Alkaloids are organic substances in plants combined with acids as salts. Caffeine and quinine are examples.

Glucosides are compounds which hydrolyse to gluconic acid—an organic substance.

20.4.1 Pepper

Pepper is the seed of *Piper nigrum*, a perennial creeper or vine, with much the same habit of growth as our black bryony. The pepper vine is cultivated or grows wild over most of tropical Asia. The fruits are one-seeded berries growing closely packed together, and when fully grown are green but on the point of turning red. At this stage they are plucked for the production of black pepper; for the production of white pepper they are allowed to ripen fully and are gathered when fully red. The dried mature peppercorns have their dried outer coating removed. In composition they are 1·5 per cent volatile oil and 6·0 per cent oleoresin. Black pepper with the maximum pungency and aroma comes to this country largely from the East Indies; white pepper comes largely from the Isle of Banka in East Indies. Other supplies are shipped from Singapore and Sarawak.

The bulk of domestic pepper is in the form of ground pepper: for table uses white pepper is usually preferred on the score of appearance when sprinkled, but in the kitchen black pepper has the advantage of aroma and pungency. The colour of ground white pepper varies according to the type or quality of the original pepper-corns and to the processes of manufacture—such as screening from pieces of husk, bleaching, tinting with turmeric, or admixture with adulterants. White pepper should have a cream or greyish tint according to grade or quality. Where flavour in food is appreciated it is better to grind as required black or white peppercorns in a small table mill; the difference between such freshly made pepper and long stored dry processed pepper is marked.

Pepper owes its pungency and aroma to an essential oil and an alkaloid (piperine) $C_{17}H_{19}O_3N$, to the extent of some 8 or 9 per cent, especially in black pepper from which it can be readily extracted by warming with milk of lime for 15 minutes, then evaporating to dry-ness and taking up with ether. The action of piperine is to stimulate the flow of saliva and the gastric juices, and in excess to promote perspiration, hence its use in the treatment of fevers.

20.4.2 Blue poppy or maw seed
Poppy seed is bluish grey in colour and is extensively used on the continent to decorate bread and rolls.

20.4.3 Capsicums and chillies
Capsicums and chillies are the fruit pods of annual plants related to the tomato, *Capsicum minimum* and *C. frutescens* respectively. When grown in the tropics they are very pungent but allied species grown in Europe either lack 'heat' or are mild. Both capsicums and chillies appear to be indigenous to Central and South America and the West Indies but are now grown widely in the tropics of both Old and New Worlds.

The large pods (38–100mm in length) are described as capsicum and the smaller pods as chillies. They are very acrid and are used for pickling or for making cayenne pepper. The colour is bright red but the seeds are yellow. Normally they are dry, shiny, and wrinkled. The aroma is characteristic and pleasant. The taste is biting but they contain no volatile oil. Capsicums are exported from India, China, Japan, Central America, East and West Indies and Africa, and chillies from East and West Africa and Java.

Cayenne pepper is prepared by grinding *Capsicum frutescens* and *Capsicum baccatum*. Nepal pepper from the orange–yellow Nepal capsicums has much more aroma than the ordinary hot pepper; it is highly esteemed but is expensive. The more pungent capsicums and chillies are largely used in the manufacture of medicated cotton wool and heat-giving liniments for the relief of muscular pains and congestion. They are also used in pickles, chutney, curries and sauces. The pungency of red pepper is due to violently active poisonous substances, which, however, in very small quantities are useful stimulants and carminatives.

20.4.4 Paprika

Paprika pepper of the higher grades is a sweet red pepper. There are two types of paprika, the mild or Spanish and the pungent or Hungarian. The mild paprika is bright to dark red in colour and the mild varieties have a pleasant sweet taste and aroma. Paprika pepper is used to garnish dishes, to colour and flavour gravies, stews and hashes, and generally for its colouring and preservative qualities by packers of meat products. Paprika was the first considerable natural source of ascorbic acid. Rose hips, which are very high in ascorbic acid, are a variety of paprika.

20.4.5 Caraway seeds

Caraway seeds are the fruits of the caraway (*Carum carvi*) belonging to the Umbelliferae, to which family also belong fennel, carrot, parsley, angelica, celery and dill. Seeds and leaves of this family are usually aromatic, containing oils which stimulate the digestive tract and are hence used in medicines as carminatives, such as dill water. Caraways have long been cultivated in Holland as well as generally in other European countries. Seeds of good quality have a bright colour, are very aromatic and yield about 7 per cent of a volatile oil. In addition to their use in medicine and for the flavouring of cakes, bread, baked fruits, roast pippins and, in Germany, cheese and soups, they are used in perfumery and for flavouring cordials and liqueurs (Kümmel).

20.4.6 Celery seed

Celery seed is used as a flavouring ingredient in celery salt and home remedies for rheumatism.

Celery seed is the dried fruit of *Apium graveolens*, 1.5mm in length, brown in colour with pale ridges. The aroma is the characteristic taste described as warm and bitter. Seeds yield 3 per cent volatile oil. Celery salt is a mixture of ground celery seed and table salt.

20.4.7 Cardamoms

Cardamoms are small dark brown or nearly black seeds contained in the capsule of *Elettaria cardamomum*, a plant allied to ginger, growing in Sri Lanka, India (Mysore and Malabar), Java and

Jamaica. The seeds lose their flavour when removed from their capsule. They are rich in volatile oil (8 per cent), are used as carminatives and to mask the taste of unpleasant drugs. They are also used
as an ingredient of flavourings for soups, sauces, cordials or 'soft
drinks', sausages, cheese, bread, cakes and curry powder.

20.4.8 Cassia

Cassia is the bark of aromatic laurels belonging to the same genus,
Cinnamomum, as that which yields the true cinnamon. Different
varieties of cassia of several tropical countries come from different
species of *Cinnamomum cassia*: China cassia, Saigon cassia, Batavia
cassia. The unripe buds are used also. They are greyish brown in
colour and cinnamon-like in flavour, containing 0·52 per cent volatile
oil, mainly cinnamic aldehyde. Cassia bark varies in thickness and
is much coarser and more woody than cinnamon. It is also distinguished from cinnamon by breaking with a short fracture, in not
being rolled into quills, and in its much darker colour. The best
cassia (Saigon) has a flavour and aroma suggesting those of true
cinnamon but it does not possess its medicinal qualities. Cassia is
valued for its flavour and relative cheapness, and is largely used in
ground mixed spices.

20.4.9 Cinnamon

Cinnamon is a product of *Cinnamomum zeylanicum*, an aromatic
laurel which grows most abundantly, wild and cultivated, in Sri
Lanka. Cinnamon bark contains a volatile oil. The tree is coppiced
and made to yield continuously, even for 100 years, willowy shoots
some 2 to 3 metres long. The shoots when two years old are cut,
usually in May, and the bark is slit down on both sides and left
for a few hours to ferment and dry. The quills so formed are graded
and bundled. Broken fragments of bark and chips from quills are
ground and distilled to produce cinnamon bark oil. Another oil is
distilled from the leaves, and, containing much eugenol, is used in
the production of artificial vanilla. Cinnamon and cassia are interchangeable in commerce, but cinnamon is used where a more delicate flavour is required.

Cinnamon is one of the most pleasant flavouring spices and is
admirable for flavouring cakes and puddings. It has also uses in
medicine as an astringent in cases of diarrhoea when taken in the
form of dry powder mixed with icing sugar. It is also used an as
internal disinfectant and is often prescribed as a relief, if not a
cure, for influenza.

20.4.10 Cloves

Cloves consist of the dried and unopened flower buds of *Eugenia aromatica* L., a tropical evergreen found in the Moluccas. For many years the Dutch held a monopoly of the clove trade but more recently Zanzibar (now part of Tanzania) and Pemba have been the principal sources of the world's supply. Other supplies come from Madagascar, Sri Lanka and the Seychelles Islands. The cloves produced in Amboyna in the East Indies are the fullest flavoured of all, containing some 20 per cent volatile oil as compared with the 17 per cent of Zanzibar cloves. The oil consists essentially of eugenol. It contains 1 per cent volatile oil. Clove oil has many uses in medicine and in perfumery as well as in domestic cookery. It is the source from which artificial vanilla is manufactured.

20.4.11 Coriander seed

Coriander seed is obtained from an umbelliferous plant, *Coriandrum sativum*, a native of the Mediterranean countries and the Caucasus. It has long been extensively cultivated in North India, Morocco and Russia, and is found semi-wild in eastern counties of England, as an escape from an old cultivation. The seed is nearly globular, about the size of a sweet pea seed; when fresh, it smells disagreeably but when ripe is very fragrant with a very pleasant warm pungent taste. It is an important ingredient of curry powder and of mixed spice, and is used as a flavouring in fancy breads, confectionery, medicine, gin, and some liqueurs.

20.4.12 Ginger

Ginger is the rhizome of *Zingiber officinale*, a native of India and China. The principal sources are India, Jamaica and Sierra Leone, although recently supplies have come in from Nigeria and Sri Lanka. The chief commercial sources are Jamaica ginger, Indian ginger, African ginger and Japanese ginger. The finest ginger is grown in Jamica; it has the best aroma and is well prepared for the market.

The normal colour of peeled ginger is yellowish buff, but it is also sold with a snow-white coating of lime, although the extra processing somewhat impairs the quality. The medium and lower grades of ginger from Africa are largely used for grinding as for making ginger beer and essence, and as an ingredient of cattle and poultry spice. High grade ginger contains from 1·5 to 3 per cent of a volatile oil and about 3 per cent of a fixed oil—hence its use for flavouring in the kitchen and as a stomachic in medicine. It also contains resinous matter which adds to the flavour.

20.4.13 Mustard

Mustard is produced by the grinding of the endosperm of the black mustard seed, *Brassica sinapoides nigra*, and white mustard seed, *Brassica sinapoides alba*; the former actually more brown than black and the latter yellow. The best white seed is grown in this country, chiefly in East Anglia. White mustard seed is some three times the size of the black seed but has less pungency and aroma. Mustard flour is usually a mixture of black and white seed flour obtaining its pungency of taste and aroma from the black seed, and its 'body' and enzymic properties mainly from the white seed.

Mustard has various uses: as a table condiment where it gives pungency to cold meat and assists the appetite; medicinally as a speedy emetic and in the form of mustard plasters or bath mustard —in these cases mainly derived from black seed.

20.4.14 Nutmegs and mace

The nutmeg tree, *Myristica fragrans*, is grown most extensively in the East Indies, and in Grenada and Trinidad in the West Indies. East Indian nutmegs are limed to protect them from pests, and are therefore superior. The fruit resembles an apricot and when ripe its outer covering (pericarp) splits and reveals a red aril, the mace, closely enmeshing the shell in which the nutmeg lies as kernel. The mace is stripped off and flattened by hand and laid out to dry, changing colour to a yellowish brown. The nutmegs in the shells when sufficiently dried over slow fires and in the sun are carefully released by the cracking open of the shells, bruising being avoided. Good nutmegs are rich in oil, containing 14 per cent volatile oil and 30 per cent fixed oil. When a nutmeg is grated the solid end should be used first so leaving the opposite cavernous end as waste.

Mace is an aril or fibrous network surrounding the nutmeg seed as an outgrowth of the seed coat. The finest flavoured mace comes from Penang and Singapore, but most of our supplies come from Grenada. Ground mace is used in the kitchen for flavouring; it should be kept in an air-tight container for the essential oil is very volatile.

20.4.15 Pimento or allspice

Pimento is the berry of a West Indian evergreen myrtle (*Pimenta officinalis linel*, called Jamaica pimento or Jamaica pepper), allied to the clove. The berry is nearly globular in shape, of rich brown colour, light and brittle, and contains two small bean-shaped seeds. The smaller berries are usually the more pungent and fuller flavoured. Volatile oil resides in the husk of the berry and may amount to 3–4·5 per cent, 80 per cent eugenol. The name allspice is derived from the supposed resemblance to a mixture of cinnamon, nutmeg and clove.

Pimento is much used in pickling, especially of walnuts, and in stews, and, when ground, in flavouring meats such as Strasbourg beef, sausage and potted meats. It enters largely into the composition of mixed pudding spice.

20.4.16 Fenugreek

Fenugreek consists of the small yellow brown angular seeds of a plant of the clover family, *Trigonella foenum-graecum* L., which is cultivated principally in Morocco and Tunis. The seeds are used considerably in veterinary practice and in poultry spices as a means of keeping animals in condition. They are rich in phosphates, iron and lecithin, and have long been used in medicine in the East. Fenugreek is an ingredient of curry powder to which it imparts colour, aroma and flavour. Its aroma is due in part to its coumarin, natural perfume—that of new mown hay—found more abundantly in tonka bean and sparingly in sweet woodruff and sweet vernal grass.

20.4.17 Curry powder

Curry powder is a condiment of very variable composition according to the fancy of the maker. The spices most generally used in its manufacture are coriander, turmeric, cumin, ginger, pepper, chillies and cardamom seeds. Some curry powders also contain fenugreek, pimento and nutmeg.

It is really a 'short-cut' preparation for Western use, as good Indian cooks prefer to combine their own spices for each variety of curry according to the needs of the individual dish.

20.5 SWEET HERBS

The sweet herbs used in the kitchen are the dried parts of plants —leaves, roots, fruits and seeds—commonly cultivated in the herb garden, which because of the flavour and fragrance due to volatile oils peculiar to the individual species are used for giving characteristic flavours to soups, stews, salads and so on. Most of the sweet herbs are native to the dry sunny soils of the Mediterranean countries but were introduced into this country at various times; first by the Romans, but more especially later by the various orders of monks. The use of sweet herbs for culinary purposes was well developed throughout the Middle Ages as adjuncts to the more pungent spices from the East, and much more so than today.

By far the great majority of the thirty odd plants cultivated as sweet herbs belong to two orders of the Labiatae and the Umbelliferae. Examples of the former are balm, basil, sage, marjoram, rosemary, mint and thyme, and of the latter parsley, dill, fennel, angelica, aniseed, caraway. Sweet herbs belonging to other orders are rue, borage, sweet bay and chives. The commonest herbs in present-day use are parsley, sage, thyme and mint.

Parsley is grown largely for its leaves, to serve as a garnishing and a flavouring, whether fresh or dried and powdered. Oil is extracted from the fresh fruits.

The leaves of sage are used as flavouring and seasoning in soups, in stuffing with onions for ducks, geese and pork; as a substitute for tea in cooling drinks; as an ingredient in herb beer; and for perfumery in the scenting of soaps. Its essential oil contains pinene ($C_{10}H_{16}$). It is of the mint family, and is the dried leaf of *Saldia officinalis*. It blends with red and white peppers and salt.

Garden thyme is a cultivated form of wild thyme of the Mediterranean coast where it has long been associated with the production of the finest flavoured honey. It is the dried leaf and flowering tops of *Thymus vulgaris*, 2·5 per cent volatile oil.

Mint occurs as three species, the spearmint, peppermint and pennyroyal; the first, *Mentha piperita*, is that ordinarily used in the kitchen (either fresh in mint sauce or in the dried form in mint jelly and sauce), the other two are medicinal herbs. Garden mint was introduced into this country by the Romans. It is commonly eaten with lamb, for it makes the meat more digestible by stimulating the digestive glands. The oil distilled from the leaves is extensively used to flavour toothpaste and chewing gums; it contains menthone ($C_{10}H_{18}O$) and menthol ($C_{10}H_{19}OH$).

20.6 COMMON SALT

Common salt consists essentially of almost pure sodium chloride (NaCl), derived in this country from natural brine springs or wells, or from deposits of rock salt, but in warm countries still mainly by the evaporation of sea water. Even in this country during the Middle Ages, salt was largely obtained by the evaporation of seawater, run into shallow ponds or salterns; traces of these may still be found in the neighbourhoods of Portsmouth, Lymington and Poole Harbour. From the centres of this sea-salt industry and from the naturally occurring brine springs at Droitwich and Northwich, ancient trackways, the salt ways, radiated throughout the country over which a considerable traffic was long carried. In those days salt had a more extensive domestic use than today as a preservative of meat, fowl and fish upon which the vast majority of the people depended in the winter and spring months for their flesh food.

In Cheshire, the most considerable area of salt manufacture in this country, brine, a 25 per cent solution of salt in water, is pumped up out of bore holes sunk in the marls of the New Red Sandstone and then evaporated in flat iron pans by artificial heat with the help of reduced pressure. According to the rate of evaporation differently sized crystals of salt separate out; large crystals of fishery and bay salts when the evaporation is slow, and small crystals as fine or table salts when it is rapid. For table use salt must be dry and reasonably free from impurities, such as the poisonous salts of barium. It contains small quantities of hygroscopic impurities which, absorbing moisture from the atmosphere, cause the salt to cake or become damp. In free running table salt this is prevented by the addition during processing of small traces of fine sodium phosphate or carbonate, or rice powder.

Besides its use at the table for adding flavour to under-seasoned food, salt has many uses in the kitchen. It is used for preserving meat, being rubbed into fresh meat as crystals or allowed to soak into it as brine. Salt here acts in two different ways: as antiseptic, killing bacterial and fungus germs; and, by reason of its water-absorptive powers related to its osmotic pressure, as a dehydrater of cells and tissues. In very weak solution—as about 3 per cent—the osmotic pressure of salt tends to stop the diffusion and so the loss of the natural salts of fish or freshly cut meat when being simmered in water; the flavour of fish is particularly improved by the addition of salt. Potatoes and vegetables generally, when boiled without salt, are flavourless, because of the loss of their natural salts, a fault which cannot be corrected afterwards at the table by the addition of salt. With good cooking there should be little or no need to add salt to food at the table. Salt plays an important role in the making of bread, not only as a flavouring but even more as a stabilizer of the gluten.

Some brands of table salt contain small proportions of such ingredients as sodium or potassium iodide in order to supply to the system iodine, which is needed for the proper functioning of the thyroid gland, particularly where the drinking water of the district is deficient in this element. Celery salt is a mixture of ordinary salt and ground celery seed.

20.7 VINEGAR

Vinegar, or 'sour wine', is formed when light alcoholic beverages, such as weak wines, cider and ale, are left exposed to the atmosphere or deliberately inoculated by the genus of bacterium called *Acetobacter*, the alcohol being then oxidized to acetic acid, the characteristic constituent of all vinegars.

$$C_2H_5OH \quad \xrightarrow[\text{oxidation}]{+20} \quad CH_3COOH \; + \; H_2O$$

$$\text{alcohol} \qquad\qquad\qquad \text{acetic acid}$$

Vinegars may be easily divided into two main classes, according as the acetic acid is produced by the fermentation carried through by *Acetobacter* and allied micro-organisms of alcohol derived in its turn by the fermentation of saccharine solutions, or whether, as in artificial vinegars, acetic acid obtained from ordinary industrial sources is simply diluted with water to the required strength and then coloured and flavoured to taste.

20.7.1 Fermented vinegars

Fermented vinegars are dependent upon *B. aceti*, which is always present in the atmosphere and finds food and a suitable medium for its activity in dilute alcoholic liquors of various origins. The bacterium cannot, however, act on strong alcoholic beverages such as port, sherry or whisky. The colour, flavour and aroma of the various types of fermented vinegar depend largely upon the nature of the original alcoholic liquor. In England, brewed vinegar is almost entirely derived from various kinds of grain and sugars— almost anything which can be made to yield a saccharine solution being used. Exceptionally, it is brewed entirely from barley malt, but more generally from mixtures of malted and unmalted barley which may be replaced by other grains such as maize or rice. In France, vinegar is made from inferior white and red wines. In the USA it is now very largely made from apple cider.

The process of manufacture of malt vinegar falls into four stages: mashing, in which the starch of the grain is converted by diastase, etc., into fermentable sugars, such as glucose; vinous fermentation, in which yeast converts the sugar into alcohol; acetous fermentation, in which the alcoholic liquor is converted by the bacterium with the absorption of oxygen into acetic acid; and clarification, in which the originally turbid vinegar is rendered clear and fit for consumption. The distinctive stage of acetification is carried out in large vessels in the form of a truncated cone the upper portion of which is filled with birch twigs, beech shavings or basket work upon which the bacterium grows, and the lower portion contains the 'wash' from alcoholic fermentations to be acetified. The wash is continuously pumped up to the top of the vessels and sprayed upon the mass of twigs, etc., impregnated with the micro-organism, when, in the presence of sufficient air, it is slowly transformed into vinegar. Acetification takes a week or fortnight to complete. It is usually stopped before all the alcohol is converted so as to allow the subsequent slow formation of esters, which are volatile compounds of the acid with alcohols, and give flavour and aroma to the refined vinegar.

A good vinegar will contain about 5 per cent acetic acid.

Distilled Vinegar Distilled vinegar is prepared by distilling malt vinegar, either pure or fortified, and comes over as a clear colourless liquid, consisting practically of acetic acid and water, but with small traces of the aromatic volatile bodies. It is more widely used in Scotland than in England, and is also sold as 'crystal vinegar' and 'white wine' vinegar.

Wine Vinegar The best wine vinegar is made from white wine and is imported from Orleans, and contains from 5 to 5·6 per cent of acetic acid. Small quantities of wine vinegar are made in this country from wine which has gone sour, or from 'wine' made here from raisins or grape juice.

Imitation wine vinegars are largely sold as wine vinegars but are simply made by diluting spirit vinegar until it contains about 5 per cent of acetic acid and then adding suitable colouring matters. Such imitation 'vinegars' can be sold very cheaply.

Special or Fancy Vinegars Raspberry and Tarragon vinegars are prepared by treating the appropriate fruit or herb, or flavouring essences with malt vinegar. These vinegars are usually sold at prices far in excess of the value of the contents.

20.7.2 Non-brewed 'vinegar'
The simplest artificial 'vinegar' consists of industrial acetic acid well diluted with water and coloured with a little caramel. Such a 'vinegar' has a harshness and pungency lacking in any variety of fermented acetic acid.

20.8   FLAVOURING AGENTS

The chief substances used as flavouring agents for confectionery purposes are essential oils, essences, liqueurs and fruit juices.

20.8.1   Essential oils

Essential or volatile oils are liquids which impart a characteristic odour to the flower, fruit or other part of plants containing them. They must be distinguished from paraffin or rock oils on the one hand and fixed or fatty oils on the other. The essential oils are only occasionally single substances; usually they are composed of several chemical substances, e.g. terpenes ($C_{10}H_{16}$), camphor compounds as well as aromatic and aliphatic alcohols, phenols, aldehydes, ketones, acids and esters. Generally, essential oils are colourless liquids when pure and with strong odours and tastes. They are volatile without decomposition and can be distilled in steam unchanged. They are practically insoluble in water but easily soluble in alcohol. On keeping they are liable to become darker in colour and thick in consistency. It is for this reason that all flavouring materials should be kept in well-stoppered bottles. This prevents loss of material by evaporation and loss of flavour by atmospheric oxidation.

Several methods are used for extracting the essential oils from plants. Among the more important may be mentioned distillation, pressing, solvents, maceration and enfleurage (taking up in oil). In the distillation process the material containing the essential oil is placed in a still with water and heated to boiling. The essential oil is distilled off along with steam and collected through a condenser. The distillate is at first milky in appearance but on standing separates out into two layers with the oil usually at the top. The water is drawn off and returned to the still or the distillation may be carried out by a continuous process. In the pressing method of extraction such as is used for oranges and lemons the oils are obtained by hydraulic presses or by hand. The usual solvent method is by means of alcohol. After extraction the solvent is distilled from the oil and recovered for further use. The maceration and enfleurage methods are used in the case of oils which are injured by a strong heat. A perfectly pure neutral fat is melted and the flowers or leaves stirred into it. The essential oil is taken up by the fat and afterwards extracted from it by alcohol. Such solutions in alcohol are frequently used in perfumery. The residual fat still contains some of the essential oil and is made use of in the preparation of pomades.

Apart from their use as flavouring materials essential oils also find application in perfumery, medicine and pharmacy. The most important essential oils used in confectionery are those derived from bitter almonds, vanilla pods, oranges, lemons, angelica and peppermint.

Essential Oil of Bitter Almonds   Bitter almond oil is obtained from the kernels of bitter almonds (*Amygdala amara*), as well as of cherry seed, apricots, peaches and nectarines. All these kernels contain also a fixed fatty oil which must first be removed. This is done by grinding the kernels to meal and then subjecting the meal to powerful hydraulic pressure. The fixed oil expressed in this way is a typical liquid fat resembling olive oil in appearance and properties. The press-cake is then ground to powder and warm water (83° C) added to it. This is allowed to cool, fresh ground almond press-cake mixed in and left to stand for twelve hours. During this steeping the glucoside, amygdalin, present in the kernels is hydrolysed by the enzyme, emulsin, into benzaldehyde, glucose and prussic acid.

$$C_{20}H_{27}NO_{11} + 2H_2O \rightarrow C_6H_5CHO + 2C_6H_{12}O_6 + HCN$$

amygdalin   water   benzaldehyde   glucose   prussic acid

When hydrolysis is complete the mixture is distilled in a partial vacuum, and benzaldehyde and prussic acid are thus separated from glucose and the residue. To remove the poisonous prussic acid the distillate is treated with iron II sulphate and milk of lime. The ferro-cyanide of calcium thus formed is insoluble and non-poisonous and is removed by filtration. Finally the filtrate is steam-distilled to obtain the oil of bitter almonds.

Finally it should be noted that it is only the bitter almond which yields an essential oil. Sweet almonds contain the same fixed oil as bitter almonds but no essential oil.

Essential Oils of Oranges and Lemons   The essential oils of oranges and lemons occur in small glands in the rinds from which they are extracted by pressure. On the larger scale hydraulic or screw presses are used, but the finest quality oils are produced by hand. One hand-method is the sponge and bowl process in which the peel is cut into halves and the oil expressed by turning them inside out and then wiping off the oil by a sponge and squeezing the sponge in a bowl. In another hand-process the rind is rotated rapidly in a round metal bowl studded with sharp spikes which burst the glands containing the oil. The extracted oil collects in a receptacle at the bottom of the bowl.

The chief regions in which these oils are produced are Syracuse,

Palermo and Messina in Sicily, while California is a more recent source of supply.

Essential Oil of Peppermint   Peppermint oil is obtained by distillation of the herb *Mentha piperita*. It is a colourless or greenish yellow liquid with a strong pungent taste and smell. Its characteristic ingredient is menthol, the remainder being a mixture of several terpenes.

20.8.2   Vanilla

The essential constituent of vanilla is vanillin, a very widely used flavouring agent. Vanilla pods from which the vanillin is extracted are the fruits of a tropical climbing orchid which flourishes in the French tropical colonies, Mexico, West Indies and South America. The vanilla beans, which are greenish yellow in colour and odourless when gathered before they are fully ripe, are subjected to a fermentation or curing process. There are two methods of curing, the Mexican and Madagascan. The former takes eight months. A specific enzyme brings out the characteristic odour by the development of vanillin, which appears as a white efflorescence of needle-shaped crystals on the outside of the beans. Vanillin is only one of the constituents of vanilla flavour. None of the others has been successfully imitated.

The beans are sun-dried and packed for export. In this form they are about 200mm long, about 6mm thick in the middle and have a dark wrinkled surface. The vanillin content of the pods is somewhere in the region of 6·0 per cent, but the proportion of vanillin is not necessarily a criterion of quality, since the fine aroma of vanilla is also due to a combination of gums, resins and oils in the form of a balsam.

The pods may be crushed to a powder and mixed with nine times their weight of sugar and used in this dry form to sprinkle over cakes, etc., or they may be broken into small pieces and steeped for several months in alcohol to which a little sugar and glycerine are added so forming 'essence of vanilla'. Vanillin can be prepared artificially by oxidation of eugenol with alkaline permanganate of potash. The vanillin is dissolved in alcohol and coloured with caramel to give artificial vanilla essence.

20.8.3   Essences

Natural fruit essences are solutions in alcohol of the essential oils and esters of fruits which flavour any goods in which they are used. With the exception of a few notable cases, e.g. vanilla essence, it is impossible to extract the distinctive flavours from fruits in sufficient quantity and of sufficient strength for flavouring purposes. The majority of essences are artificial products prepared by mixing essential oils and synthetic esters with alcohol. The aroma and flavour of such artificial essences are seldom as delicate or as fragrant as the natural product they attempt to imitate. In certain cases an artificial essence contains only a single substance dissolved in alcohol, but more usually varying proportions of several substances are used before a close approximation to the natural product is achieved. The usual method of manufacture is to mix together 70–75 parts by weight of rectified alcohol, 3–5 parts of glycerine, 5–10 parts of essential oils and esters and the whole made up to 100 parts with distilled water.

Esters associated with flavourings are shown in the table below:

Name	Structure	Flavour
Ethyl formate	$HCO_2CH_2CH_3$	rum
Isobutyl formate	$HCO_2CH_2CH(CH_3)_2$	raspberries
n-Pentyl acetate (n-amyl acetate)	$CH_3CO_2CH_2CH_2CH_2CH_2CH_3$	bananas
Isopentyl acetate (isoamyl acetate)	$CH_3CO_2CH_2CH_2CH(CH_3)_2$	pears
n-Octyl acetate	$CH_3CO_2(CH_2)_7CH_3$	oranges
Ethyl butyrate	$CH_3CH_2CH_2CO_2CH_2CH_3$	pineapples
n-Pentyl butyrate	$CH_3CH_2CH_2CO_2(CH_2)_4CH_3$	apricots

20.8.4 Liqueurs

In the preparation of liqueurs the fruits or herbs are first bruised and then steeped in diluted grain spirits or rectified alcohol. After sufficient steeping the volatile constituents extracted by the alcohol are separated by distillation and the distillate sweetened by the addition of sugar. The product is then stored in wooden casks to mature and is finally bottled. It will thus be seen that they are similar to essences and contain essential oils dissolved in an alcoholic syrup. Some very well-known liqueurs are Kirchwasser, Maraschino, Benedictine, and Crême de Menthe.

Kirchwasser or Cherry Water is prepared in the Black Forest and certain parts of Switzerland from a dark wild cherry which is fermented along with the kernel. Maraschino like Kirchwasser is also prepared from cherries, but only the pulp is used. It is one of the sweetest of liqueurs. Other ingredients such as cherry leaves, raspberries and orris roots are added in certain varieties.

Benedictine is the most famous of liqueurs and derives its name from the fact that it was originally made by the monks of the Abbey of Fécamp in Normandy. The herbs used in the original Benedictine are unknown, and since the expropriation of the monasteries in France imitation Benedictines have been prepared from nutmeg, peppermint, hyssop and angelica with the addition of a large amount of sugar.

Crême de Menthe is prepared from peppermint, sage, orris root, cinnamon and sugar. The natural green colour of the genuine article is imitated in cheap grades by the addition of dyes.

Other liqueurs which may be mentioned are Chartreuse, Curaçao, Calvados, Kümmel and Cointreau.

20.8.5 Sweeteners

Saccharin is an organic compound (2-sulphobenzoic imide, $C_7H_5O_3NS$) with 500 times the sweetening power of sucrose. It is only sparingly soluble in water which is a drawback for a food flavouring of such potency. In the tablet form saccharin is mixed with sodium bicarbonate to aid dissolution. Alternatively, the hydrated sodium salt of saccharin is prepared, being appreciably more soluble.

The small amount required to replace sugar in a made-up dish or beverage results in an economy. As it passes out of the body unchanged, it contributes nothing to the energy value of the diet, thereby providing help for those on weight-reducing diets who cannot abandon sweet foods.

Since 1970, saccharin has been the only permitted sweetener in the UK. Prior to that, cyclamic acid, $C_6H_{11}NHSO_2OH$, with its sodium and calcium salts, was gaining ground. With a sweetening power equal to 30 times that of sucrose, it provided an economical substitute and was favoured by many as having a less discernible after-taste than saccharin. The withdrawal of cyclamates in UK and USA followed publication of evidence of ill-effects from trials involving administration of heavy doses to laboratory animals. Whether this was justified is, at the time of writing, a subject of contention.

20.9 COLOURING MATERIALS

Not only are baked goods frequently made more palatable by the use of flavouring materials but their appearance is enhanced by the addition of colourings. Only colours listed in Schedule I of the Colouring Matter in Food Regulations, 1966 may be included in foods sold in this country. These fall within the following categories:

Coal tar dyes (such as are synthesized for fabric dyeing) 24 in all, giving a wide range of colours.

Caramel—from sugar.

Carmine—from cochineal insects.

Vegetable colourings—13 extracted colouring materials listed by name including annatto, carotene, chlorophyll and turmeric, plus any colouring natural to edible fruits and vegetables.

A few specified derivatives of vegetable pigments.

Mineral materials with long traditions of use as food colourings including iron oxide (bole), carbon black, and ultra-marine.

Metals in leaf or powder form—only gold, silver and aluminium for coating cake decorations.

The regulations impose limits on the uses of the above. Certain foods must not have any colouring added whatsoever: viz. meat, game, poultry, fish, fruit, vegetables, tea, coffee, cream and milk. (The only exception is that colour may be added to the skins of oranges and to the husks of nuts.) Caramel is the only colouring which may be added to bread and a few specified vegetable colourings are all that are permitted in butter and cheese.

20.9.1 Traditional colouring materials

Cochineal or Carmine Cochineal is prepared from the female insect (coccina) which feeds upon a variety of cactus (*Coccus cacti*), native to Mexico and Peru and cultivated in Guatemala and the Canary Islands. The cochineal derived from the cultivated cactus is superior to that from the wild cactus of Mexico and Peru. The former is known commercially as mestèque or grava fina, and the latter as sylvestra.

The female insects are collected and destroyed by throwing them into hot water, and are then dried in the sun or in stoves. This treatment gives the black cochineal, zacatilla. Alternatively, the insects may be placed in bags and dried in stoves without previously destroying in hot water. By this method the silvery-white cochineal blanco is obtained. The essential colouring principle of cochineal is carminic acid and a pink or red colour is produced. The usual forms in which cochineal is used are cochineal liquid, carmine and carmine liquid, and the usual mordant used in such preparations is alumina.

Turmeric or Indian Saffron   Turmeric is obtained from the underground stem or rhizome of the *Curcuma longa*, a plant of the ginger family which is native to Southern Asia and cultivated in India, East Indies and China. The powdered rhizome is used to colour curries, mustard-pickles and egg powder. It is seldom used in cakes in spite of its egg-like colour because of the presence in it of a volatile oil with an acrid taste.

Annatto   Annatto is prepared from the fermented seeds and pulp surrounding them of the plant *Bixa orellana*, which is native to South America and cultivated in the West Indies and Sri Lanka. The dye is sold as an orange paste or as small seeds with an orange covering. The colouring material, bixin, is practically insoluble in water but easily soluble in alcohol. Its chief use is in the colouring of butter, margarine, cheese and milk.

Saffron   Saffron is obtained from the dried stigmas of the flower of the plant *Crocus sativus*, which is grown in Spain, France, Austria and Italy. It requires about 100 flowers to produce 1g of dried saffron. When steeped in hot water and alcohol it gives an orange–yellow colour which is much used in cakes, pastries, cordials and liqueurs. Its colour changes from yellow to brown on gently heating (150–200° C) and it should be used fresh, for it decomposes quickly even at ordinary temperatures. Saffron is marketed as 'cake saffron'—in cake form—and as 'hay saffron', in which the stigmas are kept separate.

PRACTICAL EXERCISES

*All experiments require standard precautions. Those marked * involve particular hazards and should be supervised*

Expt. 20.1   pH EFFECTS ON COLOUR OF TEA

Prepare an infusion of tea and pour 2cm³ into each of three test tubes, A, B and C.

A   add 1cm³ water
B   add 1cm³ dilute acid   } Record any colour changes
C   add 1cm³ dilute alkali   } and check pH of each

Extend these trials to the use of different acids and alkalis and to acidic substances such as lemon juice and alkaline materials such as baking soda. Conclude whether the original results have general application.

Adapt the procedure for infusions of coffee and of cocoa.

Expt. 20.2 DETERMINATION OF THE TOTAL ACIDITY OF A SAMPLE OF
VINEGAR

Dilute 10cm³ vinegar to 100cm³ in a standard flask and titrate 25cm³
aliquots with 0·1M sodium hydroxide using phenolphthalein as indicator.
Calculate the acidity as grams acetic acid per 100cm³ vinegar.

Let Tcm³ be the average of three accurate titrations.

25cm³ diluted vinegar are equivalent to Tcm³ 0·1M sodium hydroxide
∴ 25cm³ diluted vinegar contain $T \times 0·1 \times 60$g acetic acid (60 = mol.wt.
acetic acid)
100cm³ undiluted vinegar contain $T \times 60 \times 4$g acetic acid

Expt. 20.3 QUALITATIVE EXAMINATION OF A SWEETENING TABLET

*(i) Detection of Saccharin
Mix together half a powdered tablet with 50mg resorcinol in a boiling tube.
Add about 10 drops of concentrated sulphuric acid (CORROSIVE) and heat
slowly in a water bath until dark green in colour. Cool thoroughly and
add 10cm³ water carefully and an excess of 20% sodium hydroxide solution.

Positive result Fluorescent green colour, indicates saccharin present.

(ii) Detection of Cyclamates
Crush five tablets and shake with 20cm³ cold water. Filter and acidify the
filtrate with dilute hydrochloric acid. Add a little barium chloride and make
sure the solution is clear. Add 1cm³ sodium nitrite solution (10%).

Positive result White precipitate, indicates cyclamate present.

Expt. 20.4 INVESTIGATION OF SYNTHETIC COLOURING MATTER IN A FOOD

Extraction of Colouring Matter (for example, from custard powder, fruit
squash, sweets)
Boil some white all-wool knitting yarn in dilute ammonium hydroxide
solution to remove grease. Make an aqueous dispersion of the food under
test in about 50cm³ water. Allow to sediment and note whether the colour
of the supernatant liquid is appreciable. If so, proceed. If not work with
another food containing water soluble dye until techniques are thoroughly
practised. Filter and divide filtrate into two portions to use as follows.

Detection of an Acidic Coal-tar Dye
Introduce a 20cm³ length of the wool yarn into one portion of the extract,
made acid with a few drops dilute hydrochloric acid. Boil thoroughly, then
remove the wool and wash under the cold tap. Transfer it to a small beaker
containing dilute ammonium hydroxide solution and boil gently.

Positive result Colour stripped out of wool by alkali, indicates presence
of an acidic coal-tar dye.
Save this extract for paper chromatography.

Detection of a Basic Coal-tar Dye
Introduce a 20cm length of de-greased wool yarn into about 20cm³ of the
original extract, made alkaline with ammonia. Boil thoroughly, remove the

wool and wash under the cold tap. Transfer to a small beaker containing dilute acetic acid solution and boil gently.

Positive result   Colour stripped out of wool by acid, indicates presence of a basic coal-tar dye.

Save this extract for paper chromatography.

NB. This result would suggest that a non-permitted colour had been detected. Prior to the current regulations, basic dyes were commonly used; the permitted list now only includes acidic ones.

Expt. 20.5   IDENTIFICATION OF COLOURING MATTER BY PAPER CHROMATOGRAPHY

Obtain a cylindrical glass jar with a lid: either a special purpose tank or the largest sized instant coffee jar. Cut a piece of Whatman No 1 chromatography paper which will fit within the jar in the form of a cylinder which does not touch the sides.

Concentrate the dye extract from Expt. 20.5 by evaporation over a water bath and then use it to paint along a horizontal line pencilled in about 2cm from the base of the sheet of paper. Dry thoroughly and roll into a cylinder, fastened with plastic clips, top and bottom. Vertical edges should overlap some 2cm and not touch each other. Stand the paper in the jar containing solvent to a depth of 1cm³. The most likely solvent is a mixture of:

> 20 vols n-butanol
> 12 vols water   } Solvent No 5
> 5 vols glacial acetic acid

Cover the jar immediately and leave while the solvent front rises up the paper. Remove before it reaches the top. Dry thoroughly.

Results   If the extract contained a single dye, one band only of colour will be seen across the chromatogram. Otherwise there will be a number of bands of colour. A second run with a different solvent might be needed if two bands are too close together to be distinguished. Measure the distances from the base line to the solvent front and to the centre point of each band of colour. For each colour, calculate the value of R_F from

$$R_F = \frac{\text{distance moved by dye}}{\text{distance moved by solvent}}$$

Refer to tables giving R_F values for each of the permitted water-soluble colourings in the various chromatography solvents, which will provide a good indication of the identity of the dyes which have separated out on the chromatogram.

REFERENCES

Pearson, D. (1970). *The chemical analysis of foods*, 6th edition, Churchill.
Eden, T. (1965). *Tea*, Longmans.
Roden, C. *Coffee*, Faber.
Wood, G. A. R. (1973). *Cocoa*, Longmans.

EXPERIMENTS

SECTION A

SECTION B

INDEX